The Politics
of Women's Studies

The Politics
of Women's Studies

Testimony from Thirty Founding Mothers

THE WOMEN'S STUDIES HISTORY SERIES: VOLUME ONE

Edited by
Florence Howe

Introduction by
Mari Jo Buhle

The Feminist Press
at The City University of New York
New York

Published by
The Feminist Press
at The City University of New York
The Graduate Center,
365 Fifth Avenue, New York, NY 10016.
www.feministpress.org
First edition, 2000

LIBRARY OF CONGRESS CATALOGING-IN-PUBLICATION DATA
The politics of women's studies: testimony from thirty founding mothers/edited by Florence Howe; introduction by Mari Jo Buhle.—1st ed.
    p. cm.—(The women's studies history series; v. 1)
    Includes bibliographical references and index.
    ISBN 1-55861-240-8 (cloth: alk. paper)—ISBN 1-55861-241-6 (pbk.: alk paper)
    1. Women's studies—United States—History.   2. Women scholars—United States—History.   3. Discrimination in education—United States.   4. Feminism and education—United States.   I. Howe, Florence.   II. Series.
    HQ1181.U5 P65 2000
    305.4'071'173—dc21   00-044251

The Feminist Press would like to thank the Ford Foundation and Mariam K. Chamberlain, Blanche Wiesen Cook, Helene D. Goldfarb, Jane Gould, William Hedges, Dorothy O. Helly, Nancy Hoffman, Florence Howe, Joanne Markell, Caroline Urvater, and Genevieve Vaughan for their generosity in supporting this book.

Photograph of Gloria Bowles (1990s) © Joanne Margalit. Used by permission of photographer. Photograph of Johnnetta B. Cole (1970s) © Arlene Voski Avakian. Used by permission of photographer. Photograph of Johnnetta B. Cole (1990s) © Emory University Photography. Used by permission of photographer. Photograph of Mimi Reisel Gladstein (1990s) © Cynthia Farah. Used by permission of photographer. Photograph of Nona Glazer (1995) © Robert Shotola. Used by permission of photgrapher. Photograph of Elizabeth Lapovsky Kennedy (1997) © Margaret Randall. Used by permission of photographer. Photograph of Annis Pratt (1970s) © Ann A. Straky. Used by permission of photographer. Photograph of Annis Pratt (1990s) © Olan Mills. Used by permission of photographyer. Photograph of Barbara Smith (1990s) © Marilyn Humphries. Used by permission of photographer. Photograph of Margaret Strobel (1970s) © Deborah Rosenfelt. Used by permission of photographer. Photograph of Margaret Strobel (1997) © Roberta Dupuis-Devlin, UIC Photo. Used by permission of photographer.

All other photographs used by permission of their subjects. Credits: Electa Arenal (1970s) by Gerald Cyrus, GSUC-CUNY; (1990s) by Magda Bogin. Nancy Topping Bazin (1972) by Barbara Flynn; (1999) by Andrew Carney. Josephine Donovan (1972) by Lexington Herald-Leader; (1999) by University of Maine Photography. Tucker Pamella Farley (1960s) by Emily Jensen; (1990s) by Linda Plotkin. Sue-Ellen Jacobs (1969) by Bill Jacobs; (1999) by Wesley Thomas. Nancy Porter by Joanne Penton. Kathryn Kish Sklar by Sara Krulwich.

Text design and typesetting by Adam B. Bohannon
Printed on acid-free paper by Transcontinental Printing.
Manufactured in Canada.

08 07 06 05 04 03 02 01 00   5 4 3 2 1

To the founding mothers
who could not write their essays
for this volume

SHAUNA ADIX
(1932–1998)
University of Utah

BETTY CH'MAJ
(1930–1997)
Sacramento State University, California

ELAINE HEDGES
(1927–1997)
Towson State University, Maryland

JUDITH OCHSHORN
(1928–1995)
University of South Florida

CAROL OHMANN
(1928–1989)
Wesleyan University

JUANITA WILLIAMS
(1922–1991)
University of South Florida

Contents

Preface

Everyone a Heroine

These narratives record history that few people in or out of women's studies have heard. They are private accounts of public acts requiring imagination and intelligence as well as courage. They are accounts of the agents of social change, who, in the space of a single decade, transformed consciousness on college and university campuses. To do this work, they did not often march in the streets of a town; they did not often conduct sit-ins in buildings. But in various strong, systematic, and strategic ways, they organized collective feminist power on campuses. They are part of a significant story that needs to be known, even in a dozen volumes the size of this one. For on hundreds of campuses in the 1970s and on hundreds more in the next two decades, intrepid women—students, faculty, administrators, members of the community—collaborated in a movement called women's studies. This movement has altered the curriculum and the style of teaching and produced research that has shifted the paradigms and changed the content of most disciplines.

No one denies the impact of women's studies on university life. Its detractors see it as "wrecking" or "trivializing" the curriculum. Some of its promoters strive to legitimize women's studies through its admittance as a "discipline" into departmental status. But neither of these groups, nor those who fall outside these tensions, have concerned themselves with the history of women's studies. Though one of the enormously important lessons we have learned from women's studies has to do with knowing one's history—because without it, one is doomed to repeating especially its failures—the history of women's studies has remained obscure.

The initiating moment that inspired this volume occurred during the Thanksgiving holiday in 1995 at a lunch with a "founding mother" of women's studies who, I realized only then, was not my exact contemporary but probably more than a decade older and in frail health. She had never written anything of her work in women's studies. Who would write her story? Would she agree to write it if it were to be part of a larger story? And what of that larger story? Who better could write that history than the band of hardy souls who had made it happen? I left the lunch with my head spinning. Others were in poor health. I needed to hurry were I to get all their stories. And, of course, in some cases, I was too late.

Several months later, I sent out a form letter to approximately twenty pioneers of women's studies whose addresses I knew, asking them whether they thought a collection of their founding stories would be useful. In addition to listing all their names, I wrote out some questions that had occurred to me and asked for more names and more questions. The response was overwhelming. Even people who did not want to write essays thought the idea a useful one and suggested names of other pioneers. A year or so later, I had more than ninety names, and, to each, I sent a similar form letter, but by then the questions had grown to occupy two pages of their own.

Elaine Hedges (1927–1997), founding mother at Towson State University, responded first by reminding me that the questions needed to be about collective rather than individual work. We miss her essay, as we miss those from others who died shortly before or shortly after we began this project. They include Judith Ochshorn (1928–1995) and Juanita Williams (1922–1991), both founding mothers at the University of South Florida; Shauna Adix (1932–1998), founding-mother at the University of Utah; and Betty Ch'maj (1930–1997), founding mother at Sacramento State University, California. We have dedicated the work to these founders and to Carol Ohmann (1928–1989), founding mother at Wesleyan University. Carol Ohmann was also the person in 1970 who convinced me to allow my name to be used as a write-in candidate in an election that would choose the president of the Modern Language Association. I agreed, because we both saw this only as a ploy to point to the patriarchal politics of that august body. Much to our amazement, I was elected, and so, during the early 1970s, the mothers of many women's studies programs called on me, as allegedly the "first" woman elected president of the Modern Language Association, to lecture on their campuses about the legitimacy and necessity of women's studies, not only for women students, but for the intellectual health of the whole academic enterprise.

In the 1970s, some of the mothers who wrote the essays in this volume were young graduate students or new Ph.D.'s just beginning to teach and untenured; some were my age and a few, like me, were tenured assistant professors in search of ways to improve their students' capacities to learn; a few were older, two of them administrators. During those significant years, we taught at more than thirty campuses, some of us changing jobs several times in the decade. The institutions where we taught, important to this history, are named in the table of contents. With few exceptions—Spelman College and Goucher College—they are large state universities: San Diego, Berkeley, Michigan, Wisconsin, CUNY, SUNY, the University of Massachusetts, Rutgers, Kentucky, Illinois, Arizona, Portland State, Washington, Texas at El Paso.

Today, only a few of us are still at the institutions we describe here. At least a half dozen have retired or are near retiring. I am seventy, the older ones are in their eighties, the younger ones are at least in their fifties. All have expressed, in the essays or more privately to me, the relief they feel in telling these stories, in seeing their histories on the page, in knowing that others will read about the early struggles, about the pain and the joy of building a new kind of institution, about constructing a new curriculum, and about unearthing a new body of knowledge. Many of us were not welcome as agents of change on our originating campuses, much less applauded for our work. What shocks all of us, just thirty years after women's studies began, is the amnesia afflicting most of those teaching or studying about women. Perhaps this volume will help to change that state of affairs, for although each narrative has a life of its own, collectively the story has a different power.

I want to thank Mari Jo Buhle, herself a founding mother, for undertaking the illumination of this history. I want to thank all the writers of the essays for their insights, for their ardor, for their courage—and for bearing with me through multiple rounds of editing. I thank my devoted assistant, Kelly Freidenfelds, for her collaboration on this project and for her exceptional organizing and communicating skills. Without her work this past year, we would not have this volume. I thank members of The Feminist Press staff for their work on this book: Jocelyn Burrell, assistant to the publisher, for the care and intelligence she has brought to her organizational and editorial work on the book; Jean Casella, editorial director, whom I am fortunate to have as an editor of my essays; Dayna Navaro, design and production director, for her bold design of the cover; and Lisa London, marketing manager, for her enthusiastic response to the volume.

Finally, a word about the future. We are optimistic enough to take a lesson from Sheila Tobias's presentation of *Female Studies,* that first volume of course syllabi that appeared in 1970 as "No. 1." We are calling this volume the first in the Women's Studies History Series, for which I will serve as chief editor in search of editors of additional volumes, including a volume on the development and impact of women's studies around the world.

Florence Howe   New York City
                                                                June 2000

Introduction

Mari Jo Buhle

In 1970, when scholar-activists established the first program at San Diego State University, no one could have predicted just how successful women's studies would be. Just three decades later, women's studies now occupies a prominent place within the academy. There are approximately 615 programs in the United States, and women's studies enrolls the largest number of students of any interdisciplinary field. The Department of Education has estimated that 12 percent of all undergraduate students receive credit for courses in women's studies. Although only a handful of universities offer doctoral degrees specifically in women's studies, graduate students have carved out a sizable niche for themselves within the disciplines. Between 1978, when "women's studies" first appeared as an indexing category in *Dissertation Abstracts International,* and 1985, the total number of dissertations recorded under the heading was more than thirteen thousand. Far from being a fad, as many detractors had gibed, women's studies has become an integral part of higher education.[1]

The creation of women's studies wasn't easy, but in retrospect it did seem to happen overnight. Reporting for the National Advisory Council on Women's Educational Programs, Florence Howe surveyed the field in 1976, just seven years after the inauguration of the first program. She counted more than 270 programs and 15,000 courses spread across the campuses of 1500 institutions. By then, 850 teachers were already active in designing a comprehensive interdisciplinary curriculum comprising such courses as Images of Women in Literature, Sociology of Sex Roles, and History of Women in the United States.[2] The rate of growth was swift: in 1981 Howe reported that the number of women's studies programs had increased to 350.[3]

While organizing the first programs, the founding mothers were

also busy laying the foundation for women's studies nationwide by creating caucuses within professional associations and planning panels for
the annual meetings. The Modern Language Association took the lead,
and in 1968 established the Commission on the Status and Education
of Women. Similar groups formed among historians, psychologists,
anthropologists, and philosophers. To promote publications in the
field, Florence Howe, Paul Lauter, and others founded The Feminist
Press in 1972 and soon thereafter introduced an informational
newsletter that evolved into the distinguished journal *Women's Studies
Quarterly*. In 1972 *Feminist Studies* and *Women's Studies* also made their debut,
followed by *Signs* in 1975. All these interdisciplinary journals continue
unabated, fostering feminist scholarship across the generations. In
1977, with financial assistance from the Ford Foundation, the National
Women's Studies Association (NWSA) was formed. Within a few years
the annual meetings of the NWSA were attracting between one thousand and two thousand lively participants. As Mariam K. Chamberlain
recalls, this small grant became legendary in the foundation "as an
example of how much can be accomplished with a small sum"—and with
unswerving dedication of activists.

The first ten years of women's studies were extremely heady ones.
Not only did well over half the growth in the field to date occur during
the first decade, but all of the basic institutional structures were put in
place. The writers in this volume give witness to this fast-moving chapter in the history of women's studies. They also remind us that their
effort to establish women's studies, although exhilarating, demanded
hard work and shrewd planning.

Collectively, the pioneers of women's studies represent the "come-
back" generation of women in higher education. After women first
gained admission to higher education in the 1860s, their presence
among both the undergraduate and graduate populations increased
steadily until the 1920s and then began to diminish to reach a low
point during the infamous 1950s, the decade Betty Friedan has forever
linked to *The Feminine Mystique*. By 1930 one in seven Ph.D.'s was granted
to a woman; thirty years later the proportion had dropped to approximately one in ten.[4] This figure is not comprehensive or absolute. In
this same period African American women, for instance, received
more degrees at all levels than African American men, although the
total number of African American women awarded Ph.D.'s remained
very small. Overall, though, compared with men, women occupied a

better position in higher education in 1930 than in 1970. However, the situation was changing. During the 1960s, on the heels of *Sputnik* and with the war in Vietnam revving up the economy, colleges and universities underwent a rapid expansion. The women writing in this volume stand for many others who were taking advantage of these new opportunities, although women as a group would not recover their earlier loss until 1976, when they represented 45 percent of the undergraduate population.[5]

The founders of women's studies found themselves atop a continuing and, to them, a shocking trend. They not only marked women's return to higher education but also their advancement into the ranks of professional academia. In 1970, 3976 women received doctoral degrees, and within a decade that number more than tripled. By the time that NWSA held its first national meeting, women were earning approximately 30 percent of all Ph.D.'s granted in the United States.[6]

In a variety of ways, then, the majority of women writing in this volume were far from traditional students or traditional teachers. Marilyn Jacoby Boxer, Mimi Reisel Gladstein, and Mary Anne Ferguson accounted themselves re-entry, or resumed education students, who sought to complete an education that had been interrupted by marriage or motherhood. Teachers, such as Florence Howe, joined the faculty of new institutions, such as the State University of New York (SUNY), Old Westbury, that aimed to educate men and women destined to be the first in their families to pursue college education. Inez Martinez went to Kingsborough Community College in Brooklyn, a new college established in the wake of the City University of New York's open enrollments; and Electa Arenal took a position at Richmond College, an experimental branch of the City University of New York, which opened in 1967. All dedicated themselves to helping working-class women and women of color earn a college degree.[7]

In the late 1960s, when many of the pioneers of women's studies took their first teaching jobs, there were few women among the tenured faculty to serve as either role models or allies. Like female students, female college teachers had been losing their representation on campus since World War II.[8] In fact, during the 1960s as college faculty nationally increased sharply, the proportion of women faculty members shrank. Even at colleges that took pride in their role in preparing women for the professions, such as Brown University, women represented less than 5 percent of the faculty.[9] On some campuses, the situation was worse. According to Gloria Bowles, the percentage of tenured women at the University of California, Berkeley, dropped from 4.8 percent in 1933 to only 2.9 percent in 1971, and none of them did research on women. The representation of African Americans was far less. In 1970, black faculty, including both women and men, represented only 0.9 percent of faculty in U.S. universities and 5.4 percent in four-year colleges, the majority teaching in traditionally black institutions.[10] Even in English, the discipline best represented in this volume, men gained on women as they ascended the higher rungs of the academic ladder. In the first lecture sponsored by the MLA's Commission on the Status and Education of Women, Florence Howe explained that although women represented the clear majority of undergraduate majors in English, in graduate school the proportion of women to men was reversed.[11] Among the faculty, the disparity was even greater. At Cornell University, where the second program in women's studies was established in 1972, Sheila Tobias reports that the ratio of male to female faculty was thirteen to one, with seventy-five of the one hundred faculty women in the College of Human Ecology, renamed from Home Economics in 1967.

The founders of women's studies were, therefore, pioneers in more than one way. In some cases, as Nancy Topping Bazin recalls, there were no women in a department. Far too many writers remember starting their first job in the unenviable position of being the lone woman on the departmental roster. Moreover, as most writers in the volume report, they usually began their academic careers in positions that carried little administrative weight. Rather than being regular voting members of the faculty, they represented the increasingly expedient solution to skyrocketing undergraduate enrollments: poorly paid instructors on temporary or part-time lines. Those whose spouses already worked in the university discovered, as did Barbara W. Gerber, that the laws against nepotism seemed to apply only to wives. But even in an early success story, Nancy Hoffman, just out of graduate school, landed a job as an assistant professor, and found herself turning to graduate students and faculty wives for female companionship.

By the early 1970s, though, the picture was far from bleak. Lacking institutional support, the founders of women's studies had several major advantages: a burgeoning feminist movement that gave rise to their endeavor; experience in political movements off campus; and a huge number of students eager to learn and to participate in the building of programs. These conditions together created a collective volatility. Teachers and students shared a spirited commitment to women learning together.

For the majority of women in this volume, their own graduate education or first teaching position coincided with the rise of the women's liberation movement. Although issues of women's rights and equity had circulated widely since 1963, following the report of the Presidential Commission on the Status of Women and the founding of the National Organization for Women (NOW) in 1966, women's liberation took shape later, at the close of the decade. Between 1968 and 1970, small groups, such as New York Radical Women and the Chicago Women's Liberation Union, began to organize. By 1970 second wave feminists had advanced the idea that "the personal is political." This slogan, which became the keynote of women's liberation, challenged the opposition between the personal and the political aspects of daily life by making women's own experiences the ground for feminism. Although NOW put pressure on legislative assemblies and courts to redress inequalities in the legal and economic realms, the women's liberation movement focused on such matters as sexuality, motherhood, and relationships and introduced the small consciousness-raising group as its chief organizing tool.

As the writers here attest, the first programs in women's studies bore the distinctive imprint of women's liberation. The Hunter College Women's Studies Collective issued a statement of intention that vividly illustrates this political sensibility:

> Women's studies is not simply the study of women, it is the study of women which places women's own experiences in the center of the process. It examines the world and the human beings who inhabit it with questions, analyses, and theories built directly on women's experiences.[12]

Questions of "personal politics" thus fueled the labors of the founders of the first programs. Nancy Topping Bazin recalls that she had read Simone de Beauvoir's book *The Second Sex* and Betty Friedan's book *The Feminine Mystique*, and, although finding them "enlightening social documents," could not truly appreciate what the authors had to say until "the women's movement had become part of the historical moment and culture in which I was living." Florence Howe, who had

been active in campaigns for racial equality and world peace throughout the 1960s, also remembers that her feminist consciousness developed in tandem with the women's liberation movement. Initially suspicious of feminism, Nona Glazer describes the change that came over
her after she saw the light in 1969. Like female students, female teachers often claimed that their first course in women's studies changed
their lives, sometimes in dramatic and surprising ways. As Nellie Y.
McKay puts it, involvement in women's studies rescued her from "that
state of lostness" she experienced during her first years in academia.
Women's studies emerged as the educational arm of the women's liberation movement, as Howe declares. But for many of the first teachers
and students, women's studies and women's liberation were one and
the same.

The founders of women's studies more often than not *became* feminists through the process of teaching courses, organizing programs,
and developing the curriculum. Sheila Tobias tells us that Cornell
University, where she taught, was "highly politicized" in the late 1960s
if "not yet feminist." This was true of many campuses nationwide. But
they were becoming feminist. It was therefore not unusual for graduate
students and faculty members to meet in consciousness-raising (CR)
groups. Kathryn Kish Sklar, for example, recalls her first years on the
faculty at the University of Michigan, where she advanced to a new stage
in her thinking while helping to design the women's studies curriculum. "My own understanding of my life and work was changing," she
remembers, "as I grew more committed to the emerging feminist
movement." Members of her CR group helped her draw the connection between her own experience as a woman and the history of women
she was studying. For good reason, the idea of self-discovery resonates
through these memoirs.

If feminism and women's studies developed hand-in-hand for students and teachers, the majority of teachers came to this work as seasoned political activists and were ready to transfer techniques of organizing from the community to the campus. Experience in civil rights,
the New Left's antipoverty campaigns, and the antiwar movement
stands out as a striking common denominator. This experience prepared them to wage an uphill battle to establish women's studies and, at
the same time, shaped the politics of the entire endeavor.

In the early 1960s, when most of the writers of this volume were
either undergraduates or new faculty members, racism, rather than

women's oppression, seemed to them, as it did to their contemporaries, the nation's most pressing social issue. Since the mid-1950s the civil rights movement had continued to grow; it had come to include thousands of college students. In 1960, with assistance from veteran civil rights activist Ella Baker, African American undergraduates formed the Student Nonviolent Coordinating Committee (SNCC) to fight segregation in the Deep South. In 1964 SNCC organized Freedom Summer, which brought more than one thousand northern students—black and white, male and female alike—to Mississippi to teach in freedom schools and to register voters. Outside the South, thousands more college students joined Friends of SNCC, including several writers of this volume.

The second political touchstone was the New Left movement, led by Students for a Democratic Society (SDS). SDS had formed in 1960 as an offshoot of a venerable if defunct socialist student organization and, until its division and collapse a decade later, provided a broad platform for campus protest and student radicalism. The organizational home for many of the white students who participated in the early civil rights movement, by the mid-1960s SDS was the principal campus-based group behind the era's antipoverty campaigns. Michael Harrington's book *The Other America* (1962) had made many in the United States aware that intense poverty existed alongside affluence, and in response SDS attempted to launch an interracial movement of poor people. In 1963 SDS sponsored the Economic Research and Action Project, which sent hundreds of young men and women, a few of them later national reform leaders and scholars, into urban working-class communities. During the next several years, SDS provided leadership for campus-based protests against the war in Vietnam. At its peak in 1968, SDS had 350 chapters and the allegiance of perhaps one hundred thousand young men and women.

For a significant number of the women writing this volume, their experience in the civil rights and New Left movements was (and remains) transformative. On the one hand, many learned about discrimination against women firsthand in these male-dominated political movements. Yolanda Moses, for example, recalls that in SNCC, both white women and women of color were allowed to play only secondary roles while doing much of the behind-the-scenes, day-to-day work. On the other hand, if women activists in SNCC and SDS often found themselves relegated to housekeeping chores, such as serving up coffee and sex in equal measure, they also sharpened their understanding of social injustice in the United States. And they learned how to organize.[13] Sue-Ellen Jacobs remembers that at Sacramento State College, the group of faculty and students who took their proposal for a women's studies program to the college president were "prepared for a sit-in, if necessary." As seasoned activists and budding feminists, the founders of women's studies soon identified their allies in struggle.

The stories here tell movingly of women who, with few resources, managed to secure a place for women's studies on college campuses across the country. In a few places, they found administrators eager to support their efforts. Jean Walton, who had been a dean at Pomona College since 1949, was well positioned first to increase the number of women on the faculty and then to build women's studies on a solid academic as well as financial foundation. In general, though, allies in the administration were few, and women who sought to organize the first programs were rarely able to approach administrators from a position of strength or influence.

As part-time instructors or assistant professors, they had little voice in academic affairs and found more opposition than support; many risked their own professional careers in the process. Myra Dinnerstein remembers that women in tenure-track positions were advised by their department heads that close involvement with women's studies could "deal a blow to their academic careers." Undeterred, they organized and taught the first courses, usually as "overloads," Annette Kolodny reminds us, that is, in addition to their regular teaching duties and without compensation. But what they lacked in administrative power, they enjoyed in organizational experience and sheer determination. And incidentally, they had the cooperation of large numbers of equally determined and enthusiastic students.

The writers remind us just how vital the role of students was in the formation of women's studies. Enrollment data provide the best evidence. It was not unusual for the first courses to attract more that one hundred students, and even those courses that began as small seminars often expanded rapidly beyond all expectations. In a survey of women's studies on fifteen campuses, Florence Howe estimated that by the mid-1970s, between 10 and 33 percent of all women undergraduates were enrolling in women's studies courses.[14] Elizabeth Lapovsky Kennedy confirms this impression. She recalls that at SUNY, Buffalo, when women's studies was only one year old, the Women's Studies College enrolled fourteen hundred students that year. Women students were rushing to take these courses. On many campuses, students also played an instrumental role in pressuring the administration to hire more faculty, to increase the number of course offerings, and to give formal academic status to undergraduate programs in women's studies.

Some of the most vivid memories are those of teachers who learned alongside their students. The majority recount that their own graduate education was sorely deficient in addressing scholarship by and about women. Annis Pratt recalls that in her lengthy preparation for degrees from B.A. to Ph.D., she had "not been assigned more than three books by women." Moreover, because women's studies emerged as an inter-disciplinary endeavor, the problems of working with unfamiliar methodologies were often daunting. Nevertheless, the first teachers describe what seemed at once the most exciting and the most exhausting experience of their academic careers.

Of necessity, undergraduates, graduate students, and faculty worked in harness to create the bibliographies, study guides, and assorted materials needed to teach and learn. In the absence of pre-pared reading lists or course syllabi to use as models, faculty had no other choice. There were no textbooks and very few books or articles appropriate for classroom use. The shortage was especially acute for scholarship on women of color. As Beverly Guy-Sheftall reminds us, these were days "long before writers such as Zora Neale Hurston, Toni Morrison, Paule Marshall, and Alice Walker were available to large numbers of college students." To share the precious resources, in 1970 Sheila Tobias inaugurated *Female Studies 1,* the first in a ten-vol-ume series of publications designed to assist teachers in planning courses and programs.[15]

The first women's studies courses were as innovative in form as they were in content. Because both teachers and students came to women's studies via civil rights and the New Left, they established a form of governance for the first programs that reflected their shared commit-ment to collective decision making. The *Port Huron Statement,* the found-ing document of SDS, presents a vision of "participatory democracy" by which people would be brought "out of isolation and into commu-nity."[16] The majority of the founders of women's studies—including the students—were intimately familiar with this precept. A few would not have recognized its origins, but it is safe to say that all shared the basic aspiration that every aspect of life, from personal relationships to the affairs of state, should be based upon individual dignity and democratic participation.

This shared commitment to participatory democracy effectively defined the pedagogy and structure of early women's studies in a multitude of small and large ways. It meant, first of all, that the style of teaching and the content of courses embodied the same philosophy. As several writers in this volume attest, the practice of participatory democracy also meant endless rounds of meetings and discussions of process. But undoubtedly the most memorable—and exciting—aspect of participatory democracy was the spirit of collaborative learning as well as teaching.

Faculty joined with students to inaugurate a classroom style that would flourish decades later as feminist pedagogy. At the time, though, the founders of women's studies were in alliance with others of their generation who advocated an alternative to the established educational theory that prevailed in U.S. school systems. They believed in the possibility of social change through critical teaching and learning, and, like other New Left teachers, they were especially sensitive to the ways in which conventional classrooms reproduced social inequalities. Many of these first women's studies teachers, such as Florence Howe and Nancy Hoffman, contributed frequently to the *Radical Teacher,* a journal that continues to serve as the voice of radical pedagogy. Inspired by Paulo Freire's *Pedagogy of the Oppressed,* which was translated into English in 1968, radical teachers promoted learning outside established educational institutions and advanced alternative styles of learning within their own colleges and universities. Teach-ins about the Vietnam war, freedom schools in the South, free universities in the North, and campaigns to establish black studies programs all emphasized the power of politicized learning.[17]

The first women's studies courses, whether sponsored by free universities or organized within degree-granting institutions, bore the imprint of this philosophy. Teachers and students alike agreed to focus on women and, equally important, feminist issues—"alternating between changing ourselves and changing society, following the slogan that the personal is political," Hoffman recalls.

The writers here vividly recall their efforts to apply the principles of feminist pedagogy in the classroom. For example, student-led discussions were common. As Barbara Smith recalls, she rarely lectured and instead involved students in group discussions and presentation; she says, "I remember those early classes as being delightful" for the degree of student involvement in the educational process. Nancy Porter similarly describes the intensity of feeling in the first women's studies classrooms. She remembers feeling "that we were pioneering a different sort of classroom: nonhierarchical, collaborative, intellectual yet intimate, and, above all, woman centered." Porter continues: "It was a kind of classroom that none of us had ever been in before."

It was also the most political classroom any of us had ever been in. Not only because class meetings functioned with a rotating chair, thus preventing the hierarchy of rank or the authority of any one individual; not only because many meetings ended with "criticism, self-criticism" sessions, where participants assessed the process and tried to come up with ever more inclusive forms of engagement; but also because the distance between university life and community activism was slight. Scholarship and political advocacy went hand in sisterly hand, and students and teachers alike participated in a variety of activities, ranging from consciousness-raising (CR) groups to community-based campaigns to secure contraceptive and abortion rights, day-care centers, shelters for battered women, and the Equal Rights Amendment. At SUNY, Buffalo, the founders of the women's studies program stated the following:

> This education will not be an academic exercise; it will be an ongoing process to change the ways in which women think and behave. It must be part of the struggle to build a new and more complete society.[18]

The teachers and students who shaped the first courses and planned the first programs embraced both advocacy for and inquiry about women. More than an innovative interdisciplinary endeavor, women's studies therefore emerged as an unusual program within higher education because the intention of its founders was to maintain a connection between political action and scholarship within the academy. As Margaret Strobel explains, the establishment of women's studies at the University of Illinois, Chicago, resulted from initiatives of the women's caucus of the New University Conference and of the Chicago Women's Liberation Union.

The origins of women's studies in the social movements of the 1960s, Elizabeth Lapovsky Kennedy underscores, "profoundly shaped the form and content of its curriculum"[19] and made a lasting impact. Primed by their background in the civil rights and New Left movements, the planners of these first programs determinedly made issues of race, class, and sexual orientation central to their endeavors. Although the majority were white, they shared a commitment to what today would be called cultural diversity or, in the nomenclature of the time, Third World women. "People now ask if we thought about race and class in those days," Josephine Donovan writes. "That's *all* we thought about: racism, colonialism, and imperialism. Feminism added gender to the mix." This is not to say that these early efforts were successful in their initiatives: enduring results were few. As Kennedy also stresses, despite firm commitments to anti-imperialism and antiracism, their work to undermine racism in the academy did not have long-term effects, and women of color remained underrepresented among both faculty and students. Nevertheless, women's studies programs have more consistently and directly addressed the challenges posed by cultural diversity than most other academic fields have. By 1985 more than 60 percent of women's studies programs in the United States offered at least one course on women of color. A later survey indicates that the percentage has reached 95 percent. [20]

The heroic days of women's studies are now in the past, and the playing field is changing dramatically with the rise of postfeminism.[21] Nevertheless, on many college campuses, women's studies now enjoys departmental or program status, even as the bulk of academic funding still finds its way to older, male-dominated disciplines. Women's studies has made its mark on nearly all the disciplines, transforming scholarship by moving the questions raised by the writers here from the periphery to the center. As they approach retirement, these writers take deserved satisfaction in their accomplishments, especially as they recount the obstacles they faced at the beginning of their academic careers. They recall the exhilaration of the struggle, the friendships made along the way, and the joys of working with students as eager as themselves. In not a few cases, they delight as their former students step forward to lead the next generation of women's studies scholars. Theirs is an important legacy, as Myra Dinnerstein puts it: "to be able to combine work and feminist politics: head and heart."

PART I

Naming
the Problem

The Absence of Women
from the Curriculum
and Scholarship

Florence Howe

For many different reasons, including the presence of Carol Ahlum, an intrepid work-study assistant who taught me that "routine work is not boring if it has a social purpose," from before 1970 until the late 1980s, I functioned as the historian and record-keeper of the women's studies movement. Especially after moving in 1971 from Goucher College to the new College at Old Westbury/SUNY, I divided my time among women's studies—speaking and consulting on as many as forty campuses a year—The Feminist Press, and the Modern Language Association, in addition to organizing and teaching in the women's studies program on campus. In 1973, I held a Ford Foundation fellowship to research the origins of women's studies in the archives of a dozen colleges and universities. In 1975, at the request of the National Advisory Council on Women's Education Programs, established by Congress as part of the Women's Educational Equity Act in the education amendments of 1974, I spent six months on leave visiting fifteen women's studies programs on campuses as far apart as the University of Hawaii and the University of South Florida. Ten thousand copies of the monograph summarizing my research, *Seven Years Later: Women's Studies Programs in 1976*, were distributed free by the federal government, and for some years, along with the collection of essays published in *Myths of Coeducation* in 1984, remained the only history of the movement. In the mid-1980s, for Mariam Chamberlain's *Women in Academe: Progress and Problems,* I wrote the chapter on women's studies. I have published widely on many matters having to do with education

3

and literature. I am perhaps best known as the editor of *No More Masks! An Anthology of Twentieth Century American Women Poets*. I am at work on a memoir.

In the mid-1980s also, The Feminist Press and my academic appointment moved into the City University of New York, where we are currently in residence at CUNY's Graduate Center. I am a professor of English; The Feminist Press, though an independent entity entering its thirtieth year, is one of the many institutes and centers in residence at the Graduate Center.

Learning from Teaching

Although I was a political activist through much of the 1960s, the impulse for my entrance into what eventually became women's studies emerged from teaching composition. In the fall of 1964, I returned to teaching at Goucher College, still astonished by the quality of poetry and prose written by young, black Mississippi women students who could not have parsed or punctuated a sentence correctly, yet had written memorably, with remarkable energy and conviction.[1] They had something to say, I concluded, and my privileged white Goucher College students did not. I knew that I could not transfer that "something to say" easily, for though I talked to many audiences, including students, about Mississippi's Freedom Summer, the experience remained mine. I knew I could not transfer experience. Of that, I was profoundly certain.

But I had returned from Mississippi also with a set of pedagogical tools. I would teach my composition classes, I decided, seated in a circle with my students, and from that position I would seek the theme that would unlock their abilities to write even as talking about being black in a white society had unlocked the freedom-longing voices of my black students. But what was that theme for white, middle-class females? In hindsight, it seems obvious, but in 1964 and 1965, I was not a feminist. I was a person who had rebuked young white and black women in Mississippi for "selfishly" refusing to continue sweeping floors and making coffee or for insisting that their voices needed to be heard in meetings. I told them that racism was the most important problem to be solved in white America, that once we had conquered racism we could worry about ourselves. I couldn't help repeating nineteenth-century white women's history, since I knew none. Luckily for me and for my students, I accidentally hit on a key question one day while discussing D. H. Lawrence's *Sons and Lovers.*

It happened somewhat awkwardly, as I was trying to get them to understand the idea of "point of view" by asking them to consider what the novel told them of Miriam's home life. Were there clues, I asked, to help them imagine how her parents treated her? The students were mystified. So I explained that Lawrence did not present Miriam's parents to his readers. They would have to imagine the parents from thinking about how Miriam acts in the novel. I told them that this was one way of determining that Lawrence's point of view was not focused on Miriam. I got nowhere. Perhaps I had an unimaginative class that day. Perhaps my students were still traumatized by what was for them in the mid-1960s a very unusual classroom.

Whatever the cause, their silence led me to ask, in some exasperation, the question that became key to my own development of feminist consciousness through the next several years. "What about *your* families," I asked. "How were *you* treated? Were you treated as your brother was?"

"Of course," one student volunteered at once, "we were treated equally."

We went around the circle, each student more emphatic than the one before. Even those with no brothers said that their parents would have treated them "equally." I knew at once that I was on to something, for I remembered vividly my childhood complaints about "unfairness," when I had to do all the housework, and my brother was excused even from making his own bed or picking up the dirty clothes he had dropped on the floor. But I was not, in those days, about to reveal my family's origins.[2]

Instead, I asked a series of questions: "Who took out the garbage? Who washed the dishes? Who mowed the lawn? Who got paid for family work? What was your graduation present? Your brother's? Who had a curfew? Were allowances equal?" Even as we went around the circle with each question, the students became more and more visibly agitated and defensive. Mowing the lawn deserved payment, one student said, since it was harder work than washing the dishes, and she wouldn't want to mow the lawn. Besides, another student said, her brother needed money in order to take girls out on dates. She didn't need such money, since boys paid for everything. Probably none of us in that room understood the significance of that sentence. Just before the hour was to end, one intrepid student said, "I really don't want to talk about such trivia," knowing that I was accepting of seemingly outrageous statements in class.

"Fine," I said. "Then I will assign these topics as themes for this week. I want you to write about what you are supposed to do either socially at home or on campus and what you think your brother is supposed to do socially at home or on campus, or in high school, if he is younger than you." The students groaned, frowned. No one was smiling but me. I knew I had found the subject I was looking for.

And I had, although I didn't understand that I had also found something else. For I was still quite innocent about the dailiness of sexism and the persuasiveness of patriarchy. Those words were not yet in my vocabulary, though I had by then published a review of three of Doris Lessing's novels, including *The Golden Notebook,* and had read *The Second Sex.* I needed years of discussion in the composition classroom, as well as the experience of some events outside the classroom, before I could call myself a feminist.[3] When an intrepid reporter named Malcolm Scully, who had come to visit my composition classroom early in 1970 to interview me, wrote in the new *Chronicle of Higher Education* that I was "teaching consciousness," I was insulted and insisted that I was teaching writing, that students in my class were gaining information that allowed them to write more clearly and profoundly.[4]

Scully's front-page story brought me forty-eight letters from teachers all over the country who wanted to know exactly what I was doing in my classroom. Rather than answer each of them separately, I wrote a seven-thousand-word mimeographed "letter," which I continued to mail as a response to other requests. In October of that year, I was invited to Wesleyan College to talk about my freshman writing course, now called Identity and Expression. One of the editors of *College English* then asked for permission to edit my mimeographed letter into an essay for publication in that journal. And so the idea of what was, though I could not for years have called it that, a feminist composition course spread its news as part of what was clearly by 1970 a burgeoning women's studies movement.

From 1965 until 1971, when I left Goucher, I continued to experiment with my freshman English classes, adding fiction by women writers each term to the staples of Lawrence's *Sons and Lovers,* Ralph Ellison's *Invisible Man,* and Simone de Beauvoir's *The Second Sex.* Until 1969, my course was the least popular section of Freshman English.[6] The grapevine told students what themes faculty used to teach their composition courses, and students did not want to read "lady" writers, who were, of course, all inferior to any man. One rare student, who announced that she wanted to be a writer "like D. H. Lawrence," was profoundly important to raising my consciousness, for without pausing to think, I said, "But you never could be 'like D. H. Lawrence.' He's male and you're female." She and the class were shocked. *I* was shocked. But I then began to understand what still kept me from writing. In my family I had been taught that I was not male, and in college I was taught that only males were good writers.

After 1964, I also began to make changes in the Introduction to Poetry course I regularly taught each year. Placed in charge of Goucher's Poetry Series, I had begun by inviting four male poets, including Robert Lowell, who, in 1963, had at first offended me by bringing along with him Adrienne Rich, and insisting that she read a few of her new poems. I learned quickly that she was a person beloved in Baltimore, and I was ultimately gratified to be invited by the *Baltimore Sun* to review her ground-breaking volume, *Snapshots of a Daughter-in-Law*. Following that experience, I altered the design of the series by inviting one woman poet each year: Marianne Moore, Denise Levertov, Muriel Rukeyser, and Anne Sexton. Of course I wanted my students to read these poets, and I couldn't help noticing that they were not often included in anthologies I used, or in other anthologies I began to review. I had to type and mimeograph their poems, or order small volumes to go along with the anthology I still could not label "male-centered." During these years I also began to ask the women poets to hold a writing workshop for student poets the morning after their reading. It was probably those workshops that led me to the idea of creating a project for teaching in Baltimore's high schools by the best students in my poetry class each year, some of whom were to become poets, others teachers.[7]

By 1969, the year that the women's movement was making headlines that freshman students had seen, my course was the first to fill, and students were eager to write about "women," not "girls." Other students in my literature classroom began to ask me questions I had not asked myself. Nor could I answer them. "What were 'real' women like in the eighteenth century? Did women go to college? Did they write books? Why are there no women writers in this course?" The library was no help. Even art history was no help: I returned to class with slides of Hogarth's *Shrimp Girl* and paintings of elegantly dressed and coiffed patrician women by famous masters. What was I to do about my ignorance?

Several other events external to my life as an assistant professor helped me. In 1969, I was appointed one of the first two cochairs of the Modern Language Association's Commission on the Status and

Education of Women, and shortly thereafter asked the Executive Council for permission to divide my time between the formal study of the status of women faculty in five thousand English and Modern Language Departments—a given in the commission's mandate—and the curriculum. I knew something had to be done about the literary curriculum, but I didn't know quite what. Because I had by now published three essay/reviews of Doris Lessing plus an interview with her, editors at three university presses wrote to ask whether I'd be interested in writing a book about Lessing. "No," I responded, "but I'd like to talk with you about another project." In each case, and later also at the *New York Review of Books*, I described what I thought my students and I needed: a series of small, pamphlet-sized books written by distinguished women about other women—in history, in the arts, in politics, and perhaps even in science and other areas of life. I mentioned that I could see Doris Lessing writing on Olive Schreiner, or Marianne Moore writing on Emily Dickinson. The editors or publishers were clearly intrigued, but in each case, the financial officer of the press or the magazine intervened, always with the same statement: "It's a great idea, but there's no money in it."

By late June of 1970, I was discouraged enough to consider giving the whole thing up, when my ex-husband suggested that I do it myself. Thus in mid-July I decided to find collaborators among Baltimore's women's liberation group. Twenty-five women thought the idea was fine, but they were all too busy, they said, with their magazine, *Women: A Journal of Liberation*. I left in a fury and returned home, determined to forget the whole idea.

At Cape Cod with family for a month, I worked on the study of English departments for the MLA meeting in December, and I prepared my courses and finished other writing assignments. Hence, when I returned to Baltimore to clear out the curbside mailbox usually stuffed only with junk mail, to my surprise—and then horror—there were a hundred or more envelopes addressed to "The Feminist Press" at 5504 Greenspring Avenue, Baltimore, Maryland 21204. Fury does not aptly convey the mixture of emotions I felt as I read the letters. Apparently Baltimore Women's Liberation had included, in their July newsletter, an announcement about "The Feminist Press," stating that its publishing goals were to be "biographies of women and *children's books*." How could this have happened, since I had never mentioned children's books? I fussed and fumed for more than a month, then mimeographed a long letter, describing "the confusion," the mixed messages, and stating that if more than twenty people turned up on November 17, 1970, and agreed to work together on this "project," there would be a Feminist Press. If not, I would return the small checks and dollar bills—amounting to about one hundred dollars—and we would forget the whole thing.

Many more than twenty people turned up, including Cynthia Secor from the University of Pennsylvania. From Baltimore, there were two Goucher students, Barbara Danish (who wrote our first children's book) and Laura Brown (now on our board of directors), Elaine Hedges from Towson State University (who stayed closely involved with The Feminist Press until she died in 1997), Mary Jane Lupton from Morgan State College (who wrote the first of our small biographies), and many of the women from Baltimore Women's Liberation, one of whom, Judy Markowitz, volunteered to manage the distribution of our books from her garage in Columbia, Maryland. For a year, we met monthly about how to respond to all the mail we were getting, how to begin to think about contracts, and how to raise money enough to publish the first children's book, *The Dragon and the Doctor*. While I was always present at meetings, I did not feel in charge, certainly not around children's books, and we tried to make all decisions by consensus, with different people taking turns chairing.

In fact, I had many other things to work on, even beyond my teaching, for the MLA Commission met four times a year, and I still had to write the study of women faculty, both for a scholarly audience in *PMLA* and for a more general one in *College English*. I had also begun to be invited to campuses to talk about the status of women or women's education and the development of women's studies, and I could not speak without writing a new lecture. When, for my ex-husband's sake, we decided to move out of Baltimore, and I had accepted a job at Old Westbury, I fully expected that The Feminist Press would remain a Baltimore project, and that I would come down for meetings once a month, since I still needed to go to the dentist in Baltimore.

But despite its youth, no one would volunteer to keep it, and so it moved with me to a hallway in a temporary building on the Old Westbury campus where I had a desk, a chair, and a small bookcase. It was not long before a group of New York publishing women were eager to help, and soon the Baltimore group was coming to meetings in New York, or we were traveling to Baltimore. We would still have been working only on biographies and children's books, but by then Tillie Olsen had given me her tattered copy of *Life in the Iron Mills*, a novella published anonymously in the *Atlantic* in 1861 and only recently discovered to be by a woman named Rebecca Harding (Davis). My reaction to that story spelled the mission of The Feminist Press to this day: If that amazingly brilliant story had been "lost" for more than a hundred years, what else had been lost? Was it not our business to find that "lost" literary output by women? Would not that search also reveal the lives of these women and the history of half of the human race?[8]

With Tillie Olsen's Literary and Biographical Afterword, we called this volume "Reprint No. 1" when we published it in 1972, aware that its publication was to change the ultimate purpose and achievement of The Feminist Press, for we were publishing symbiotically with the development of women's studies. We would—we were conscious of the mission—supply the classroom with literary volumes by women that should always have been there. By then, Elaine Hedges had given us *The Yellow Wallpaper* by Charlotte Perkins Gilman and Tillie Olsen had given us *Daughter of Earth* by Agnes Smedley, both of which we published in 1973. By then, too, with the blessing of the Baltimore and New York groups, who were still meeting monthly, we had in place a Reprints Advisory Board of young scholars eager to put their mark on what was clearly going to shape the future feminist curriculum, not only for women's studies but for literature, history, black studies, and other academic areas.[9]

Though it is not easy to portray, only a very small portion of my life was focused on The Feminist Press during this period, for I had a full-time teaching job that included not only heavy administrative responsibilities but the management of a grant from the National Endowment for the Humanities meant to support the organization of an American studies program, into which I wanted to place a women's studies program. The State University of New York College at Old Westbury, a new and experimental campus, organized not into departments but interdisciplinary programs, was unique in other ways as well. The campus profile for faculty and students had been deliberately set by President John Maguire: each was to be recruited in a pattern that came to be known as 30-30-30-10: 30 percent white; 30 percent black; 30 percent Hispanic; and 10 percent other, which meant Asian American. Moreover, the student body was to be drawn from the local Long Island population, at least half of which was working class, émigrés from Brooklyn and Queens seeking a better life for their children. Further, the college was committed to encouraging older students to apply, giving them "life experience" credits. Thus at least two-thirds of the students were "nontraditional," and at least half were working class.

What was I to make of a campus so politically, culturally, and academically different from staid, white Goucher College, where I had not been allowed to call my composition course *Women* and Identity, for that, I was told in 1969, would be "offensive." When I began to teach at Goucher in 1960, I had been the good daughter, a rare young woman on a faculty largely made up of older and younger men. Just three years later, accused of encouraging students to break the (racial) laws of Baltimore, I became the bad daughter. Eventually, during my last few years, I was still further isolated from a faculty and administration determined not to be touched by feminism.

At Old Westbury in 1971, I was older even than President John Maguire, and definitely the senior woman, the token female full professor, and one of very few white full professors. Although I had no Ph.D., I had political credentials as an organizer, and professional credentials as a published writer and newly elected second vice president of the MLA. Moreover, I arrived with what were perceived as professional, rather than political, projects: The Feminist Press was welcomed by John Maguire, as was the Clearinghouse on Women's Studies, an outgrowth of the MLA's Commission on the Status and Education of Women. By 1972, The Feminist Press was also producing—and I was editing—the *Women's Studies Newsletter.* Everyone also expected me to organize a women's studies program. It could have been an assignment.

I should have enjoyed it, since all the white women on the campus wanted a women's studies program. Seemingly, there was no one to oppose us. But I was not happy to be isolated from women of color, most of whom were teaching in the writing program where I had also expected to teach. But no one there knew or cared about my work at Goucher—or, indeed, even in Mississippi, for that was history—and the identity politics of the campus called for blacks to teach blacks, if not all the time, then certainly in the writing program.[10]

The major teaching that fell into my hands was Introduction to Women's Studies, a course I first designed for the fall of 1972. Not surprisingly, I used what I had learned at Goucher to organize the syllabus:

> This course will introduce the resources that clarify perspectives of history, our contemporary lives, and our visions of the future. Some of these reasons are inside us, our experiences and present states; others are to be found in history or in literature by or about women, including fiction, autobiography, and poetry, as well as selections from feminists (and anti-feminists) past and present. We will write some literature of our own.[11]

When I began the next paragraph with the sentence, "We will focus on who we are and the work we have done and plan to do," I knew that the students I would be meeting in these classes were totally different from those I had taught for eleven years. There were generally at least sixty students in this introductory course, most but not all of them women, no more than 50 percent white. Only one-third were the age of Goucher students; one-third were twenty to forty; and one-third over forty. And more than half were working class, a high percentage of the white students Italian American Catholics opposed to abortion, then the hottest feminist topic. Politics and political action were rife on Old Westbury's campus, but the women's studies program decided early on that abortion was one area reserved for discussion. Not that there were no "actions." Some of our students described their taking in of women whose families were opposed to their pregnancies, but who wanted to have their babies. Some of our students helped others to get abortions. No class passed without some debate on this topic. But no votes were taken, no manifestos circulated for signatures. We understood that both camps considered themselves feminists.

While the course was ostensibly "mine," various members of the women's studies program faculty, drawn from programs beyond American Studies, team taught from time to time. One of the results of this team teaching was *Witches, Midwives and Nurses,* the ground-breaking pamphlet by Deirdre English and Barbara Ehrenreich, followed by *Complaints and Disorders: The Sexual Politics of Sickness.*[12]

The syllabus for this introductory course, organized developmentally to follow the course of a woman's life, listed topics to be covered: playing with dolls and other games in childhood; brothers and sisters in families; mothers and fathers, and their children; going to school, friends; early sexual awareness and early sexual encounters; high school and the future; work or love; relationships with men/women; marriage, housework, motherhood; jobs and the future. To begin with, we used Toni Cade Bambara's book, *The Black Woman: An Anthology,* though eventually we added *Woman in Sexist Society: Studies in Power and Powerlessness,* edited by Vivian Gornick and Barbara K. Moran. Students also read fiction, some of which I had also used at Goucher. But the differences were startling. With regard to *The Awakening* by Kate Chopin, Goucher students thought appropriate the suicide of twenty-eight-year-old Edna, since, as they so clearly put it, "Her life was over." She didn't want to be married to her husband, her lover had left her, and so what could she do with her life but leave it. Even her two children, the students insisted, would be better off without her.

At Old Westbury, these older students were so puzzled by the ending that they asked me whether the printer could possibly have rewritten it. They assumed that no writer would want to kill off Edna, for she had all that these students were searching for: she had talent, she had education, she had "her" children, as they would put it. "So what if her lover had left her," one students said. "She could get another." As for her husband, he had enough money to keep her living comfortably even divorced. Finally, as one student put it, "No one with as much consciousness as Edna would have killed herself."

In addition to the middle-class literature I had taught at Goucher, I had working-class texts I could assign; hence, we could talk about class as well as gender and race. We read *Coming of Age in Mississippi* by Anne Moody and *Tell Me a Riddle* by Tillie Olsen. By 1973, I could teach *Daughter of Earth* by Agnes Smedley side by side with *Sons and Lovers* to make palpable the differences gender makes in the lives of working-class young people. But Smedley also provided a lesson about race, for all the African Americans and some of the white students assumed that Marie was black, since her family's poverty was so stark that she had to go out to do housework at ten. Because she was so heroic a character, moreover, the African American students wanted to claim her, but it was significantly important for black-white relationships in my classes that she was white, though with a partly Native American father.

As the 1970s moved forward, however, I traveled more and more, for single lectures or for a week's or a summer's residence on other campuses, helping women's studies programs begin, or consulting—sometimes for the administration—about their future direction. I traveled for six months at the end of 1975, spending a week on each of fifteen campuses to write a monograph for the federal Department of Health, Education and Welfare on women's studies.[13] I had also assumed heavy responsibilities at the Modern Language Association, where, though I no longer chaired the Commission on the Status and Education of Women, I had been given the Clearinghouse on Women's Studies to manage. Only midway through the 1970s did I think to place it under the umbrella of The Feminist Press, which also needed more and more of my time, as it took on not only large publishing projects, but initiated a series of in-service courses called Sexism in School and Society for public school teachers in the New York area, some of which I taught.

Throughout this period, my teaching anchored me. In every essay I wrote for the scores of lectures I gave during those years, I used examples from the classroom to illuminate the importance of the curricular revolution occurring in all fields. Because my students mirrored the multicultural realities of U. S. society, they taught me as much as I taught them.

One year, to vary the classroom format, we organized panels on sex and money. To get a good mix of age, gender, class, race, and sexual preference, we needed at least nine or ten people per panel. Innocently, we had theorized that it would be very difficult to recruit students to talk about their first sexual experience, expecting that at least half of them would drop away, given the topic. But all appeared on the prescribed morning, and were totally unembarrassed as they described their early sexual lives in more graphic detail than the faculty cared to hear. Analytic discussions followed the presentations on subsequent days, along with readings. When we moved on to money, we assumed that we would then be able to make significant connections between the two themes. To our surprise, half the panelists did not turn up for their session, and those that did were remarkably brief. One white, middle-class woman in her forties described a generous family inheritance she had used to put her ex-husband through medical school, where he had found a new partner. When asked why she had not used the money to put herself through medical school, she could only shrug. Further, the question itself generated only silence from a class that had been full of comments, questions, and analyses about sexual behavior a few weeks earlier. I should not have been mystified, for had I ever been willing to talk about my family's poverty? My father's occupation? My mother's working, and even my own work life as a child and teenager? While historians and literary faculty like me were, in the 1970s, reading as much as we could of feminist scholarship in psychology, sociology, and anthropology, we were not astute about economics, nor had we begun to touch on fiscal policies of banks and other lending institutions, or differential scales of pay for gender-classified work, including the professions.

If I have any regrets about this crowded period, it is that I did not have the skills or the knowledge to teach and write more about social class. It took several years of magical time with Tillie and Jack Olsen for me to understand all I had missed throughout a lifetime spent hiding my working-class roots. And my students continued to teach me as well.

Some of them also began to work at The Feminist Press, first as work-study students, and then as paid staff. Three of them—Tamar Berkowitz,

Jean Mangi, and Jane Williamson—coedited *Who's Who and Where in Women's Studies,* published with funds from the Ford Foundation in 1974. By mid-decade, we had moved out of the large office I had been given for women's studies, which we had filled with six work spaces, into a small cottage in a remote area of campus. There, until 1985, Feminist Press staff continued to be a medley of Old Westbury students, usually nontraditional in age, and middle-class housewives seeking training to enter new careers, though leavened with two or three publishing professionals willing to commute out of New York City to join so dedicated a workspace.

By the end of the 1970s, the symbiosis between the needs of teaching women's studies courses, especially in history and literature, and the publishing mission of The Feminist Press had thoroughly melded. The project that engaged The Feminist Press from 1974 until 1981 was called Women's Lives, Women's Work. We imagined and designed twelve texts on topics key to women's studies and needed in high school classrooms if women were to be perceived as historical subjects and employable. We hoped we would be able to initiate changes in the high school curriculum as rapidly as we had in college literature courses, but of course we were naïve about the intransigence of schools.[14]

At a tenth-year gala celebration at Manhattan's Town Hall, in 1980, board member Elizabeth Janeway clinked champagne glasses with me, saying, "Here's to the next ten years." And for the first time, I had to think about the future of The Feminist Press. Could I leave it and return full-time to the pleasures of the classroom? For two years I tried separation—in the Midwest in visiting appointments—and tried to give most of my attention to women's studies students and faculty, first at Oberlin College, then at Denison University, and other institutions that were part of the Great Lakes Colleges Association, where I was visiting professor. Early in 1980, intrepid Mariam Chamberlain, then at the Ford Foundation, whisked me off to Europe for a three-week visit, saying that it was time to think about women's studies internationally. She meant women's studies and The Feminist Press. And by then I knew that I was caught.[15]

In retrospect, the 1970s were a golden age for women's studies and the women's movement in general. My own re-education owes much to my students and colleagues, and as the 1980s turned into the 1990s, I learned not only from my students but also from authors, colleagues, and board members that The Feminist Press, evolving with women's studies, was to be my future.

Nancy Hoffman

I came to Brown University in 1996 to be director of the Office of the President, and then became secretary of the university, but in July 1998, I returned happily to full-time teaching as senior lecturer in education. At Temple University in Philadelphia, I was vice provost for undergraduate studies (1993–96), presidential fellow, and, prior to that, director of the university honors program with faculty appointments in English and women's studies. I have also been academic services dean at the Harvard Graduate School of Education (1986–90), program officer at the Fund for the Improvement of Postsecondary Education (1979–81), and a founder and faculty member of the University of Massachusetts, Boston, College of Public and Community Service in the 1970s and 1980s. At the University of Massachusetts, I also ran the Center for the Improvement of Teaching. I have also taught English and comparative literature at the University of California, Santa Barbara, at Portland State University, and at the Massachusetts Institute of Technology. I have a B.A. (1964) and Ph.D. (1971) in comparative literature from the University of California, Berkeley, with a specialization in the Renaissance. I can claim *Spenser's Pastorals* (Johns Hopkins University Press, 1979) from my literary days, and *Women's "True" Profession: Voices from the History of Teaching* (Feminist Press, 1981), which was the beginning of my work in education. With Florence Howe, I edited *Women Working: Stories and Poems* (Feminist Press, 1979). I have also coedited two volumes of *Women's Studies Quarterly: Women, Girls and the Culture of Education* and *Women, Race and Culture;* and a third, on gender in grades K–12 and teacher education, is in progress. At Brown, my current courses include Urban School Reform, Women and Teaching, and Literacy and Community through the Arts. I am on the board of The Feminist Press; serve as convenor of the Pew-funded project, Restructuring for Urban Student Success (focused on restructuring the first year of urban universities); and work in and around urban high schools and universities.

Teaching Across the Borders of Race and Class

My "mothering" of women's studies began on the West Coast, instigated not by academic intellectuals but by radical student activists, of whom I was one. Our goal was to open up the university to scrutiny, to challenge institutional power, and to take some for our own purposes. Although many of us were students and young faculty members, we were also outsiders whose prior political activities had been off campus. We saw the youth on campus as ripe for radicalizing and organizing. For me, the women's studies classroom became the place where politics and intellectual interests could come together, where you could teach in the radical style set out in Paulo Freire's *Pedagogy of the Oppressed*. This essay, then, is the story of working out ideas for women's studies through teaching practices; it is also the story of dealing with race and ethnic diversity.

I grew up in the civil rights movement of the early 1960s as an organizer of poor people. I was also an antiwar activist. The thread of meaning from an early age, and the tradition in my atheist Jewish family, was to fight against discrimination and for integration in a world that granted privilege to whiteness. As a student at Brandeis University from 1960 to 1962, I picketed Woolworth's in Harvard Square and went on a very early antiwar march from Brandeis to the Watertown arsenal, a weapons storage site. In 1962 I was twenty years old, married, and a student of literature. I moved to Berkeley, where I completed my B.A. and Ph.D. in comparative literature while becoming increasingly involved in civil rights activity. This was the Berkeley of legend: I arrived just after the Auto Row sit-ins in San Francisco, as protesters attempted to force the automobile dealers on Van Ness Avenue to hire black salespeople. A serious student of classics and the Renaissance, I lived a divided life quite deliberately—working by day as an undergraduate grader and teaching assistant for several exceedingly bright English professors and spending evenings and weekends first as a member of and then as a leader of Bay Area Friends of the Student Nonviolent Coordinating Committee (SNCC) in San Francisco. My husband and I spent the summer of 1965 working for SNCC in Mississippi; I was a birth control educator on and around plantations in the northern part of the Delta.

Looking back at my upper-division years at Berkeley and the three years of graduate school that followed, I realize that my story will be familiar to many women. I was an excellent girl student: obedient, smart, on time, reliable, and an insightful, close reader of literary texts. I was also attractive and thus came to confuse in my own mind the reasons for my success: was it due to my brains and academic promise or was it that young male professors fell in love with me? From those years, an essay of Sally Kempton's called "Cutting Loose" inhabits my mind: If you were pretty, asked smart questions, and flattered male intellectuals, Kempton had written, you could succeed, but there was damage to be calculated, and it was gender damage. At the end of the essay, Kempton asked, "How can you fight an enemy that has outposts in your head?"[1]

My outposts were well established; I participated in the flirtatious atmosphere in exchange for assurance of my academic talent. Later I came to think that some of the young male faculty had been so busy being smart and getting to be junior fellows at Harvard during graduate school that they were in a state of arrested development when it came to "girls." Ten years or so younger than they, their smart female graduate students could be flattered and flattering. And without feminist analysis, there were no words for the situation except those our mothers used to describe their dubious power: we women manipulated men with our female wiles. It was only in the 1970s, when I had become a member of the Modern Language Association's Commission on the Status and Education of Women and was researching an article on sexism in letters of recommendation that I confronted directly the fact that physical attributes mediated the assessment that male faculty made of female job candidates. One of my own letters said, "She is pretty, some might say beautiful"; while that of another job seeker said disparagingly, "She is the wheel horse of any committee she serves on."

With my composer husband, I spent 1967–68 living in Paris during *les années soixante,* participating in political rallies from Copenhagen to Milan. By the spring of that year, I had hepatitis, and I spent several months in a rented farm house outside of Geneva recuperating. Still not exactly strong, I returned to Berkeley in the summer of 1968 to find "the movement" in shambles, and antiwhite sentiment at an all-time high in what had become a nationalistic civil rights movement. Tensions were increasing in my marriage as I began to write my dissertation and apply for academic jobs while my husband's anti-institutional sentiments persisted, along with his anger and his commitment to anarchism. Our movement work that year included raising funds and helping gather food for Cesar Chavez, leader of the grape strikers' union drive, and getting involved in unionizing my own profession—graduate students—into the American Federation of Teachers. In both these activities, I distinctly remember priding myself on being the only woman included in the conversation, the only one trusted to organize. My framework for analyzing political situations thus far was New Left Marxist: class and race were the salient categories.

In the spring of 1969, I took a job in the English department at the University of California, Santa Barbara, and moved there during the summer of what would be—although I didn't yet know it—my first year of life as a feminist. By then, the West Coast youth movement was fragmented by racial tensions, drugs, antiwar violence, and that brand of drop-out individualism called "do your own thing." The borders between what had been Marxist or at least coherent left political analysis and activities and the hippie, druggy, free sex, free love ethos began to blur. Star intellectual graduate students destroyed their minds with drugs: one of our friends went slowly mad, living in a room stacked with newspaper clippings about the war. He had to be taken home to Queens by his mother. Others killed themselves or disappeared—especially those without institutional affiliations who drifted loose—questioning everything and having no discipline to which to return. Southern California was astonishing in that period. In the crisp fall days, the Channel Islands gleamed off the coast of Santa Barbara; John Birch Society members sleuthed the until-then conservative campus looking for subversives, among whom I numbered. Slowly, sleepy UCSB was becoming a hotbed of student conflict and activism.

My entrance into feminism was influenced by my isolation as one of a very few young women faculty at UCSB. I was a twenty-six-year-old assistant professor whom my department colleagues thought of correctly as a radical graduate student. Having no female colleagues as role models, I chose as friends female graduate students and faculty wives. Furthermore, because my prior history of radicalism led me to gravitate to the leftists in the sociology department rather than to my colleagues in the English department, early on I sought out Dick Flacks, a sociologist from the University of Chicago, who also had recently moved to UCSB with his wife, Mickey Flacks. A chronicler of leftist youth movements and the target of a physical attack in Chicago because of his North Vietnam sympathies, Dick had attended the same leftist summer camp as I in the late 1950s. Early in the fall, Mickey organized what we called back then a consciousness-raising (CR) group composed of faculty wives and myself. A number of us were movement activists who had done our share of typing, making coffee, and other support activities. We met once a week, exploring what it meant to say that the personal is political—mainly groping for language to explain perceptions and feelings that had been hitherto inchoate. I do not think that I had ever before talked to anyone—let alone a group—about my intensely personal feelings, but R. D. Laing and Doris Lessing—the writers we were reading at the time—were opening questions about sanity and madness that challenged our perceptions of the cost of "normality." Although such talk seemed self-indulgent at times, given the war, poverty, and my still-unfinished dissertation, it was the kind of conversation from which there was no turning back.

In that group, I dared to think about the question of whether women's situation was in any way analogous to that of blacks, to raise the issue of the dual oppressions of black women. As I recall, we also talked about who did the dishes, kept the kids, cooked, shopped, and created domestic comfort; how we looked, how we cared or did not care about what we wore; how our intellects were not valued; and whether pulling magazines with demeaning images of women off of drugstore shelves was, indeed, a useful political act. That fall also, several undergraduate students from a new group called Concerned Women (CW) persisted in trying to persuade me that there should be a course about women at UCSB and that I should teach it. Despite belonging to a CR group, I was still reluctant to get involved publicly in women's issues, clinging to the view that movement work was incompatible with and politically superior to studying myself. Finally, I agreed, and my department chair gave his permission for a special topics course. "I like those pop courses, " he said. And so Women and Literature was on the books. The university was in turmoil over the war and student radicalism, and a course on women was not threatening. The problem was what to teach. This was 1969–70, and it was not at all apparent that one might study images of women in literature.

From my years of study in English and comparative literature, I had almost no knowledge of women writers. I had read Pearl Buck in junior high school, *Jane Eyre* in high school, *Middlemarch* in a course on the novel, Emily Dickinson under a tree in graduate school, and a few obscure female French Renaissance poets: not the makings of a syllabus, especially on a campus moving from deep conservatism to very left student activism. A small group of students from CW met with me on Sunday mornings for breakfast, after which we went to the UCSB library and looked up women writers in the card catalogue.[2]

The texts chosen, and the educational philosophy and practices decided on by students with my support, reflect the deeply political moment in which these students and this professor came together. There was a counterpoint in the group's movement between the time set aside for class discussion and time for organizing, striking, demonstrating, and bailing people out of jail. Starting in the fall of 1969, UCSB students began to organize against the nonrenewal of the contract of a popular anthropology professor. The wrongs against Bill Allen soon stood for all that was wrong with university authority, with the Reaganite government of California, and with the Washington war machine, which was preparing for the invasion of Cambodia. The semester was punctuated with the arrests of one hundred students, with my own departure from class at one point to bail a student out of jail, and with deeply fatigued students preparing for the legal defense of their compatriots. By spring, UCSB had moved from idyllic surfer campus to tinderbox. Students burned the Bank of America in Isla Vista, the student ghetto. The underground group the Weathermen (the violent offshoot of Students for a Democratic Society), attacked a National Guard arsenal, and I was asked to move out of my rented house because my police officer—landlord said I was harboring criminals.

In good early feminist fashion, the first day of Women and Literature began with personal statements: "I feel this terrible passivity in myself and it frightens me," said a young woman with a pink bow in her hair. We then moved into a discussion of passages from Anaïs Nin's

Diary and Lessing's essay "A Small Personal Voice," both of which became touchstones for what was to follow. The Nin image of feeling like a shattered mirror stood for a fragmented identity with a touch of narcissism. The Lessing statement that the writer should "voluntarily submit...*his* [emphasis mine] will to the collective, but never finally" provided a way of thinking about demonstrations just outside the door. We went on to read *The Golden Notebook, The Second Sex,* selections from *The Mandarins,* Susan Sontag's *Esquire* essay "Trip to Hanoi," and Mary McCarthy's book *Hanoi.* These last two works were immediately put to use as various students tried to apply what they could from the lives of revolutionary women in North Vietnam to becoming revolutionaries in Southern California. Amusing as this comparison seems now, I believed with these students that the youth revolution would result in some measure of socialism in the United States. Alternating between changing ourselves and changing society—following the slogan that the personal is political—as the quarter moved along, we read *I Never Promised You a Rose Garden* by Hannah Greene, *The Ha Ha* by Jennifer Dawson, and *A Spy in the House of Love* by Anaïs Nin. We attempted to deal with race and gender by comparing the oppression of white women with the oppression of black men in LeRoi Jones's *Dutchman;* we then read the same book from a Marcusian perspective, which saw alienation and oppression as the modern condition. There followed classes on Sylvia Plath and Anne Sexton, Gertrude Stein's *Three Lives,* and, finally, Virginia Woolf's *A Room of One's Own.*

Woven within the discussions were larger issues of the emerging academic feminism of the era: Why have so few women written at all? Are women's works valuable, as "true" as men's are? How are gender and racial oppression related? When I presented my proposal to the English department to make Women and Literature a permanent offering, I argued that women were painfully underrepresented in academia because of overt discrimination; that our thinking suffered from masculinist bias; that women's history was absent from the curriculum; and that women learn what men think of them, not what they think of themselves. I argued as well that women lacked intellectual confidence and that they must learn to take themselves seriously.

In the spring of 1970, my marriage ended. Finding Santa Barbara isolating and lonely, I spent the summer in Berkeley and then moved to Portland, Oregon, where, with little more than a casual interview, I was hired in the English department of Portland State University (PSU).

Here, with my colleague Nancy Porter, we enabled women students to build a women's studies program, one of the first in the country. Ours was a grass-roots movement: Nancy Porter calls it not a program but an action. As one of the chief architects and organizers, I can see now that we applied community-organizing skills to the student community. Our essays were full of dismissive statements about academia and the career-mindedness of our East Coast colleagues. We felt morally superior about the fact that we sought no legitimacy from the university's administration. In a wonderful series of sentences published in *Female Studies: Volume 6,* (Feminist Press, 1972), a PSU undergraduate writes, "One comment about women's classes; the women in them eat. . . . It takes away from the sterility. . . . We are non-academic. For this, at least, we must also be intelligent" (p. 198).[3]

Collectivist practices characterized women's studies at PSU; I was also trying to incorporate into my academic life the justice morality of the civil rights movement, along with a class analysis of society. Although my first bout with women's studies involved inward-looking and leftist works, the subsequent syllabi anticipate what is today called multicultural curriculum. These courses provide some evidence that the early women's studies movement was not as oblivious to race and class issues as some have concluded. As I do in my classroom today, I raised issues about race and racial conflict in the classroom. By 1972, my course in women's autobiography included Anne Moody's *Coming of Age in Mississippi,* Maya Angelou's *I Know Why the Caged Bird Sings,* Emma Goldman's *Living My Life,* Paule Marshall's *Brown Girl, Brown Stones,* and, as secondary sources, Goldman's *Anarchism and Other Essays* (1911) and *The Black Woman: An Anthology* (ed. Tony Cade Bambara, 1970). This last title is the first book of which I am aware to examine women's liberation from a black perspective.

In 1972, married for a second time, I moved to Boston, where my husband had been hired by the mayor's office to oversee the desegregation of the public schools. I joined what was called the Literature Section at the Massachusetts Institute of Technology. Although MIT hired two other young women in literature in 1972, the atmosphere at the institute was completely stifling. To be a female humanist was to be not only invisible but actively negated. By now I was becoming an expert not at long-term institution-building, but at "growing" women's studies wherever I happened to land. MIT, however, was not fertile ground. Teaching had become activist feminist work for me, and

I attempted to apply what I knew in the fairly flexible sections of Writing and Experience, the required composition course I taught. Young and still inexperienced as a teacher, my attempts to provoke my students into suspending their rationality and instead writing from feelings and intuition resulted in a year of the students testing me, and I, the young woman professor, finding myself either frustrated with their resistance or unnerved and ill prepared to deal with the personal writing they did produce. Although during that year, our savvy, risk-taking group of young feminist faculty proposed a large-scale collaborative course called Sex Roles and Literature, I felt useless as a faculty member: the gulf between me and the scientist boys was too great.

That spring, I became a member of the planning team for a new college to serve city adults at the University of Massachusetts, Boston. Admitting its first class in September 1973, the College of Public and Community Service had the explicit goal of changing the quality of life for poor people in Boston. Like several other competency-based higher education institutions begun during the late 1960s and early 1970s, CPCS took its cues from the alternative schools movement, from the pedagogy of the civil rights movement's freedom schools, from the preliminary work on adult learning that preceded *Women's Ways of Knowing,* from the experiential learning movement, and from the successes of the lively community organizations in the Boston, Cambridge, and Somerville area. With an average student age of thirty-six, it also began with a fundamental premise of feminist pedagogy: that you should build an education program based on the prior learning and needs of students. Students' wisdom, we believed, derived from advocacy for a disabled child, a struggle with an alcoholic mate, neighborhood organizing for a stop sign or the clean-up of a vacant lot, or refusing to comply with the welfare department. The B.A. program consisted of a series of competencies that students were required to demonstrate using portfolios, projects, and documentation of skills and knowledge—woman-friendly methods of assessment—rather than high-stress, one-shot exams.

Two-thirds of the one thousand students at the College of Public and Community Service (CPCS) were female, and at least half the faculty were. In effect, instead of having women's studies courses or a program, we created a poor women's institution in which gender issues figured across the curriculum; our majors—human growth and development, legal education services, and housing and community change—encompassed the low-paying, feminized helping professions, and the school's philosophy embraced the notion that personal and political change are entwined. What is interesting, then, and very much in keeping with work I have pursued throughout the decades, is that rather than fight for women's studies in an institution resistant to change, I helped to create a school in which there was an explicit commitment to support and empower poor women and to deal with issues of racial difference. The first few years of the college were trying, but not for reasons of feminism. Busing had begun in Boston, and the college became one of the few places where working-class blacks and whites from the neighborhoods could meet on relatively neutral ground. Feelings were raw. Louise Day Hicks, the antibusing president of the city council, was a neighbor of Southie students. The unveiling of Boston's racist history to a wide community made for serious tensions. Our students were parents of black children who were being bused to white neighborhoods, and of white children who were being kept out of school or sent to hastily established private academies. Class antagonisms were rife and the alliances were not attractive. J. Arthur Garrity, the remote federal judge who ordered desegregation, lived in wealthy Wellesley; whites and some blacks felt that affluent suburbanites were pulling the strings that pitted poor against poor.

Like many of the struggles that involve poor people, women and children suffered the greatest hardships and had the potential for greatest growth. I worked closely with the Citywide Educational Coalition, an almost all-female organization that employed some CPCS students as parent organizers. In an article about the coalition, I profiled a white antibusing staffer, Judy, who recounted going to ask a principal to clean up a school. "He called us 'girls,'" she said, "and told us while it was nice we had gotten out of the kitchen to see him, he couldn't do a thing to help us. I'd never asserted myself against authority. I couldn't imagine being nervy enough to confront a principal." But Judy learned quickly to stick up for herself, to cool racial tensions, and to withstand the emotional and physical trauma of being cursed, stoned, and attacked. Judy landed in the hospital three times.

The kind of women's studies I developed at the college were about using literary texts—I taught *Their Eyes Were Watching God* and *Coming of Age in Mississippi* and *Life in the Iron Mills*—to create a basic reading and writing community where students could actually speak about themselves, their families, and their experience in relation to books. Books could validate their feelings and perceptions: if domestic violence appeared in the pages of a book, then it could be spoken about, it could be real, as could racist violence and the silencing of the white working class.

With spotty primary and high school records from de facto segregated schools, CPCS students brought with them all the qualities of typical, tentative adult learners, the women especially. Community organizers who had fought city hall did not necessarily take easily to skills of academic analysis. We did not theorize about feminism; indeed, some of my colleagues of color were hostile to the term. Yet across the curriculum and in the many independent projects students carried out, we took note of the situation of women, and of women of color particularly. Massachusetts's welfare rights organization, the Coalition for Basic Human Needs, was born at CPCS, and our students worked in and involved us in such organizations as Aid to Incarcerated Mothers; Older Women's League; Women for Economic Justice; and Women, Inc. (a residential drug treatment program for women and their children). I sponsored a Women's Day in 1973 at which there were workshops called Managing Money and Myths about Motherhood, Women, and Power. The centerpiece was a poetry reading that foregrounded race and class diversity, and within that diversity, the necessity of representing women's self-identification precisely. A poster in my handwriting has these carefully inscribed words: "Jackie Silva [one of the poetry readers] is a Third World person who happens to be a black woman. She teaches about prisons and women and has been writing for years."

I taught at CPCS from 1972 to 1978, and again from 1982 to 1985.[4] The CPCS years stand out for the painful memories of struggles with the intersection of race and gender in teaching, in personal relations, and with colleagues. CPCS had very few faculty who remained outside of diversity politics, but there were substantial differences among us. Given that almost everyone had an openly political agenda and that most were radical Democrats or socialists, the cacophony of voices was constant. Almost nothing was decided without discussion and dissension. The faculty socialist collective had splits within it; there were struggles about the school's unionization, about the quality of student work, about the content of the curriculum, about office space, and especially about college leadership.

Gender issues were an undercurrent while race roiled the waters into frightening waves. For example, the founding dean, a white southerner with a civil rights background, was followed by an acting dean, also white, a returned Peace Corps volunteer and Harvard-trained lawyer. It seemed appropriate, then, in a school serving a large minority population, that CPCS should seek a person of color as the next dean. Most of the African American, Latino, and Asian American faculty said, however, that they would only support a nonwhite dean candidate; the whites were divided between those who agreed and those who, although hoping for a strong nonwhite candidate, argued that we should not preclude the possibility of a white who could adequately represent issues of minority students and faculty. The latter group of whites, among whom I number myself, were resisting identity politics. Such divisions tainted relationships, especially between women; the men were less bonded across races to start with and had less to lose in these conflicts. There was talk at one point of whether I should be teaching Black Women Writers, for example, or chairing a panel discussion on race issues.

White women like me, who had tolerated quite a lot of criticism to stay engaged in civil rights, simply kept working, whatever our blind spots, and got a bit tougher. The personal cost in self-doubt and hurt notwithstanding, there was something totally right and persuasive and clean about working at CPCS with women during those years. I had incredible freedom to experiment in teaching; the work was as real as it gets in academia; and literature evoked ancient and deep passions in the students. I could struggle for weeks to get a class to understand that the "I" voice in a novel was not the author's; simultaneously, a student could (and did) fall in love with Zora Neale Hurston's Janie in *Their Eyes Were Watching God,* rename herself after the character, and decide that henceforth she would be treated by the men in her life according to her own protocol for egalitarian relationships. I taught Poetry and the Female Consciousness, The Myth of Success in America, and courses in family history in which we traced generations of women from slave ships and Ellis Island records and Massachusetts census data. I developed an advanced American studies course about the relationship between the suffrage and abolitionist movements that went straight at the racism of some of feminism's founding mothers, and to the prescience of those few women, white and black, who saw the power in common cause. With an economist colleague, however, I was also engaged in planning a neighborhood learning center that would teach low-income people sufficient economics to enable them to take advantage of community economic development funds for their neighborhoods. And, like the majority of the faculty, I played informal case worker intervening with the welfare department, the Massachusetts Rehabilitation Commission, the housing courts, the food banks— whatever the emergency of the student at hand. When I left CPCS for Washington, D.C., to work on the staff of the Fund for the Improvement of Postsecondary Education in 1979, I was more a community organizer than a professor, more a feminist activist than a theoretician, and more identified with the condition of poor women than I had been before—or have been since.

Perhaps the coda to this essay should be a brief note about the Modern Language Association's Commission on the Status and Education of Women.[5] From 1969 to 1974, I was a member, and was cochair with Elaine Reuben for a couple of years. The story of the commission is probably a more familiar founding-mothers story than the one I have told. Suffice it to say, the commission kept me anchored to a profession that at times seemed pretty meaningless against a backdrop of racism, racial conflict, and poverty; it gave me Tillie Olsen and Florence Howe and Adrienne Rich; it was a place to meet women who were in the tormenting process of coming out; and it gave me some choices about the woman I could become without giving up my political commitments—at least not in full. I suspect, although I remember myself rather little as a commission member, that I gave some of CPCS to the commission. And that's how I mothered women's studies.

Sheila Tobias

At the time of the Cornell Conference on Women (January 1969), I was thirty-three years old with an already checkered career behind me: graduate of Radcliffe (now Harvard/Radcliffe) in 1957 in the history and literature of modern Europe (mainly Germany); four years of journalistic work in Germany; three years of graduate study of history ("all but dissertation"); work in the civil rights movement and the antiwar movement; volunteer for Eugene McCarthy; researcher for ABC and NET television; and goad and gadfly to a talented man with whom and for whom I had come to Cornell in 1967.

In the summer of 1970, just after teaching the first course in women's studies at Cornell, I was asked to be a candidate for a newly created position at Wesleyan University, which had voted the previous year to go coed. The position allowed me a perch from which—throughout an eight-year period—I was able to shepherd Wesleyan's new women students, oversee the hiring of new women faculty and staff, introduce imaginative new policies (on nepotism, maternity, and women's health services), and collaborate with other token women like myself to forge a New England network featuring job search and referral, off-the-job training, and national activism in the service of women's studies, affirmative action, and gender equity in education.

It was at Wesleyan that I uncovered "math anxiety" and started a program and wrote a book. That book changed my life's course once again, because it presented me with the opportunity to be a public educator, unconstrained by institutional affiliation and able to teach, write, speak, consult, and work on short-term assignments—at will. I chose as my special beat the patriarchy: arenas in which men dominate or predominate numerically. I have written books on mathematics teaching and learning, war, militarism, military spending, and science; and I have written articles on politics and women's war work. My most recent book is *Faces of Feminism: An Activist's Reflections on the Women's Movement* (Westview Press, 1997).

Beginning in the 1960s

In the spring semester of 1970, at Cornell University in upstate New York, a new course, The Evolution of Female Personality: Its History and Prospects, sprang forth fully formed, fully accredited, and fully enrolled with two hundred students in the first class. The campus did not know it, but the course was unique not only in its content but in its origins: unlike the ordinary, professor-generated segment of a traditional curriculum, Female Personality had been forged by a *collective,* a self-appointed group of thirty staff women, graduate students, and adjunct faculty, most of whom were, like the women whose nature and history and status the course was designed to explore, on the margin of academe. Where did the energy come from, the sense of urgency and of entitlement to invent and launch such a radical feminist program of academic studies on an Ivy League campus—a program that (although we did not know it at the time) would expand and garner ever more student and faculty support throughout the next thirty years?

Cornell University was coeducational in name and charter from its founding in 1862 but, as historian Charlotte Conable found in researching *Women at Cornell,* despite a handful of outstanding women graduates, Cornell had not evolved commensurate with its founders' ideals.[1] Still, the women who called Cornell their alma mater included Ruth Bader Ginsburg, '54, the first woman member of the Columbia Law School Faculty and second woman appointed to the Supreme Court; Susan Brownmiller, '56, who would, as a mature feminist scholar, write the ground-breaking *Against Our Will: Men, Women, and Rape;* and Constance Cook, '41, LL.B. '43, a leading advocate of abortion reform in the New York State Legislature, of which she was a member.

For women students arriving to take their limited places in the late 1960s, Cornell felt more like a bastion of male chauvinism—a term just then coming into common parlance. With enrollment in Cornell's Arts College limited by trustee mandate to one female for every two males (because, it was argued, the men's dormitories in which the extra women would have to be housed were equipped with urinals; more likely, because women did not contribute as much to the alma mater's ever hungry coffers), Cornell's several colleges seemed to exaggerate the traditional notions of what was "male" and what was "female." There was an engineering school, more than 90 percent male, and a Home Economics College (in 1967 renamed the College of Human Ecology) traditionally "female" in its curriculum and regressive in its expectations of what educated women would do with their lives. And the veterinary college, until it attempted in the late 1960s to deny admission to the daughter of a Cornell trustee, had never enrolled a female undergraduate on the spurious grounds that women could not lift large animals (as if men could).

In the late 1960s, Cornell was a highly politicized community, but not yet feminist. That is, there was little appreciation by the radical men (and women) among the student body and on the faculty that the unequal status of women on the campus was also political in nature. Overt admissions quotas, differential parietal rules, and inadequate representation of women on the faculty (100 women out of a total faculty of 1400, with nearly 75 of the 100 in the College of Human Ecology) was clearly the result of overt discrimination combined with what we would now call sexist bias in the recruitment and promotion of women faculty and staff. Thus an androcentric curriculum was linked to the inadequate representation of women on campus, and their invisibility and lack of power made of coeducation, as Charlotte Conable was to conclude in her 1977 study of women at Cornell, a "myth."[2]

The antiwar movement had made deep inroads into the Cornell community. Undergraduates and graduate students, enthusiastically supported by a sizable minority of the Cornell faculty, rallied locally, burned their draft cards, marched on Washington, and, after the late Allard Lowenstein stopped at Cornell on his way to a "Dump Johnson Democratic Convention" in the fall of 1967, Democrats on and off campus organized to elect a propeace delegation to attend the infamous Democratic National Convention in Chicago the following year.

The Cornell community was educated and inspired (if sometimes terrorized) by its African American community. Black students had been recruited to the campus since the early 1960s, and Gloria Joseph, later to become the life partner of the poet Audre Lorde, was the point person in Day Hall (the building that housed the campuswide administration), trying to get the overwhelmingly white Cornell faculty and student body to understand the sources of black students' anger and alienation, and to do something about campus racism in the curriculum and culture. Those issues caused a deeply divisive crisis on the campus in the spring of 1968 when the black students "took over" the student union (Willard Straight Hall). But one positive outcome was the establishment soon thereafter of a significant black studies program under an African American director—a program that would serve as a model for women's studies.

By the fall of 1968, however, campus activists were tired. The previous spring had seen the retirement of Lyndon Johnson from the presidential campaign, the assassinations of Martin Luther King Jr. and Robert Kennedy, and, finally, in November, the election of Richard Nixon, which ushered in not peace in Vietnam but the so-called Vietnamization of the war.

Numerous women at Cornell and elsewhere were trying to make sense of the intensity of the past several years and to decide where to go from there. As Sara Evans tells it in her book about that period, the exposure to activism in the student and antiwar movements had not been an entirely positive one for young women.[3] Still, nothing might have happened on our campus had not circumstances conspired, as it were, to give us the time and space to host a conference on women.

In 1967, the Cornell faculty in its wisdom had tinkered once again with the academic calendar. Faculty have few inalienable rights vis-à-vis administrations. One is to define graduation requirements—hence the endless wrangling over core curricula; another is to determine the academic calendar. For years, students had been railing against the post-Christmas continuation of the first semester. They wanted to be done with their classes before Christmas. Contributing toward an earlier first-semester start-up was an increasing sensitivity (even before the 1973 Arab-led oil embargo) to the country's dependency on foreign oil that, in wintry Ithaca, translated into high heating bills during January.

So, in an effort to end first semester before Christmas and to save on heating, the Cornell faculty came up with the idea of a "January term," which, though not attracting much of a populace of either faculty or students, could be used—the spirit willing—to try out new interdisciplinary subjects or pedagogies. I was assigned by my boss, the vice president of academic affairs, to "coordinate" January term, that is, to encourage and provide administrative support for whatever courses and activities individual faculty cared to mount. To get the ball rolling, I proposed that my office (lowly though it was—I was only the assistant to the vice president) be allowed to develop one campuswide program to stimulate others.

What the subject of that program should be, I hadn't yet decided, but I was reading, as were many women of my age and stage, in the *New York Times* and elsewhere about the advent of a new feminist movement and the founding in 1966 of the National Organization for Women (NOW). As I wandered the campus in fall 1968, talking to faculty and department chairs about possible January Term activities, I heard that the College of Human Ecology had invited Dr. Esther Rauschenbush, a Sarah Lawrence College educator, to speak at the college during those weeks, and I saw a chance to spark January term with a Conference on Women. The dean of the college was worried that in the middle of January few people would be on campus to attend Rauschenbush's talk. He and I knew that Sarah Lawrence College was (and remains) a women's college and that Esther Rauschenbush was a pioneer in continuing education for women. Would he be willing, I asked, to feature Dr. Rauschenbush within a larger conference activity, one centered on women's education and jobs? He would, and so I set about creating a planning committee of women I knew on the staff, in the graduate school, in human ecology itself, and elsewhere on campus to plan what was to become a four-day meeting.

In preparation for that event and as a way to measure community interest, our planning group decided to invite someone from the nascent feminist movement to speak on campus two months before the January conference. Our guest turned out to be Kate Millett, and in early November 1968, a medium-size group of women (and some men) in a charming small auditorium in Cornell's Goldwin Smith Hall were treated to a reading from *Sexual Politics* (still in manuscript). Nothing had prepared any of us in the audience for this sudden encounter either with Millett's theory of patriarchy or with her person. But one thing was obvious even then: nothing on the Cornell campus or in our lives would ever be the same.

We hadn't gone looking for Millett. No one in our group had known of her work at the time, and she hadn't gone looking for us. We had first wanted Ti-Grace Atkinson to be our speaker. Atkinson was also not yet well known, but she had written an article about something called "the new feminism" in no less a publication than the *New York Times Magazine;* she was a "philosopher" by training, which we thought would suit our academic environs; and she was listed as a task force coordinator for NOW. However, when I sought her out in early fall at her New York apartment, Atkinson declined our invitation, explaining to me, with the patience reserved for the unenlightened, that she did not speak before "mixed audiences" (audiences, it took me a while to comprehend, that included men). So, unless I could restrict the attendance, she recommended as a substitute the head of the nascent New York NOW Task Force on Education, a doctoral student in Columbia University's literature department named Kate Millett.

Two years later, after *Time* magazine featured Millett and her book in a cover story remarkable for its attention to a movement as young as the New Feminism, everyone would be familiar with the broad outline of Millett's theories of patriarchy and sexual politics. But as we soon-to-become feminists sat transfixed by her presentation on that cold fall day in 1968, we already knew in our bones that history was about to be made and that we were going to be a part of its making.

Millett came back to Cornell in January 1969 to "star," you might say, in our Conference on Women. In typical movement fashion, she persuaded us to let her trade in her prepaid airplane ticket for a rental van so that she could bring a small delegation of New York feminists to our rural campus. Among them were six radical women from New York City's self-styled cabal the Women's International Terrorist Conspiracy from Hell (WITCH). We also brought in Betty Friedan, who was still touring the country with her book *The Feminine Mystique* and leaving protofeminists everywhere in her wake. Millett's group was waking up student radicals to a variant of that same message. The high points of our conference would be the debates among the new feminists on our panels, the male radicals, and the academics.

"Yes, we do studies of sex differences," one Cornell anthropologist intoned during one of the sessions. "We know that men play tic-tac-toe to win, women to tie." The WITCHes hissed, the crowd cheered the hissing, and the radical men cowered as the imported feminists pointed out that in men's "socialist heaven," women poured the coffee, ran the mimeograph machines, and played groupie. A feminist critique of radical men's politics was *long* overdue.

But so was a critique of the curriculum. Going to college, we began to grasp as the four-day conference unfolded, was itself socialization for inferiority. Insofar as the curriculum mentioned women at all (and, for the most part, women's lives and accomplishments were omitted), it marginalized both their problems and their contributions to literature, history, the arts, and the behavioral sciences. On a college campus, feminist political organizing clearly had a teaching function as well. But to replace what was missing, we had to offer courses on women and women's issues, which is what we set out to do after the conference was over and how The Evolution of Female Personality—the first women's studies course at Cornell—came to be.

In the early 1970s women were inventing new ways of working together. Patriarchy, according to feminist theory, involved hierarchy; women's work need not. True to our subject, we course planners fashioned ourselves into a collective, a team with no captain, who met regularly, first in a loosely organized seminar with undergraduate students (spring 1969), and then by ourselves (fall 1969) as we formally decided on a sequence of topics for our course.

Who were we? All of us were academic in that we held bachelor's and some postgraduate degrees and were all working, in one capacity or another, at Cornell. All of us were well read, curious, good thinkers, and able writers. But, as was common in those waning days of the feminine mystique, the glass ceiling was very low. Most of us were underemployed at Cornell, either because we had followed a partner to the isolated campus or because we didn't know how to demand what we deserved. I had come up from the City College of New York's history department, all but dissertation, as we used to say, from Columbia University, only to be given a typing test by an assistant to the head of personnel (herself an underemployed woman professional). I had landed a better job than either she or I had anticipated, only because a Cornell task force had recommended the creation of an undergraduate advisory committee and that committee needed staff.

Others in our group held low-paying or temporary positions, with titles, as we began to notice, that usually began with the letter *a*. We were assistants, associates, acting, or adjuncts, with one exception, Professor Joy Osofsky, a regular member of the faculty in the Department of Human Development and Family Studies. Jane Camhi ran an international affairs program, not as director but as coordinator. Jennie Farley, the wife of a faculty member, was returning to graduate study, having brought up children and worked as a part-time journalist for most of her postcollege years. Barbara Francis (later Richardson) was an English major transformed by Jane Gould at Barnard College, for whom she had worked in New York, into a feminist social psychologist seeking a graduate degree. Patricia Latham Lamb, later an author and editor of a collection of letters between women, was then an Africanist just beginning to discover in herself a literary scholar. Joanna Russ was then as now a brilliant science fiction writer.

The collective met regularly for ten weeks and managed to create a syllabus, reading list, and course of lectures out of virtually nothing. To be sure, there were books about women, some biased and some good but dated. To our continuing surprise, the search for reading material revealed to the collective that although we came from disciplines as diverse as sociology, literature, and biology, we had read many of the same books. But there was no structure, no "story line," not yet any agreed-upon topics in women's studies. We had to sculpt a new field for ourselves and, eventually, for our students.

Different disciplines hold different standards of truth. When Pat Lamb, the literary scholar, delivered a miniversion of a lecture she proposed to give in the course on the character Daniel Deronda, from the George Eliot novel of the same name, Jennie Farley, studying for a Ph.D. in rural sociology, wondered aloud how it was possible to generalize about Victorian womanhood from "a sample of one"—and a fictional one at that. We also analyzed old topics from new points of view, such as my content analysis of *Playboy* magazine's much-touted "philosophy." I remember analyzing the discrepancy in age, education, earnings, and class origin between the typical *Playboy* reader, as described by the publisher, and of the monthly "Playmates,"—as described by themselves. Playmates were always younger, less educated, poorer, and significantly shorter than the men who bought the magazine, *Playboy* was accommodating men's superiority fantasies quite as much as their libidos.

If course material was scarce, colleagueship was not. All over the country in that first year of the new decade, feminists who were scholars and scholars who became feminists were beginning to locate "lost women" in history and literature and to do important new research about women and men, employing and sometimes having to modify the techniques of social science.[4] We were in touch with these other women and used sources such as KNOW, an underground feminist press in Pittsburgh, to augment our reading list. By late fall 1969, we had a course.

But who would mount it, and how long would it take for us to get it approved? Except for Joy Osofsky, none of us held faculty rank, and she was very junior. But she had a colleague in the Department of Human Development and Family Studies (again the College of Human Ecology would, despite itself, come to our aid) who offered to be our Trojan horse. "We'll call it my course and you'll teach it," Harold Feldman promised, and so women's studies had an academic home. Feldman and his wife, Margaret, who taught psychology at neighboring Ithaca College, were activists in a number of radical movements (including an effort to provide college courses to men incarcerated in a nearby federal penitentiary). But, more important, Feldman was a family sociologist who knew how ideologically biased his own field had become. He didn't mind tweaking his staid colleagues either, and so, as promised, he allowed our course to sally forth under his official sponsorship, keeping himself on the sidelines.

Thus, unlike most of the early women's studies courses at colleges and universities, which had to be masked as special topics seminars, or sponsored by dormitories or free schools, our course, The Evolution of Female Personality: Its History and Prospects, had the benefit of official sponsorship and therewith required no formal approval by a collegewide committee. Still, we had no listing in the 1970 spring semester course catalogue. Who would know about the course? Who would enroll? I moved quickly and, just before the semester began, purchased ad space in the *Cornell Daily Sun*. It was "gross," I was told the day after the ad appeared, to advertise a campus course. I agreed (after the fact), but the ad had an impact. Two weeks later, two hundred students, male as well as female, signed up for The Evolution of Female Personality, and within two years, substantial student support made it possible to launch a full-fledged women's studies program at Cornell.

We were not alone. Within a year, I located sixteen new college courses taught from a feminist perspective whose syllabi I compiled into what became the first of a series of course catalogues of women's studies.[5] Within a decade, there were hundreds more.

The excitement of women's studies remained for me throughout the thirty years during which I frequently taught gender and politics in the subject itself. The recovery of suppressed women writers and scholars gave rise to insights into disciplinary bias. This, in turn, raised questions as to why gender-related issues had been overlooked in the first place, and exciting scholarship ensued. Every discipline has felt the effects of the new scholarship on women, even the hard sciences and mathematics. My contribution, such as it is, has been to extend this critical stance to the patriarchy itself, particularly in fields where men traditionally dominate: mathematics, science, military strategy, and military weapons. In this work, I have found wonderful feminist colleagues with whom to collaborate and from whom to learn.[6]

But unlike some of my cofounders, I have always tried to work with men and in ways that demonstrate to all who attend my classes that when women, feminism, and women's issues are *not* included, the story is incomplete.[7] Never have I wanted to look out over a class that was made up only of women or only of feminists already sharing my feminist outlook. Learning, for me, resides in the confrontation between closely held views and new material. My students need to be confronted with countervailing views—that's why I always assigned a unit on the antifeminist Phyllis Schlafly—and so do I.

In introducing my gender and politics class at the University of California, San Diego, during the 1980s, I would proffer a special welcome to the male students present, urge them to stay, and, as a way of underscoring my open-mindedness, say this: "You will find that there is room for all points of view in this class with but one exception: You must believe, or at least allow me to persuade you, that the subject is important." Most stayed.

Jean Walton

My early years in Pennsylvania included, between 1935 and 1948, three degrees in mathematics (B.A., Swarthmore College; M.A., Brown University; and Ph.D., University of Pennsylvania) interspersed with two working positions, teacher of mathematics in high school and assistant dean and instructor of mathematics at Swarthmore College.

These activities led to an offer from Pomona College in Claremont, California, of a position as dean of women, with faculty status and an opportunity to teach mathematics. My thirty years at Pomona, from 1949 to 1979, provided many opportunities for personal growth and increasing responsibilities: four sabbaticals, including a Fulbright lectureship in Japan and a year as consultant to the Danforth Foundation; experience as dean of students in this coeducational college during the tumultuous 1960s; and leadership in the 1970s, including my work in women's studies, as the Claremont Colleges were facing the implications of the new feminism.

I took on other responsibilities after my retirement: 1) fund-raising for a senior center in Claremont and work on the city's Committee on Aging, which was responsible for the new center's program; 2) active participation on various Quaker committees in the Claremont Friends Meeting and the Pacific Yearly Meeting; and 3) joining the governing board of directors of a local retirement community as an elected resident member, and later serving two years as president of the residents' council in that community.

Two awards have been particularly memorable: the Scott Goodnight Award "for outstanding contribution as a dean" given in

1974 by the National Association for
Student Personnel Administrators
and the honorary doctor of science

degree presented by Pomona College
at their commencement in 1994.

The Evolution of a Consortial Women's Studies Program

In early September 1971 I drove away from Claremont, thirty-five miles north and east of Los Angeles, heading for Interstate 10 and a long drive across the country, aiming to spend a sabbatical semester looking for answers to a basic question: What has been the impact of the new feminist movement on the educational experience of women students? I wasn't sure how I would proceed, but I knew that I felt isolated and out of touch with these new developments as I worked at Pomona College, the admittedly excellent but strongly male dominated coeducational college where I was dean of students. I had some uneasiness and uncertainty as I started out, but the dominant feeling was one of excitement mixed with a faith that if I could get back East, where the action was, I would certainly learn a great deal.

I started work at Pomona College in 1949 as dean of women, with an opportunity to teach a course each semester in mathematics. The college had decided to look for a dean with an academic background, and I had no doubt that my Ph.D. in math was a major factor in my appointment. I enjoyed the teaching and the generally good relations with the largely male faculty, but my primary energies and responsibilities were focused on the women students and their activities.

In my early days it became clear to me that even in this excellent liberal arts college, the educational experience for many of our very able women students fell short of what it might be. The climate of expectations for them was low, and many of them felt unsure of their purpose in being in college. I tried, without much success, to discuss my concern with my male colleagues. Even though, in those early days, I retained remnants of the unquestioning acceptance of male authority with which I had grown up, I was not reassured by their comfortable failure to see any problem. "But, Jean, I don't understand what you're talking about. We treat our women just the same way we treat the men."

In fact, my underlying concern kept growing. Unanswered questions loomed larger and larger: What are the college's goals for women? We speak of educating for leadership, but what does leadership mean for women? Should we be dealing with the pressing dilemma that women face in thinking about marriage and career? How do we begin to discuss the real difference between the experience and expectations of our men students and our women students? Nourished by many conversations with women students, by what reading I had been able to find, and by memories of my own undergraduate experience at Swarthmore College, where I got A's in my math courses but never thought of myself as a potential career mathematician, these questions and others like them persisted and grew, leaving me at the time with a gnawing concern that needed development and some resolution.

When I started on my trip to seek some answers, I knew that I was fortunate to have four sisters living in different locations across the country. Each provided a comfortable home base for a time, a place for mail and messages as plans developed, home cooking, and, above all, some relaxation and loving support as I faced a challenging undertaking. I stopped first in Boulder, Colorado, and began the process of visiting bookstores, buying books, talking to individuals whose work seemed interesting, listening to new ideas, and asking for advice and suggestions. From the beginning, the possibilities before me grew at an ever-increasing pace. Everyone was as excited as I was about the new feminism and what it might mean for education, and everyone was generous about sharing. I had plenty of unplanned time. When someone said, "You should talk to so-and-so," I could find that person and make arrangements for a conversation. Or when someone said, "You might find it helpful to read such and such," I could find that book and read it.

I moved on across the country, hearing new names, gathering books and articles, encountering new ideas, and trying to absorb all that I was hearing. The sense of openness and sharing continued. Many spoke of the value of their consciousness-raising groups, and I chuckled internally at the time, thinking of my consciousness raising in my many one-on-one conversations with different individuals: a different process, with regard to my own consciousness raising, but very effective in my case, one of the most important effects for me was my growing understanding that much in my early experience was shared by other women, that difficulties I had attributed to my own inadequacies might indeed have had their roots in cultural traditions.

By the time I reached the East Coast, I had an extensive list of people I was eager to see. Some of these were Pomona graduates with whom I had corresponded about my trip and who had expressed an interest in sharing ideas about my concerns. Others were individuals whose names had been mentioned several times in my earlier exploratory conversations. One of these was Florence Howe, and I was pleased when I was able to arrange a visit. Now the publisher/director of The Feminist Press, about which I have since learned a great deal, she was, in my eyes, on that first visit primarily a professor who illustrated the power of women's studies by making vivid for me in our conversation how feminism can enlarge and enlighten teaching.

Another example of a visit that led to a long-term association came about because I had seen a news article that the Association of American Colleges was starting a Project on the Status and Education of Women, and that Bernice Sandler had been appointed director. I was able to reach her in her office in Washington, D.C., and we had a stimulating conversation about her goals in this new effort. I left determined to find a way to stay in touch with her, even though my own office was three thousand miles away. I learned from her later that my visit was, in fact, the first in her new position, and that our conversation had been a memorable one for her as well as for me.

During my long journey home in January 1972, I needed the time alone to reflect on the intense experience of the previous few months. There was much that was new to me in the feminist ideas I had been considering. It seemed important to sort out the relationship between these new ideas and my own core Quaker values before I embarked on the many conversations I would have when I returned on the college. One thing became clear. I felt both commitment and urgency about the challenge of women's studies to include the experience and perspective of women in curricular materials.

As time went on, my reflection was increasingly focused on plans for my return to the college. I kept asking myself how we could stimulate new thinking at Pomona and bring about the level of change that was needed. I knew that we needed to build a coalition of those who would be ready to join the effort, and it was clear also that we would need to prepare and circulate good written materials about the new feminist movement and its growth on campuses across the country. In my final written report on my sabbatical I included two strong recommendations for immediate action: 1) undertake vigorous recruiting to achieve a significant increase in the number of women on the faculty; and 2) arrange courses, seminars, and lectures to open up full discussion on the campus of the various issues raised by the new feminist movement. I added a third, unwritten, recommendation directed to myself. I had to remember that these two formal recommendations to the college administration, important as they were, would accomplish nothing in themselves; that change in this college would come only slowly; that we would need to exert constant pressure; and that I would somehow have to manage to keep myself from being swallowed up by my responsibilities as the dean of students.

My friends have told me since that I seemed a different person when I returned to the college. I know that I had a deep concern and a sense of urgency to act on it. Not long after my return I was asked to speak about my trip at a meeting of the "Little Men," a faculty group open to all faculty except those few who happened to be female. I took this invitation seriously. Support from these men would be important; many of them I had considered my friends. They were indeed friendly, in a casual, social way, but I had come to recognize more clearly that they had rarely allowed me to be a true professional colleague. On the whole, they remained friendly after this event. It is possible, of course, that for some my comments stimulated some new thinking, but to my regret, there was no clear and vigorous response, no attempt to engage me in serious conversations about issues I had raised. Our relationships seemed unchanged.

In the summer of 1972, the president of the college established the Commission on the Education of Women with a charge to study and make recommendations concerning equal employment opportunities for women and curricular responses to the needs of women. In addition to myself and an assistant from my office, the commission had eleven members, seven faculty and four students, about equally divided between males and females. We were fortunate to have some funding available for our initial efforts. A few months earlier, the college had received a generous gift from an alumna who had been present at one of my meetings with former graduates. She had expressed her support of the ideas I had discussed and, as it worked out, the Anonymous Woman Donor's Fund became the initial source for our yearly budgets.

The next few years were difficult, for it was hard to see definable results of our activities and to measure progress. An early decision of the commission accentuated the difficulty, but it was a decision in which we believed. We agreed that we did not want to survey the institution, write a final report on the status of women, include a list of recommendations, and see the report filed. We chose rather to concentrate on specific issues and to stimulate action on a particular issue as it was needed.

In 1972, when the commission was formed, we all shared a strong sense of urgency regarding the need to recruit more women to the faculty. As I look back now at the intervening years, great progress has been made, though the change was very slow at first. We were not in a position to take action ourselves but did what seemed possible with the hope of encouraging action by others. We talked to deans, department chairs, and members of the Affirmative Action Committee, and we wrote to women's caucuses and committees of the various professional associations. We were successful in achieving approval from the faculty and the Pomona College Board of Trustees of new faculty policies that might make employment in this academic community inviting to potential female candidates: provision for child care leaves, the possibility of arranging a reduced load for an interim period without losing regular faculty status, and so on. Robert Voelkel, then dean of the college, was a strong supporter of our goals, and his efforts were important in gradually increasing the number of strong female candidates for faculty positions.

Our Anonymous Woman Donor's Fund made it possible in those early days to bring in the outside help needed to offer some new courses focused on women. Jan Jaquette, of the political science department at Occidental College, was with us on a part-time basis in the fall of 1973. Carlotta Mellon, with a doctorate in history from Claremont Graduate School, was appointed in the fall of 1974 to a full-time, non-tenure-track position as assistant professor of history and women's studies (she resigned at the end of the first semester to take a position on the staff of California governor Jerry Brown). Carol Ireson, with a doctorate in sociology from Cornell University, was appointed to a similar full-time position in the fall of 1975. She was with us for two years and gave us invaluable help. We did not have sufficient funds, or the necessary support from the college, to keep her, and she resigned in 1977.

During those early years, these three women carried the responsibility for coordinating an introductory interdisciplinary course on sex roles, working with faculty members at the college and using a few guest speakers as well. Mellon and Ireson each also offered a course in her own discipline. These courses were all well received, with good enrollments and positive evaluations by the students.

While she was at the college Ireson was very helpful in increasing our contacts with faculty women in the other Claremont Colleges who shared our interest in women's studies.[1] We knew during that period that there were isolated efforts similar to ours on some of the other campuses, but we did not know one another well. It seemed difficult to bridge the gap. We understood and appreciated the vision behind the creation of this group of colleges: separate colleges, close together geographically, independent institutions and yet cooperating with one another in some areas. At the same time, we knew well how strongly each of the colleges guarded its independence. The demands of our own separate positions in our colleges were very real, and the possibility of a major joint effort seemed remote.

We had occasional lunches in the Faculty House, which served all the colleges, to meet with visiting women speakers. Florence Howe, Sheila Tobias, Sandra Bem, and others visited during this period, and each occasion brought a lively group of women from all the colleges. We said frequently that we should get together more often, but no one found the necessary time and energy to bring this about. Carol Ireson was helpful while she was with us. During the spring of 1977, she worked with Sheryl Miller, anthropology department at Pitzer, who took the initiative in producing a brochure listing all the women's studies courses to be offered in the Claremont Colleges in 1977–78. This listing, with course descriptions included, mentioned five at Pitzer College, four at Pomona College, one at Claremont Men's College, two at Scripps College, and one at the Chicano Studies Center. Thirteen additional courses, listed by title only, had a significant component devoted to some aspect of women's studies. This brochure, distributed widely in all the colleges during the registration period, was the first instance of shared publicity from the colleges about women's studies activities.

In the fall of 1976, we made a serious effort to achieve within Pomona College a regular budget item supporting our ongoing women's studies program. We knew that the Anonymous Woman Donor's Fund would not last much longer, and we had by that time several years' experience with which to document the value of the program. Margaret Dornish, religion department at Pomona, then chair of the commission, wrote a strong statement presenting the recommendation, and we also prepared materials to be used in our discussions with the college's Educational Policy Committee. We heard positive statements about what we were doing, and received encouragement to continue and offers to help us find grant money from outside sources to make the continuation possible, but we did not achieve firm financial backing from the college. Nothing in writing gave the reasons. My impressions are that there was little real understanding or acceptance of the need. Some said, "It seems too early," and added that it might be a passing fad; their recommendation was for us to aim for visiting lecturers rather than permanent faculty appointments.

As it turned out, their offer to assist us in finding additional outside funds was very helpful, and in the spring of 1977 the college was awarded a grant by the Bertha LeBus Charitable Trust "to enable the Commission on the Education of Women to invite, for extended periods, distinguished women who have made notable scholarly contributions in the emerging field of Women's Studies."

The commission developed considerable interest in bringing to the campus as our first LeBus lecturer the noted feminist historian Gerda Lerner. Because of her very crowded schedule, and our limited budget, we had to settle for a two-week visit in February 1978. She agreed to give a public lecture and to conduct a short, condensed seminar for undergraduates; and, more generally, she agreed to advise us how to move forward in our efforts to advance women's studies at Pomona.

Her initial lecture, "The Challenge of Women's History," and the two subsequent open discussions on "Where do we go from here?" were all well received and attracted considerable attention. Lively interest on the campus, eager talk by students, and efforts to take part in her seminar all pointed to the vigorous response we had hoped for. Even if nothing else had happened, we would have judged her visit a success.

How limited and narrow our hopes were! I doubt if I will ever forget that moment when she and I sat down together soon after her arrival to go over the schedule we had prepared for her. She looked at it carefully, asked a question or two, and then said, "I don't understand. When am I to meet the women from the other Claremont Colleges?" I mentioned, rather weakly, that they had all been invited to her public lecture, but my inner reaction was shame. How could I! How could I not have seen the need and the potential for this moment? She put it quite bluntly: "You've asked me here to advise you about the future of women's studies at Pomona. How can I do that if I don't have the opportunity to get acquainted with the women at the other Claremont Colleges?"

We were wiser than we knew in inviting Gerda Lerner to our campus. She was able to do what she did for us because she combined, in a way few people can manage, a direct, forthright, energetic manner with a very deep caring and concern for the people with whom she was working. Furthermore, in our situation at Claremont, our mistake was one that could easily be corrected. We arranged a time and place for a meeting and did all we could to spread the word. It didn't take much. Interest was high, sparked by the realization of Lerner's strong intercollegiate perspective as well as by the great individual needs. We had a packed house. She had told me, "You can introduce me if you like. Otherwise, leave the meeting to me."

What she did was simple and yet had profound implications for the growth of our women's studies program. She asked each person to introduce herself and say something about her strengths, interests, and greatest needs. It was a powerful and moving occasion. Again and again we heard variations on one theme: I feel so alone; there is no one to talk to about the things I care about. So many of us caring so much about the perspective of women's studies, and yet feeling so isolated, needing colleagues, needing communication. So many of us, so close together, not knowing how to reach one another.

We knew by the end of that meeting that we had to get together and build a program for the Claremont Colleges as a whole. Our impetus to do so was surely strengthened by Lerner's statement to us at the end of her visit: "If you work together, you have the combined strength here to develop a first-class program." We knew that we would have hurdles to overcome in building an intercollegiate program; her statement helped us formulate a vision that would launch us into the effort.

We all knew the forces that had kept us apart and that would be a continuing challenge as we moved ahead. The primary one, as mentioned earlier, is that the colleges, though close together geographically, have always been strongly independent institutions. We considered the specifics behind the statement. Each college makes its own curricular and budget decisions and there is normally considerable variation in the results. There were then six presidents, six deans, six committees on appointments, promotion, and tenure, and even six separate boards of trustees. (A seventh institution has been added recently.) There is no one person at the top but rather a Council of Presidents, which each president chairs in turn according to a rotating schedule. The various joint operations and services which existed when we started our discussions had been worked out slowly, and sometimes painfully, by the council in its regular meetings. We recognized one great strength of the situation for our purposes; namely, that, with few exceptions, students in any of the colleges are free to register for courses at the neighboring colleges.

We were full of energy as we gathered to begin our planning. We recognized that our first need was to be clear for ourselves, and to make clear to others, what we were aiming for. How would our joint effort fit into the six-college picture? Given that each college had its own programs and its own procedures for reaching curricular and budget decisions, it became clear to us that our goal could only be to coordinate our various efforts, and to help one another through our joint planning, in the development of women's studies on our respective campuses. This would mean that programs on our different campuses would probably follow different time schedules and take different forms. In fact, this had already begun to happen. Pitzer College, for instance, with an organized effort by a substantial group of faculty, had by 1975 established a women's studies major and created an introductory course, Women in American Society, which was being taught regularly by Ann Stromberg in the sociology department. Our Commission on the Education of Women at Pomona College had made arrangements for scattered courses for several years, which had been well received, but we had not yet considered a concentration in women's studies, nor had any of the other colleges.

Our first move was to have representatives selected by the various colleges form a Coordinating Committee, which I agreed to chair. During the spring, the Council of Presidents officially recognized the entire group of women's studies faculty (approximately sixty in June of 1978) as the Intercollegiate Women's Studies Field Committee. This step, of course, did not give us any power or any funding, but it provided some legitimacy and a solid base for any action we could manage.

It was an exciting time at first, with an abundance of vigor and enthusiasm and new ideas coming from every direction. As it happened, I was on a sabbatical leave that spring and decided without difficulty to lay aside the personal project I had planned. Others were all teaching full-time but shared the conviction that this was an important moment that we must not lose. We made an effort to reach faculty members in all the colleges who had some interest in women's studies, and to collect information from them about courses, research areas, and possible participation in women's studies activities. This work led to another brochure in the spring of 1978 listing all the women's studies courses to be offered the following year. (The new list, not surprisingly, showed growth: twenty-seven courses, in contrast with the thirteen courses listed the previous year.) We had no budget but sought help, successfully, from the various admissions offices to meet the modest cost.

Inevitably, some of our first energy began to sag as we moved beyond that exciting spring of 1978 and into the second full year. With leadership from Debby Burke, psychology department at Pomona, we had made some good progress in developing a Women's Studies Colloquium Series, but had been unable to do much to strengthen our library resources. I was back into my full-time work at Pomona, and it was hard for all of us to maintain momentum with too little time to do what we needed. Gradually, the decision grew that if we were to accomplish anything, then we had to get help. In December 1978, the field committee made the decision to submit a request to the Council of Presidents to establish and fund an office of women's studies coordinator.

As the Coordinating Committee prepared the proposal to the presidents, we had some informal conversation about my retirement, which, as was widely known, had long been scheduled for June 1979. The other members of our committee asked me how I would feel about being the coordinator if our proposal to the presidents were successful. They understood that I couldn't say anything definitive, but I could, and did, say that I would surely be interested in exploring the possibility if the situation developed in that way.

All of us on the Coordinating Committee at that time had considerable experience with the intercollegiate structure of the Claremont Colleges system, and we also knew of the complex procedures laboriously developed to handle some recently authorized joint appointments in the Black and Chicano studies, theater, and the joint science departments. It seemed important for us to proceed as we had started the year before. We made it clear that we were seeking a coordinator position; appointments, promotion, and tenure would be left to individual departments and colleges, as would decisions concerning majors, concentrations, and minors. We spoke of our need for administrative coordination and support to help us plan together and help one another in our various efforts in this rapidly growing field.

Even this proposal, modest as it was, did not come easily. Two of us were invited to attend the critical meeting of the Council of Presidents, where the decision would be made. For a long time the debate seemed to center on the difficulty of establishing a new joint service or program, which by previous agreements would automatically require sharing all costs according to a complex formula. Not much was said at first about the merits of the proposal (pro or con). Comments such as "My board has made it clear they do not want me to bring a recommendation for another joint program" increased my feelings of frustration and concern. It seemed entirely possible that we were about to lose our needed support, and for the bureaucratic reasons.

I will be forever grateful to John Chandler, then president of Scripps College, who spoke up suddenly, saying, "This is too good an idea to let it die on the issue of the joint program. Let's not do it that way. I volunteer Scripps as the lead college. We'll provide an office and general supervision and some of the necessary funding. If some of the other colleges will help with the funding, I think we can proceed with the program as outlined." The presidents of Pomona and Pitzer spoke immediately in support of this idea and promised some help with funding; the other colleges supported the idea.

This meant, of course, that there was no required formula; the amount of funding for the office, the contributions from the other colleges, and the appointment of the coordinator would all be in the hands of the Scripps president. He circulated an official announcement late in May 1979, telling of the establishment of the position of women's studies coordinator, and the appointment of myself to the position. "The basic responsibility of the Coordinator," he wrote, "will be to facilitate the mutual assistance and joint planning to which we are committed, without losing sight of the fundamental understanding that the Women's Studies programs on the different campuses will not all take the same form."

He also listed, in general terms, five more specific responsibilities, dealing with curriculum development, public events, the vitality of the women's studies faculty, library holdings, and sources of outside funding. The inclusion throughout the document, in fact, of phrases such as "if possible" and "if the budget will allow" led to an unmistakable conclusion: we would be starting on a shoestring budget. We would have to find a way to translate these goals into specific activities and, at the same time, find the funding to make the activities possible.

The transition from my position at Pomona to my new part-time work at Scripps was not an easy one for me at first. I had been at Pomona for many years and, on the whole, felt recognized and appreciated. My work had been very demanding but satisfying, constantly changing and developing; I never had enough time and was always facing some immediate need or new crisis. Then, after the personal pleasures of the retirement festivities and a good vacation, I moved a few blocks up the street and started work in a small office on the Scripps campus, with a telephone, a bare desk, a tiny budget, and limited secretarial help. I had John Chandler's letter with his listing of five specific responsibilities, but little else. I was unnerved by the silence, the day-after-day, continued silence. I knew that it was up to me to initiate the work in this office. I surely had all the time I needed to think and plan, but I had to acknowledge to myself that I was without any clear sense of how to get started. It was a strange and disorienting experience, and somewhat frightening at first.

My primary support, naturally, was the other members of the Coordinating Committee. We had worked together to create this office, and had developed strong relationships. The other committee members were, as they had been before, committed to our long-range goals but also immersed, just as they had been before, in their own jobs on their own campuses. I, in contrast, had an even greater, and perhaps more anxious, desire to move ahead, and also had more free time than I had known in years. We had to find a good balance after these changes, and I had to allow this to happen. Gradually, my sense of inner tension lessened, a sense of movement and possibility returned, and plans began to emerge.

From that slow beginning in the fall of 1979 until now, the summer of 1999, the intercollegiate program has grown steadily, though not always evenly. I was active only in the very early stages of the program's development, retiring from the coordinator's position in June 1983. The Coordinating Committee recommended at the time that the new coordinator be a faculty member from one of the colleges who would teach half-time and work half-time as coordinator. This arrangement turned out to be a good one. The current coordinator, Jane O'Donnell, is the fifth since I left the office, with different colleges and disciplines represented in the various selections.[2]

Our first efforts in 1979 were in response to two urgent, continuing needs. The first was to strengthen the Women's Studies Colloquium Series, with its reports to the entire academic community on the research in the growing field of women's studies. With our limited budget, funding was a constant problem, but the strong response from the community always encouraged us to continue our efforts. We owe a large debt to the great goodwill shown by our speakers, with their willingness to accept a token honorarium and on many occasions to plan a talk in Claremont when other commitments brought them to Southern California.

The other immediate need was to respond to the feelings of loneliness and isolation so movingly expressed at the meeting with Gerda Lerner by the faculty members already involved in women's studies. Our goal was to provide an opportunity for an intellectual, intercollegiate, multidisciplinary gathering of those interested in a serious exploration of women's issues in a congenial environment. We were able to find some local grants and developed a continuing seminar program, starting in the spring of 1980 and continuing through the next two years. An informal buffet began each session, followed by a lecture and then discussion of the talk and the assigned readings. The response was positive, with appreciative comments about the "network of colleagues" and the "deepened friendships."

A third major focus of our work, the curricular structure of women's studies, developed during my early years and has continued to grow.[3] We knew at the outset that our goal was not to build a defined intercollegiate major program, but rather to offer a solid and trustworthy women's studies curriculum that the individual colleges could use with confidence to set up their own individual programs. We had very early a rapidly growing list of women's studies courses available, but this was only a collection of the courses that individual faculty members had chosen to offer in a particular year. It became essential for us to evaluate and then, in time, to regulate what we were offering.

By the fall of 1982, we had a permanent Curriculum Committee, with Sue Mansfield, history department at Claremont McKenna College, as the initial chair. They developed working statements distinguishing introductory, upper level, and seminar courses and designated each existing course as belonging to one of these categories. As new courses were suggested, the committee developed a policy by which courses with their descriptions would have to be approved for inclusion in the intercollegiate program. In another development, the committee recognized the need for more advanced interdisciplinary courses, and between 1986 and 1989, with the help of funds from a Mellon Grant, produced three advanced courses titled The Politics of Gender: one in the social sciences; one in humanities; and one in science, technology, and public policy. These interdisciplinary, multicultural courses were created and taught by various faculty teams from across the colleges and have become vital, key components of the major programs now offered by Pitzer, Pomona, and Scripps Colleges.

After leaving the position of women's studies coordinator, I moved on to other things, with my primary energies directed elsewhere. I remained in Claremont and kept in touch with my friends in the women's studies program, but I was not at all close to the daily activities or the issues the group was facing. From my limited perspective, two public moments stand out, marking stages in our development as a program. The first was early, in the summer of 1982, when we received the report of the Review Committee, which had been mandated by the presidents when they established our office in 1979 with the proviso that it be reviewed in a few years. The committee report presented evidence of "significant accomplishment" and recommended "the continuance and strengthening of the office and program." In their response, the presidents regularized women's studies as a joint academic program. Scripps continued as the lead college, with operating authority delegated to the deans of the participating colleges. Not a major step forward, to be sure, but it gave us somewhat more legitimacy and clearer lines through which to express our needs. Throughout the years since then, there has been a gradual increase in budget and support staff.

The second moment that stands out for me occurred much later. In September 1997, I rejoiced with others over the inauguration of the Intercollegiate Women's Studies Teaching and Research Center. This center, with its central location and attractively furnished space, is a visible acknowledgment of the solid base of our program in the Claremont community. I know well that it is the fulfillment of a long-held and actively pursued goal.

I have not been close enough to the program to give any valid summary of the issues faced and the decisions made as the Intercollegiate Women's Studies Field Committee moved ahead between these two public moments that I remember so well. I know that the environment in which we started (a few women faculty who were widely dispersed, lonely, and needing colleagues) has changed dramatically. The changes are exciting but, of course, raise new questions, and new issues. Maintaining the intercollegiate and interdisciplinary emphases of our program, dealing with issues of diversity, building good relationships with the ethnic studies programs, and participating in and supporting the National Women's Studies Association: all of these have been and will be essential in developing our program. In a recent conversation with the current coordinator, I asked her what she saw as the most difficult problem at the moment. Her answer was quick and clear: "Managing the core courses." With 90 percent of our women's studies faculty appointed to, and dependent for tenure on, traditional disciplines, many of them—especially the younger ones—find it difficult to get permission to teach interdisciplinary courses. It will take a continuing high level of intercollegiate planning and cooperation to staff the central core of courses needed for the major programs.

I think back to Gerda Lerner's words more than twenty years ago: "If you work together, you have the combined strength here to develop a first-class program." She never said it would be easy, and it hasn't been. The consortium makes a great deal possible, but it adds great complexity and moves very slowly. The balance has been favorable for us. I hope it will continue to be so.

As I reflect on my own experience in the intercollegiate program, I realize that my colleagues and I barely scratched the surface of what it takes to create an ongoing program. Nevertheless, my work as a women's studies coordinator meant a great deal to me. I remember well the joy I felt in the friendships that I developed with my colleagues on the Intercollegiate Field Committee, with whom I shared so much. During much of my early working experience, first in mathematics, and then as dean, I felt quite isolated, on my own. For a long time, I wasn't even really aware what I was missing, but it became clear during those later years. I feel very fortunate to have had the opportunity at the end of my working career to enjoy the pleasure of working hard as one of a group of congenial colleagues, a group with many differences, but with a shared goal.

PART II

Overcoming
Barriers

Ridicule,
Reluctance,
and Refusals

Nancy Topping Bazin

In 1978, I arrived at Old Dominion University in Norfolk to direct the first women's studies program in Virginia, having already coordinated programs at Rutgers College and the University of Pittsburgh. From 1985 to 1989, I was chair of the English department at Old Dominion.

In 1994, I was one of eleven in Virginia to receive an Outstanding Faculty Award. That summer I was a visiting scholar at Indiana University's Institute for Advanced Study and, during spring 1995, a fellow at the Virginia Center for the Humanities. In 1996, I received the Charles O. and Elisabeth Burgess Faculty Research and Creativity Award. That same year, Old Dominion University designated me an Eminent Scholar; of the honors I have received, this is the one that has pleased me the most.

I have participated in faculty development projects in postcolonial literature, Third World studies (with trips to the Ivory Coast, Tanzania, and Morocco), and East Asian studies (with a trip in 1989 to Japan and China). In 1998, I went to South Africa for a seminar sponsored by the Council on International Educational Exchange (CIEE).

I have published two books—*Virginia Woolf and the Androgynous Vision* and *Conversations with Nadine Gordimer*—and more than forty articles. In addition to essays on writers Margaret Atwood, Edith Wharton, Marge Piercy, Flora Nwapa, and Mariama Ba, my articles have been focused primarily on curriculum transformation, women's studies, and authors Doris

Lessing, Buchi Emecheta, Bessie Head, Virginia Woolf, and Nadine Gordimer.

On January 1, 2000, I retired from my position as a professor of English at Old Dominion University.

The Gender Revolution

In the fall of 1958, when I arrived at Stanford University to begin a Ph.D., the all-male faculty of the English department were still grumbling in the corridors about the last woman they had hired. They had found her too assertive, so they did not want to repeat that mistake. Later, at a session on getting jobs, the department chair told us that females would be hired "at one level of university lower than what they deserved." In 1960, like the other silent students, I accepted that pattern as the way the world worked. Yet the injustice of it did not escape me. Another graduate student at Stanford told me how, on the day she received her Ph.D., her department chair had taken her aside and said, "You know that your husband will always come first, don't you?" After I had my Ph.D., I, too, accepted the social attitude articulated by this department chair: my husband's interests and career came first; mine must always come second—if at all.

In 1962, while leading the lonely life of a housewife and mother in Paris, I read Betty Friedan's *The Feminine Mystique* and Simone de Beauvoir's *The Second Sex*. I found them enlightening social documents but was not ready to comprehend what they could suggest to me personally. Nor did I fully grasp the feminist nature of what I was learning as I wrote my doctoral dissertation on Virginia Woolf's novels. Nevertheless, Woolf's insights were preparing me to become a feminist teacher and women's studies director. In the 1960s, I *understood* intellectually what Woolf was saying. However, not until the early 1970s, when the women's movement had become part of the historical moment and culture in which I was living, could I *feel* what she meant.

In Paris and later in Princeton, New Jersey, I lived according to my belief that children must be cared for by their own mothers. From 1962 until 1970, I was a stay-at-home mother who worked on her dissertation in the evenings. Because I saw the caretaking role as mine alone, for a long time I thought I could not justify a daytime babysitter because I earned no money to pay for one. Gradually, I realized that I was working for my husband and, because the children were his responsibility, too, he could pay for a babysitter. Thus for a short while, I had a babysitter for two afternoons a week. However, when we traveled to Chile and Algeria during summers so that my husband might teach, I had no relief from child care. My progress with my intellectual pursuits was slow; I had too many distracting obligations, including long visits from my husband's French family. My husband, my children, and my husband's family came first; my mother, my dissertation, and I came last. Not surprisingly, writing my dissertation took me ten years.

Without having a name for it, I was writing feminist literary criticism. Connecting the feminine with the psychological state of mania and the masculine with depression, and relating both to Woolf's aesthetics, I was working with the concept of androgyny. My book on Virginia Woolf was about ready to go to press in 1972 when I decided that "androgyny" was a word that was "coming into being" along with the feminist movement and that I should refer to the ideal of the androgynous vision in the title.[1] Pioneering feminists created their own concepts and learned directly from doing rather than working consciously through theories and strategic plans. We discovered our goals and methods as we made our way through the unknown. Because of this process—perhaps the only one possible in 1973—I published a book titled *Virginia Woolf and the Androgynous Vision* without including a chapter on *Orlando*.[2]

In August 1970, at age thirty-six, I was hired to teach at Rutgers College. At that time, Rutgers, the state university in New Brunswick, New Jersey, consisted of five separate colleges: Rutgers College for male students; Douglass College for female students; University College for evening students; Cook College, primarily for agricultural and environmental studies students; and Livingston College, a new, experimental college that enrolled one-third black students, one-third Hispanic, and one-third white. Except for University College, which used the Rutgers College facilities at night, the colleges were quite separate geographically. The five English departments had little contact with one another. Furthermore, the mathematics and science departments of Rutgers College were across the river in Piscataway, a bus ride away from the humanities and social science departments. Therefore, as an assistant professor at the all-male Rutgers College, I was quite isolated. At that time, of the 440 faculty on our two Rutgers College campuses, only 44 were female; of those 44, only 10 were tenured and 4 or 5 of those 10 were in math and sciences on the other side of the river.[3] Like the male students and professors, I became so accustomed to male bodies around me that once, glancing up from my book in the library, I recall doing a double-take when I saw a young woman walking by. A female body was still rare enough that it stood out as "abnormal."

Several male students came to me in 1970 and expressed their concern about having a female teacher. One reason was that they could no longer swear in the classroom; I assured them that neither happiness nor learning were dependent upon using profanity. I was shocked, however, at the boldly disrespectful comment of a student who wrote that he would like to "come into my orifice," a play on the word *office!* I was the third woman to join the full-time faculty of the English department; the other two were not then feminists. When one of the two women faculty came to my class and saw the film *Women on the March,* she said the images of the women demonstrating in the streets for the right to vote made her want to demonstrate in the streets *against* giving women the vote! A male colleague asked me why I did not wear jeans and an old shirt—his stereotype of feminist apparel. I purposely dressed to avoid fitting into such a stereotype.

My desire to teach a course on images of women in literature was inspired primarily by attending two conferences and reading two books. First, in December 1970, I went to the Modern Language Association Convention, where my dormant feminist consciousness blossomed for the first time. Attending sessions on women's literature, hearing a speech by Elaine Showalter, and, later, reading her 1971 article on the way the reviews of works by Charlotte Brontë and George Eliot changed once their female names were revealed, finally awakened me.[4]

Another formative experience was my attending the Women in the Arts Symposium, April 21–30, 1972, at State University College in Buffalo. Included were exhibits, plays, performances, and films by women and talks by female painters, architects, dancers, poets, critics, and opera singers. Being in this all-female and feminist environment for ten days was an extremely liberating—even ecstatic—experience; I emerged from it a different person. The absence of men had enabled me to talk freely with other women. I saw how women could express their inner, uncensored feelings in diverse arts.

Other moments of illumination came in a variety of ways. For example, through reading Kate Millett's *Sexual Politics* and then rereading the chapter "Independent Women" in Simone de Beauvoir's *The Second Sex*. I suddenly could envision the meaningful role that feminist literary criticism might play in my life. I could finally make sense of much that had puzzled me. My personal life, my political interests, and my professional life became connected. Furthermore, although I had always been interested in teaching, I now had a reason to want to publish. Feminist scholarship befit my concerns and feelings.

The title of my first women's studies course was Female Roles and Feminine Consciousness in Literature; in my class I had eighteen Rutgers College male students and three female students, who came by bus from Douglass College. Given the makeup of the class, I emphasized how sex roles hurt both men and women; but I also explained that, although the men might be damaged, they had power and money that women did not, thus creating enormous differences in the degrees of their privilege and suffering. The literature provided convincing evidence of this. The best device I discovered to convey what I meant by a patriarchal society was to have them imagine what a matriarchal society would be like. There would be a female president, a female vice president, a cabinet that was all female, a Senate that was all female except for one man, a House of Representatives that had 423 women and twelve men,[5] a military that was mostly female, engineers, scientists, and religious leaders most of whom were female—all this when half the population (or at least 49 percent of it) was male. Even the diehards had to admit that such a society would seem quite sick and that the male domination in 1971, equally bizarre and unbalanced, was unlikely to change rapidly.

In one especially interesting hour, we talked about why few representations of giving birth existed in literature. Because men knew little about the birth process and most writers were male, the absence of this topic was not too surprising. But then I asked poet Alicia Ostriker to read to that class "Once More Out of Darkness," her long poem about birth. A stunned silence followed. The men began to raise their hands to say that if birth was as she described it, they were never going to get a woman pregnant. Then, the women raised hands and said that they never wanted to get pregnant! Alicia and I were shocked by the response, because we had found her poem to be an honest, nonfrightening description of the birth process.[6]

Except for a half-dozen faculty at Rutgers College, I began that first course in an environment that was, at its best, indifferent and, at its worst, hostile. Nevertheless, the response to the course by both male and female students was extremely positive. In that course and in those that followed, I found that students reached a consensus that women were not by nature inferior and that valid reasons existed for the women's movement; those were not attitudes that characterized the general population in the early 1970s.

In 1972, the first women students would be admitted to Rutgers College. The Women's Equity Action League and Ruth Bader Ginsburg (then a Rutgers-Newark professor) had clarified the imminent danger of lawsuits, thereby convincing the reluctant Board of Governors in 1971 to vote in favor of coeducation.[7]

The dean appointed me to a committee to plan for the arrival of women on campus. The administrators were concerned about the dormitories and athletic facilities. What would women do without walls between the showers? I suggested that all students—male and female—might appreciate having privacy. The physical education faculty were perhaps the most nervous about the prospect of female students. As one of the few female faculty members on the committee, I was sent to talk with them. They admitted that professors had taught them in their graduate studies that women could not roll on their chests, that you could not throw a ball at a woman for fear it would hurt her breasts, and that women could not swim during menstruation. Assuring them that such notions were myths, I told them that many female students would be capable of becoming excellent athletes.[8]

During a meeting with the academic dean, a history graduate student dared to suggest that perhaps the curriculum should be changed. For example, she had searched and found nothing about the women's suffrage movement in her American history books. Incensed, the dean immediately stood up, slammed his hand down on the table, and proclaimed very loudly, "If this curriculum has been good enough for the boys, then it is good enough for the girls!" That terminated the conversation.

Female graduate students in the English department took their own initiative in creating a women writers course called Literature and the Feminist Imagination. They designed the course, selected the texts, and asked me to teach it. Although the graduate adviser actively discouraged students from signing up for it, the course filled with thirty students.

Meanwhile, on the undergraduate level, my strategy was to get courses started in various disciplines and then seek approval for a Rutgers College Women's Studies Certificate, modeled on what already existed at Douglass College. I persuaded other faculty to teach courses on women. Many were reluctant, because they feared it would hurt their prospects for tenure. Among the faculty who chose to teach for women's studies were Ann Parelius (Sociology of Sex Roles and Sociology of the Family), William O'Neill (History of American Women,), Judy Stern (Psychobiology of Sex Differences), John Bird (Sex and Pregnancy), La Frances Rose (The Black Woman), Ann Bodine (Language and Sex Roles), Jim Reed (Women in American Medicine), and Elizabeth Platt (Ancient Near Eastern Religions, a course on gods and goddesses and their relationships to sex roles in those cultures). Some courses were developed by teaching assistants (for instance, Jill Kasen in the sociology department and Atina Grossman in the history department), and sometimes we crossed college boundaries: I taught literature and history courses with historians Judy Walkowitz (from University College) and Dee Garrison (from Livingston College). I met with department chairs individually to explain the new program and why it was good for men as well as women. After I had talked at length with many people, we finally had enough courses (six or seven per semester) to offer students an eighteen-credit certificate.

Without an official appointment, without released time, without a budget, and without an office other than my own in the English department, by January 1972, I was "coordinating" the Rutgers College women's studies program.[9] Eventually, in the fall of 1973, I took my proposal to the faculty-governing body for the college. Although some male professors expressed skepticism, the program had cost nothing and it already existed. So they approved it without delay.

Throughout the seven years I was at Rutgers, from 1970 to 1977, I moved from teaching courses in which 80 percent to 90 percent of the literature was by men to courses in which half the writers were women to courses composed of only women writers. My women writers course, consistently attracting about sixty-five students, earned a secure place in the department. In those days, student reactions to such courses were unusually intense and personal. For example, when students observed that often female protagonists had so few socially approved options or opportunities for change that they committed suicide and that even women writers—including Sylvia Plath, Virginia Woolf, and Anne Sexton—had killed themselves, a few began leaving suicide notes on one another's dormitory room doors. One student even attempted suicide. When students became aware of how many women in Victorian fiction died in childbirth, their right to have birth control took a historical context that was new to them. Discovering lesbian, black, or immigrant literature enabled students to speak out about their feelings and have other members of the class understand. In addition, student enthusiasm about the course moved them to participate in activities outside the classroom. When contemporary women writers visited the campus, students eagerly attended their readings to learn more about women's experiences; as opportunities opened up for women, these writers could create female characters who had choices. A few students from the course joined together to create a rape crisis center in New Brunswick. Others fought to get gynecological services for women on campus. Many became activists.

Women writers courses were always the most rewarding to teach. I saw lives change because of such courses. Joy, self-confidence, career changes, escape from bad relationships, a new assertiveness, and pride in being a woman were common by-products. Student comments included the following: "Eye-opening course! This class was very stimulating and opened my eyes to new views. Very thought provoking." "My awareness of women's issues has increased and has caused me to re-examine my life with the new knowledge I have gained."

In spring 1972, in honor of the arrival of the first female students to this male college, the dean asked me to set up the Rutgers University Women's Series. Eight others and I planned thirty-three programs for 1972–73, without a cent from the dean. Alberta Arthurs, Dennis Cate, Gerri Frazier, Susan Gliserman, Carol Keon, Susan Nash, Joyce Wadlington, Joan Walsh, and I raised money from twelve funds and campus organizations on the Rutgers College campus and set up cosponsorship arrangements with other Rutgers University campuses. In September 1972, we held a symposium in the Rutgers College Student Center that included panels, talks, the women's theater group Earth Onion, a feminist art exhibit by Eva Cockcroft, and a feminist film festival. With the first hundred dollars raised, we invited Toni Morrison to do a reading; she was a newcomer to the literary scene, having just published (1970).[10]

In 1974, I was one of several cofounders of the Rutgers University

Women's Research Institute, located in a house near the Douglass College campus. Our immediate goal was to encourage more research by women faculty in all five colleges of Rutgers University in the New Brunswick area. Therefore, serving as its first director in 1974, I gathered information about who was doing what research and set up a series of faculty talks instead of inviting only outside speakers for the Rutgers University Women's Series. Not having tenure, Guida West, the woman who succeeded me the second semester of that first year, and I were holding the institute together until Mary Hartman of Douglass College would have tenure and become director the following year.

Because Kate Ellis at Livingston College and Elaine Showalter, Elizabeth Meese, and Adrienne Rich at Douglass College shared my feminist literary interests and because women in other fields gained an interest in women's studies, gradually, during my seven years at Rutgers, I came to feel much less isolated. However, within the Rutgers College English department, all but three of my colleagues still assumed that feminist literary criticism was a passing fad. Only those three believed that a variety of approaches to literature would enrich the department. Since the others were not yet reading feminist scholarship and criticism, to them, my creative efforts for women and women's studies were not of value. Therefore, in 1975–76, when I came up for tenure with a book, two articles, an annotated bibliography, and a draft of several chapters of a second book, I did not get it, even though the department chair had stated at a meeting with the junior faculty of Rutgers College that a published book was the requirement for tenure.[11]

When I speculate on why tenure was denied me, I guess at many factors, including a lack of respect for the new affirmative action policy written the year before (in 1974–75) and the evident hostility of some of the powerful senior men in the department. Unlike my younger male colleagues, many older ones seemed to have a special problem accepting me. When I was in a room with them, they treated me as if I were invisible. The ultimate example occurred one day when one of the departmental powers was walking down the steps and I said, "My book just came out from Rutgers University Press." He did not even turn his head toward me but kept on walking. The woman standing with me, the wife of another senior colleague, exclaimed to him, "She *said* her book just came out!" He ignored her, too, and continued on his way. He was evidently not at all pleased that I had a published book, because it qualified me for the tenure he did not wish to grant. Another factor in my not getting tenure was perhaps the undemocratic nature of the department. I was hired by the chair without consultation with anyone else; the department had no hiring committees and no general meetings on policies.

After I was denied tenure, I looked at the letters that had been sent to outside readers of my work. The department chair had chosen three of his close friends, all of whom had recently given talks on campus. Although the names were blacked out, I could easily read them beneath the black marks. The letters also revealed that the chair had not sent (or mentioned) any of my published works to the readers, but merely the draft for the beginning chapters of the new book. I considered filing a grievance, and I had some faculty support across the five campuses, including Adrienne Rich, then at Douglass College. However, when I talked to Elaine Showalter, head of women's studies at Douglass, she discouraged me from appealing the decision. At another university, a well-known female professor who had made an appeal had just died of cancer, and stress was rumored to be a factor. Showalter mentioned that, as well as the stigma she felt a grievance would place on me in terms of getting hired elsewhere. Considering the times, her opinion was convincing. Because even the preliminary steps in exploring the possibilities of an appeal had caused me a great deal of stress, I decided that I would stop looking back and move on with my life.[12] But I had to do that alone, for my husband and I had separated in 1974.

Looking for a job in 1976–77 as the single mother of a four-year-old daughter and an eleven-year-old son was extremely discouraging. Budgets at all universities had been severely cut; not one advertisement appeared for an associate professorship in my literary field. I applied for more than two hundred jobs in all areas of university life—very few were academic—and had no luck. With two children now dependent on me, I became increasingly anxious.

Late in July 1977, I was offered a half-time administrative position in women's studies at the University of Pittsburgh, with the security of a three-year contract. This was not ideal, but half a salary (plus adjunct pay for a course each semester) was better than no salary. I worked happily at the University of Pittsburgh for one year as coordinator of women's studies within the framework of a well-established program. That program had financial difficulties (the dean refused to replace money for new programs cut off because the program was no longer "new"), and it struggled with a broken promise that five faculty would be given joint appointments with women's studies (the number was down to two plus me). However, broad support for the program existed among both faculty and students. Because of this support, I was welcomed with a kind of warmth that had not existed at male-dominated Rutgers College. The presence of large numbers of female faculty— including tenured ones—and female students made a world of difference. Because men were accustomed to having women around, no one felt that women were trespassing on male territory. The dean, whose field was chemistry, had little concept of interdisciplinary study and gave minimal financial support; however, he did recognize me as an official head of a program. In that position, I was treated with respect. I even had a large office and a secretary.

Whereas the dean at Rutgers College in the 1970s seemed to perceive women's studies as a potential threat,[13] by contrast, the dean at the University of Pittsburgh saw women's studies as an asset to the university. By the time I moved to Old Dominion University as an associate professor of English and director of women's studies in August 1978, times had changed some more. Affirmative action was well established at Old Dominion, a relatively young and flexible university, and the dean, Heinz Meier, felt a strong commitment to making women's studies a success. When I began teaching there in the fall of 1978, he and his wife, Regula, invited the entire faculty of the College of Arts and Letters to their home for a reception in my honor.[14]

At Old Dominion University, I focused on curriculum and faculty development. Despite some pockets of opposition,[15] by the 1980s, the tide was turning. Gradually, most people were ceasing to applaud sexist behavior. What remained to be done was a transformation of the university. In 1980, I persuaded our affirmative action officer and members of the University Affirmative Action Committee to support the idea of affirmative action in the curriculum.[16] I postulated that a university commitment to the principle of equality would lead to hiring faculty with expertise on women, minorities, and non-Western peoples. Therefore, I wanted this commitment written into the mission statement of the university. After a series of meetings, President Alfred Rollins and two vice presidents of the university acknowledged the following: 1) the need for a curriculum that would reflect the perspectives of and include materials about women and minorities as well as Third World and non-Western peoples; 2) the need to hire faculty with expertise in these fields; and 3) the appropriateness of including within the university mission statement a commitment to the ideal of equality. What followed during the late 1980s was a rewriting of the university mission statement along these lines (approved in 1989), and a revision of General Education requirements that made approval of the designated courses dependent upon the inclusion of material by and about women as well as minority and non-Western males. Departmental monitoring of syllabi by a committee encouraged compliance by all faculty. In addition, the English department, in 1986, placed in the new catalogue a requirement for all majors to take a course devoted to women, minority, or postcolonial writers. Thus the strategic plans of the university, the college, and the department made commitments to the ideals I had set forth in 1980. My idealistic words had become institutional language.

My wildest dreams of the 1970s had come true. Yet naïve students and faculty who think that the women's issues they care about have been permanently solved and an increasingly conservative student body and public (weary of being "politically correct") have the potential to undermine what has been achieved. As I retire at the turn of the century, I must rely on the young to determine what will prevail.

Barbara W. Gerber

I was born and educated in western New York. I first planned to become a physician but succumbed to the constant assertions of science professors in the early 1950s, whose message was, "Girls are a waste of time in medical school: they take seats away from men, who are going to make a career of medicine; women will have to quit to raise a family." I switched to sociology-anthropology and then became an elementary school teacher through graduate work. Once in the field of education, I moved into another graduate program focused on school counseling and worked in guidance at the high school level for a few years. Not yet satisfied in the educational sense, I began a doctoral program in counselor education, after which I became a college faculty member. I was active in my field of counseling psychology throughout my career but became enlivened by the new scholarship on women that occurred starting in the late 1960s.

I was active in the National Women's Studies Association (NWSA) from its inception. During those years I served on the governing board, was treasurer for three years, chaired a major revision of the constitution, and, under that new constitution, served as the fifth president-elect and president of NWSA. My last major activity as president was having the June 1998 conference on the campus of the State University of New York, Oswego. It involved planning and preparation for more than a year, and it was accomplished by people who were all working or studying full-time. Clearly, it would have been impossible without excellent support from my local and national women's studies colleagues who, with grace and persistence, put their shoulders to the wheel, helping to create a wonderful confer- ence. I retired at the conclusion of the fall 1998 semester. I am working on several writing projects and looking forward to traveling.

Moving from the Periphery to the Center

In late 1963, with encouragement from members of my dissertation committee at Syracuse University, I removed the female respondents from my data set and put that raw data into an appendix of the dissertation. The women's performance on the psychological instruments I was using to test my hypotheses had been, at best, confusing. I recognized fully the irony of that action ten years later at a college administrators' conference. I was the third member of a panel that featured Peggy McIntosh and Elizabeth Minnich. During the discussion following our formal talks about bringing women and girls into the curriculum, I related that story to illustrate a point being made by one of the other panel members. Although it was not the first time I had told the story, this audience and the panelists encouraged and supported me in redefining it from a feminist viewpoint.

After that point, instead of remaining somewhat chagrined, as I had been about my dissertation, I was able to summon a bit of post hoc outrage about it. For ten years I had been mulling over various hypotheses that might explain why data generated by the female subjects were less definitive than those by male respondents. In that mulling, the now obvious had been elusive: that the instruments I used in my study were designed by men, who had also determined the scoring and the meaning of those scores. Their supposition of objectivity about measuring basic human traits was wrong; actually, what was being measured was much more culturally determined than it was inherent, and men were more likely to have developed such skills and information than were women, because the male culture encouraged boys and actually discouraged girls in their development. However, when I tried to share that with one of the committee members with whom I was still in touch, he did not, as they say, "get it," even though it was, by then, 1974.

Late in the spring of 1964, the dean's secretary called to say, "He wants to see both of you." Okay, I thought, getting married was going to be more of a problem than either of us had anticipated. My fiancé and I were to be married in June, and the dean indicated that he could not have two people from the same family as members of the School of Education, especially in the same department. He offered alternatives: I could move off tenure track and teach full-time or part-time as an adjunct; or I could take a position as research associate, from which I could teach and do research and grant writing but could not be tenured. When I asked why the alternatives were for me only, he said that my soon-to-be second husband was already established and he did not want to lose him.

It had been difficult to manage our developing relationship during that academic year: we had been discreet, perhaps even secretive, on campus. Some friends and colleagues were aware of our relationship after a conference in Boston in March 1963. There for several days, we had switched roommates, obvious because we were all in one suite. Concerned that I was imposing on my female colleague, she and I talked privately for more than an hour before I was satisfied that she was willing. Considerably later, I learned that her agreement had been somewhat reluctant. So was mine, but I acknowledge having been a bit driven by the eagerness of both men, who had made the suggestion and were openly excited at the prospect. Today we might see this suggestion as sexual harassment. The men were full professor and department chair, and director of guidance: the women were a new assistant professor (myself) and an advanced graduate student.

During the 1964–65 academic year, I was still becoming aware of discrepancies between men and women with respect to power, privilege, and pay. In the fall of 1964, I was notified by the dean that I was being removed from my tenure-track appointment at Syracuse University, as he had indicated in the meeting in early May. At this time, he said that he had devised a way to give me the 10 percent raise that I had earned but was no longer eligible for; he had added it to my husband's salary. At first I was stunned. I had no idea what to say or do. It reminded me of a circumstance in 1959, when my first husband and I bought a house. We were with the loan officer reviewing the credit application and income statements when he told us that my salary was of no consequence, because I might leave work at any time due to pregnancy. I had responded that we already had a child and were unlikely to have a second. In return, he admonished me, saying that one never knew. He also said that the bank considered only the salaries of wives who were nurses, but if I had a note from my physician, they might reconsider their stand on my salary. The loan was approved without having to resort to medical testimony about my fertility. That experience had left me equally as stunned as I was in the dean's office five years later. When we had received the title and mortgage papers, I examined them to find that I was nowhere to be found on the document; the deed was made out to *William J. Gerber and one!* I vowed then that I would never be party to another mortgage unless my name was in full print.

I was also very angry about the nepotism rule, which took away an opportunity to continue pursuing my career at Syracuse University. I continued to teach and began looking in the central New York area for an academic position, because I was overeducated for secondary schools. My husband was annoyed about the incident but frank about disagreeing with me regarding my leaving the university. "What difference is it to you?" he asked. "You can still do everything you want to do: teach, do research, write; and you don't have to do the other stuff. You have the best of it, and as long as I am here, you have all the privilege and none of the burden. Settle down and enjoy yourself." I was not angry with him about the circumstances, but I certainly was angry. Still, I could not fathom the systemic nature of the circumstances. I felt personally affronted and I wanted to leave. I had no intention of remaining at an institution where I was unwanted.

In the spring of 1965, I received an offer to become a member of the psychology department at the State University of New York, Oswego, where academic growth was the byword. I willingly plunged into planning for an expanded graduate program with the chair, two senior faculty, and several other recent hires. Best of all, I found that there were other women in the department with whom I was going to work. It was a very exciting time: new programs were being developed across the campus, buildings were going up, and the student population was expanding. By 1968, I had been promoted to associate professor and had received tenure. That year, five of us left the psychology department to establish a separate graduate department in counselor education.

My husband and I had settled into a comfortable house in between Oswego and Syracuse with my husband's two boys and my daughter. The children were then ten, thirteen, and sixteen. We managed our lives by scheduling our teaching such that one of us was home after school and for dinner every night. Weekends, we focused on the chil-

dren and their athletic endeavors. The two younger ones skied competitively well into their teens, and the oldest was headed toward becoming
a professional golfer. Life was hectic but sweet. I had achieved more
than I had ever imagined, and I was respected and liked by many colleagues and students. During the 1960s, I had also become a civil rights
activist. I had marched, been tear gassed, spoken out, and wished that I
could go to the South to register voters. At the time, that was impossible: I was too encumbered by family and a major responsibility for
teaching summer sessions as well as during the year.

I had read *The Feminine Mystique* while poolside at the country club,
supervising my kids, and I resonated with much of what Betty Friedan
described and discussed. I talked a few times with my husband about the
issues, but he seemed to find it much less interesting than I, so I did
not burden him further. However, when feminists such as Friedan,
Karen DeCrow, Gloria Steinem, Florynce Kennedy, Robin Morgan,
and others began to be invited to our campus to give talks, I easily
found many like-minded women with whom I could discuss these
issues. During the early 1970s, an intensity of feeling captured many of
us. I felt connected: this was the movement in which I belonged, not on
the periphery, but in the center.

I returned home one evening in the winter of 1972 after having
driven Gloria Steinem and Florynce Kennedy to the airport following
their inspiring speeches at Oswego, and said to my husband, "I think
this women's movement is going to change my life." I had absolutely no
idea of the extent and depth of the changes I was forecasting, nor could
I have imagined them at the time. In the next three years, both my personal and professional life goals and circumstances underwent major
reorganization.

In the spring of 1969, Oswego's president had called all women faculty members together to share his concerns about the upcoming
Middle States and National Council for Accredidation of Teacher
Education (NCATE) reaccreditation reviews. He indicated that those
accrediting bodies were interested in receiving, as part of the campus
self-study, data about women students and women faculty. He asked
for volunteers from among the group to form a committee to address
those issues, and within a few days after the meeting several of us were
sent letters of appointment to the president's Committee on Women,
which was empowered to seek data and prepare the needed reports. In
an eighteen-month period we discovered shocking data, discussed the

implications, and finally completed the reports requested by each accrediting organization. And we continued to meet and discuss; we extended the group to include almost all women faculty and many staff members. We were eager to discuss plans to rectify situations of inequity we had found in gathering data for our reports. We scheduled information-gathering sessions with members of the administration, seeking their commentary on what we had found. Probably the most egregious inequities were to be found in admission criteria to the college: for women, they were considerably higher than they were for men, because the college wished to maintain a ratio of two-thirds men to one-third women.

Following the campus visit of the Middle States team, and at their recommendation, the president hired an affirmative action adviser, whose husband taught in the history department. Patti McGill Peterson had been teaching part-time while completing her dissertation in political science, and she had been active on our committee. We advised her to insist on a full-time salary, and that she be allowed to continue teaching her course, Women in Politics, as part of the job. Her appointment as assistant to the president for affirmative action was announced, she was empowered to create an Affirmative Action Advisory Committee, and she continued teaching. Several of our group became initial members of her advisory committee; she also used our group as a sounding board, as well as suggesting that we raise issues that she felt were important but were not appropriate for her advisory group to raise. The President's Committee on Women was beginning to be political.

We stayed in existence as the president's committee for at least two more years, meeting regularly, well after the submission of the reports. Some of us Oswego women had become involved at the state level in forming the organization known as the SUNY Women's Caucus. At that time, we detached ourselves from the president's office in a formal manner. I was chairing the local group at the time; we wrote a letter of thanks and appreciation to him for having convened us and indicated that, although we were planning to continue meeting, we were officially severing our ties with his office, to become the Oswego chapter of the SUNY Women's Caucus. We felt that remaining a residual committee of the President's Combined Self-Study Group would narrow our focus and limit our credibility as a force for change with respect to women's conditions of employment, curricular issues, changing differential admissions criteria for women, and so on. We then extended our committee membership to all women employees in recognition of the strength in inclusivity across campus. I thought that our most important action was to get a group moving, which included myself, that was interested in planning a women's studies program for Oswego. Other members of the caucus worked on other projects.

The women's studies program planning took place during the 1971–72 school year and into the next fall. Members of the planning group were not limited to faculty members: we were enriched by the presence of members from student services, the clerical staff, the student body, and the community. In the spring of 1973, we prepared and sent forward, to the SUNY central office in Albany, a letter of intent to flesh out the design and put the curriculum in place. At that time there were two or three courses focused on women being taught each semester; they originated in the history, English literature, political science, and philosophy departments. The courses offered were usually entitled, Women and . . ." After we sent off the letter of intent, we waited until we received permission from the SUNY central office to proceed. We received a favorable response during the fall 1973 semester, and our subcommittee of the caucus began meeting very frequently in hopes of getting ready to send a full proposal through faculty governance that academic year. We added new course outlines to the mix of those already extant. We also encouraged departments to extend their offerings to include women's issues and concerns in courses past the introductory level. And we began the unanticipated lengthy political work of seeking support from departments and other administrative entities for a women's studies minor program at Oswego.

The committee prevailed upon our newly appointed provost, Virginia L. Radley, to grant assigned time for a faculty member to coordinate the work to be done in lobbying for new courses in various departments; we chose a member of the philosophy department, Christine Pierce, who had recently published an essay on feminist theory in the *Monist*. Our group decided that her academic credentials were the ones that were strongest in support of our goals. She served from 1974 to 1976, as director of women's studies, working to establish lines of communication among faculty and departments from whom we wished approval for courses. Several of our courses moved successfully through the department and college approval processes. In May 1976, at the end of her term, we had nearly every course in place at the department level, but we had made little or no progress toward program approval; the proposal had been languishing in a council of the Faculty Assembly. Christine Pierce was taking a leave, and I became the second head of a program still awaiting campus approval.

During 1974–75, I served as interim dean of graduate studies after the dean took an appointment in mid-September at another institution. This was my first exposure to administration, which I found challenging and particularly educational. In 1975–76, I took my first sabbatical leave. I had applied for a National Science Fellowship to study the psychology of women during the academic year 1975–76, as part of the sabbatical, and was accepted into a year-long workshop with Judith Bardwick. We met early in the fall for a two-week residential session; we were given a short bibliography and several reading and writing assignments, which were due at the late spring week-long residential session. Each student was to complete her reading assignments, write an annotated bibliography, and design an undergraduate course that she could offer during the spring session. We shared our course outlines and bibliographies and discussed the feeling of excitement and sense of empowerment that we had experienced in the workshop. It was, for me, a wonderful intellectual experience, as I was already more than ten years postdoctorate and believed I was in need of credentials in this area of study.

My personal circumstances were undergoing changes, too. My husband and I were unable to maintain a reasonable marital relationship because of the rapidly widening disparity between our goals. He, being older than I, was thinking about an early retirement in a few years, while I was savoring the experience of providing academic leadership and giving serious consideration to moving in that direction. We divorced without much rancor. At that time the children were twenty-one, eighteen, and fifteen, and they seemed to manage the situation reasonably well. My daughter and I moved into a large house, which we shared with friends. Within a few months my mother, whose health was failing, also came to live with us. Our household looked and felt like an old-fashioned three-generation extended family, which was made up of my mother, three parents, each working; and three teenagers in high school.

I returned to campus in the fall of 1976 to become the director of women's studies, ready to move the approval of the women's studies program through campus governance. I was also eager to teach

Psychology of Women, and to take my course through the governance procedures, adding a permanent, as distinguished from a special topics, course to the psychology department curriculum. I was again destined to be stunned by the reception I received from my psychologist colleagues, who saw no reason to approve such a course. They were sure that this was just a fad, and they compared Psychology of Women to a favorite topic of a retired senior faculty member: mob psychology. The Curriculum Committee stalled for nearly a year. Halfway through, they asked me to attend their meeting to discuss the course, which I did. By then I was teaching Psychology of Women as a special topics course, and planning to offer it regularly. The section scheduled for the fall of 1977 had filled almost immediately after registration opened, and had developed a waiting list of considerable proportion. In late April I spoke to the Curriculum Committee chair about the progress of their approval. He told me that perhaps the course would be approved sometime in the fall. I told him that there were more than fifty students registered or on the waiting list and that if the committee did not see fit to approve the course then I would cancel it, go to the student newspaper with an apology, and give reasons pointing to his committee for my having canceled the course. The course was reported out of committee to the department in the next meeting—and it was approved. I actually very surprised myself with my courageous response. But by then, I knew that my promotion to professor had gone through both the department and the dean's office.

It took the Oswego women's caucus, the women's studies planning group, and both the former and the current director of women's studies five years, from the sending of the letter of intent to Albany, to get our proposal for a women's studies program through Oswego college governance. There were many very politically charged meetings with male colleagues before we garnered the votes needed to move the women's studies proposal out of committee. I went to meetings regularly, during the 1977–78 academic year, to answer questions.

Finally, in the spring of 1978, the full Faculty Assembly approved our program, and we of the original group who were still on campus celebrated. The victory was particularly bittersweet: we had been constantly working against a resistance that took the form of interminable questions and requests for justifications at every level. In that interim, our actual course offerings had increased to include one or more sections of communication studies, psychology, sociology, anthropology, and health and physical education each semester. But the majority were still of the "Women and . . ." type.

We were very hopeful as we put the administrative structures of the program into place. We established an advisory board consisting of representation from community, faculty, professional staff, and students; we held regular meetings; and we chose a liaison to the campus Women's Center to help facilitate extracurricular program planning. In the summer of 1978, I resigned as director of women's studies to take another position in academic administration. I continued to serve on the Women's Studies Advisory Board; was a guest speaker in classes; and created and team taught for four semesters Women and Management, which has since been staffed by women faculty from the School of Business.

During my 1975–76 sabbatical year, I had become aware of a national group of both academic and community women organizing for what subsequently developed into the National Women's Studies Association (NWSA). I was aware of women's concerns groups in several academic associations, and of the Berkshire Conference Group among the historians. I had attended several New York state and East Coast meetings in the early 1970s, where the major topics were developing women's studies curriculum and how to solve the political problems of getting a program started. I quickly became convinced that curriculum development involved as much political sophistication as it did knowledge of content, at least in the area of women's studies.

Although I had been very aware of, and committed to, the issues of diversity since my undergraduate studies in anthropology and sociology, my experience at the 1977 NWSA Founding Convention intensified my belief that unless *much* more attention was paid to racism and class bias along with sexism, women's studies organizations were going to be rife with conflict and short lived. Following the 1981 NWSA conference, which had racism as the theme, nine white women associated with women's studies at Oswego, including myself, formed an antiracism group that met weekly, using a curriculum that had been discussed at the conference and that focused on white racism. Our meetings continued through the 1981–82 academic year. In the following years, we easily bonded to lobby for the recognition and inclusion of diversity in the curriculum and in aspects of student affairs programming on campus. In 1985, I reviewed my work of seven years as an academic administrator and decided that the classroom was where I wished to be. I returned to teaching Psychology of Women, along with graduate courses in counseling. I was again active in the governance of women's studies at Oswego. In 1988 we took the opportunity presented by a new president and administrative regime to lobby successfully for a separate budget for women's studies and assigned time of two courses per semester for the director of women's studies. We also managed to get the reporting structure altered such that the director reported to the provost's office as distinguished from one of the deans.

I know that my career as a college faculty member and as an administrator was very favorably affected by my involvement in women's studies. First, I was reinforced within women's studies for my focus on diversity, and that gave me the strength to initiate mainstreaming diversity issues in my disciplinary courses. Also, I found a "honing ground" through developing women's studies at Oswego and in my work within NWSA to develop my leadership skills, which might otherwise have lain dormant in the largely patriarchal college community. Women's studies also provided me with an unparalleled opportunity to engage in a new field of study, and I have reveled in it. During the academic year 1997–98, the Oswego women's studies program moved through governance a letter of intent to offer a major; permission was granted with very little opposition. In fact, it was almost easy to convince the All-College Curriculum Committee. The letter of intent was filed with the central administration; the faculty have moved to the full fleshing out of a major in women's studies. Participating in that activity, albeit mostly from the sidelines, was, as I moved toward retirement, a very satisfying thing.

Annis Pratt

I was born in New York City in 1937 and grew up there during World War II, turning thirteen in 1950. I attribute my intellectual self-confidence to my all-girls' and all-women's schooling from first grade all the way through college, after which it was impossible to believe that I was inferior because I was a woman. At college, we talked about the desegregation movement in Little Rock, heard speakers on race relations, and tried to understand the impact of segregation on us all as students our age began nonviolent protests against it. In my junior year I joined a group committed to social action for civil rights, and I've never looked back.

My senior thesis was on William Blake, who once declared that he preferred creating his own systems to pondering those of other people. Taking that statement as my mantra, I spent my scholarly career creating a system to examine archetypical elements of literature, leading to *Archetypical Patterns in Women's Fiction* in 1981, and in 1994, *Dancing with Goddesses,* a comparison of women and men poets.

I have, however, always enjoyed creating literature more than writing criticism about it: known at one point as a Georgia poet, I arrived at Spelman College as their director of creative writing. Recently, I've become a Unitarian poet, performing "Dancing with Elements to a Rhythm in Jazz" (accompanied by a jazz pianist) and "The Wingra Symphony," set to a concerto by Handel at the Birmingham, Michigan, Unitarian Church.

I love canoeing and kayaking, using my river adventures in Wisconsin and Michigan to write *The Marshlanders,* the first novel in an ecofeminist trilogy.

Imploding Marginality

One afternoon in November 1969 I was sitting in my office at Spelman College, leafing through Eugenia Collier's *Black Literature: A List of Bibliographies,* which I had picked up at a College Language Association meeting the previous spring. There had been an exciting forum on the opportunities and problems of teaching black literature at that Virginia Beach conference, where Nick Aaron Ford, Donald Gibson, and Charles Ray had debated with the audience of teachers from predominantly black colleges about the exclusion of black writers from American literature courses. Then the phone rang on my desk. It was Mrs. Micklebery, the Spelman librarian, calling from downstairs.

"Are you putting together the black bibliography for the English department?" she asked. "You *really* ought to come down here," she continued, with the lilt of excitement that infects a librarian who has just opened boxes and boxes of new acquisitions, "You've just *got* to see what we have just finished shelving: a foundation has donated a *huge* selection of materials on women, both black and white!"

Down I went. I still remember the smell of all those books that day, from brand new paperbacks such as Arna Bontemps's 1963 anthology *American Negro Poetry* and Margaret Walker's *Jubilee* to rows and rows of names entirely new to me: Phyllis Wheatley, Mrs. Frances E. W. Harper, Harriet Tubman, Ida B. Wells, Gwendolyn Brooks, Margaret Danner, and Naomi Long Madgett. Pamphlets about Harriet Tubman and Sojourner Truth had pamphlets about Susan B. Anthony and Lydia Maria Childs for neighbors; Jane Addams on the position of women and suffrage leaned companionably against books about black women abolitionists, Margaret Sanger's crusade for birth control, and Ida B. Wells' courageous stand against lynching.

The Curry collection had arrived at a time when Spelman faculty and students were finding empowerment in their historical heritage: here was a treasure lode to help me teach it! Excited for my students, I felt for my own intellectual life a kind of lonely hunger. Though I looked forward to reading African American books in order to prepare new courses, I did not feel comfortable about building my career upon the cultures of people that my ancestors oppressed.

We had arrived in Atlanta in the summer of 1964—my husband, Henry, our daughter Lorien, and I, pregnant with our daughter Faith— for Henry to teach at Emory University. And it was in Atlanta that discrimination came home to our house. I became a part-time lecturer at Emory University in 1965. I loved teaching poetry courses to Emory students, and when an assistant professorship opened up in my field, I assumed that I would be considered for it. But the chair of the English department told me that I could not even apply, because Emory had "feelings about nepotism," namely, about husbands and wives employed on the same campus.

I spent several weeks in shock and despair before it occurred to my husband and me that I was experiencing discrimination on the basis of both gender and marital choice.

"Why don't you call Betty Friedan in New York City?" suggested Henry, who had no intention of seeing me back off from our dedication to an equal marriage. "Perhaps this new National Organization for Women can tell us what to do."

"NOW is backing an amendment to an executive order," Betty barked cheerfully over the telephone. "Why don't you and Henry convene a NOW chapter for Atlanta? In the meantime, we are looking for ways to prohibit universities from discriminating against women."

For two years before that November 1969 afternoon in the Spelman library, I had been channeling my rage against Emory into feminist activism. In the fall of 1967, I began teaching at Spelman College, where my new colleagues educated me in the black literature with which they had long been familiar. The English department chair, Dr. Richard Carrol, urged me to attend College Language Association meetings, where professors from predominantly black colleges met to share bibliographical materials. With the help of colleagues such as Dr. Carrol and Dr. June Aldrich, I retrained myself in order to teach black literature to my increasingly proud and self-confident Spelman students, a project in accord with the mission of the college to educate black women separately from men and from whites, providing four years of sisterhood with one another, to strengthen them for their futures in a white, male world.

It was a heady, exciting intellectual atmosphere at the predominantly black Atlanta colleges in 1967 and 1968, like that of the French Revolution when Wordsworth wrote, "Bliss was it in that dawn to be alive," except that it was somebody else's dawn I was alive in. My students were abandoning passive acceptance of oppression and the desire to assimilate into the majority white culture. Catalyzed by profound events into a rejection of oppression, they were immersing themselves in their black heritage in order to establish positions from which they could go on to take their place in U.S. society.[1]

Then, one rainy April evening in 1968, Spelman students' depth of anger against majority white culture was renewed and intensified. Later that week, I stood behind Martin Luther King Jr.'s coffin as a faculty usher at the viewing held for the public in the chapel, with plenty of time to contemplate what my people had done to this brilliant theologian dedicated to integration, nonviolence, and compassion. Now even more Spelman women abandoned assimilation to transform themselves into African American women.

In a parallel process, I left behind my last shreds of conformity to the gender norms of the 1950s, channeling my anger into organizing and demonstrating on behalf of women. I had emerged from the more passive acceptance of my gender role, felt as a teenager in the 1950s, into anger at how Emory had treated me. Later, I had forged alliances with other feminists to fight sexism, but I had lived in mere opposition to patriarchy, not yet strengthened by my selfhood as a woman.[2]

Nor had I found a way to connect my newfound passion for feminist activism with my own literary scholarship. In all my years studying for my B.A., M.A., and Ph.D. at Smith College, the University of Wisconsin, and Columbia University, I had not been assigned more than three books by women. Now, walking up and down the new metal shelving filling what had, only the week before, been an open reading area, breathing in the heady smell of recently unboxed books, I was galvanized by material on Greek and Roman women, West African women, career women, African American women, Italian American women, feminism, and family planning in Victorian England. Here was a research topic that I could passionately research for the rest of my scholarly life: women!

Though the term *women's studies* had not yet been coined, I spent the winter of 1969 creating a course and a textbook, both called *The Woman Question: Prehistoric to Present.* Just as Spelman students were gaining fresh strength from the study of their African heritage, re-empowering themselves against the discrimination they had been experiencing their whole lives, I wanted to start women off with good news about their accomplishments. Although it was perfectly clear that there had never been a "golden age of women" (certainly never a "matriarchy" of women dominating men the way men dominated women in patriarchy), there was plenty of material in the Curry collection to empower women.

When I made the rounds of New York publishers with my multicultural feminist textbook proposal, I found no takers. I know now that it was too far ahead of its time to interest them. In the summer of 1970, I used the materials I had collected to teach my first Woman Question course, at the Atlanta YWCA. That fall we moved north to Detroit, where I did not look for a job right away, but took the year off to help our daughters adjust to the new environment and to read more widely in women's literature. Our house had room in the basement for a huge mimeograph machine, on which I printed *As We See it NOW,* Detroit NOW's first newsletter. The house had bedrooms for both daughters and, best of all, a library adjacent to our bedroom, painted in a dusky rose.

In was in that library that I sat down to immerse myself in women's literature. Having heard about the Commission on the Status of Women in the Profession of the Modern Language Association, I had corresponded from Atlanta with Florence Howe, who had asked me to present a paper on an MLA panel in New York. For my presentation, I invented "The New Feminist Criticism*s,*" a play on the New Criticism, a fashion of the 1950s, making it multiple in hopes that feminist scholarship might be eclectic enough to include the archetypal criticism that I had decided upon as my life work.

Then sex discrimination came, once more, to our house. In the fall of 1970, I had begun looking for a job in the Detroit area and had written to apply to the University of Michigan, Dearborn, which had advertised a full-time position. In November, the chair of the English department phoned to say that there was a position open, and that I might be interviewed either in town or at the MLA convention. I had heard nothing by the time I went to the convention, and it was there that members of the Commission on the Status of Women in the Profession warned me that the UM, Dearborn, campus had a reputation for hiring women on a part-time basis in order to keep their salaries and benefits at a minimum.

I heard nothing until February, when the chair phoned to offer me a part-time position to start in five days. I replied that, as a professional literary critic and professor, I did not take jobs on five days' notice. I phoned him again in April to inquire about the full-time position, only to be told that there was one part-time opening for the following year, but that "the woman who came on five days' notice has the edge over you for that position." It was painfully clear that I had once more come up against sex discrimination, so I filed a complaint against UM, Dearborn, with both the Department of Health, Education and Welfare, and the Michigan Civil Rights Commission.

Although I was called in for an interview, ordered by the Michigan Civil Rights Commission, at the Dearborn campus, their English department easily found a way to get around my complaint, which was denied. The fact that I had filed a complaint against a Michigan university was made known to every Michigan university I ever applied to, and that was the end of my ever being employed full-time in Michigan. I was turned down for one position after another for the next fifteen years, even for openings specifically in my field or when the departmental chair clearly wanted to hire me. Thus began a painful life for me and my family as I became a commuting professor-partner-mother, prevented from ever teaching in the state where my husband lived.

NOW and the civil rights movement saved my professional career. On October 13, 1968, NOW had persuaded Lyndon Johnson to amend Executive Order 11246, which prohibited federal contractors from discriminating on the basis of race, color, religion, and national origin. Now the order would also cover discrimination based on sex. In January 1970, on the basis of the amended order, Bernice Sandler, who had been working part-time at the University of Maryland but was refused consideration for full-time openings because, she was told, "You come on *too strong for a woman*," filed a huge class action case against all universities through the Women's Equity Action League. Sandler's brilliant strategy against the same kind of discrimination I had been suffering from frightened the University of Wisconsin, Madison, into looking about for women to hire, and thus, in June 1971, I was offered a visiting assistant professorship with assurances that I would immediately be considered for a regular tenure-track job.

One of the principal reasons that Wisconsin was open to hiring women in 1971 was the moral suasion of Kathryn Clarenbach, the widely respected head of the Wisconsin Commission on the Status of Women and the first coordinator of NOW after it was convened in June, 1966; and because of the pioneering work of Joan Roberts, an assistant professor of educational policy at the University of Wisconsin, Madison, who had put in place a Wisconsin Coordinating Council of Women in Higher Education. Between them, Clarenbach and Roberts had persuaded the Wisconsin university system that its mission included teaching and scholarship about women, which paved the way not only for hiring more women faculty but for the development of women's studies programs.

On my first day in Madison, I was told by two new mentors (one male and one female), editors of *Contemporary Literature,* who were responsible for my being hired and to whom I told my story, that if I ever mentioned my case against the University of Michigan again, I would never get tenure. They instructed me to wear dresses and skirts instead of the denim outfits and suede boots I loved so dearly, and to keep as low a profile as possible in the English department. I calculated that it would take only two years, and that with tenure in hand, I could be as active as I wanted on behalf of women. I knew that without tenure, I would be of much more limited use to women.

It was harder than I thought to go demurely about my teaching in those vulnerability-creating skirts. There had been sexual harassment against graduate students and secretaries in the department. I promised them that the minute I got tenure, I would do something about it, and the very next morning in November 1973, I reported this unacceptable behavior.

Meanwhile, administrators had been trying to block the demands of the Association of Faculty Women for an end to discrimination against academic women and for the establishment of a women's studies program. In 1970, Joan Roberts began teaching Education and the Status of Women, the first women's studies course on campus, which was broadcast over the university radio station. Subsequently, Roberts devised another course, Sex Socialization and the Status of Women, in which women faculty collaborated with one another and consciousness-raising took place. These courses met with scorn and derision from other faculty, who saw the subject of women as unimportant.[3]

In March 1974, Joan Roberts, though widely published and boasting an excellent teaching record, was denied tenure. Bravely (and backed by courageous students, who marched and demonstrated on her behalf), she called for an open hearing, where the shameless lies and overt duplicity of male academics were displayed before a huge audience and the news media. When Roberts' department chair baldly insisted that she did not hold a publishing contract for her most recent manuscript, she beckoned a student holding a telephone onto the stage, dialed her publisher, and handed the phone to her chair amid triumphant cheers from her supporters. Repeatedly denied tenure, she took the University of Wisconsin, Madison, to court in a case that was settled in 1978 for a mere $30,000. She subsequently received tenure at Syracuse University, where she became chair of the Department of Child and Family Studies.

Energized by this blatant injustice against a highly accomplished feminist scholar, we increased our pressure upon an administration reluctant to establish a women's studies program. Elaine Reuben, an English department member, had been teaching a pioneering interdisciplinary course since the fall of 1971, along with Joyce Steward. By the time I joined the group in January 1974, Alice in Academe had existed for three years under the auspices of an experimental program called Contemporary Trends. Starting out with this voluntary unit was a good way of proving the seriousness of women's studies on the campus.

Alice in Academe was taught by a collective, consisting of a faculty sponsor, who did the grading, and several teaching assistants, each leading a group of twenty students. When my turn came up to sponsor the course, we called it Herstory: The Changing Role of Women in Society. With *Our Bodies, Ourselves* by the Boston Women's Health Collective as our text, Barbara Bitters, Diane Sachs, and I integrated the personal and political, leading students to arrive at feminist analyses through exploring their own lives as women. This experiential pedagogy intrinsic to women's studies integrated head and heart in a manner that provided the foundation for the teaching method I would use from then on.

As I review my Herstory syllabus, however, I notice that we heaped bad news upon our students from the first day: we talked of stereotypes without going on to explain how women can empower ourselves, we detailed Simone de Beauvoir's dreary exposition of womanhood without contradicting her, we outlined Betty Friedan's "problem that has no name" without suggesting any solutions to it, and we discussed Phyllis Chesler's definition of madness as an inevitable outcome of patriarchy without outlining saner ways of living. We heaped the same account of patriarchal horrors upon our students' heads in the course Women in Literature, which I taught every year in the English department. Instead of starting with women's self-affirmative writings, I chose books (*The Awakening, The Bell Jar, The Yellow Wall-Paper,* and *The Golden Notebook*) either by or about women who a) went mad, b) committed suicide, or c) were seriously depressed.

Meanwhile, the Association of Faculty Women and the ever-increasing number of students who wanted to take women's studies courses continued to pressure the school to establish a department or program. Obdurate, recalcitrant, and devious, the university administration was finally persuaded to appoint a Chancellor's Committee on Women's Studies in the spring of 1974, only to choose the summer to do this—when they thought activists would be gone—so that they could pack the committee with their allies. What I brought to the women's studies movement in this crisis was my cynicism about the motives of administrators and an ability to anticipate the tricks and ploys that they might use to try to trip us up. Not all of the administrators trying to prevent women's studies from being established were men: there were assimilated women anxious to stay in the good graces of the academic patriarchy who joined in the effort to quash us.

Jacqueline Macaulay (a sociologist the university refused to hire, who later became a civil rights lawyer) was astute and wily, with a good head for knowing which way university administrators would leap.[4] That summer, she and I devised a counterstrategy: a rota to make sure that one of us was in town at all times should the bureaucracy put forward one of their nominees for the Chancellor's Committee on Women's Studies. This way, we won our fight for a balanced committee, which convened in the fall to put a women's studies program together.

During those early days of organization, I was not as effective within the women's studies community itself as I was in agitating for the establishment of a women's studies program on campus. Courageous as I might be in the face of institutional deviousness and male chicanery, I found myself incapable of dealing with women's anger. That rage was, in part, a passing on to one another of the emotion-laden hostility visited upon us by colleagues, whose irrational attacks came as a terrible shock to our expectations of decent academic behavior. Many of my feminist colleagues felt more at home than I did in the atmosphere of argument and counterargument, verbal fisticuffs delivered with a snarling eloquence and dialectical cut-and-thrust typical of (patriarchal) academic culture.

As the years went by, I still fled the room when that kind of verbal violence began to fly, but I was able to bring my skills at consensus building to meetings of the women's studies program. I would sit back and listen to all the points of view until I heard a fragment of consensus begin to emerge, and then propose a motion to bring varying views into harmony. When things got difficult, I would make a joke and break the tension.

I regret that, in my early years as a feminist activist, I used to get the equality that I so fiercely desired confused with sameness: I wanted equal pay for equal work, and I wanted to be hired and promoted on my merits without consideration of gender. I wanted my chance to be the same kind of college professor that men were, using my intellect in the same way, writing similar kinds of books and articles. Being a woman was a difference I would leave behind at the ivory gates of a genderless community, which would accept me on my merits and where I could take my place in a culture of ideas and teaching, free at last from discrimination. Getting ahead by conforming to the dominant culture was hardly unique to women: this was my version of the American dream, which valorized assimilation.

Although my admiration for my African American students' refusal to "pass for white" should have warned me away from assimilating to academic culture, that is precisely the position I took. On the chancellor's committee, as we had designed the new women's studies program we had seen our African American studies department as a model to avoid: we had not wanted to "ghettoize" ourselves, we told one another; a separate department would "weaken our position." Still following my academic version of the American dream, I was among the chancellor's committee's strongest advocates for gaining access to academe by establishing a program rather than "marginalizing" ourselves as a separate department. The women's studies program was established that way: each faculty member was granted a 51 percent appointment in her "home" department and 49 percent in women's studies.

Looking back at the twenty years in which women's studies faculty had to conform to departments to get tenure, I think that a separate department of our own might have been better after all. The academic culture of huge research institutions is structured upon patriarchal modes of domination and competition, tempting even women's studies professors to allow their emotional and relational skills to atrophy in order to adapt to it. I consider this (unconscious) masculinization of the self responsible for the stressed lives many women's studies professors live in academe as well as for the restriction of their syllabi to patriarchal abuses and reactions against them. Because women's studies faculty had to assimilate to win tenure by getting serious about whatever academic theory or research technique was fashionable in their departments in the 1980s, many humanities faculty got caught up in deconstruction. I thought it very odd to see feminist faculty burning the midnight oil to assimilate the ideas of European males questionably occupied during World War II, schooling themselves to devalue the very things women's studies cared about most—women, bodies, selves, and the natural world.[5]

Would the bonds among women have remained stronger if we had established our own department to hire faculty with 100 percent appointments? I think that a separate women's studies department could have fostered greater validation of our differences from men, tolerated scholarly ideas not in fashion, and provided a more mutually empowering community for women. Realistically, however, I know that it is possible that, given enormous institutional pressures to conform, faculty from a separate women's studies department might have felt compelled to "pass for patriarchal," a decision that no self-respecting Spelman woman, joyously embedding herself in African American difference, would have tolerated for a moment.

I never forgot that it was the civil rights movement to which I owed my professional career: in 1981, when it became clear that affirmative in action was still the order of the day on the Madison campus, Jacqueline Macaulay and I surveyed departments to see if women were being hired and promoted, and developed charts to detail our findings. We were members of a union for faculty and academic staff, United Faculty Local 223 of the American Federation of Teachers, through which we brought our charts of noncompliance to the attention of the Office of Federal Contract Compliance (OFCC).

When I saw federal agents coming out of their interview with the present and past English department chairs, I felt the frightening clarity of walking my talk that is the heady terror of active commitment. On the one hand, I felt entirely at peace with myself at having committed my principles to action; on the other hand, I was terrified out of my mind at standing up against a huge research university. Although the OFCC had assured me anonymity, my heart was in my throat when I sat in departmental meetings when women faculty who had been kept back for years began to move toward tenure, accompanied by an angry roaring from men not in the inner circle, who did not know that their more powerful brothers were being forced by the federal government to promote women.

Things did not go as well for me in the English department after that as they did for the women my action had helped. When my cover was inadvertently blown by a colleague who let the university attorney see one of our charts with my name on it, I was marked as the whistle-blower, held at arm's length by my English department, and ostracized from university committees for the rest of my career. Although I used the extra time to give workshops on pedagogy for women's studies, to sponsor a support group for women artists, and to develop the English Ph.D. in women's literature, as the years went by, the isolation and powerlessness this shunning brought about saddened me profoundly.

Titling articles "Post Cards from the Volcano," "Scratching at the Compound," and "Dancing at the Edge of the World," we who dared to stand up for women against institutions dead set against us articulated our position in academe. During those years, I chronicled academic women's struggle to get ahead in a column called "Dancing through the Minefield," which appeared in both *Concerns* (the journal of the Women's Caucus of Modern Languages, which I edited) and *NWSACTION*, (the newsletter of the National Women's Studies Association).

In my classes, meanwhile, women who had been marginalized by gender felt their gender margins implode as they became more centered in their lives as women. Through exposure to symbols of feminine power, they claimed control of their own sexuality and discovered in themselves an intellectual inventiveness, a love of community, and a marvelously creative but practical competence. Though I emerged from class after class delighted at my students' transformation, my energy to continue this intensive kind of teaching went unreplenished. It was as if many wires were going out from me, with no fresh voltage from what Mary Daly used to call "the cosmosis of sisterhood" coming in. Where was the energy source I had thought the women's studies community would provide?

By the late 1980s, I was spiritually dehydrated from isolation while, both in English and women's studies, women faculty were too busy to stop tearing about, even for a chat. I felt that I was dying for lack of gossip, that web of words and embracing patter through which women replenish one another. Those are the reasons why, in 1990, I took early retirement. It turned out to be a very good choice, enabling me to return to full-time writing; to launch a newsletter of tips and tactics for women faculty, *The Strategist;* and to rejoin the fight for racial justice in the Detroit metropolitan area. I finished my last academic book and began a trilogy of ecofeminist novels and *The Peripatetic Papers,* humorous sketches about my life as a commuting professor. I have continued my feminist activism as disbursements coordinator of NWSA's Academic Discrimination Task Force, which I administer from my home.

In June 1995, I attended the NWSA convention in Oklahoma, where I told an auditorium full of feisty feminist scholars that when we grittily persist in our friction against the obdurate academic oyster, we become like pearls, gleaming and shining. Why, when we emerge at last from all this conflict with the powers that be, would we want to become oysters? We are not oysters, we are pearls strung on a gold chain: brilliantly intellectual and heart-whole sisters, whose power and effectiveness reside in the golden strand that binds our lives together as women.

Josephine Donovan

I was born in Manila in 1941 and grew up as an "Army brat" on various military posts throughout the United States, as well as in Germany and Turkey, with my parents, brother, and sister. I received my B.A. degree, cum laude, from Bryn Mawr College in 1962, majoring in history, with my junior year spent in France and Switzerland. After graduation I worked for various publications, including short stints at the *Washington Post* and (as a "copy desk girl") at *Time* magazine. In 1967 I received an M.A. and in 1971 a Ph.D. from the University of Wisconsin, Madison (both in comparative literature).

My scholarship has been primarily in the areas of feminist literary criticism, feminist theory, women's literature (early modern and American), and animal defense theory. Most recently, I published *Women and the Rise of the Novel, 1405–1726* (1999); *Beyond Animal Rights: A Feminist Caring Ethic for the Treatment of Animals* (1996); and *Animals and Women: Feminist Theoretical Explorations* (1995) (the latter two coedited with Carol J. Adams). My work also includes *Feminist Theory: The Intellectual Traditions of American Feminism* (1985; rev. ed., 1992; 3d rev. ed., 2000); *New England Local Color Literature: A Women's Tradition* (1983); and *After the Fall: The Persephone-Demeter Myth in Wharton, Cather, and Glasgow* (1989).

I am a tenured full professor at the University of Maine in Orono and live in Portsmouth, New Hampshire.

A Cause of Our Own

When I first heard about "women's lib" in the late 1960s, I didn't pay much attention. I knew only that some women in New York had taken to burning their bras and refusing to let men open doors for them.[1] I was then actively and passionately involved in the antiwar movement, and such concerns seemed trivial. Villages were being napalmed, atrocities committed, and "body counts" enumerated daily in the news. My political imperative at the time was to end the Vietnam war. People now ask if we thought about race and class in those days. That's *all* we thought about: racism, colonialism, and imperialism. Feminism added gender to the mix.

My final year in graduate school at the University of Wisconsin, Madison, was 1970–71. As I was preparing for my doctoral exams, an event occurred that some have called the end of the antiwar movement, the August 1970 bombing of the Army Math Research Center at the UW. I lived only a few blocks from the bomb site and was jolted awake by the blast—in more ways than one. I had long been uneasy about the violent rhetoric of the New Left, which had intensified through the summer of 1970 on the Madison campus. The willingness of extremist groups—the Weather Underground, for example—to endorse violence seemed to me to compromise the cause. I had joined a group called the Nonviolent Alternative and worked with the American Friends Service Committee in their pacifist antiwar activities.

My antiwar commitment was not irrelevant to my becoming a feminist. The New Left was dominated by macho men who were nevertheless insecure about their masculinity. One of the more celebrated pieces of graffiti on a construction fence at the UW—"Antimilitarists Have Balls, Too"—humorously highlighted this anxiety (it ostensibly referred to an antimilitary ball that was held in protest against the military [ROTC] ball). Meetings and rallies were dominated by men; women were invisible at worst, subordinate at best. I theorize that the violence endorsed by the New Left was a way radical men had of "proving" their manhood, which, in this country, is virtually synonymous with militarism and violence.

It came, therefore, as a surprising and delightful idea that women should have something to say about how things were done, that we women might have a different modus operandi, that we women might, in short, have a cause of our own. "Goodbye," as Robin Morgan wrote at the time, "to all that."[2]

My first serious exposure to feminist ideas occurred by chance. One evening in the summer of 1971, after typing all day on my dissertation, I happened to turn on WHA-TV, the local PBS channel. In progress was a panel discussion about women's liberation; the panelists were Miss Wisconsin, a Catholic priest, and Elaine Reuben.[3] Not surprisingly, I found myself agreeing with Elaine more than the others, and figured that if such an intelligent, articulate person could be for it, there must be something to the women's movement.

My interest thus aroused, I decided I would have to look further into "women's liberation." Soon thereafter, I picked up a paperback copy of Kate Millett's *Sexual Politics,* which I began reading in the evenings as I typed my thesis by day. By the time I had finished typing the thesis (which was entirely about male authors), I was beginning to realize that there was a whole new way of looking at literature—and at life. I had to admire Millett's audacity in taking on then-chic male authors and thereby taking on the whole male literary/critical establishment.

I finished my Ph.D. work in the summer of 1971, taking my thesis orals in August and receiving my degree the same month. I don't know if the term *role models* had been invented yet, but I had three on my orals committee: Germaine Brée, Cyrena Pondrom, and my dissertation director, Fannie LeMoine.[4] I have often said that I would never have made it through graduate school without the intellectual stimulation, inspiration, and nurturing of Fannie LeMoine, professor of classics and associate dean of humanities of the UW Graduate School at the time of her death in August 1998. Germaine Brée's work helped me to realize that academic writing could be objective and accurate and, at the same time, politically engaged and relevant. Without that understanding—which feminist research, at its best, embodies—I would never have chosen an academic career.

I assumed my first tenure-track position in September 1971 as an assistant professor in the honors program at the University of Kentucky. I was teaching great books courses, such as The Greek Worldview and The Medieval Worldview, and I still had not heard of women's studies. That idea I first encountered in a lecture/presentation by Gloria Steinem and Florynce Kennedy on September 22. I was standing next to Suzanne Howard, then an assistant professor in the

School of Education, when Steinem spoke about the idea of teaching courses devoted to women's literature, history, and so on. Sue and I looked at each other. "Why not here?" we said.

Shortly thereafter, we organized a Women's Studies Committee, and I began planning my first women's studies course, Women and Literature, which I taught in the spring of 1972 as a junior-senior seminar to about fifteen students, a few of whom I still correspond with. I recently encountered one of them, who remembered it as a "magical" course. Also, that fall I went to a Midwest Modern Language Association meeting in Detroit, where I learned about the first two volumes in the *Female Studies* series; there I found marvelous syllabi with dozens of works by women, many of which I had never read.

So I began reading, and, in fact, barely two months after receiving my Ph.D., I found myself embarked upon what was essentially another, self-directed, Ph.D. program, reading literally hundreds of works by and about women's literature, history, and culture. There had been but three women on my comparative literature doctoral exam (we had to put together three lists of one hundred works each as preparation for our exams): Hrotsvitha of Gandersheim, a tenth-century playwright; Louise Labé, a French Renaissance poet; and Virginia Woolf. Three out of three hundred. And, of course, we learned next to nothing about women in my undergraduate years at Bryn Mawr (class of '62). So I had a lot of reading to do.

It was in preparing for and teaching my first course in feminist theory (spring 1973) that I discovered the amazing body of eighteenth, nineteenth, and twentieth-century theorizing about women. Mary Wollstonecraft's *Vindication of the Rights of Woman;* Margaret Fuller's *Woman in the Nineteenth Century;* Sarah Grimké's *Letters on Equality;* Charlotte Perkins Gilman's *Women and Economics;* and Virginia Woolf's *Three Guineas:* all these were new to me and revelatory. I was particularly taken by the idea that women were in some sense different from men and, indeed, had a separate history, culture, and, yes, value-system. The latter idea, still controversial, has become a major vein in contemporary feminist ethical theorizing. I began to see that my antiwar/pacifist commitments and my newly awakened feminist interests were integrally related. *Three Guineas* remains the work that most nearly expresses the feminism I embrace.

These first feminist courses were unlike any I've taught before or since. It was truly a revolutionary period: everything was being questioned; everything was experimental. We had the sense of being on the threshhold of a new world. The excitement and energy were overwhelming. It was a period, as Ti-Grace Atkinson wrote, of "unlimited hopes, of seemingly endless horizons."[6]

Not only was the subject matter new, but we also wanted to transform the university, to make it more democratic and egalitarian.[7] I held most sessions of my first feminist theory course (spring 1973) in my apartment. (There were about ten in the class.) Class sessions were informal and filled with laughter; they often opened with narratives of personal experience. We got to know one another as friends and, indeed, political comrades. I was only about ten years older (in some cases, less) than the students, and I was learning feminist history and theory along with them. I assigned each student a major figure in feminist theory; that student was supposed to become an authority on her figure. Each class period—it was a seminar that met weekly for three hours—was then devoted to a major feminist: Sarah Grimké, Margaret Fuller, and so on.

Occasionally, we had class projects. When we discovered that the UK library held a complete set of *The Forerunner* (Charlotte Perkins Gilman's magazine), we all went over, each of us taking a volume, which we skimmed and reported on to the others. That way we "discovered" *Herland,* Gilman's utopian novel, and many other gems. One time, we took the first hour of class to picket and leaflet a Kentucky Wildcats basketball game because of the use of "Kentucky Kittens," women students who were used as "hostesses" in the recruiting process.

The blurring of boundaries that we experimented with in that class—between student and teacher, between class and life, and between academics and politics—I now consider a mistaken idea. Students and teachers are not and never will be equal. The reason is that we operate in an institutional context where teachers have more power. So long as that context of power relations exists, this will remain the case. Even, however, if that context were abolished, teachers, by virtue of their knowledge, would remain on a different plane than students, and this is as it should be. We are there to guide and teach them, and although friendships may often result, a certain distance should be maintained while the course is operative. I also now feel that it is inappropriate for a course to undertake overt political activity such as picketing.

In the early years, there was often the temptation to run a class like a consciousness-raising session. That temptation remains but should be resisted. This is not to say that no personal, experience-based information should be used; on the contrary, such material is often relevant and engaging. But it should not dominate the course. I also have given up the use of journals, which I initially used. I found that students too often revealed painful, deeply complex personal experiences, which in many cases I felt unqualified to respond to and certainly unable and unwilling to "grade."

Yet the women's studies courses I teach today remain different and nontraditional, and students still seem to feel an energizing sense of excitement, of discovery. Classes are informal: when possible, we sit in a circle. Although I provide background information, the class time is mostly dialogue and discussion, and each student in upper-level courses is responsible for directing a portion of a class period. I never give timed, in-class exams, but rather assign papers on a specific question or issue, which function as take-home exams. The question of who passes thus boils down to who is willing to put time into the work. Of course, grades are still assigned on the basis of intellectual quality and writing ability—not on how sincere a feminist one is—and I occasionally feel conflicted about this.

Meanwhile, in the early 1970s, more and more women's studies courses were being offered at UK. Following a suggestion of Kimberly Snow, an assistant professor in the English department, we used to publicize forthcoming classes on huge posters, plastering the campus with them during preregistration. In late 1972, the Women's Studies Committee, which I chaired, developed a proposal for a women's studies program. On March 15, 1973, it was dutifully and unanimously rejected by the Academic Affairs Committee. The speed of the committee's action brought to mind Susan B. Anthony's sarcastic comment about the judge's decision in her celebrated civil disobedience trial in 1873: he had exhibited the wisdom of forethought, she noted, having rendered his opinion without having to hear her arguments.

I was chagrined by the committee's decision, because I thought we had prepared an intelligent, well-written, and well-reasoned proposal. I soon came to realize, however, that, to paraphrase Mae West, "reason had nothing to do with it." As Catharine Stimpson explained to me on a visit to campus shortly thereafter, "You didn't have the numbers." It had been, alas, a matter of power. This realization about the academic world has been one of the hardest for me to accept. I am still astounded that a place allegedly devoted to thoughtful inquiry, the pursuit of knowledge, the careful examination of evidence, operates largely like any political institution on the basis of who has power, who has the numbers—*not* on who has the most intelligent plan, the most reasonable argument, or justice on her side. Women's studies has been successful, not because it is an exciting, intellectually challenging, and rigorously demanding field of scholarship and knowledge, or because it is right and just, but because we have the numbers. It's still a matter of "body count."[8]

One interesting discussion—in fact, the only serious discussion—I had with a tenured male faculty member about the UK women's studies proposal occurred with a professor of geology, who suggested that we deflect accusations that women's studies teaches a party line by comparing women's studies to biology. There, too, a particular hypothesis—evolution—has been agreed upon by scholars, and that—not creationism—is the theory they teach. So, too, in women's studies, indeed in every field, scholars come to a consensus about the dominant paradigm (to use Thomas Kuhn's term) in their field. In women's studies that paradigm is feminist, and there is nothing inappropriate or unacademic about rejecting antifeminist material.

The UK administration did finally decide to give us separate space—the upper floor of an old house on the edge of campus—for the Women's Studies Committee and for a Women's Center. The Women's Studies Committee had a part-time secretary, Bonnie Stirler, who was an ardent feminist and devoted to the concept that work and home should be integrated. She could often be found baking cookies in the house's kitchen. Occasionally, someone would call and a student would answer, "Oh, Bonnie can't come to the phone. She's washing her hair." It was fun to have a space of our own like this, but the fact that such an "unprofessional" atmosphere was tolerated by the administration signified how marginal and trivial women's studies was in its eyes.[9]

Meanwhile, in the early 1970s, women's studies scholarship continued to grow nationally. Because the University of Kentucky hosted an annual Kentucky foreign languages conference, I asked if I could chair two sections on the newly emerging field of feminist literary criticism. Surprisingly, the conference planners agreed to my idea, so I wrote to every feminist critic I had heard of (I sent out perhaps seventy-five form letters), inviting them to submit proposals. Eventually, I narrowed the field to about ten, which were presented at the conference on April 27 and 28, 1973. One of these sessions was devoted to feminist critical theory; its highlight was the now-famous dialogue between Catharine Stimpson, then an untenured assistant professor at Barnard, and Carolyn Heilbrun, a professor at Columbia; it was included, along with several other papers, in a book I edited, *Feminist Literary Criticism: Explorations in Theory.*[10]

The women's movement affected my personal as well as my professional life, and by 1974 I found myself involved with a member of my support group, Anne Barrett, in a partnership that lasted fifteen years. When Anne accepted a position at the University of New Hampshire in 1975, I decided to move with her, thus giving up my tenure-track position at UK. I was, in fact, scheduled to come up for tenure in 1976; the director of the honors program, Robert O. Evans, said he was confident that I would receive tenure and urged me to stay, but, many would say foolishly, I decided to resign my position. I later recounted this story to Germaine Greer in a job interview. She remarked candidly, "You must either have had enormous nerve or been an awful fool." In retrospect, I'm afraid it was a bit more of the latter than the former.

In truth, I didn't take academia very seriously at the time. I still don't, but I have become much more aware of how important status and rank are to academics. Without the protection of tenure and the status of academic rank, you are extremely vulnerable, and no amount of intellectual brilliance or accomplishment can overcome the stigma. I was oblivious to all this in 1975, still high on the feminist euphoria of the day.

A rude—indeed brutal—awakening awaited me at the University of New Hampshire, where I was appointed the first women's studies coordinator in 1977. This three-year ordeal remains by far the worst, most humiliating, and enraging event of my professional as well as my personal life. If I could rerun my life and erase just one experience, this would be it. Not only did it dash much of my faith in feminist solidarity, it frankly lowered my opinion of human nature. The rank viciousness, faithlessness, and contempt I experienced there I still find appalling.

I learned that powerlessness "invites" abuse. While I had been a tenure-track assistant professor at UK, I made the mistake of accepting the rank of non-tenure-track lecturer at UNH (on a one-year renewable contract). Even though it now seems foolish and naïve, I accepted the position thus for a number of reasons. One, of course, was that I was committed to the growth of women's studies; another was that I wanted to be in the same area as my partner; a third was that I needed a job; and, finally, I was told by feminist members of the Search Committee that this was the best deal they could get out of the administration, that it was this or nothing—no women's studies at UNH. So I took the position.

The first indication of the kind of harassment that was in store for me came when, soon after I started the new position in September 1977, the dean called me into his office. Women's studies was then located in a tiny, dingy office in the basement of the appropriately named Murkland Hall. On the main floor was the spacious, brightly lit dean's suite. The dean had the grade list from a course in feminist theory I had taught that summer at UNH in the philosophy department. He wanted to know why I had given so many A's. I realized right away that it was just a matter of petty harassment and replied that I gave them because the students—many of whom were advanced philosophy majors—deserved them. I also told him that I thought it was a violation of my academic freedom to be harassed by the administration about my grading decisions, that his behavior was particularly suspicious in view of my having just begun as women's studies coordinator, a position of which he did not approve. He replied that he had just chosen my course at random. I shook my head, amazed at his cynical sangfroid. Such, then, was the welcome to my new job.

Shortly thereafter, I got a rude letter from the chair of the philosophy department demanding an explanation about the grading in the course. I responded with a vehement memo dated October 4, 1977, protesting this appalling treatment. I was, in truth, amazed to find my professional credentials and judgment held in such contempt, because, in fact, I had—and have—a reputation for being a somewhat rigorous grader. I noted in the memo that it had been my experience that "women's studies courses attract highly motivated and intelligent students" and that, in any event, the students had earned whatever grades they received.

This was the first time in my professional life that I had encountered sexism in such a raw form. I suddenly realized with dismay that my association with *women*'s studies meant, in the minds of these administrators, that I was intellectually, academically, and professionally suspect. It didn't matter that I had attended elite schools, had a distinguished academic record, had outstanding letters of reference, and that I had published with a major university press. No, I was the barbarian at the gates, who had to be beaten back and intimidated in any way they could think of.

After three years of this kind of unrelenting treatment, I decided that I needed a year off.[11] Because I did not have a permanent position, my "leave" consisted in resigning my position in 1980, in hopes that I would get the job back permanently upon my return. In my absence, however, the Search Committee hired someone else. Such was my reward for being the "founding mother" of the women's studies program at UNH.

Thus began for me seven years in the academic wilderness. Although I applied for literally hundreds of jobs, it was not until 1987, when the cultural tide had turned in favor of feminism and women's studies, that I finally obtained once again a regular academic position—in the English department at the University of Maine.

I soon learned that intramural squabbling among women's studies faculty at UM had prevented the development of a women's studies program there. Evelyn Newlyn had been hired the same year, however, and one of her charges was to develop a program. Shortly after her arrival, Evy, who became a good friend and comrade, drew up a proposal for a program, which we managed to get through the deeply divided Women's Studies Committee by one vote in 1988. A women's studies program was thus finally instituted that year at UM.

I have since come to realize that the academic Moloch requires the sacrifice of a female body—preferably a lesbian—in order for the establishment of a women's studies program to proceed. I played that role at UNH; Evy, unfortunately, had to play it at UM. In a budget-cutting move the following year, the administration reduced her position to half-time, and she was thus forced to leave. Like me (at UNH), she did not have tenure (in fact, had given up a tenured position to accept the UM job), and, like me, she was run over. Such, then, was *her* reward for being the founding mother of women's studies at UM. In truth, had it not been for Evy, there might still be no program at UM. "You should-n't complain," my colleague Marie Urbansky once told me sarcastically. "They used to burn us at the stake."

Although Maine was a bit laggard, it was clear by the mid- to late 1980s that there had been a sea change nationally in academics' attitudes toward feminism and women's studies. You could sense that we were suddenly "in": we had won. I could feel the change myself in the different way in which I, as a feminist, was treated—i.e., with respect. It was a strange but welcome experience to find other academics actually listening to what I had to say—not only listening, but taking notes!

In reflecting on why I became a feminist and an ardent promoter of women's studies, I must first ask why my generation of women rediscovered feminism, and why in fact the second wave of feminism occurred. I have long thought that World War II was an important causal factor. Not the idea that Rosie the Riveter became liberated during the war, because it was not Rosie's generation, for the most part, that embraced feminism. Rather, it was the generation of Rosie's daughters. Many of us were children during World War II in women-headed households with fathers away. Our first awarenesses were of competent women managing perfectly well without men, exercising female authority. This was my own case: I was four when the war ended. My father had been in the Far East for the duration (as a Japanese prisoner of war). Until 1945, my household had consisted of my mother and grandmother, with myself and my siblings, living together in an apartment in Greenwich Village in New York City. I suspect that many in my generation of women grew up with similar experiences. Hence for us the norm was female power and authority; we were ready for its reassertion as we entered adulthood in the late 1960s.

The second factor that connects World War II with the emergence of the second-wave women's movement is the Holocaust. Many of us grew up hearing with horror about the war's atrocities, especially the Nazi concentration camps, but also, in my family, the Japanese treatment of their POWs.[12] Like many in my generation, I was powerfully determined from my early teens on never to be a "good German," never to allow it to happen here. The animus for the antiwar movement, I believe, stemmed largely from this determination. And I think much of the moral energy that has infused second-wave feminism and the institutionalization of women's studies must similarly be seen as a response ultimately to the Holocaust and other atrocities of a century that has seen more than 100 million people killed in war and in genocide. Susan Sontag once remarked, "Virginia Woolf was altogether correct when she declared . . . that the fight to liberate women is a fight against fascism."[13] That fight continues.

Inez Martinez

I grew up hiking the mesas and mountains bordering Albuquerque, New Mexico. The Southwest's landscapes are in my blood and color most everything I see. They're surrounded now, in my mind, by ocean, jungle, plains, cityscapes, and forests. Lucky enough to be born into a United States so filthy rich even Mexican American tomboys could be educated, could be self-supporting, and could travel, I have grabbed my chances. I've come to love the Earth and am sustained by its beauty.

My structured learning has come through university programs (my B.S. and M.A. are from St. Louis University, and my Ph.D. is from the University of Wisconsin, Madison, all in English), through postdoctoral fellowships, through Jungian therapy, and through a Jungian group that has met weekly for more than twenty-five years to try to create a community of people seeking to realize their possibilities, individually and as a group.

Public acknowledgments of my work have come in the form of scholarly fellowships and grants; publications; elections to faculty governance bodies, including a time as chair of the Community College Caucus of the City University of New York (CUNY) Faculty Senate, a caucus I helped found; an invitation to coteach the women's studies pro-seminar, required of students seeking a certificate in women's studies at the CUNY graduate school; and a New York Foundation for the Arts Fellowship for fiction. Private acknowledgments, I am grateful to say, have come from many students.

My realized dreams include having published a novel, *To Know the Moon;* having

built a house in woods I own with
women friends from my youth; sharing my life with an emotionally

generous lover; and having good
friends.

An Odyssey

I once dreamed I taught at the ideal college.
It was surrounded on three sides by water.
When I woke up, I realized Kingsborough
is surrounded on three sides by water.
Oddly, for me, this exemplar of patriarchal
culture has been the place to be.

I came to Kingsborough Community College in Brooklyn, New
York, during the height of the Vietnam antiwar movement; I might
say *because* of the Vietnam antiwar movement. My political history had,
with the exception of my feminism, been a series of lurchings. Most
recently, I had moved from being a persuaded but theoretical socialist—
a status I had reached during a journey around the world third class—to
being an antiwar activist—a transformation accomplished by the police
riots in Madison, Wisconsin, in 1968. This move involved a plate-level
shift in my understanding of governmental and media forces. A
chronic overachiever, at graduate school on one memorable day I
waved greetings to my friends as I hurried to class. They were among
those sitting in against Dow Chemical's holding interviews on campus,
protesting Dow's making profits on napalm being dropped in Vietnam. On my way up the stairs of Bascom Hall, I heard what sounded
like shots, and I rushed to the window. From there, I saw students in
the courtyard, dashing helter-skelter, trying to run from helmeted and
masked police, who grabbed and clubbed them. I watched the frenetic
smashing of clubs against students' bodies through columns of smoke
trailing through the air: tear gas fumes. By the time I joined the growing crowd on the lawn in front of Bascom, word of injured students was
everywhere: two on their way to the hospital, one with a split uterus,
another with a popped eye. That night I watched the news and heard
reporters describe a "student riot."

That day and the following ones of organized resistance led me to do

some research on the origins of the Vietnam War. Even as I was studying for my comprehensive examinations, I began a course of further
reading (I had taken a course in the philosophy of communism) in
Marx and Engels, followed by study of works by various supporters of
anticapitalist revolutions. I was particularly moved by Harry Magdoff's
The Age of Imperialism. I began to study the recent histories of Cuba,
China, and the U.S.S.R. I became an activist. I wanted the United
States to live up to its stated ideals of equal opportunity and justice for
all. I thought of my life's meaning in terms of working toward a more
just world.

Accordingly, when the City University of New York began its unparalleled effort to extend higher education to all high school graduates, I
signed on. It was 1970, and by that time, women veterans of the civil
rights and antiwar movements had learned that a more just world
included equality for them and had begun organizing themselves. An
early form that organizing took was women's studies. However, none of
the women with whom I worked politically in the early 1970s ever conceived of their own emancipation apart from a more general politics
seeking to end unjust wars, racial injustice, and the political dominance of the profit motive in deciding issues affecting the common
good. My friends and I saw women's studies as but one part of feminist
efforts to transform society.

The feminist part was easy for me. I had always despised the way
women were treated and portrayed as inferior. As a little girl, I had not
wanted dolls and had envied my brother his toys—a wooden rocking
horse, a softball. I had wanted adventure. I admired being brave, being
honest, honoring your word, and helping those in need of help. While
growing up, my heroes were Sir Lancelot, Robin Hood, and Joan of
Arc. In fact, I resisted various gender pressures—such as dressing in
uncomfortable, vulnerable ways or pretending to be stupid, cowardly,
or inept in a crisis—to conform to ideas of female sexual attractiveness.
Imagine my surprise—and my joy—to discover a number of women who
felt as I did! All of a sudden, I wasn't alone: I was part of an ever-
growing and international movement—or perhaps, movements.

The carpet bombing in Vietnam; the assassinations of Malcolm X,
Martin Luther King Jr., and Bobby Kennedy; and the explosion of
ghetto riots in the United States all motivated me to put politics at the
center of my life. I threw my life against what I saw as evil and triumph-
ing. I took courses with Stanley Aronowitz at the Alternative University

in New York City. I worked as a volunteer for the left-wing newspaper the *Guardian,* and went to cover a women's organizing event at Columbia University, which led to my joining a consciousness-raising (CR) group. This group eventually decided to become politically active and, after having read William Hinton's book on the Chinese revolution, took its title, *Fanshen,* as its name. There I met Elizabeth Diggs, who had as friends Roberta Salper and Vivian Rothberg. In San Diego, Salper had pioneered a women's studies program, and so through her and her connections with Diggs, my New York friends and I were informed early about women's studies as an academic endeavor. In Chicago, Rothberg had organized an umbrella organization for women activists. Diggs and I attempted to emulate the work of the Chicago women by forming a community group in our neighborhood called Half of Brooklyn. Part of that group's activities included CR and study groups. In the CR groups we discussed our experiences of growing up female, and in the study groups we read and discussed books such as *Rosa Luxemburg Speaks.* In other words, feminist educational work was not to be split between the academy and the community. We thought of women's studies as a means of changing consciousness that was to be pursued wherever we could.

In an effort to embody our dreams of community, in 1970 Diggs and I joined with Lucy Gadlin, an organizer we had met through the New University Conference, a leftist political organization of academics, to form a communal living situation. A crucial part of our vision of political work was its embodiment. We wanted to form both a living-situation community and a working political community. We had originally intended to have five adults in our home, but practical concerns limited us to three. We made some effort to pool funds. I, for example, shared the expenses of sending Diggs' and Gadlin's children to school. We attempted to integrate our other political work into our communal life by offering our home as the center of our political reference group of nine women. This group was the second stage of the CR group, Fanshen, that had formed at Columbia. Some of the membership was the same as in the CR group, and some of the membership was new. We all met regularly and discussed our organizing efforts. We attempted to practice "criticism and self-criticism." It was from this group that the idea of holding a national conference about women's liberation and higher education was born. Our home was a place that feminists visited. I recall, for example, evening discussions with Ros Baxandall,

Juliet Mitchell, and Meredith Tax. Perhaps predictably, our commune lasted only one year, because our child-raising philosophies differed in ways not amenable to discussion. Our efforts were further hampered by the fact that we all spent at least five nights a week organizing—in addition to our full-time jobs. Living together with anyone in a close way, particularly at the beginning, requires rivers of attention, and we were focused on our other political work.

Diggs and I, in fact, were taken up by teaching, she at Jersey City State College as director of women's studies, and I at Kingsborough Community College as an English instructor trying to help open admissions students to get educated. In 1972 she and I, together with our political reference group, including Ann Kaplan, Betty Levy, and Nan Maglin, organized a conference called Higher Education and Women's Liberation. We called it a national conference, although it was really an East Coast affair with people coming to Washington Irving High School in Manhattan, where it was held, from no farther than Boston and Baltimore. To illustrate how thoroughly our feminist work was shot through with a more general politics, we there introduced as one of the organizing ideas the *People's Peace Treaty,* a document for people in the United States to sign to indicate their wish for peace with the people of Vietnam.

Similarly, my own women's studies work at Kingsborough was not limited to academic business. I was not only trying to get syllabi to include women authors and, together with Sharon Leder, to get the library to carry more books by women, but also helping hundreds of female students, almost all African American, to be able to stay in college and get their degrees instead of being flunked out or forced by monetary pressures to quit.

In 1971, I had been assigned two sections of remedial English students who were all majoring in nursing. Toward the end of the semester, they told me they were failing two courses that would effectively send most of them away from the college. One was a biology course where, they claimed, the labs had nothing to do with the class presentations, and where passing or failing examinations had less to do with what they had learned in the classroom than in being able to write essays on questions such as "What is life?" The other was a nursing course, the passing of which was prerequisite to taking any further courses. If students failed that course, they would not be able to take it again for a year, because it was offered only in the fall. Thus they would not be able to take any courses toward the nursing degrees in the spring. Of course, they said, they didn't have the financial resources to add a semester to their program of study. From the biology department, they wanted an examination based on their classroom learning and more coherence between their laboratory and classroom work. From the nursing department, they wanted the needed course to be scheduled also in the spring.

I suggested that they call a student meeting and discuss what to do. They called a meeting, and, I think to everyone's surprise, certainly to mine, more than three hundred students arrived. Then several of them escorted the chairs of the nursing and biology departments to the meeting, so that the students could express their grievances. The results for the nursing students were, happily, good. The nursing department faculty made available the course that the students needed; the biology department faculty made more clear the connections between laboratory work and class work. In addition, the English Skills Laboratory developed materials specifically geared to learning biology as a way of helping students develop needed writing skills. Eventually, a course prior to the required biology course was designed specifically for nursing students who had not been adequately prepared in high school.

For me and the two colleagues, Beverly Keith and Rhoda London, who also taught nursing students and who encouraged them to organize on their own behalf, the event was fraught with long-term consequences. Keith was not reappointed. London and I were both threatened with non-reappointment. London was eventually reappointed, although she left Kingsborough shortly thereafter. I was threatened with having my name spread across the country so that I would not be able to teach again. On the advice of my political reference group, I went to my chair, Jack Wolkenfeld, and asked for help. He arranged meetings with colleagues from the biology department (these meetings led to the changes that helped the students), and he went to bat for me with the other chairs. I was eventually sent a letter announcing that I was being reappointed but that I had to demonstrate that I could be adequately professional. I was later told that my reappointment was helped by the fact that the chairs were trying to force the then-president to resign. His wanting to get rid of me apparently motivated a number of chairs to vote for my reappointment.

This incident was, for me, at the heart of women's studies. Although transforming curriculum to make gender, color, and class intellectually visible was key, the first priority had to be helping women get the education they needed in order to obtain economic independence. As the aftereffects of the nursing students' criticisms and requests made clear, listening to students' articulation of their needs was crucial to their being able to succeed.

Almost losing my job, however, combined with a conflict with other members of Half of Brooklyn about goals left me exhausted. In the community, Elizabeth Diggs and I had been trying to establish women's studies courses so that we and others could learn more about economics, history, and politics. We had led a group from Half of Brooklyn in a national march on the Pentagon in protest of the Vietnam War. These priorities were not the felt needs of the women coming to the meetings. Their interests ranged from how to get their landlords to take care of the apartment buildings they lived in to how to get their husbands and boyfriends to treat them as equals. My passions were education and ending the Vietnam War. We discussed these differences during a meeting in which other women undertook to lead Half of Brooklyn, leaving me free to withdraw. Relieved, I turned my energies exclusively toward my college teaching.

My teaching style was demanding. Although I knew that many feminists were trying to undo hierarchy in the classroom, I never believed it possible. I knew more about reading, writing, literature, and political economy than my students. What I didn't know was their own experience or the way that their imaginations could create patterns of meaning. I used my authority to try to enable them to discover and express their perspectives and to learn to think strategically. As one student said, it didn't matter whether you were male or female, black, white, or any shade of any color, in Professor Martinez' class, you were expected to think. One student told a friend of mine that I was the first teacher ever to take her seriously as a thinking person. In my heart, I believed that trying to be the best person I could be in terms of intellectual honesty and inquiry, courteous kindness, unconventional authenticity, and dogged pursuit of consciousness would be the best kind of teaching I could offer. I also thought it would be the best refutation of stereotypes about being female and Mexican. Further, I believed that seeing women able to assume authority would help students break out of gender hierarchies. In my efforts to empower my students, I thought of the knowledge and questions I had to offer as part of what might help them. I did not, in other words, participate in the feminist pedagogical trend of the teacher effacing herself. In fact, I thought that trend was embraced so heartily partially because it fit so well the understanding of women as servants of others. In the 1970s I resisted ascribing the word *feminist* to particular pedagogical approaches, and I still do. Any teaching approach that helps students realize themselves and become critical of socialization and of social structures that have inhibited their possibilities for maturation and for community seems, to me, to deserve encouragement.

During the first couple of years, before I had persuaded my colleagues to adopt a course on women and literature, I offered feminist materials to my students as part of the readings assigned in composition courses. These consisted of both classic and contemporary texts. We read chapters from Simone de Beauvoir's *The Second Sex* (1948), Mirra Komarovsky's *Blue Collar Marriage* (1962), and Ruth Herschberger's *Adam's Rib*, which was republished in 1970. We also read Ann Moody's *Coming of Age in Mississippi* (1967). My students, by and large, were primarily interested in ideas that they could apply to their own relationships. Thus, for example, many of them were taken by de Beauvoir's idea that mothers tend to have an investment in daughters' replicating the lives they've lived, whereas fathers tend to see daughters as more human than other women and to want more for them than gender roles prescribe. In terms of the concept of sexism, students were most influenced by the example offered by Ruth Herschberger of Robert M. Yerkes' experiment on dominance between chimpanzee mates. She quotes Yerkes' decision to include in his data only "typical" behavior rather than actual frequency of occurrence. Thus he eliminated all observations of "Lia and Pati [two females] because they are highly dominant."[1] Herschberger's ploy of having one of the chimps speak about the unfairness of the experiment, together with the information about the omitted data, persuaded many students that "knowledge" could be distorted based on assumptions about gender.

By 1973, the course Women and Literature was in place. There were many challenging moments. I recall the male student who said he that would turn in his work and try to pass the course if just once I would wear a skirt. I didn't. He dropped the course. My chair indicated that any department faculty member could teach the Women and Literature course, and, in fact, assigned it to a man who had just written up study materials for another course that included neither women writers nor topics of particular relevance to women's lives. I had deliberately written a course description that a feminist scholar of literature might use with texts of her own choosing. Because the other courses in the English department were the private property of one professor or another, I had specifically wanted to open up the teaching of this course, so that students would have the advantage of various feminist faculty. Also, I hoped in this way to begin to build a community of feminist faculty. I met with the other teachers, and we agreed to press our chair with the idea that only faculty who had published in the field could teach the course. Ultimately, he agreed. To this day, the course Women and Literature is the only course, other than general or introductory ones, that is shared by department faculty members. We also had to struggle to keep the course consistently offered each semester. We made the argument that, because it was the only course to focus on women writers specifically, it must always be offered. My colleagues and I won that skirmish by being confrontational.

Kingsborough students, however, never organized themselves into a powerful movement, not even on issues such as the imposition of tuition. Most of them worked. Many of them had families. They were not 1960s dropouts, suspicious of materialist versions of the American dream. They were, by and large, first-generation college initiates, students of all the colors there are. Even students of color—and perhaps those students most of all—were interested in gaining a college degree for its monetary and prestige rewards. Learning about sexism, imperialism, and institutional racism was knowledge that most of them considered subordinate to their immediate practical priorities.

Yet Kingsborough students, in 1974, became the workers who made possible a turning point for women's studies on campus. With their help, particularly that of Michelle Krug, under the auspices of Mary Rothlein, assistant to the new president, and Betty Caroli, a history colleague, I organized a three-day conference on women that included student presentations; a women's theater troupe; feminist writers, lawyers, psychologists, and artists; a karate demonstration; continuous film presentations; and a women's dance band. The students took responsibility for all the technology required: setting up the mikes, the lighting, and the film projectors and screens. They divided among themselves the hours of running the projector. They set up the cafeteria for the dance, cleared the area for the outdoor karate demonstration, and, in general, made the conference happen. Teachers brought classes to the various presentations, so that more than one thousand students heard speakers or saw a film. The speakers included Kris

Glen, Diane Schulder, Pat Mainardi, and Deirdre English, and the films included *Black Women, Janey's Janey,* and *Salt of the Earth.* More than two hundred students flocked to the concluding dance with the all-women's band. That conference made gender and issues of sexism part of the college community's consciousness.

For twenty years after 1974, women's studies survived and grew at Kingsborough because of individual feminists. Various faculty created courses in women in American history, women and psychology, women and work, and images of women. Eventually, individuals created courses in women's issues in biology, health, and sociology. There was, however, no women's community on campus, apart from the City University of New York (CUNY) Women's Coalition, which had unfortunately divided feminist faculty in its battles regarding union elections. Further, Kingsborough continued as a bastion of hierarchical patriarchal power. Department chairs were almost exclusively male. The president and the dean of faculty, the dean of administration, and the dean of students, that is, all full deans were male. Permissions for just about everything depended on the goodwill of the president, who virtually controlled the college governance body. There was no student union or faculty senate. In short, organizing at Kingsborough was just about impossible.

Thus feminism survived at Kingsborough because of the persistence of individuals. Nonetheless, feminist consciousness was being fed by various streams. Women's History Month, first led by Vera Mattingly and Fran Kraljic, and, more recently, by Carmen Rodriguez and Hope Parisi, brought many female professors into planning events ranging from art exhibits to lectures to performances. The CUNY Women's Coalition, led originally by Isabelle Krey and then later by Carol Flomerfelt and then still later by Joyce Miller, helped gather the evidence for the sex discrimination suit that CUNY women faculty eventually won. The Women's Center, run by Krey, sought respectability for women's issues through such events as yearly Women of Distinction Awards. A student club, Equality of the Sexes, eventually gave way to the Women's Studies Club, which helped sponsor events such as the Clothesline Project, a display of T-shirts that students painted to protest publicly against violence against women. A presidentially appointed committee led by Rodriguez undertook to educate the college community about sexual harassment. Finally, in 1994, a women's studies program was established.

The latter was accomplished through a neat coming together of political expediency and years of survival by feminist faculty. CUNY had a chancellor, W. Ann Reynolds, who favored women's studies programs, and Kingsborough's president, Leon Goldstein, a political virtuoso, not only agreed to hire Patricia Hopkins, the wife of the newly appointed president of Brooklyn College, but he offered her the opportunity to lead a committee to form Kingsborough's women's studies program. Hopkins had already organized two other women's studies programs, and she told me later that Kingsborough had been the toughest nut to crack. She and the other committee members decided to take the existing women's studies courses and call them a program. The committee then formed a search subcommittee and sought a director for the new program from existing faculty at Kingsborough. I was one of those who applied, as was Fran Kraljic, a historian from the social sciences department. After months of silence, the two of us discovered through a memo sent to the college that we had been appointed codirectors. In 1994, more than two decades after many feminists had started organizing and teaching at the college, Kingsborough became the only community college at CUNY to offer a women's studies program.[2] In other words, the existence of committed individuals, many more than I have been able to include in this memoir, sustained feminist teaching and learning throughout the years until institutionalization became possible.

Let me not leave the impression that women's studies at Kingsborough exists in nirvana. Only about four hundred out of eight thousand-plus students are exposed to women's studies questions, frameworks, and information in any given semester. The number has doubled from what it was when the program began, but obviously, women's studies courses are not merely marginal: they are absent from the experiences of most Kingsborough students. Neither Kraljic nor I have any way to influence hiring, promotions, or teaching quality. We influence curriculum only through persuasion. Frankly, the success of the program has depended on the excellence of our colleagues and on the inherent worth of women's studies. The success of the program also bears witness to the continuing desire among a conscious minority of community college students for the kind of education a women's studies program can provide. Those students existed in the 1970s; unheralded numbers of such students continued to take women's studies courses throughout the 1980s and early 1990s. Even more are choosing to take these courses today, at the turn of the century. Let me end by quoting a student, Jacqueline Gonzales, who in the spring of 1998 took a course in analytical reading and in writing research papers whose theme was gender justice:

> Being able to take part in a Women's Studies course in English has enabled me to become aware of many issues that involve women. I was not aware of the Beijing Conference, led by women activists and the NGOs. . . . I was intrigued by the chapters from the Gilligan reading pertaining to differences in the moral concepts of men and women. I have come to realize how women are being exploited in a number of different ways. Women are exploited by governments through prostitution and by corporations through tourism and sweatshops, and the list goes on. Women's Studies . . . has raised my interest in becoming part of women's activism.

PART III

Inventing
Successful
Strategies

The Power of Groups,
Planning, and
Publicity

Mimi Reisel Gladstein

L ooking back, I think the difficulties I have had to overcome have made the accomplishments that much sweeter. Although I married too young, had children early, and arrived only serendipitously at a career choice, it's all worked out well. If I had been the eldest son instead of the eldest daughter, I probably would have attended Harvard or Stanford and become a doctor or a lawyer, which I don't think would have been as satisfying as teaching literature. Although my undergraduate degree prepared me to be a high school speech and drama teacher, I have never done that. Instead, I teach twentieth-century American literature at all levels in the university and love what I do.

Recognition of my teaching and research has been most gratifying. In 1975 I was named the El Paso Women's Political Caucus Woman of the Year in Education, and in 1988 I received the Burlington Northern Award for Teaching Excellence. The John J. and Angeline Pruis Award for Teaching Steinbeck and the Burkhardt Award for Research on Steinbeck are national honors that I cherish. I spent a year as a Fulbright professor in Venezuela and five months as a senior Fulbright professor in Spain. Both were peak personal and professional experiences. Currently, I am associate dean for the humanities in the College of Liberal Arts at the University of Texas at El Paso (UTEP). Prior to that, my administrative jobs ran the gamut from director of the western cultural heritage program to executive director of the university and communitywide celebration of UTEP's diamond jubilee. All aspects of the profession inspire me: teaching, researching, and writing. My books include *The Ayn Rand*

Companion (1984), *The Indestructible Woman in Faulkner, Hemingway, and Steinbeck* (1986), *Feminist Interpretations of Ayn Rand* (1999), coedited with Chris M. Sciabarra, and *The New Ayn Rand Companion* (1999).

The Deodorant of Success

W e don't hire housewives," he told me, surprised that I would ask for a job. How presumptuous of me, his tone seemed to suggest, to think that I could join the ranks of university professors, a profession that had a decidedly masculine image in those days: tweed jackets and a pipe. The English department chair's response to my mid-1960s query about a possible job at the University of Texas at El Paso (UTEP) was in keeping with the tenor of the times. Regaining my composure, I asked if there was anything I could do to make myself employable. "Get a Ph.D. from another university" was his retort, and I'm sure he believed that this would be an impossibility for a married woman with three children. The closest university was some three hundred miles away.

My master's degree qualified me for part-time employment in the freshman English program, he suggested. I could be hired, on a semester-by-semester basis, to teach a class or two of freshman English, if enrollment warranted it. Nothing secure, he cautioned. Often the call to teach would come on a Sunday night, twelve hours in advance of the Monday morning first meeting of the class. Such was the beginning of my university teaching career.

My decision to take my three children and go away to work on my Ph.D. scandalized the community. We were, after all, the products of *Redbook* and the *Ladies' Home Journal.* Their prescriptions for married women's behavior did *not* include going away to college. Magazine and television messages of the time suggested that I should be the most fulfilled of women. I had all a woman could want: a husband, a nice little house in the suburbs, and three children. My floors were clean enough to eat off and there was no ring around the collar of my husband's shirts: my life should be complete. Nevertheless, there I was, suffering from "the problem that has no name." Betty Friedan described it tellingly in *The Feminine Mystique,* which, coincidentally, was published about the same time as my initial job query. My problem was that I had not read Friedan. What I had read was Ayn Rand's *Atlas Shrugged*. Her arguments against the sacrifice of a greater for a lesser value and her scathing portrayal of parasites and "second-handers" stimulated my rethinking of the traditional life of a woman, particularly the idea that a woman achieved her identity through her husband or her children rather than through her own accomplishments. To be the best that you could be at whatever it was that you excelled at was one of her themes. Dagny Taggart, Rand's heroine, was a self-actualized, competent woman who would not give up her railroad for any of the three men she loved. Some years later, when the students in my Women in Literature course became depressed by the portrayals of neurotic, frustrated, and thwarted women and the limited possibilities for women in what Carolyn Heilbrun called "the masculine wilderness" of American literature, I recalled my reading and experimented with teaching *Atlas Shrugged*. The article I wrote about it, "Ayn Rand and Feminism: An Unlikely Alliance," was published in *College English* in 1978.[1] It turned out that I wasn't the only feminist who found positive implications in Rand's philosophy. A 1970s interview with Billie Jean King revealed that she considered *Atlas Shrugged* "the book [that] really turned me around."[2]

Most of the other literature of the time, particularly the nonfiction, presented me with only one pathway to fulfillment, and that was through a man. The materials I was reading counseled me on managing my time so that I could have the house clean, have the children fed, and look pert and appealing upon my husband's return from work. Women who "let themselves go" lost their husbands to women who didn't. It tickles me now when I think of how well we internalized that rationale for male faithlessness. Years later, when Tom Hayden strayed in his marriage to Jane Fonda, I remember thinking that he could hardly be excused on the basis that one of the top fitness gurus in the country had let herself go.

Edith de Rham's *The Love Fraud* was also a revelatory work for me. She argued that women were victims of a fraud that exploited their love and convinced them to concentrate on pleasing men while men concentrated on their work and careers. Hers was a devastating critique of that societal commonplace and an injunction against "the staggering waste of education and talent among American women."[3]

Nevertheless, in El Paso, Texas, in the mid-1960s, there were no precedents, no role models, for me. My parents, my friends, and my colleagues all expressed their qualms about my plan to go away to school. My father remarked that he had not raised me to be an irresponsible wife and mother. My mother warned me not to expect any help from her. If I chose this selfish path, I was on my own. They were confounded by my behavior. I had always been the dutiful daughter. Later, in the acknowledgments for my dissertation, I noted the contradictions inherent in their expectations. They had raised me to strive for the best that was in me, and they were never satisfied with less than a first-place performance—but then they were surprised that I should pursue this ultimate educational goal.

My women friends pointed out that my husband was a very attractive man and that it was dangerous for me to chance leaving him to the wiles of those who might take advantage of my absence. The most galling warning came from the department chair, a man who had just been divorced by his wife of twenty-two years and was in the process of marrying a twenty-one-year-old student. On the eve of my departure, he came to my office to ask me if I had thought carefully about the effects of this separation on my marriage. I choked down my retort that *he* was hardly in a position to be giving *me* marital advice.

The department included a number of male M.A. instructors, most of whom were enrolled in out-of-town Ph.D. programs. Each was expected to take a leave of absence to fulfill his residency requirement, usually one year. That alternative was not presented to me. I was told that should I leave to study, I would have to resign and take my chances that a job would be open when I returned. The path to professional advancement for the men with master's degrees was also eased by the existence of a forgivable loan system. Money was advanced for the pursuit of the Ph.D. with the stipulation that the loan would be forgiven if the person returned to teach at UTEP for a stipulated period of time once the degree was granted. My request for such a loan was met with disbelief. "We couldn't possibly give one to you. You have a husband to support you," huffed the vice president of academic affairs. I was gratified that my application to be a teaching assistant at the University of New Mexico was accepted. At least I would have some funds to support my studies. My husband was conflicted about my plans, and his men friends did not help, offering such unsolicited testimonials as, "I wouldn't put up with a wife deserting me."

Though it sounds outrageous now, it was standard procedure then.

And though I was vaguely unhappy with my treatment, my consciousness had not been sufficiently raised, in those pre-ERA and pre–affirmative action years, to fully understand the nature of the discrimination I was experiencing. I *assumed* that if a woman wanted to do something out of the ordinary, she simply would have to work twice as hard as men did and overcome all the obstacles placed in her way. The discrimination continued in graduate school. The director of the graduate program at the University of New Mexico, though he had never seen me before and had my excellent academic record before him, informed me that although I had been accepted into the Ph.D. program, he had voted against it. That is a daunting experience for a neophyte graduate student. When I expressed astonishment and asked about the reasons for his decision, he mumbled something about "discontinuous students," which meant that I had not followed the traditional pattern of going straight from high school to college to graduate school. I had taken time out to marry and have children and teach physical education for one year in public school. I didn't fit in. I did not look like a graduate student. My school costume was not sandals, faded and patched jeans, long hair, and beads. I looked like a refugee from the supermarket in my bouffant hairdo, heels, and hose.

At home in the suburbs, I was the odd woman out, going to school rather than being part of the coffee klatch crowd. At graduate school I suffered from a kind of reverse discrimination from the activists on campus. I looked like a member of the establishment, a "square," not one of them. They didn't know what to make of me. Looking back on it, I must say that the contradictions and ironies of my particular situation added a crucial layer to my enlightenment. I learned how easily people who were discriminated against could discriminate and how prejudice works both ways. It was a bracing and stimulating time of change.

Most of the events that define that revolutionary period that we have misnamed the 1960s did not occur until late in that decade and in the early 1970s. The year 1968 was a watershed. Defining events, such as the riot at the Attica State Correctional Facility in upstate New York and the killing of four students at Kent State University in Ohio by National Guard soldiers during an antiwar protest, took place in the early 1970s. Texas passed the ERA in 1972. My matriculation at the University of New Mexico (UNM) took place from 1968 to 1973, the height of that era. It was a time of national antiwar demonstrations and civil rights marches by and for diverse populations. At UNM, eleven students were bayoneted by the National Guard during an antiwar protest in front of the student union. I refused to teach in the ROTC building because of persistent rumors that this or that student group was planning to blow it up. It would have been hard to avoid having my consciousness raised.

I finished my year in residency in 1971 and returned to full-time teaching at UTEP. There was no position waiting for me, but then, in the first week of classes, one of the professors received a grant, and I was hired as a last-minute replacement. The time away had changed me considerably. I had always been an individualist, opposed to discrimination, and had acted against segregation in small ways. My sorority house at Oklahoma University, for example, invited black women students who could not find lodging in the then-all-white town of Norman to lodge with us. But before UNM, I had never been prepared to work with women to organize against discrimination and fight for equity on a large scale.

Our battle at the university began the first year of my return, 1971. Maureen Potts and Holly Cabarrus (Hollis Elkins), two newly hired instructors, made a study of the English department budget and presented their work to other women for review. We were astounded to see how poorly we were paid in comparison with men with similar—or inferior credentials. The sense of benevolent paternalism we had experienced had lulled us into a blind acceptance of our situation. When we began to ask questions, we were often treated as ingrates. And there was no consistency in the rationales proffered by the administration in response to our queries. Professor X was the sole support of his family was the reason given for his salary, which was considerably higher than that of a woman of equal rank and seniority. Our quick retort that Professor Y was a single mother, with greater expenses because she did not have a wife at home to take care of her children, was met at first with censorious silence. Then the administration replied: Surely, we could see the difference in the professionalism of the two. We could: *she* consistently got higher merit evaluation ratings than *he* did. A male colleague and I, both ABD (all but dissertation) at the time, cochaired an important committee and cowrote an article that was published in *College English.* We both received the same merit category, but his raise was three times mine. In this case, he was a single man. As it turns out, these blatant disparities ended up helping our cause, because they provided incontrovertible evidence in our subsequent suits against the university.

We formed a group, the Women's Committee of the English Department, joined by all but one woman in the department, an African American colleague who insisted that the discrimination she experienced was caused not by her sex, but by her color. She did not remain in the department long, taking a job at another university. Though I was only an untenured instructor at the time, I was elected chair. The esprit de corps was warming. Rank was forgotten as senior professors, tenured associate professors, and untenured instructors all worked together to develop our call for change. First we presented our recommendations for resolving the inequities to the department. By that time we had a sympathetic chair, but he had neither the funds nor the power to adjust salaries and rank. It did not help our cause that he was at odds with the dean.

We began to expand our call for equity to include more of the campus community. Further research uncovered appalling data. Even in the cafeteria, women servers were paid at a lower rate than the men serving on the same line. The same was true for janitorial workers. It seems that if a man mopped floors, his work was dearer than that of a woman who mopped the same floors.

Some of the senior women in the department had warned me that as an untenured instructor it was not wise for me to head this group. My instincts were the reverse. If they were going to get rid of me, I thought, I did not want to go quietly. I remember thinking I'd just as soon be hung for a sheep as for a lamb. In the ensuing flurry of lawsuits and public protests, my name and face became inextricably linked with women's issues. When I suggested to a colleague who was barking detailed instructions to his young wife about exactly how he wanted her to type up his research that he might do it himself, he turned on me with the only half-joking pun, "I've had enough of your women's lip."

I was regularly interviewed on television and in the newspaper. The president of the university told my husband that I was his chief antagonist on campus. Though he insisted that there was no discrimination at UTEP, he was forced to set up a committee to investigate "gender-related inequities." Not unexpectedly, the committee recommendations were tokenism at best. Minimal adjustments were made to a few salaries, especially those of the most vocal of us. We were not bought off. We continued our protests. The inadequacy of their initial remedy was proven by the fact that two further rounds of salary adjustments had to be made.

At about that time, Eleanor Duke, a senior biology professor, was summarily dismissed. Her firing was so blatantly sexist that the American Association of University Professors (AAUP) took up her cause. The Department of Labor was called in to investigate. Eleanor was a full professor and she filed suit not only for herself but also for all similarly situated women at the university. We met with and worked with her to gather evidence and to help the labor department attorneys understand the intricacies of academe. The resultant class action suit, which took many years to settle, taught us much about the law. By the time it was settled, most of the inequities it addressed had been resolved. Naturally, the settlement provided only a small percentage of the real loss in salary and merit money. I used my meager check to buy a printer for my computer.

Ironically, the only women's studies course being taught at UTEP when I returned from UNM in 1971 was Women in History, taught by a male professor, Eugene Kuzurian. With little resistance, perhaps because of the pending lawsuits, I created Women in Literature. The main text was Mary Anne Ferguson's *Images of Women in Literature.* Student response was very positive. A follow-up course was requested, so I developed Biography and Autobiography of the Female Experience. Estella Portillo Trambly, one of El Paso's early successful Chicana writers, often spoke to my classes. Lorraine Hansberry's *To Be Young, Gifted, and Black* and Maxine Hong Kingston's *Woman Warrior* were syllabus staples, along with Mary McCarthy's *Memoirs of a Catholic Girlhood* and Gertrude Stein's *Autobiography of Alice B. Toklas.* Endorsements from students in that course must have brought me to the attention of the Junior League, which then asked me to teach a course to their provisional members. I am embarrassed to admit that I first met that class of women full of prejudices about Junior League types, whom I expected to be vacuous socialites. Instead, I found women eager to expand their perceptions, and receptive to feminist theory. Many of those women went on to become community activists, and some returned to school, developing businesses and careers. It was a heady time for course development. Ruth Kern, the only woman lawyer in town at that time, and I team taught Literature and the Law. Then I developed Language and Gender, an interdisciplinary graduate course. I was invited to churches to give lectures on women in the Bible and Mary Daly's feminist theology.

In 1973, I took the battle out of the classroom and into the synagogue. Eva Fige's *Patriarchal Attitudes* and Mary Daly's writings were quite helpful in that situation. My daughter was reaching the age of bat mitzvah and, like her brother before her, she had gone to Hebrew school and learned the requisite prayers and chanting, but unlike her brother, she would not be called to the Torah. I went to the rabbi, who was surprisingly sympathetic but afraid to challenge a century of tradition. He took the case to the Religious Committee, which took the case to the board of directors, which found it such a controversial subject that only a meeting of the whole congregation would suffice to decide the issue. By this time my father, a synagogue trustee, was on my side. So was the synagogue's reigning religious scholar. It was a heated battle. Biblical citations were hurled back and forth. The synagogue membership voted to allow women to be called to the Torah on special occasions: a compromise, but a first step. When my daughter became the first girl in our synagogue to read from the Torah, and I the first woman called to the Torah in honor of her bat mitzvah, the rabbi winked at me and commented, "The walls are still standing." Even one of the elderly men who had been most opposed turned to his son with an approving comment about our chanting of the prayers.

Other complications attended my introduction of women's issues to the university, particularly in women's studies courses. For one thing, I had gained the enmity of numerous men in the community. Some women, drawn to those early courses because of their own "problem with no name," were looking for answers. The results were often uncomfortable for their marriages. Rather than face the problems, some husbands found it easier to see me as a troublemaker. My doctor's wife took my course and subsequently sued for divorce. He reprimanded me severely. Another old friend, also a doctor, blamed me for the discord in his marriage. At a party, after a few drinks, a man accosted me with a harangue about my inciting women to leave their husbands. He was a bit taken aback when I punctured his characterization of me as a bra-burning man hater out to destroy the American family with the information that I had three children and a twenty-year marriage. On the other hand, the fact that my marriage had lasted through a difficult redefinition meant that many women sought my advice when their marriages were in trouble. Adopting the role of therapist is seductive but should be resisted you are not a professional. I resisted. Marriages are as individual as the people in them. What works for one couple won't work for another. I was lucky: my growth and my husband's growth accommodated each other. He and my eldest son are now two staunch feminists.

One of my favorite philosophers, Elizabeth Taylor, once said, "There is no deodorant like success." By the mid-1970s, I was beginning to experience the validity of her dictum. The Scarlet Woman who had left her husband, uprooted her children, and gone away to school now had a title. There were few women doctors in El Paso in those days—M.D. or Ph.D. The title did a lot to help me further the agenda of women's studies. It gave me a kind of credibility, amusingly enough, especially with male medical doctors. I convinced my gynecologist that women should sign in under their own name, not their husband's name.

On campus, the deodorant of our success had stimulated the hiring of more women and the creation of a women's studies program, the first, to my knowledge, in Texas. Working with a coordinating board of Kathy Staudt, Lois Marchino, and Gay Young, I was its first director. Our organizational strategy was to manage the program jointly and to rotate the director's position, bringing new women on board regularly. One of our first events was bringing the exhibit Texas Women: A Celebration of History to our campus for a month and arranging for all public school students studying Texas history to see it. It added a little "herstory" to counter the prevailing presentation of Texas as strictly man's country. Ann Richards and Liz Carpenter attended our opening reception. We also created our own El Paso exhibit to honor local heroines. One, a bullfighter in the 1940s, proved her heroism a few months after the reception by saving some people in a burning apartment building.

In subsequent years, when I was selected chair of the English department, I incorporated the strategy of group governance that we had used in the women's studies program to administer the department. Rather than chairing the department on a top-down basis, as all previous male chairs had done, I created a Steering Committee that met weekly, so that all sectors of the department could participate in decision making and share information. Maybe it was so successful because most the members of my administrative team were women. Whatever the reason, the department has continued to use that structure, though most people have forgotten its origins.

It was exhilarating to fight to establish equity, to create a program, and to incorporate women's texts into the curriculum. It is gratifying that nowadays, most young colleagues, male and female, come out of graduate school thoroughly grounded in feminist criticism. They've passed me by in their knowledge of recovered women's works. I even have to wait my turn to teach Women in Literature, which I created. But if that is the price I have to pay for our success, I count it as as small one.

Kathryn Kish Sklar

In the summer of 1972, when I helped create women's studies at the University of Michigan, I was also revising my dissertation for publication. That combination of writing and organizing has persisted in my career. My published dissertation, *Catharine Beecher: A Study in American Domesticity* (Yale University Press, 1973; Norton paperback, 1976), received the Berkshire Prize for the best book written by a woman historian in any field. After moving to the University of California, Los Angeles (UCLA), I chaired the Faculty Advisory Committee of the women's studies program for five years. In 1978 I organized the Workshop in the Teaching of U.S. Women's History, which since then has annually attracted college teachers to UCLA from throughout the West and Southwest to discuss teaching strategies and innovations. After moving to the State University of New York, Binghamton, I organized with Gerda Lerner in 1989 a national conference of scholars in U.S. women's history to discuss graduate instruction in the field. With Mary Rothschild I am now organizing an oral history archive to document the emergence of U.S. women's history as a field of academic study.

In the mid-1970s I became interested in women's collective action in the Progressive era, which so far has led to the publication of several articles, four edited books, and *Florence Kelley and the Nation's Work: The Rise of Women's Political Culture, 1830–1900* (Yale University Press, 1995). This book received the Berkshire Prize in 1996, and in 1998 was named the Outstanding Book in Nonprofit Organizations and Voluntary Action by the Association for Research on Nonprofit

Organizations and Voluntary Action. I am currently writing a sequel volume.

With Tom Dublin I have constructed a web site, Women and Social Movements in the United States, 1776–1976. We have developed a model that we think others can follow in making more women's history accessible to college and high school teachers via the World Wide Web (http://www.womhist. binghamton.edu).

The Women's Studies Moment: 1972

Looking back on my part in the founding of the women's studies program at the University of Michigan in the spring of 1972, I am struck by both the power and the fragility of memory. Although folklore and the memories of friends say that I was central to the creation of the program, I chiefly remember the subjective aspects of the process. Yet my powerful memories of hard work and tears do not alone constitute a meaningful record. Because no papers related to that distant event survived—in my records or in the program's files—and because no newspapers recorded our labors, my account relies on the reports of friends as well as my personal memories.[1]

Context was everything in the early 1970s, of course. The hurricane of social and political change blew especially fiercely in Ann Arbor between 1969 and 1972. During those years it became possible to think of women as serious subjects of academic study, and to try to incorporate their study into the academic curriculum. Three stages of intellectual development prepared me to seize opportunities opened up by the winds of change. First—more visible in retrospect than apparent at the time—I became an intellectual in the late 1950s. Second, I became a historian in the early 1960s. Third—although I didn't name it at the time—in the late 1960s I became a historian of women. My own emergence as a person equipped to teach the history of U.S. women occurred just before the women's movement created a demand for such courses. Yet my route to this conjunction was anything but linear. To discover my interest in history, I first had to invent myself as a dissenter. To cultivate my interest in women's history, I had to reject alternative paths to a "marketable" future. If I had tried to prepare myself for a recognizable "career" during college or graduate school, I would not today be a historian of women, nor would I have been in a position to nurture women's studies.

Like other colleagues of my generation who shaped the emergence of U.S. women's history as an academic field, I became an intellectual before I became a historian.[2] Seeking shelter from the vacuous paradigms of 1950s womanhood in intellectual activity, particularly in reading books, during my last years of high school I read shelf-loads of European literature in the local library. Starting with Austen, ending with Zola, and with lots of Camus and Dostoyevski in between, I sought a meaningful ethical alternative to the Presbyterian church membership that had guided my early adolescence.

In college, my friendship with Robert Sklar helped this exposure to social criticism ripen into a personal commitment to social dissent. As a junior at Princeton in 1957, Bob Sklar had used his position on the college newspaper to expose the right-wing political activities of the Catholic chaplain and prompt his removal from campus. *Life* magazine documented Bob's dissent with a full-page photograph. We married after he graduated, and I left college thinking that I would become a bohemian intellectual.

My bohemian interval was brief but intense. Bob's work as a reporter for the *Los Angeles Times* brought us into direct contact with the city's structural injustice. For example, he witnessed and wrote extensively about a dramatic show of force in the county courthouse by the Nation of Islam in 1959. Hundreds of African American protesters—men dressed in black suits and women in white saris—lined the hallways of the courthouse, protesting the forced removal of families from their homes in Chavez Ravine, the area designated for the construction of what became Dodger Stadium. Yet no non-Muslim newspaper, including the *L.A. Times,* carried a word about the event. This and other disillusioning insights into our own culture prompted us to give up on U.S. society. We expatriated in 1959, thinking we might not return.

In Germany we studied the transition from fascism to democracy. I attended the lectures of Professor Karl Dietrich Bracher at the University of Bonn, and read systematically in German history, trying to answer the question, Why did German society become so demonic in the 1930s? Just before emigrating, our first child, Leonard, was born. In our cold-water attic flat, I washed diapers by hand and basked in the glow of my liberation from middle-class respectability.

Halfway through our first year in exile, "the German question" became less compelling. Like many expatriates before us, we began to ask new questions about our own culture. My reading shifted from German to U.S. history. Historians from Charles Beard to Richard Hoffstadter provided compelling answers to questions about the thwarted potential of U.S. society. Oscar Handlin's 1951 book, *The Uprooted,* showed me that history could be as compassionate and as powerful as any novel by Zola.

Exchanging distance for engagement, Bob and I decided to seek degrees in American history at Harvard. He completed his Ph.D. and I my B.A. in 1965. Our daughter, Susan, was born in the spring of my junior year. When I expressed my desire to major in the History and Literature Program, one Radcliffe dean hinted that I lacked sufficient "flair" to be admitted to that posh program. By excelling in the program I tried to place myself above her barb.

By graduation day I felt that I had absorbed a near-toxic dose of history by men, about men, and for men. Although I had resumed my undergraduate studies with the goal of eventually completing a Ph.D. in history, the male dominance of the historical profession looked too much like the male dominance of Harvard's academic culture for me to imagine that I might be accepted within the profession. So I decided to pursue a Ph.D. only if I could study something with greater personal meaning than my undergraduate work had permitted. That something became the history of U.S. women.

My dissenting stance as I entered graduate school in 1965 had everything to do with the excruciating choice that I had made throughout my undergraduate years between my physical and spiritual engagement with my children, and my intellectual commitment to the study of history. Tears often sprang into my eyes when I entered the Radcliffe library for a late-evening stint of study and yearned to be at home. Yet I also knew that my intellectual work was an essential ingredient of my personal happiness. By focusing my graduate studies on women, I hoped to narrow the gap between those two delights. And indeed a dialogue did emerge between them: they became integrated rather than discontinuous parts of my life.

When Bob's job offers allowed us to choose between continuing to live in Boston and moving to Ann Arbor, I emphatically preferred the midwestern option. The University of Michigan proved liberating in many ways. Supported by national fellowships (a Woodrow Wilson and a Danforth) that allowed me to remain independent of departmental authority and obligations, I moved quickly through the program and completed my Ph.D. in four years. My dissertation committee chair, John Higham, encouraged my focus on women, though neither of us ever mentioned the professional suicide that this presumably entailed. I was, after all, a faculty wife, and could not be expected to become a serious contender on the national job market; faculty wives taught locally at a former teacher's college in nearly Ypsilanti. With no one to please but myself, I did as little U.S. history as the rules permitted, completing Ph.D. fields in colonial Latin American, medieval economic, and European diplomatic history, and went so far into art history that I almost didn't get out. Sylvia Thrupp, a distinguished Canadian scholar of medieval economic history, was the only woman member of Michigan's history department. She set a fine example of personal and intellectual independence that I was too young to emulate but nevertheless drew courage from.

By driving my children and babysitter from archive to archive and motel to motel in a car that lacked air conditioning, I researched my dissertation on Catharine Beecher in the summer of 1968. In the 1969 ceremony that awarded my Ph.D., President Robben Fleming warmly acknowledged the tireless support of the "wives" of the Ph.D. candidates, and asked them to stand. This underscored the oddity of the few women who received degrees that day. Bob joined the standing wives.

Meanwhile, social protest was transforming the Michigan campus during these years in ways that eventually nurtured the revival of feminism and—amazingly enough—created a constituency for the skills that I had been cultivating. Protests against the war in Vietnam led the way in this metamorphosis, buttressed by the Black Action Movement (BAM), which brought the fervor of the civil rights movement to campus.

In the spring before I arrived at Michigan, students and faculty in Ann Arbor moved into a vanguard position within the national antiwar movement by staging the first teach-in about the war, sparking a national teach-in in Washington, D.C., two months later.[3] Such protests were not without risks. As an untenured member of the history department in 1966, Bob Sklar helped students resist the U.S. attorney general's intimidating practice of issuing a list of allegedly Communist-front organizations that should be banned from campuses. When protesting students needed a faculty sponsor so they could found a new local chapter of a proscribed organization (the W. E. B.

Du Bois Club), Bob agreed to serve and recruited others as faculty cosponsors. The university promptly sent all of the faculty names to the House Un-American Activities Committee in Washington, D.C.

This was one of many occasions amid the turbulence of the late 1960s and early 1970s when the university demonstrated its capacity for acting without conscience. Yet although we never entirely trusted university administrators, somehow we also viewed them as reformable. The more we protested against their policies, the more engaged we became in the process of changing the university, and the more we believed in its capacity to change. Flawed as we believed it to be, the university became "our" institution.

By the time I began teaching in the fall of 1969, the war had become a life-and-death issue to male students, who were at risk of being drafted. This was especially true at the working-class institution where I began to teach introductory courses in U.S. history, Eastern Michigan University (EMU) in nearby Ypsilanti. The student body at Ann Arbor was overwhelming middle class, drawn in part from the managerial class of the automobile industry, whose sons were usually able to evade the draft through medical and other exemptions. Students at EMU came from the working class; their families often included automobile factory line workers. Few EMU students sought or received exemptions. At Ann Arbor, antiwar protest was openly expressed everywhere: in the student newspaper, on tables laden with manifestos in the student union, and at frequent rallies held at the university's central concourse in front of the library. The president of EMU prohibited protest and censored the student newspaper.

Unwilling to cooperate with the process by which students could be drafted if their grades put them on probation, I announced that all my students would receive an A. Senior colleagues began to snub me in the hall. My grading practice also brought me to the attention of student journalists who wanted to challenge the university's censorship of their paper; I agreed to provide faculty support for their decision to print proscribed antiwar opinions. When these students were promptly expelled and drafted, I could do little to help. Deeply shaken, I concluded that I had to leave EMU, and sought a teaching a position at the University of Michigan's Residential College. There, under the benign rule of Dean James Robertson, who believed in open debate and experimental learning, I began teaching in January 1970. A year later I taught my first women's history course.

Michigan's elite status came under attack that spring by the Black Action Movement (BAM), which sought to increase the numbers of black students at the university. BAM eventually negotiated an agreement with the regents to raise black enrollment to 10 percent by 1973–74. A classroom strike helped achieved that goal.[4] I joined the relatively small coalition of white faculty who supported the strike. Only two members of the history department supported our multiracial picket line to keep classes closed. I had chosen sides, and it was not a side that endeared me to my departmental colleagues. As an undergraduate member of the Congress of Racial Equality (CORE) in Boston, I had experienced CORE's requirement that its white members reflect upon and accept the bitter truth of their own racism: I had learned to understand how my identity as a white, middle-class student was part of the problem. At Michigan I was grateful for the chance to become part of the solution.

In the thick of this activity in the fall of 1970, feminism began to emerge as a force on campus. That October a teach-in celebrating the centennial of women at the university brought together women from across the political spectrum, including Michigan congresswoman Martha Griffiths, President Robben Fleming's assistant Barbara Newell, and radical feminist Robin Morgan, as well as other scholars, activists, and politicians. Catcalls and cheers from the audience of six hundred interrupted the introductions, and Morgan urged the audience to join the speakers on stage and break down the "antiwoman" and "elitist" structure of the program. A tumultuous session followed with lively discussion of the Equal Rights Amendment, radical lesbianism, and the nature of women's liberation.[5]

That year a group of Ann Arbor women, including a leading attorney who had been prominent in the Democratic party but now turned her talents to women's rights, Jean Kings, organized a local chapter of FOCUS on Equal Employment for Women, and filed a complaint with the U.S. Department of Health, Education and Welfare (HEW) against the university for sex discrimination. FOCUS was inspired by Bernice Sandler of the University of Maryland, who in a speech at Ann Arbor urged women to develop new strategies for improving the status of women on campus through the use of Executive Order 11246. That order, issued by Lyndon Johnson in 1968 as an extension of Title VII of the 1964 Civil Rights Act, prohibited federal contractors from practicing sex discrimination on pain of the withdrawal of federal contracts. After gathering ample evidence of the university's discrimination against women, in May 1970 Ann Arbor FOCUS submitted one of the first sex discrimination complaints against an academic institution under Executive Order 11246. This complaint was the first to be investigated by HEW, and the first under which government contracts were delayed.[6]

The university responded by creating a Commission for Women, which in 1971 found that women made up only 6.6 percent of the faculty and 5 percent of full professors. Early in 1971 the university established the Office of Affirmative Action, and in the fall appointed a director. In 1973 HEW approved the university's proposed plan for improvement in the representation of women among faculty and withdrew its sanctions.

Although at the time we took it as a sign of our uphill battle, it probably helped us that our first courses on women were offered against this background of university resistance to affirmative action mandates. Certainly, the emergence of feminism on campus created a constituency for the academic study of women. At the same moment that FOCUS posed serious financial challenges to the university, it became possible to think of women as serious subjects of academic study. My first women's history course in the spring of 1971 occupied one of the college's largest rooms, and yet there were not enough seats for all the students. The totally unexpected had happened: my study of women as historical agents had carried me to a time and place where I was teaching courses about women as historical agents.

Although occasional courses on women had already been taught in some departments—especially one on the psychology of women in the psychology department—courses on the history of women broke new disciplinary and cultural barriers, not only because the history department was so male dominated, but also because the course helped women students enlarge their understanding of themselves as human beings by seeing themselves as historical agents. Gerda Lerner has since explained what we somehow then intuited: that a group without a history is a group without a full human identity. Studying the history of women with my students became an empowering way to discover our humanity as well as to study subject matter that was challenging and fun.[7]

Lynn Weiner, a student in the 1971 course, who went on to become a historian of women herself, remembers the course as "transformative," because it showed that history consisted of the stuff of everyday life. Guest speakers included a pair of English midwives, who discussed the historical significance of their work. In many ways the course was a combination of women's history and women's studies. Because very little had been written about women by professional historians, we drew on other perspectives. In addition to Eleanor Flexner's *Century of Struggle: The Woman's Rights Movement in the United States* (1959), we read Charlotte Perkins Gilman's *Women and Economics* (1898), Thorstein Veblen's *Theory of the Leisure Class* (1899), and autobiographies such as Emma Goldman's *Living My Life* (1931). For women of color, we drew on contemporary writings, such as Toni Cade's *The Black Woman: An Anthology* (1970). This mix, we were sure, was producing new knowledge about women. Meanwhile, my own understanding of my life and work was changing as I grew more committed to the emerging feminist movement. One important vehicle in this process was a consciousness-raising group that in the winter of 1970–71 brought together a cadre of about a dozen faculty, faculty wives, graduate students, and at least one undergraduate. Many were on their way to becoming well-known scholars in their chosen fields. Yet regardless of their academic position or sexual orientation, each had a story that revolved around her identity as a woman. In that group we used the Chinese method of "speaking bitterness" to learn how our experience was collective rather than individual. Fusing the personal and the political in life-altering ways, that group helped me understand my own experience as part of the history that I was studying. And when the time came to advance women's studies on campus, it fueled my commitment to women's collective action.

The cultural visibility of my course made me an obvious person to organize a campus coalition to establish a women's studies program, but the idea that I should do this was not my own. Lydia Kleiner, a graduate student in English with a work-study award, convinced Student Services to hire her in the summer of 1972 to investigate the creation of a program. She recruited me to work with her, and together we contacted everyone who was active in feminist politics or feminist intellectual work on campus. Women's studies was growing by leaps and bounds by the summer of 1972. First launched at San Diego State University in 1969, women's studies was institutionalized at Cornell in 1970–71, and that year fourteen regional conferences were held.[8] So Lydia and I felt that Michigan had some catching up to do.

A robust coalition took shape, embracing other junior faculty like myself, some senior faculty, graduate students, and undergraduates. Success hinged on our ability to hold together our diverse ranks. One of the strongest lessons of women's history, I thought, was the power of women's collective action. But for that action to be effective, we needed to agree on our goals and on the methods to reach them. Coalitions like ours were fragile because, in the turbulent campus politics of the moment, groups were constantly torn apart by internal differences.

And our differences were quite apparent. We included undergraduate lesbian activists who viewed compromise as the agent of the devil, young mothers who worried about meetings that stretched beyond the limits of their child care resources, and socialists who doubted the utility of gender as a category of analysis. Crucial to our success was the inclusion of senior faculty, who were unused to spending August afternoons in long, sweaty meetings. In this regard, we owed a lot to Professors Libby Douvan of the psychology department and Norma Diamond of the anthropology department.

To be effective within these meetings, I had to surrender my own desire to control their outcome and let "feminist process" take its course. But because I grew increasingly invested in having us produce a document that I thought the dean would accept, I had a definite point of view: principles mattered less to me than getting official approval. That is, I figured that whatever we said on paper mattered less than the dean's endorsement of our courses and program. We could shape our practice to suit our needs later. At one point in our discussions, I remember hiding tears of frustration by going to a window and pretending to look outside. Part of my pain on that occasion also came from knowing that my children were expecting me elsewhere.

Miraculously, however, our meetings eventually produced a design for the program, which we took to the dean. Luckily for us, the dean of the College of Literature, Science and the Arts was Frank Rhodes, who later served for many years as president of Cornell University. He helped us obtain the needed bureaucratic approval. In the fall of 1972, Gayle Rubin, a central figure in our coalition and a graduate student in anthropology, coordinated the first women's studies course, Introduction to Women's Studies. A variety of faculty and graduate students and I lectured in the course.

From that moment forward, the program flourished. Sustained by a broad coalition of faculty and students, rooted in departments but cross-disciplinary in spirit, and supported by a friendly dean, it became one of the strongest programs in the Midwest, and probably in the country.

Yet as respectable as that program now appears, it emerged from circumstances that challenged "respectable" opinion. We did not support women's studies as a way of advancing ourselves within the university. On the contrary. We identified with the oppositional stance of those who had been and were still making trouble for the university by insisting that it become more humane and diverse.

Those of us who founded the women's studies program at the University of Michigan drew on the energy of FOCUS and others who protested against the university's historic discrimination against women, but mainly we traveled under our own steam. As an academic project and a curricular innovation, women's studies would, we hoped, change the way knowledge was created. We also thought that the program would advance the interests of women faculty and students in new ways by consolidating their energy outside traditional academic units— units that often opposed the study of women even more vigorously than they opposed the hiring of women faculty.

Because our women's studies activism in the summer and fall of 1972 occurred at a time when the university was under serious pressure to remedy its documented discrimination against women, it would have been outrageous for university officials to reject our proposal, but it also would have been consonant with university policies and attitudes. In December 1971, President Robben Fleming had argued that women could not excel in academics because they "wanted both a family and working life." Fleming also insisted that the "deep and historical pattern" of sex discrimination was not the university's responsibility to reverse.[9]

In the fall of 1971 the history department responded to the growing demand for U.S. women's history by creating a tenure line for it. I kept teaching the course while they kept searching for someone (else) to fill the position. In 1973, with my book in press at Yale, they hired a person who had barely begun her dissertation. (Later she moved into administrative work.) I left Ann Arbor to accept a tenured appointment at the University of California, Los Angeles.

While this exile from Ann Arbor was beneficial in the long run, in the short run it felt agonizingly painful because it meant separating from my family. Bob had grown up in Southern California and did not want to return; my daughter Susan insisted on staying with him in Ann Arbor. Although Leonard later joined me in Los Angeles, his ambivalence meant that I had to decide to go alone. When I boarded the plane to fly from Detroit to Los Angeles, my body refused to follow my mental commands. I had to be assisted to my seat and wept inconsolably during the long flight.

At UCLA, when I chaired a committee appointed by the dean to design a women's studies program in 1974–75, it seemed almost anticlimactic when compared with the struggles I had weathered in Ann Arbor.

Gloria Bowles

After leaving the University of California, Berkeley, in 1985 and teaching at Stanford, the University of California, Santa Cruz, and the University of California, Davis, finishing *Louise Bogan's Aesthetic of Limitation* (Indiana University Press, 1983), and I came to a fork in the road. After much soul searching, I decided to leave academe and devote my work life to writing. The search was for a more personal voice. I edited my journals; an article, "Going Back Through My Journals," (*NWSA Journal*, Summer 1994) describes that process. Now I have a manuscript ranging from 1961 to 1988, which serves as raw material, for a yet-to-be-published novel and also for *Living Ideas: Women's Studies at Berkeley, 1973–1985*, which I am currently completing.

I have been traveling widely. I lived in Singapore for two months, where my novel takes place, studied conversational Italian, and traveled in Italy. Now I am learning Spanish, which I have tried out in Mexico, Ecuador, and Spain. My next book will be about the adventure of learning Spanish, understanding foreign cultures, and discovering new things about myself as well. I enjoy my house in the Berkeley hills and the Northern California life of great food, friends, coffeehouses, and culture as well as striking natural beauty, that outdoors which beckons me to garden and swimming pool.

From the Bottom Up
The Students' Initiative

In the spring of 1973, I underwent seven days of Ph.D. examinations in comparative literature encompassing all of German literature and French, English, and U.S. literature in the modern period. And yet there was not a single woman writer on the voluminous reading lists for those exams. My success at those exams made me feel confident enough to end an unsuccessful seven-year marriage. Those exams also, by virtue of their unifying flaw, propelled me into women's studies. I began attending meetings of the University of California, Berkeley, Comparative Literature Women's Caucus, founded by Marsha Hudson a year before, meeting in living rooms to discover women writers and to talk about the strains of graduate student life.[1] Some among us had formed a translation workshop and were translating women poets from around the world, which would yield *The Other Voice: Twentieth Century Women's Poetry in Translation.*[2]

The caucus had mounted one of the first women's courses on campus: Comparative Literature 40, Women's Literature, taught each quarter. The caucus had demanded that it be allowed to choose instructors from among the graduate students. We listened to proposals for the course, filled with a sense of discovery, as we sat in a circle on the carpeted floor of the comparative literature library surrounded by sheaves of papers and stacks of books by women. One quarter, my proposal was chosen. I taught Women's Literature in fall 1973. More than two hundred students applied. Somehow I had to select twenty.

I had taught for two years in French and another two in comparative literature's composition courses. But to prepare for Women's Literature, I had to start from scratch. All that study and yet I had never read, to say nothing of taught, women writers. Moreover, Women's Literature was personal. We saw our lives reflected in the words of these writers. I loved the male writers I had read—Horace, Goethe, Rilke, Ungaretti—but now I realized that I had often felt removed from their experience. There was nothing wrong with this. We read literature in part to understand lives different from our own. In contrast, I felt close to women writers. Sometimes it was because I shared their experience, and sometimes it was just that they had done it, had put words into print against great odds.

I wanted to admit students' personal reactions to women's writing to the class, but I didn't want us to talk only about our lives. This was a university class, not a therapy session. I was experimenting with a new kind of teaching, one that allowed emotional response as well as distance, as we tried to glean authorial intention and appreciate artfulness.

What I remember is this: the meetings of the class in my living room and the faces of the women, the light in them. How we felt special together because we were doing something new, uncharted. Little ships on an ocean, going we knew not where.

By day I tried to find time to work on my dissertation, a perfect comparative literature topic: "Images of Decadence in the Poetry of Stefan George and Stéphane Mallarmé." At night I sprawled out on the red corduroy couch in the alcove by the fire and clandestinely read U.S. women poets for the first time: Teasdale, Rukeyser, and Rich. *No More Masks!*, an anthology of modern and contemporary U.S. women poets, edited by Florence Howe and Ellen Bass, became an instant treasure. Finally, I decided to bring my nocturnal reading into the light of day. I changed my dissertation topic.

Through Women's Literature, I met a brave undergraduate, Ellen Carlton, who was trying to do an independent major in women's studies. She had to find courses, find an adviser, and come up with a coherent thesis topic. Berkeley had (and has) twenty thousand undergraduates and ten thousand graduate students. Ellen was on her own. I identified with her. At the University of Michigan, and then at Berkeley, I had managed to find a few professors with whom I could talk. But their attention to teaching worked against a culture that prized publishing above all. Berkeley, especially, took itself seriously as a "prestige" university. It made me furious that students were treated so badly. It felt natural to hold out a hand to them.

Ellen was a visionary. In 1973, there were a handful of courses on women at Berkeley. Most were not regular offerings, because they were taught by graduate students. Women's Literature and the Sociology of Women were the most popular, drawing hundreds of applicants. The percentage of tenured women faculty had sunk from 4.8 percent in 1933 to 2.9 percent in 1971. Now we were seeing a slow trickle of assistant professors into the most progressive departments. In 1973, of a faculty of 1480, there were 86 women, 41 of them untenured. Of the 45 tenured women, none did research on women. It was risky for an assistant professor to place women at the center of her intellectual agenda, and only two, Barbara Christian and Arlie Hochschild, dared to do so.[3]

The heyday of radical educational and political action for which Berkeley had become famous had ended. By 1973 the institution had settled back into its comfortable academic remove from social issues.

Ellen and I and some of the women from my Women's Literature course hatched a plot. We named ourselves the Women's Studies Committee and called regular meetings.

The fact is: students at Berkeley started women's studies.

We did not know that women around the country were having similar thoughts.

Our committee found more students who were trying to organize individual majors and brought them together. We started a newsletter, *Woman,* and included in it a quarterly list of women's courses.

Organizing came naturally to me. I had grown up in the small town of Plymouth, Michigan, midway between Detroit and Ann Arbor. My father had started the first Democratic Club in this Republican village. One of my brothers, Franklin, was named for Roosevelt. In fourth grade I stood before my class, reading from the bright blue sheet in my hand a campaign pitch for Adlai Stevenson. Dad took me to fund-raising dinners for the Americans for Democratic Action (ADA), then considered leftist. In early 1960, he got me into a meeting of the Michigan Democratic Committee, where I met a handsome young senator from Massachusetts who was about to announce a run for president. As an undergraduate at Ann Arbor, I gave myself heart and soul to the *Michigan Daily,* which put civil rights on the front page. Once married and in graduate school, I retreated. But I came up after exams to find feminism and a healing of what I called my private/public split.

Like Ellen Carlton, I had to find a new thesis adviser. I had not taken any courses in the English department, but it was there that I had to look in 1979 for someone to direct a dissertation on U.S. women poets. My department was upset: why was I abandoning my privileged education in European languages? I wasn't: all that was still a part of me. But it felt wonderful to come back to my own language. Finally a young assistant professor, Carol T. Christ, who had been teaching a course on sexual identity in literature, agreed to be my dissertation director, even though, as she pointed out, she knew nothing about my subject matter. I was just grateful to find someone who would not obstruct my work.

The Women's Studies Committee expanded to include administrators. In 1974, Betty Jones, in the College of Letters and Science, suggested that we aim for a group major, which brought together existing courses to create a new major. The university liked this structure, because it didn't cost any money. I wrote a draft on the Smith Corona I'd won in a journalism contest in high school, and ran off purple mimeographed copies in the comparative literature office. In April 1974, we passed around the first proposal for a group major in women's studies at Berkeley to interested faculty, administrators, and students. It was signed by three student members of the undergraduate Women's Studies Committee—Susan André, Lynn Witt, Marti Dickes, and myself. We noted that seventy-eight colleges and universities offered programs in women's studies; by now, we knew something about organizing in other parts of the country through the *Female Studies* syllabus series from KNOW and the *Women's Studies Newsletter*, published by The Feminist Press. We set out our intellectual goals:

- to critically examine assumptions about women held by each academic discipline
- to test these assumptions in the perspective of current research and individual experiences
- to examine traditional and changing sex roles in various cultures
- to explore new alternatives for women and men in our society

We found some faculty sponsors: Natalie Zemon Davis, a professor of history, who had given us a small grant from her teaching award; Carol T. Christ, my dissertation director; and Arlie Hochschild, an assistant professor of sociology, my next-door neighbor, and feminist coconspirator. I slipped drafts of the proposal under her door and got them back under my door with red jottings and words of encouragement.

I could never figure out whether Dean Anne Kilmer, who routed our proposal through Letters and Science, agreed with our objectives. But we were learning how to work the system.

Predictably enough, Letters and Science turned down our first proposal in October 1974. Many of the students on the Women's Studies Committee had graduated. It was clear that we needed to seek broader faculty support. So I went around campus begging faculty to sponsor our efforts. In April 1975, Carol, Arlie, and I submitted a second version of our proposal. The Letters and Science committee wanted a biology requirement, so that students would hear "the other side." So in the summer of 1975, Carol, Arlie, and I wrote a third version. We were lucky: Carol was now on the Executive Committee of Letters and Science. In the fall of 1975, a group major in women's studies was approved. We would have to wait another year for it to go into effect.

We now had a major—but no money. I decided to apply for funds to the Council on Educational Development (CED), which gave seed money to new programs. Carol was pessimistic: "Maybe you should go elsewhere if you want to pursue women's studies," she said. But a visit to the vice chancellor, Mike Heyman, a law professor with a liberal reputation, was fruitful. I argued that the major would fail without coordination. He agreed to shepherd a request for funding for a coordinator, core courses, and administrative support through CED.

Through all this organizing, and its attendant anxiety, women's poetry nurtured me. After reading scores of volumes, I had settled on Louise Bogan, Denise Levertov, and Adrienne Rich for my dissertation. I finished "Suppression and Expression in American Women's Poetry" in May 1976. Three women graduated with Ph.D.'s in comparative literature that year with dissertations on women writers.

One day in June I heard a knock on the door. It was Arlie, with a letter in her hand and a big grin. I perched on the edge of my couch. "We got it!" she said. "We got the money for women's studies."

Our office opened in July 1976. I became the first coordinator. A friend and I took plants and a Judy Chicago poster to my gray office. Our new home was in special programs, all those interdisciplinary programs the university didn't know what to do with.

In the fall, we were immediately inundated with requests, and we attempted to fill an enormous gap no one had known was there. The Women's Center, established in 1972 as a service unit, helped us to handle every possible request regarding women. In 1977, Carol taught Introduction to Women's Studies, focusing on her specialty, Victorian literature. I taught the senior thesis seminar, adding to my load as half-time coordinator; I was also teaching three seminars in

Strawberry Creek College, an experimental interdisciplinary program on campus. I was in a vulnerable position: my women's studies appointment was not on the tenure track and was dependent from year to year on CED funding.

Because Carol thought we should make the program highly visible, we mounted one lecture series on research on women and another featuring women writers. Feminist research was in its rudimentary "Women in . . ." phase. We also wanted to increase our support from other women faculty. But it wasn't so easy to get them involved. One day I visited Laura Tyson, who then specialized in Eastern European economies. She was taken aback: "I should be interested in women's studies because I'm a woman?" She had a point. Sue Ervin-Tripp, a professor of psychology famous on campus for her advocacy of women, put it another way: "I support the idea of women's studies. But it isn't my research focus. The university should appoint faculty who specialize in feminist research." She would become one of our most active advocates. Several assistant professors said they applauded our efforts but couldn't say so publicly, because they would be ridiculed for an interest in research on women. Others agreed to be listed as members of our Resource Committee but could give no time to it. Still others ignored my phone calls.

Seven women graduated with B.A.'s in women's studies in 1976. I found a friend in the CED office, who helped me with the request for a second year of funding, which included comprehensive documentation and evaluation of the first year. We got the money.

In June, I went with a friend to Mendocino and bought myself a beautiful silver-and-carnelian necklace "for surviving the first year of women's studies." The work load had been far more than I had ever anticipated. A year before, I had written in my journal, "The conflict I feel is between this super busy administrative work and the other, emotional side, the writing." By November I was resigned to not writing.

Above all, I was strategizing. I now knew the cast of characters who would decide our fate. From my father I had learned how to scope out the political landscape. Politics was the major subject of discussion at our dinner table in the 1950s. Besides his work in Democratic politics, Dad was a labor arbitrator and later a judge. I watched as he assessed competing claims and got people to work together while gathering support to counter certain opposition. After the first year of women's studies, we had a few faculty solidly behind us, and we also had the vice chancellor with us. My immediate boss, the dean of special programs, William B. Slottman, was kind and supportive of me, but passive. He wasn't taken seriously, because he cared about students and had taken on the amorphous special programs. His boss, Provost Rod Park, was extremely ambivalent about powerful women. And I was pretty sure that the new chair of CED, Donald Riley, who studied learning theory in a lab and to whom I would address my yearly funding proposals, did not much like the ideas of women's studies.

Moreover, we possessed an energetic group of students who wanted to participate actively in the program. They mounted our first jubilant graduation party. They asked for a broad and more political introduction to women's studies, as well as more core courses. They were right: the major lacked intellectual coherence. Most courses were taught by faculty from traditional departments, so students were plunged into sociology, anthropology, and African American studies without adequate background, without the benefit of a discipline. As one graduate, Taly Rutenberg, put it to me years later, "I got the critique before I got the substance." For two quarters I worked with students to plan a large lecture version of Introduction to Women's Studies. For the first time, I immersed myself in multidisciplinary research on women. I loved it. I had always enjoyed putting ideas in context: this had been one of the attractions of comparative literature. I had reveled in the intellectual exchange among disciplines at Strawberry Creek College, where I could pursue a problem approach to inquiry and draw upon the insights of history and the social sciences, even if sometimes I could not bear the language, the jargon, in which they were delivered.

I learned from my students, who had been active in the women's movement during all those years I was in college. Together, we searched for materials and produced a massive photocopied reader, which included readings from the second wave of feminism and the suffrage movement, every article on women of color that we could find, and analyses of sex-role socialization. Women's Studies 10 was a smashing success, with more than two hundred enrolled. I would teach that course eleven times.

"Every major issue faced by early women's studies was an issue of governance," Marilyn Boxer has said.[4] Governance was a problem we returned to time and again. In 1976 faculty wanted students to be actively involved. I had just emerged from student life and wished to change for others what I had found inadequate. So we brought together a student-faculty committee to choose a lecturer to teach the two-quarter thesis course; another committee advertised nationwide for a one-quarter class in feminist theory. Carol, Arlie, myself, and others decided to formalize student involvement in governance and announced a plan for a student-faculty governing board. In the second year, as Carol went on leave for two years to have a baby and write a book, we held an election for student members.

This new board then proceeded to have enough meetings in one year to last a lifetime. We found faculty to serve on it: Dorothy Brown, a new Ph.D. from English, who had been selected to teach our thesis course; Robin Lakoff, tenured in linguistics; and Francine Masiello, an assistant professor in comparative literature. Students brought enormous energy to the board. They even had meetings about our meetings. They called for methodology courses in literature and social science methods, and talked an English professor into teaching the first of these.

But the board also had real problems. Through an election fluke (graduate students were defined as either students or faculty), jubilant students had more votes than faculty. My relationship to the board, despite guidelines devised through hours of meetings, was fuzzy at best. I had one vote like everyone else, and was supposed to carry out the board's wishes. Nonetheless, students were wary of me. On the one hand, I had relinquished some power to create the board. But on the other, I had an official post. One energetic major, a mother who had returned to school, wanted to be me, or at least was certain that she would be a better coordinator than me.

Moreover, although the board was real enough to us, it was, in university terms, "unofficial." We were espousing egalitarian governance in a university, a hierarchical, status-conscious organization. At the end of the second year, students won the vote to ask our funder for $110,000, almost four times what we had been getting, "because women never ask for enough." I took the point but I found the request tactically unwise, because I felt it—or its size—would antagonize the chair of CED. We got our usual modest stipend.

I had to come to terms with my new role as a member of the faculty. I had vivid memories of my lack of power as a student. But I had now been at Berkeley for more than ten years. I knew the institution well.

My experience told me that women's studies was on the wrong track if we wanted to survive and flourish.

Another lesson was emerging. I realized that in some subtle ways I had been backing away from my own power. I had truly believed in the idea of coordinating: standing in the middle helping and directing, but letting many participate, many speak, many have power. But in a hierarchical university, I was the one held responsible.

So I made a terrifically difficult decision. Supported by the faculty, I insisted that I would hold a veto power over the board. If I had a veto, I could overrule board decisions I considered unwise, such as the request for a budget of $110,000. The students said no and then did something memorable. They did not attack the women's studies program publicly because they had lost power in it. Instead, they resigned from the board. In effect, the board was dissolved. We left it with our new knowledge and deep exhaustion from all those meetings. I learned that students want and need limits and that it was up to me to establish such boundaries.

In the fall of our third year, I got asthma for the first time, a kind of fallout from the rough year. Colleagues asked if I wanted to carry on. Of course I did. It was not in my nature to give up so easily. I went back to the drawing board. I found ways to continue to include students in our work by helping them form a support group for re-entry women (a population that, in 1978, one of the vice chancellors said was not "significant") and writing a grant for a course, Women's Studies and Careers, to be cotaught by a student and myself. And I strategized for the future, as I profited from the experience of a new comrade-in-arms, Barbara Christian, who taught in the Afro-American studies department. The remaining ethnic studies programs, on the other hand, had been thrown together in a division, and their shaky institutional status exacerbated conflicts among them. In special programs, where women's studies was housed, other marginal programs, such as film studies and environmental studies, kept themselves marginal with a faculty of nontenured lecturers.

Women's studies, I decided, would take another path. We persuaded permanent faculty to teach in our program, thus showing the university that those to whom they had given their imprimatur through tenure found the field viable. I continued to encourage departments to offer new courses on women. Florence Howe came to campus and advised us to form a faculty advisory board; it was officially appointed by the provost and included two liberal men and some women who lent us their names and other women who gave generously of their time, forming a core governance group. Robin Lakoff was elected chair. I started a feminist pedagogy group, so that more experienced teachers could help those mounting a women's course for the first time. The faculty new to women's studies came to our noon meetings in shock at how very different it was to teach students who expected a women's studies course to be relevant to their lives.

In 1978 I initiated a new seminar, Theories of Women's Studies. This was the thinking behind it: I had regarded women's studies as a temporary pursuit. We'd all go back to our disciplines eventually. But now we had an intellectual revolution on our hands. To thrive in the university, we had to develop a solid intellectual rationale for our work. At Berkeley, power resided in the departments, which were more or less seen as "disciplines." So my new course was rooted in both practical and theoretical concerns. It first attracted graduate students and professors from foreign countries. We invented as we went along, because there was little written on the subject, treasuring articles on the study of women in the disciplines beginning to appear in the new women's studies journal *Signs*. The following year our syllabus included some new articles on women's studies.

In 1979 I organized a session called Is Women's Studies an Academic Discipline? for the first convention of the National Women's Studies Association (NWSA) in Lawrence, Kansas. I delivered a paper with that title; Sandra Coyner delivered a paper that boldly asserted, "Women's Studies Is a Discipline." This was the first draft of her state-of-the-art argument. Renate Duelli-Klein, a Swiss biologist doing a B.A. in women's studies at Berkeley, had been thinking about questions about feminist methodology. Renate and I began a productive collaboration. We coedited *Theories of Women's Studies I*, produced with a forest green cover by the women's studies department at Berkeley in 1980. Orders came in from programs around the country. The blue *Theories of Women's Studies II* on feminist methodology would come out a year later. Finally, the books were combined into one book, *Theories of Women's Studies*, and published by Routledge and Kegan Paul in 1983. The 1983 version sold more than ten thousand copies. [5]

The annual meetings of the NWSA saved me. I had support at Berkeley, but no one who understood my specific experience as the head of a controversial program without the protection of tenure.

Those NWSA gatherings—I gave papers at every one from 1979 to 1985—were essential to the collaborative thinking that helped me chart our future. And the work on all three books about theory assuaged somewhat my major frustration as coordinator: a lack of time to write.

We managed to get four years of support from the CED, unusual for a fledgling program. But we couldn't move toward permanent Letters and Science funding without an academic review and had, in fact, been begging Provost Rod Park for one. In 1980, I had convinced the academic review unit of the Associated Students to include us in their rankings of fifty undergraduate programs on campus. We ranked third. The faculty advisory board wrote to Rod Park, pointing out that, despite an increase in courses, majors, and enrollments, we had received no increase in support. He responded by threatening to abolish the coordinator position, the easiest way to get rid of women's studies.

Finally the provost decided to rehire me and to review the program. I was jubilant that we had made the transition to Letters and Science money. In spring 1981, the fifth year of the program, a review committee was finally appointed. We managed to get a couple friends on it, including Susan Ervin-Tripp, who had been an active member of our board; it was headed by Marian Diamond, a distinguished scientist. I prepared voluminous documents, gathering together teaching evaluations, the CED budgets and reviews, and feminist research that coincided with the academic interests of the committee. Students and faculty joined together to press our case.

In August 1981 I was handed an overwhelmingly positive report, which recommended tenure-track faculty, including positions for which Dorothy Brown and I, both lecturers in the program, could apply. We were praised for our esprit de corps. When asked what they had gotten out of the program, students replied, "Confidence."

I remained at Berkeley as coordinator until 1983, and taught until 1985, when I was ousted by a new director not previously associated with the program. Besides the students I helped and who remain good friends, I regard the collaborative work on *Theories of Women's Studies* as a significant contribution to the field. Up to now, the academy has been reluctant to reward interdisciplinary work. The lack of elaboration of ideas first proposed in our book, however, is dangerous. Discipline-based research and postmodern theory dominate, threatening the long-term survival of our field. However, as new graduate programs seek to define women's studies, scholars are returning to *Theories* as the basis for a renewed exploration of women's studies as a discipline in its own right.

The greatest impact of women's studies is upon those who partici- pate in it. All the institutional barriers and constrictions cannot efface the magic of the women's studies classroom, the magic of dis- covery before the lamp and the book in the solitary study. This was our revolution.

Margaret Strobel

I came to women's studies in the 1970s through African history and through socialist feminist politics via the New American Movement. My entire post-Ph.D. career has been spent in women's studies, first at the University of California, Los Angeles (1975–78), and then briefly at San Diego State University (1978–79), and since then at the University of Illinois at Chicago (UIC) (from 1979 to the present). I have written about African women; gender, race, and empire; and the Chicago Women's Liberation Union. These seemingly disparate topics are connected by my interest in women's activism and organizations and in the intersection of gender, race/ethnicity, nationality, and class. I like working collectively on projects. I am coeditor of a series, Restoring Women to History, which includes four volumes that synthesize the scholarship on women in Africa, Asia, Latin America, and the Middle East. Committed to developing Chicago women's history as well, I serve on the editorial board of *Women Building Chicago, 1770–1990: A Biographical Dictionary,* a collaborative project between UIC's Center for Research on Women and Gender and the Chicago Area Women's History Conference. I also helped initiate Don't Throw It Away! Documenting and Preserving Organizational History, a project to encourage grass-roots organizations to save their documents. I am professor of women's studies and history, and interim director of the Hull-House Initiative. In Oak Park, Illinois, where I live, I worked on K–8 education as a member of the Multicultural Advocates Committee, which addressed issues of gender, race/ethnicity, and religion in the schools, and I ran two failed campaigns for the Common Sense Party to get progressive candidates elected to the village board.

The Academy and the Activist
Collective Practice and Multicultural Focus

My career in women's studies began serendipitously. I had not been involved in developing the proposal for the women's studies program at the University of California, Los Angeles (UCLA), although I had been active in feminist organizing in the Department of History as a graduate student and had been a teaching assistant for the first course in (U.S.) women's history in 1971.[1] The women's studies program at UCLA was approved by the Academic Senate in April 1975; I filed my dissertation, a study of Muslim (Swahili) women in Mombasa, Kenya, from 1890 to 1973, the following month. I was facing unemployment, because jobs in African history were scarce. The women's studies program's organizing committee needed to hire an interim director who could, on a couple months' notice, implement the program's proposal and get the courses started. After that, the plan was that a famous scholar could be hired to run the program. Because there were few young Ph.D.'s with dissertations on women in the Los Angeles area in 1975, and because I had administrative experience in helping to found and run the New American Movement's Socialist Community School,[2] I was hired as the program's first (interim) director. I stayed for three key years, 1975–78.

From African history I brought to women's studies an international, non-Western emphasis that was especially rare in the 1970s. From the New American Movement (NAM), I brought experience in developing and maintaining an organization, a commitment to institutional democratic and collective processes, and a dedication to linking "the academy and the activist," the title of a session at the 1979 conference of the National Women's Studies Association (NWSA) that I helped organize.[3] My knowledge of the emerging field of women's studies came from reading anthropology and the women's liberation literature coming out of the feminist movement, in particular the work of people who came to be identified with socialist feminism. I was young, inexperienced as a teacher, and, in some ways (by inclination and political perspective), poorly socialized into academe. As a result, rather than working within UCLA's structure to carry out a bold plan to develop

the program (we had no such plan), I concentrated my efforts as director on perfecting the program's courses and building institutions outside the academic mainstream, such as NAM's Socialist Community
School, the Pacific Southwest Women's Studies Association,[4] and the
West Coast Association of Women Historians.[5]

UCLA's women's studies curriculum had two quarter-long core
courses: an introductory course and a senior seminar. I taught both of
these, as well as a course on African women. A mere ten weeks long, my
introductory course (Women's Studies 100) made no attempt to be
comprehensive. I drew on an eclectic batch of books and articles that I
had read in the course of becoming a feminist. Stressing international
comparisons and incorporating material on U.S. "minority women"
(whom we now call women of color), the syllabus focused on the
themes of sex roles and stereotypes, family structures, work, and political mobilization.[6] It did not address sexuality very extensively.
Heterosexual myself, I discussed lesbian issues in two contexts: lesbian
separatism as a political position and homophobia of, for example, the
Chinese Communist Party. As an undergraduate, I had studied
anthropology and history at Michigan State University and attended
programs at the University of Nigeria, Nsukka, and Delhi University.
Hence I felt comfortable teaching about what we then called Third
World women. Although I understood the critiques of, and supported
many of the cautions regarding, white U.S. women like myself
researching and teaching about Third World women, I believed that it
was important to get this material to women's studies audiences.[7]

The multicultural elements of my teaching also derived from my
political activities in NAM, which involved me in reading about, thinking about, and agitating around international affairs and issues of
importance to U.S. women of color. For example, I represented NAM
on the Coalition to Stop Forced Sterilization, a group that provided
political support for a class action case by several Latinas against Los
Angeles County General Hospital. In that work, we linked the lack of
informed consent there to the history of, for example, testing contraceptive drugs on women in poor countries. In addition, I taught a
course on women in Africa, Asia, and Latin America for NAM's
Socialist Community School in the mid-1970s, undaunted by the
scope of the task. There, guest lecturers joined me in discussing such
topics as population control, forced sterilization, the involvement of
women in national liberation struggles, and the incorporation of

women's issues into those struggles and their ideologies (or their omission from the same).[8]

The primary change that I made in the three years (1975–78) that I taught the introductory course at UCLA was to introduce more material on Chicanas and on China. This emphasis reflected my own efforts to work with several women from UCLA's Chicana Studies Center and with Lucie Cheng Hirata (now Lucie Cheng), then the director of UCLA's Asian American Studies Center. We cosponsored lectures; we lectured in one another's courses; and an undergraduate research assistant from the women's studies program worked on Lucie's bibliography project on Asian American women. At a time when few publications existed on Chicanas, I showed *Salt of the Earth*, a 1953 film about a mining community's strike in New Mexico produced by leftists blacklisted during the McCarthy period. After the screening of the movie, I invited Debby Rosenfelt to lecture on her interviews with the women twenty years after the strike.[9] The themes of the film paralleled those in the novel *God's Bits of Wood*, by the Senegalese Marxist Ousmane Sembène: the separation in consciousness between male wage earners and their wives, the importance of these women's participation to the success of the male workers' strike, and the resultant change in both women's and men's understanding of themselves and their community. Through Debby, I was invited to join a women's tour of the People's Republic of China in the summer of 1977, which contributed to my friendship with Lucie Cheng Hirata.

In the ten-week senior seminar that I taught each year, I encouraged students to select a topic related to women in Los Angeles for an original research paper. The syllabus directed undergraduates to graduate students and colleagues of mine at UCLA who were beginning research on local topics. I invited students to research and write about the contemporary women's movement in Los Angeles. As with the introductory women's studies course, my political activity outside UCLA contributed significantly to my conceptualization of the senior seminar. I learned from reading, discussions, and political work in my NAM chapter nearly all of what I knew about Los Angeles and Southern California.

At UCLA, the women's studies program had a faculty advisory committee of female and male faculty, tenured and untenured. These included scholars with research interests in women and others who had been involved in UCLA's Commission on the Status of Women.

Members' political views covered a wide range, and, as a result, the program lacked the coherence and clarity of vision I found at the University of Illinois at Chicago (UIC), when I arrived there in 1979.[10]

UIC's women's studies program grew out of the collective efforts of dedicated faculty and students, drawn overwhelmingly from the ranks of the left wing of the women's liberation movement. The founding mothers resonated with feminism for the same reasons that we have heard in many stories from that period. Judy Gardiner describes their initial encounters with feminism: "I and a few other women involved with New University Conference, a politically radical but not feminist group, found ourselves defending the Women's Liberation Movement against charges that feminism was trivial, exclusively personal, or divisive to left activism. As we defended feminism, we began to study it and join local women's organizations."[11]

Women's studies in Chicago developed out of not only the women's caucus of the New University Conference (NUC) but also the Chicago Women's Liberation Union (CWLU). Together, the groups sponsored in February 1971 a citywide conference, Women's Liberation Studies. Participants discussed how to mobilize support for women's studies and to avoid cooptation by conservative institutions, such as universities. CWLU members envisioned the union's Liberation School as a way to connect theory and practice and to maintain an activist edge to knowledge about women.[12] Operating in a context where there was interest in women's liberation but few experts who could be hired to teach courses, Liberation School organizers discussed offering the courses and having universities give credit for them, as with extension courses. Cooptation was a real concern. Some of the earliest courses on women in the Chicago area were taught by CWLU member Jenny Knauss at Mundelein College, a Catholic women's college that has since been incorporated into Loyola University, Chicago. College administrators saw the popularity of the courses but were threatened by Knauss's content. So they fired her and established a more conservative women's studies curriculum. "There was a direct attempt," she stated when I interviewed her about the CWLU, "to coopt the work that I . . . and other students had been doing, frame it into something which was actually a marketing tool for the college, eliminate all the stuff on sexuality, . . . and professionalize it."[13] The women's studies program at Northwestern University emerged out of the work of CWLU members Ellen DuBois and others, who were heavily influenced by the militant struggle that resulted in the approval of the Afro-American studies program there.[14]

In 1970, UIC feminists had formed Circle Women's Liberation as a chapter of the CWLU; the next year, they decided to focus on campus-based goals but remained as individual members of the union.[15] Their affiliation with CWLU was intended to be a statement of their commitment to an autonomous socialist feminist movement[16] that was not dominated either by the men of the New University Conference (NUC) or by the Socialist Workers Party, a leftist group also active on campuses that, in the view of many in the women's liberation movement, was not to be trusted.

Circle Women's Liberation had a five-point program, seeking to establish a child care center, a research archive in the library and a research center, an academic women's studies program, an advocacy/services women's center, and gynecological services as part of the student health plan. Because it was the early 1970s, this program included such notions as free abortion on demand and free twenty-four-hour day care for children of students, staff, and faculty. To their credit, however, the "founding mothers," their male supporters, and subsequent feminists at UIC managed to institutionalize much of that early program, even though it was not in the sweeping form initially sought. The first accomplishment was the formation of Circle Children's Center in 1972. The organizing group achieved their victory by holding "baby-ins" at key administrators' offices, circulating petitions, and then donating toys to and cleaning the space provided for the center.

The women's studies program itself began in 1972 with a day-long teach-in on Susan B. Anthony's birthday, February 15. Borrowing the teach-in technique from the antiwar movement, the founding mothers organized a day of speakers and workshops to point out the need to put women into the curriculum. Holly Graff, a graduate student in the Department of Philosophy at the time, recalls, "People came—I remember even the men of the [communal] household [in which I lived] came—just because they honestly wanted to hear about this. . . . [Women's liberation] was not something that at the time was common knowledge or was commonly understood among people on the left."[17] It was standing room only in every workshop.

Eighteen months later, a collective of faculty and students from Circle Women's Liberation received permission to teach an experimental course. Beginning in fall 1973 with the first course, Women's

Studies 101, American Women Today, UIC's women's studies program was developed by a collective of faculty, graduate students, and undergraduate students, joined occasionally by community women, who selected the course topics, assignments, books, and speakers. Despite the relative homogeneity of the organizing group in terms of race and sexual orientation (most were white and heterosexual), the course structure emphasized a plurality of voices and small-group discussions. In the early days, meetings of the Teaching Collective, as it was called, lasted late into the night, merging consciousness raising, political education, and course preparation. Because membership was by invitation only, the Teaching Collective had a high degree of consensus regarding anti-imperialist and largely socialist feminist politics. This consensus in political orientation changed in later years, as subsequent cohorts of students became less militant women's liberationists and, in part, as more people became involved, each bringing her particular concerns. The Teaching Collective grew more diverse as lesbians joined, followed later by women of color. The collective, and the Women's Studies Committee, which administered the fledgling program, continued through the 1980s to operate on consensus and engage in evaluative "criticism and self-criticism"[18] at the end of each meeting.

The experience of working as feminists in Circle Women's Liberation and the Teaching Collective was enormously transforming for the faculty and students involved. Sandra Bartky, a philosophy professor who had been active in the NUC and in the civil rights movement before that, reflects, "The act of organizing a political group and having responsibility for defining its politics was incredibly empowering . . . . I know that the really transforming experience for me was in that small, face-to-face collective, Circle Women's Liberation. I think I got a whole new sense of myself."[19] Jo Patton joined Circle Women's Liberation in 1975 as an undergraduate: "I had been in . . . a small liberal arts college that supposedly had this very loose kind of teaching style that involved a lot of student-professor communication. But I had never seen anything like the [Teaching] Collective. I enjoyed it tremendously; I think I learned a lot."[20]

By 1977, the initial course had been joined by Women's Studies 102, Women in Other Cultures,[21] Women's Studies 103, Women in [U.S.] History, Literature, and the Arts; and others crosslisted between the women's studies program and the departments. The Women's Studies

Committee secured approval for a minor in women's studies, two 25 percent teaching assistants, an office, and a staff person to handle the administrative work of the program. The committee hired as administrative assistant Marilyn Carlander, who had participated in the Teaching Collective and Circle Women's Liberation and graduated with the first individualized major in women's studies. Part of the effort to bring the women's studies program into being, she pursued an M.A. in philosophy while staffing the office. Some faculty members still taught courses on overload; in other cases, the women's studies course counted toward a faculty member's course load in her department. In 1978, the dean agreed to conduct a national search for a director.

At that time, Debby Rosenfelt, Emily Abel, and I were organizing the program for the first national conference of the National Women's Studies Association (NWSA) following its founding convention in 1977, to be held in June 1979 in Lawrence, Kansas. I recall that when we received UIC's panel proposal for the conference, Learning from Our Mistakes: Women's Studies in a Multicultural University, we were ecstatic, because we had received so few proposals that involved women of color or addressed racism. Here was a panel of faculty, staff, and students, including an African American panel member and a Mexican American panel member, talking about their collective teaching and learning in an urban university that served working-class students. The conference program describes the session as seeking "to expose and discuss the problem of racism in teaching women's studies courses at the introductory level."

In January 1979, my San Diego State University (SDSU) colleague Bonnie Zimmerman returned from a visit to Chicago with news that UIC's women's studies program was searching for a director. My husband, Bill Barclay, had a tenure-track position in SDSU's sociology department, but he was willing to move if I got a job with tenure. So I applied to UIC. By then, my book, *Muslim Women in Mombasa, 1890–1975*, had been published by Yale University Press,[22] and I had had three years of experience directing UCLA's women's studies program. In order to present a politically neutral application, I omitted from my curriculum vitae the citation for the article I had published in *The Radical Teacher* comparing teaching my course on African, Asian, and Latin American women at Los Angeles NAM's Socialist Community School with teaching about African women at UCLA.[23] Because UIC's women's studies founders read *The Radical Teacher,* they eventually realized that Margaret Strobel not only had all the requisite academic qualifications but also shared their political vision. I arrived at my new job in September 1979, having made the enviable leap from part-timer to associate professor; it was my first tenure-track position. My appointment was 100 percent in women's studies. Because my women's studies colleagues and I were inexperienced, and no one savvy about how departments grow advised us otherwise, I did not bargain for anything for the unit or myself when I took the job.

We retained the collective operation of the program for many years. I taught in the Teaching Collective most, but not all, quarters. I reported to the dean *and* the Women's Studies Committee. I never met with the dean by myself: we always sent at least two of us. In part, this decision was a statement of collectivity; in part, it stemmed from our desire to have as many individuals present as possible to interpret his remarks and his intent. In the context of the hierarchical culture of the university, however, the practice probably both marked us as eccentric and detracted from the administration's sense of me as a unit head. The Women's Studies Committee made all policy decisions and rotated responsibility, for example, for chairing and taking minutes of the meetings. Until part of the budget lines of two of the founding mothers (Judy Gardiner and Sandra Bartky) were transferred into the women's studies program in 1984, the only budgeted personnel besides myself was Marilyn Carlander. Between the two of us, we had only a rudimentary division of labor. From time to time, UIC faculty members and administrators mistook one of us for the other; because we were both white with shoulder-length brown hair, casual dressers, and feminists, we "looked alike."

In 1981–82, during a period of serious fiscal problems, the associate dean of Liberal Arts and Sciences proposed a plan to eliminate Marilyn's position as administrative assistant and transfer our courses and me, trained as a historian of Africa, into the sociology department, which at the time had no international emphasis. Women's studies program faculty, staff, students, and supporters spent the year fighting this plan. We engaged in a variety of tactics, including organizing committees, national letter-writing campaigns, and speak-outs; lobbying the trustees; and kicking the issue up into the office of the vice chancellor for academic affairs, who we felt was more likely to negotiate a settlement than was the dean.

It was a terrible year. Students had established a committee that was to operate autonomously from the faculty. Two faculty members who had taught as members of the Teaching Collective (on overload, for one of them) were denied tenure that same year. I was pregnant for a second time and due in March; our first child had been stillborn in 1980. At the lowest point in the struggle, the students and faculty met in a particularly painful meeting. It occurred three days after I had had a stress test to be sure that my daughter was still alive in utero. The students described how they felt deserted by the faculty and criticized us for not caring enough about the program. The evidence: we hardly ever attended their meetings. We faculty said we had understood the autonomy of the student committee to be real, not fictive. With particular insight, one student noted that they were treating us as if we were their mothers, at one moment saying, "Stay away, stay away," and the next saying, "Help us, help us." (One does not usually think of this dynamic when referring to the role of being a mother of a women's studies program.)

Our program had for so long involved students in empowering ways and de-emphasized status and role differences that the students had little sense of unique faculty contributions or problems. We described what sacrifice was involved in teaching on overload in women's studies, what losing a tenure decision meant for an assistant professor and for the program, and how we faculty had been fighting the denial of tenure as well as, but not linked to, the demolition of the program. I indicated that stopping the dean's proposal was not enough: we needed to convince him that women's studies was valuable. Hence I had spent part of the year writing a grant proposal to the Fund for the Improvement of Postsecondary Education to hold a summer institute in 1983 for people interested in incorporating material on women of color into their courses on women. It is a testimony to our collective commitment, and to the strength of the bonds we had forged throughout the years, that we walked out of that meeting still united.

We won.[24] The vice chancellor solved the dean's budget problem by forming a short-lived Council for Women's Services, which I chaired, and funding a 50 percent staff position to which he appointed Marilyn Carlander. Within a few years, that money ended up reverting to the women's studies program. We saved the program; I got the grant;[25] and my daughter was born safe and sound. Nonetheless, because the associate dean who had initiated the plan to cut the program was later appointed dean, we felt we had to fight an uphill battle for respect. We wanted to grow.

Although we believed that we did not have the strength, resources, and administrative support to launch B.A. and graduate degrees in women's studies, we felt that there was much to gain from continuing our two-pronged strategy of broadly influencing the university, and strengthening feminist constituencies and units. Circle Children's Center and the women's studies program were under way (we added a graduate concentration in 1984). Gynecological services for students were adequate, and we had gotten in place policies and procedures for dealing with campus victims of rape. UIC's Special Collections Department housed the Midwest Women's Historical Collection, the core of which was developed by librarians in the late 1960s by building upon the papers of residents of Jane Addams' Hull-House, which is still located on the UIC campus and open as a museum.

The final parts of the founders' five-point program remained to be established, however: we did not have a research center or a women's center. To achieve the former, women's studies and other liberal arts faculty worked with faculty from the College of Nursing, who were engaged in developing a women's health concentration, which is now nationally recognized. We eventually gained approval in 1991 for a Center for Research on Women and Gender. Someone from women's studies, typically both Marilyn Carlander and I, served on the Chancellor's Committee on the Status of Women (CCSW) each year and chaired it or one of its subcommittees. A task force of CCSW developed a proposal for an Office of Women's Affairs, formally approved by the chancellor in 1994, which serves as an advocacy, programming, and service unit for female faculty, staff, and students. CCSW has consistently had both white women and women of color in its leadership, and our work with it has kept women's studies connected with issues of importance to staff women. In our curriculum and conferences, we continue to link research and activism.

In my teaching at UIC, I foster these connections among the classroom, research, and activism. The senior seminar closely resembles my first undergraduate research seminar at UCLA. In the past dozen years, I have become involved in studying women in Chicago.[26] My interest in analyzing feminism in a particular locale (and in the question of how to create and nurture organizations devoted to social change) has led me to teach UIC's senior seminar with a focus on women's organizations in Chicago. Each student looks at the records of an organization, interviews past and present participants, and writes up an analysis of the organization that takes into account the organization's history, changing mission and structure, accomplishments, and challenges. A student selects an organization related to her interests; frequently, she ends up joining the organization or volunteering there. In another course, History and Archives, I place students with community-based groups to help organize their records. Whether the records remain in house or are donated to an archival repository, the resulting collection makes available—both to the organization itself and to researchers—the history of the grass-roots activity that feeds social movements but often goes unrecorded because of an absence of documents.[27]

Still, the 1990s is not the 1970s or the 1980s. The Women's Studies Committee's debate about the Teaching Collective illuminates the changing context in which we were operating and our struggle to respond. The Teaching Collective had been a hallmark of our program. On the one hand, there was evidence of how important the experience of being a Teaching Collective member had been to some of our students. One undergraduate Teaching Collective member who, at the first class meeting, was so shy that she could not introduce herself without trembling, stood at our 1982 speak-out to save the women's studies program and gave a five-minute extemporaneous speech about the importance of the program. Student members routinely learned important skills: envisioning a course, chairing meetings, developing consensus (or at least identifying and minimizing areas of disagreement), leading discussions, reading and evaluating essays and papers, and contacting speakers. As they moved to other organizations, they took with them a critique of hierarchical and undemocratic structures. Teaching Collective members often participated in panels we organized for NWSA or regional women's studies conferences, thereby developing public speaking skills. The close relationships that developed in the Teaching Collective gave our students a sense of connection to the university community that most UIC students, most of them commuters, did not have. The ideology of the Teaching Collective emphasized that students and faculty all contributed, and some of the students brought particular abilities or life experiences that enriched the course.

On the other hand, because the members of each Teaching Collective developed their own course within the broad catalogue description, there was less opportunity to build expertise throughout time than with the traditional method, in which a course was taught and retaught by a single individual. Courses were built around numerous guest speakers in order to include many voices and to avoid giving the faculty member a primary position as expert, above the undergraduate students and graduate teaching assistant in a hierarchy. As a result, it was difficult to connect the topic of one week with that of the next. Although some students in the course found this multitude of perspectives enlightening and exhilarating, for others it brought merely confusion. Sometimes students in the Teaching Collective felt betrayed by the rhetoric of the equality of faculty and student contributions, which was at odds with the reality. As women's studies developed as a field and research proliferated, faculty Teaching Collective members often knew very much more than student members, unlike the early days of the Teaching Collective, when faculty and students often were reading the same material for the first time. Although the student Teaching Collective members found the designing and teaching of a course to be new and exciting, for the faculty member it became repetitious. I and others came to believe that, although the Teaching Collective was a wonderful experience for undergraduate student Teaching Collective members, according them a special and intense experience, courses taught collectively were less wonderful for the students taking the course.

Other factors pushed us to eliminate the Teaching Collective as well; they illustrate the complexity of balancing our feminist principles with efficiency and a division of labor. From one perspective, our introductory courses were expensive. A faculty member and a 50 percent teaching assistant taught an introductory course of seventy-five students, in a Teaching Collective that typically also included administrative assistant Marilyn Carlander. If we were to count Marilyn's Teaching Collective time in her thirty-seven-and-one-half-hour week, then seventy-five students were being taught by three paid instructors. If we did not, she worked overtime, and we would not be able to convince an administration that had sought to terminate her that she should be paid extra for doing work outside what they expected of an administrative assistant. The question of overtime work raised the related issue of job satisfaction and unalienated work: Marilyn enjoyed teaching and often did work overtime, because she had a political commitment to women's studies. Was it more important that we use our resources, that is, staff time, efficiently or that she (and the course) benefit from her teaching? That question was tied to the larger issue of the division of labor within the office. When I first arrived and the program staff consisted of Marilyn and me, plus a work-study student, it made sense to have a minimal division of labor. As we added faculty and additional work-study students and office work increased, many saw the need for the administrative assistant to function as an office manager.[28] Put another way, should we prioritize Marilyn's participation in the Teaching Collective as more important than her work running the office? In the end, for a host of reasons, we ended the Teaching Collective.

Overall, I find it hard to evaluate definitively my work and that of our program. Often I feel buoyed by our successes. We have carried out the initial strategy of influencing general education and a broad range of students, as well as securing several differentiated but not conflicting nodes of feminist activity. Unlike some other institutions, where such nodes become the locus of competing ideologies or personalities, we experience little friction within the women's studies program or among various campus units working on behalf of women. Although feminists at UIC have faced personal and political disagreements, these have not destroyed the units. Moreover, I believe that it is unlikely that our women's studies program would be targeted for elimination or downsizing. As faculty, we have been elected or appointed to many of the key committees on campus. Individually, we have gained recognition in our fields and, on campus, for our teaching. Our teaching assistants routinely win awards and fellowships. Throughout the years, the program has regularly asked for and been given small but significant resources, and we have helped bring strong faculty to units other than women's studies.

At times, however, I am unsure. Other programs around the country are allowing students to earn Ph.D.'s: have we been too cautious? I wonder if I conflate our individual professional successes with the legitimacy of our program. Do university faculty and administrators really see women's studies as a legitimate field, or do they merely tolerate our unit because they see how hard we work and what productive citizens we are? Have we asked for too little throughout the years? Why did it take until 1999 for us to secure a line in the budget for lesbian/gay/bisexual/transgender studies within our program?

Personally, I think of myself as having changed very little throughout the years. I still believe in largely the same politics that I did when I arrived at UIC. Never predisposed to militant gestures, I am probably more pragmatic than before and a better strategist and tactician, though I believe I have not sacrificed my principles: I think hard about *how* to say what I believe, but I rarely consider *whether* to say what I believe. I cannot take on the university regarding every one of its actions with which I disagree, but I have spoken out, including on the occasions when doing so threatened my own personal interests.

In a very real way, however, I am different. I am not an outsider to the institutions of my profession or marginal within my university. For example, after many years of feeling alienated at American Historical Association (AHA) conferences, in the 1990s I was elected to the AHA's Executive Council and served as the Annual Conference Program Committee chair. Within UIC, the early sign of my marginality in the eyes of the dean was unmistakable. In fall 1980, during the course of my second year here, my book was awarded the prestigious Herskovits Prize by the African Studies Association. That academic year the dean proposed a below-average salary increase for me. (I asked him if you had to win two national prizes in a year to qualify as an average scholar at UIC.) He later reconsidered and gave me an average raise; perhaps he had received a discreet call from the campus affirmative action officer of whom I asked the procedure for filing a complaint of sex discrimination. Nonetheless, the message as to the value of my work and presence to the institution was clear. The proposal, the following year, to destroy the program merely depersonalized that message.

The climate at UIC for women's studies, for women, and for me personally, *has* changed for the better in the past twenty years, even though problems remain. I do not often recall those early put-downs to myself or the program, but neither do I view my individual successes as indications that all is well for women's studies, women, or feminists at UIC. I take as my motto two sayings. One, printed by NAM on note cards sold to raise money in the 1970s, comes from the Italian communist leader Antonio Gramsci: "Pessimism of the mind, optimism of the will." The other comes from an anonymous cartoon I pasted to the door of my office years ago. It shows a young girl wearing a feminist symbol on her T-shirt, leaping into the air, and saying, "Never give up!"

Mary Anne Ferguson

When my father lost his inherited fortune and then his health to inherited tuberculosis, my family moved in 1918 from a mansion in Charleston, South Carolina, to poverty in Asheville, North Carolina. My father spent ten years of his life on a porch in a sanatorium. I was valedictorian of my high school class and went on to Biltmore Junior College for a year before transferring to Duke University. I graduated in 1938 as an English major, and earned a master's degree in English in 1940.

I married that year and worked for Douglas Aircraft in Oklahoma City during World War II. After the war I taught, first at the University of North Carolina, later at the University of Connecticut, and still later at Queens College in New York City. After my first marriage ended, a casualty of the war, I married Alfred Ferguson in 1947 and moved to Ohio Wesleyan University, where he was a professor of English. We had three children, and I taught freshman English part-time until 1961, when I began to commute to Ohio State University's Ph.D. program.

After teaching a year at Ohio University, I moved with my husband to the University of Massachusetts in Boston. My husband died in 1974, and I retired as chair of the English department in 1986.

My publishing includes a medieval monograph and scholarly essays, critical essays on contemporary women writers, and five editions of *Images of Women in Literature*. Two of my daughters are English professors, and the third is a singer and piano tuner. I have seven grandchildren and live now in Pittsburgh.

Awakening

This is what I hear you saying," said Elaine Reuben, and, in three minutes, summed up the rambling brainstorming that had taken eight women an hour. We were the Commission on the Status of Women in the Profession of the Modern Language Association of America (MLA), the prestigious professional organization for college English and modern language faculty. Between 1970 and 1973, when I was on the commission, we might have been discussing how to elect more women as leaders of the programs at the annual meeting; or how to change the pyramidal structure our research had shown to be the way women were grouped in the academic ranks, with many at the bottom and few at the top; or how to publicize the discrepancies in salary between male and female faculty at the same rank. Although the commission was definitely my consciousness-raising group about such issues, it was also more. Listening to Elaine, I became aware of a kind of thought process of which I had been entirely ignorant: *hearing* the meaning underlying what seemed like fairly random and quite wide ranging ideas. She not only summed up: she saw the direction in which we were moving. And while summarizing, she subtly guided us to the next step in recognizing where we were going. I had great respect for her mind and wanted to imitate her, wanted to go beyond sudden insights that bounced off another person's ideas, which had been my usual mode of "thought." My consciousness was raised not only about issues but about myself. As I practiced imitating Elaine in other settings, such as department meetings, I became more adept and assured at leading meetings. The commission had helped me to develop self-esteem, in which I had been almost totally lacking.

In 1969 the MLA's members in Denver had witnessed a revolt against the status quo: a radical leftist was elected president, and the commission had been created, with Florence Howe as one of the first two cochairs. I promptly wrote to her and suggested that nepotism rules caused many women to occupy the base of the pyramid, teaching largely freshman English or introductory foreign language courses, often working part-time and almost always at substandard wages and without benefits. As a faculty wife, that had been my experience.

Though I had taught full-time in several universities after World War II, I had taught English 101 part-time for fifteen years at Ohio Wesleyan University, where my husband was a professor, both of us in English. One year, because of a faculty member's sudden illness, I was allowed to teach a sophomore literature survey. This was a revelation: the hard work of preparing material was infinitely more interesting than the drudgery of grading an unending stack of papers (only years later did I perceive composition as a matter for philosophical thought); and I reveled in reading for the literature course. With my husband's encouragement, I decided to get my Ph.D. from nearby Ohio State University: I assumed—naïvely, as it proved—that advancing beyond the M.A. would mean that I would teach a larger proportion of literature courses. I was already forty-five, and this seemed like the right time. I loved studying, focusing on Old English in order to be as far from my husband's specialty in American literature as possible. But when I received my degree in 1965, that precaution proved useless: Ohio Wesleyan decided that it had a nepotism rule that prevented my teaching full-time.

In 1968 I began to commute between Ohio and the new University of Massachusetts, Boston, where I had been hired as assistant professor. In 1969 my husband joined me as a full professor there—with tenure, of course; but within two years, they too "discovered" that they had a nepotism "law" and reduced me to two-thirds time. The next year a new chancellor realized that this was illegal and gave me a terminal appointment. My husband was very angry. For my sake, he resigned and moved to a prestigious research professorship at Ohio State, which had given me a year's fellowship. We traipsed back to Ohio with five thousand books and a child still in high school. It was at that point that I wrote to Florence Howe, offering to lick stamps or do anything to help the commission: the personal had become political.

Florence's response was to invite me to join the commission, to help plan the first forum at an annual meeting. I was to read papers submitted and help choose the panelists. I had never thought of myself in such a position; my self-esteem, though very wobbly, was beginning to stir. When I met with Florence at her vacation spot on Cape Cod, she warned me that as a commission member, I would probably be tarred with the same brush that labeled her a radical leftist: she had not only been involved in the small revolution at the MLA, but had been very active in the civil rights movement. Though at the time I did not understand what such labeling might involve, I admired her ability to perceive the possible usefulness underneath my naïveté, and her generosity in warning me. I accepted her invitation and for three years served on the commission.[1]

In 1970 I was fifty-two; I had three children and my husband was a distinguished professor. This "respectable" front was useful to the commission for whom I served as representative to MLA committees, as well as the MLA Women's Caucus. I was pleased to be useful, but I saw that the commission needed more diversity. I was the first to suggest that we initiate a rotating membership, which would mean that some of us would have just one more year to serve. From the beginning, the commission had questioned the male-centered curriculum we had all studied. We agreed that the curriculum needed to be changed to reflect the presence of women in literature. Tillie Olsen's "One Out of Twelve" talk at the 1971 MLA forum suggested that only one out of twelve anthologized American authors was a woman. At a rare dinner meeting of the commission (we worked hard, usually having sandwiches during our meetings), I remember distinctly having a full-blown idea: I would collect "images of women" that had had an impact on me in the literature I knew and use them in a course at my university.

Known in my department as a curriculum innovator in early English literature and in a very popular course, History of the English Language, I was trusted when I proposed a new course, even though it was in nineteenth- and twentieth-century literature, in which I was not a specialist. Long years in freshman English as well as general reading had acquainted me with a wide range of stories and poems with memorable women characters and speakers. I found useful course outlines and bibliographies shared by women faculty published by an organization called KNOW.[2] In the *Women's Studies Newsletter* I saw Tillie Olsen's lists of works by and about women. I put together and photocopied enough material for a sophomore course called Images of Women in Literature, to be given credit toward the English major.

My students proved to be a tremendous resource: they brought in their favorites. I no longer saw myself as an authoritative figure with a Ph.D. and much information to impart; nor did I feel like Socrates, hoping to elicit from students what I already knew. Seeing myself as a student among peers, I soon changed my teaching style. We sat in a circle (I longed to be young enough, like some of my colleagues, to sit on the floor!). I organized students into small groups that caucused to give a report to the class for discussion. We soon perceived that most of the images were negative and began to seek reasons for the depression we often felt in our reading. Once I stopped in the middle of a class and asked, "Do you really want to read this?" They answered that it was better to read and discuss others' images of women together than to accept them passively. Our questions led to a more than sophomoric discussion of literary matters, such as the reliability of narrators and authors' techniques of persuasion. We became sensitive to tone and setting; we saw that imagination was important in going beyond realism.

I longed for a better understanding of the relationship between literary images and personal lives.[3] I came up with a plan to organize the mostly negative images of women found in literature from many countries and times around the concepts of stereotypes and archetypes— images that persisted over time in many cultures. No single textbook contained more than two of the pieces I had photocopied, and I finally realized that I had a critical mass of material that might be of interest to others: I had an anthology. The selections could be grouped around a few stereotypes: wife, mother, sex object, single woman, and "liberated woman"—though it was difficult to find many of the last category, ultimately subtitled "What Price Glory?" When I approached publishers in 1972, five expressed interest: my idea was timely and could make money for somebody.[4]

From Elaine Showalter, who published a major review of literary criticism about women in the first issue of *Signs* in 1975, and Carol Ohmann, I learned the importance of women authors as a focus and included more and more in the subsequent four editions of my anthology. I soon perceived that it was naïve to think that women authors always rose above the stereotypes; my criterion for selection became works that used, but at the same time subverted, stereotypes. I included stories about lesbians, and about mixed-race marriages, and by black authors. Alice Walker's poem "Beyond What" seemed to sum up what I was trying to do. She proposed going beyond the stereotype of romantic love and merging identities to an equality based on looking each other in the eye—separate *and* equal. My final edition (1991) ended with "Woman," a poem by the "disappeared" Guatemalan poet Alaïde Foppa. She specified most of the negative stereotypes in lines beginning with "NOT," and concluded with an affirmation of women. Though my original approach became dated in the minds of feminist critics, some reviewers saw that I continued to change and grow. The awakening begun on the commission has, I believe, continued over the years.

In 1971, when my course in "Images" began, there were two other courses about women at the University of Massachusetts, Boston[5]; by the fall of 1972 there were eleven. We decided to launch a program in women's studies, which would award a certificate to students with other majors. We started our campaign for approval with a formal evaluation by a professional research group of all the courses offered; our provost Dorothy Marshall's use of her own funds to initiate and publish this research raised the program's credibility. Students judged them as more demanding and more difficult than their other courses. The faculty already involved came from nine departments, who noted the heavy enrollments of these courses. Because departments depended on student enrollment for obtaining new faculty positions, we had little difficulty winning approval for our proposal.

In spring 1973, our campaign was approved by the university and the program began offering its own courses, with a certificate and a senior internship. Our courses drew so many students that in 1974 the university allowed us to hire a coordinator. The program was governed by a board of directors consisting of four students and four faculty, elected by those taking or teaching a course in the program. At this point the National Endowment for the Humanities offered the administration a choice between a grant for our program and for another new program on law and justice. We realized how marginal we were when the administration chose the other program; but when their funding expired, so did the program. We, in the meantime, supported by the provost, had sufficient funding from the university to continue regular offerings.

We were very idealistic in allowing such wide participation in managing the program, and soon found that it did not work out well in practice. The system left us vulnerable to manipulation by a small group of students wishing to impose their own order. I spent some of the bitterest moments of my life—walking the beach for days—when I was not elected to the first board, though I had been a "founding mother." I seriously considered abandoning women's studies and returning to my "real" specialty, Old English. Soon, however, investigation showed that the ballot box had been stuffed. Eventually, a new election was called and I was elected to the first board. It was not until several years later that I learned that the fraud had been instigated by a cabal of students who were enemies, in an indirect way, of my husband. He had been elected copresident of the University Senate, with a student as his partner, who was the real target of the dissidents. It was bitter even years later to realize that the betrayal had been managed by a student who had done clerical work for women's studies, before we were allowed to hire a faculty coordinator.

This experience confirmed my sense of the political nature of women's studies. Hence, in administering the growth of the program, we were very careful not to offend those who might become our allies. Many faculty were eager to offer a course that would count in their departments as well as in the program; it was a way of attracting students. I remember one English professor who was astounded when women students rebelled against his syllabus because it included no women authors; he was so taken aback—and realistic enough—that he offered the protesters a tutorial in which they studied only women authors of the period.

We established guidelines for the inclusion of women's studies courses: the course had to include the study of a critical mass of women; though we had no party line defined as feminism, we required that all courses in the program make known to students the blossoming of scholarship on women occurring in many fields. The program enrolled fifty students in its first semester. From the beginning in 1974, the faculty coordinator emphasized activities as well as courses as part of the program: a speakers' series, film showings, a weekly radio show, and a women's athletic program highlighted the importance of women students at the university. The program cooperated with nonacademic programs, such as Women in Career Options, Affirmative Action, the Day-Care Coalition, and the Women's Association. A program for returning women students, funded by the Carnegie Foundation, was very active, because the university attracted many women older than twenty-five who had put their husbands through college or graduate school or had for other reasons delayed their own education. As the only state university in Boston, we offered a quality education at a relatively modest fee. It was obvious that women's studies benefited the entire university.

As we sought out faculty to offer new courses, we in women's studies realized that there were many departments with no women (or male feminist) faculty. Along with our colleagues of color, we lobbied for a policy of affirmative action. There was strong opposition: many saw it as a return to the hated quota system, which had historically limited the number of Jews in prestigious universities. Because of my experience on the MLA Commission on the Status of Women in the Profession, I understood that the Executive Order mandating affirmative action was aimed at inclusion, not exclusion: it did not specify quotas but established goals for balance. With the help of secretaries who gave us information about faculty status and salaries, a (woman) professor of psychology who could analyze data, and a (woman) professor of anthropology who had long been an adjunct at Harvard and perceived the issues well, I launched a research study of the distribution of women faculty in all departments. It revealed, of course, the pyramidal structure that the commission had documented: women were clustered in the lower ranks, but only in a few departments (including English) was there a significant proportion of women. Our report caused a furor but, ironically, not because of any sense that women were being exploited: rather, the Humanities and Social Studies Divisions were horrified to discover the difference in salaries between them and the Science Division. Thus the administration was forced to embark on a program of equalizing salaries as well as obeying the Executive Order. Our study convinced the administration that we needed an Affirmative Action Office. I also perceived that the issue for women was tenure: there were many women on the faculty (for example, they were 28 percent of the English faculty), but they were vulnerable without tenure. For blacks, as my colleague James Blackwell in sociology realized, the issue was entry into the university. In looking back on my career, I think that helping to tenure women was my greatest contribution to the university and to the position of women faculty elsewhere. Instead of only six tenured women full professors in the university in 1972, by the late 1970s there was a critical mass.[6]

In 1973, when our program began and the first edition of my anthology came out, I wasn't sure exactly what women's studies was: perhaps it was a perspective within disciplines; perhaps it was a category of thought. It did not seem to be a separate discipline, though there is much precedence for new disciplines in academe, psychology and sociology among them. I felt that I needed to get another Ph.D.—in psychology, specifically: how did the literary images relate to the reality of women's lives?—and I certainly wanted to know more about literary theory. Fortunately, I had a daughter studying English at Yale who was being exposed to avant-garde French literary criticism; she guided me through a reading program and congratulated me on finding Luce Irigiray nearest my own thought. Still, it was difficult to see our program as more than merely multidisciplinary: what was the overarching concept that gave unity to courses on women in history, English, sociology, psychology, economics?

To answer such questions, in 1975 I used a grant from the National Endowment for the Humanities to organize an interdisciplinary course on women. For the first semester, I was able to pay professors of anthropology, biology, psychology, and sociology to coteach a course on women. It didn't work out very well: each discipline had a perspective, but the professors couldn't really talk to one another, much less give students an answer to questions such as "What is women's studies?" or even "What is woman?" The biologist's analysis of elephant seal mating seemed to have no relevance to humans; when asked to explain, he only repeated what he had said. For the second semester, I tried a different approach: I hired experts in American literature, history, and art to help me organize a course called Pioneer Women: The Myth and the Reality, which I would teach alone. Centering the course on Willa Cather's Nebraska novels set in the 1890s, I was able, I thought, to show that Cather's fictive women approached our sense of reality more than did the decorative images of the (male) artists and even of diarists and letter writers, whether men or women. In using realism as a criterion for evaluation, I knew that I was resisting current French theory, but the approach seemed intuitively right to me and my students: we were concerned with life even more than with literature per se. The literature often served to raise consciousness among us, and discussion about our life experience and the keeping of journals to record our reaction to the literature became a mode of pedagogy. Though at first as many as one-third of the students were men eager to know about women, gradually over the years this proportion dwindled as even a literature course shared in the backlash against the women's movement: it definitely was considered political by all of us involved. I continued to teach this course for twelve years; it counted as a seminar on historiography in American studies, as a literature course, and as a women's studies course: it was, in fact, interdisciplinary.

Initiating this course broadened my perspective and led to changes in my anthology and in the "Images" course; it clarified the difference between multidisciplinary and interdisciplinary, but it still did not answer my question about an overarching concept of women's studies.

This issue became the topic of major debate among women's studies theorists—those in France trying to establish difference as the major criterion for defining *woman* and those in England and in the United States emphasizing as their major concerns the equality of women and the need for action to promote their welfare. I felt that "either/or" or binary thought was intellectually reductive. Although equality does not assume sameness as a necessary condition, difference seems apolitical. I remain convinced that an activist politics focusing on justice for women—and men—must be the goal, if not the definition, of women's studies. The issue has still not been settled to my satisfaction. I continue to follow with special interest new discoveries about male/female physiological and mental functions; though finally women's health is seen as different from men's, the distribution of characteristics along a continuum weakens the either/or approach.

In the late 1970s, what seemed to many a disaster turned out to be serendipitous for women's studies. The legislature forced the university to fight for its life against Boston State College—of which many legislators were alumni— to be the only four-year public institution in Boston. The university won the fight and had to find places for all the Boston State College personnel with Ph.D's. The result was that two of their faculty were given to women's studies, with tenure. In 1979 we won tenure for the first professor specifically in women's studies. With three tenured faculty and the coordinator's position, the program was now in a position to become a department. We had feared that becoming a department would mean being relegated to a ghetto; but with tenured faculty, that fear seemed less threatening. Finally, with the help of a feminist male provost, we were granted status as a department, with a budget and a major in women's studies. The program has continued to attract majors, and many students take its courses as electives. On its twenty-fifth anniversary in 1998, it had much to celebrate.

My awakening on the MLA commission changed my life. I was promoted to full professor because of my women's studies activities; the profits from my book became important after my husband's death in 1974. The circle of friends begun on the commission widened over the years. Because of my own growth, I was able to contribute to major curricular and policy changes at the University of Massachusetts and, to some extent, to the growth of women's studies throughout the country. I am among the few early founding mothers who profited in every way from my involvement.

PART IV

Providing
Feminist
Scholarship
For Texts,
Teaching, and
Other Scholars

Electa Arenal

The summer of 2000 will mark my completion of a three-and-one-half-year term as director of the Center for the Study of Women and Society and coordinator of the Women's Studies Certificate Program at the City University of New York (CUNY) Graduate Center; it will also mark the culmination of a teaching career that began in 1957–58, when I was invited to teach Spanish 1 as a junior at Barnard College.

It was my translations of and critical work on Cuban and Central American women poets, especially Claribel Alegría and Gioconda Belli, that led to a Norwegian Government Research Council grant to teach at the University of Bergen, which, in turn, resulted in my being selected to serve as director of their Center for Feminist Research in the Humanities (1992–94). There, in long-distance collaboration with Amanda Powell, I completed the introduction and annotations for Sor Juana Inés de la Cruz's celebrated self-defense *The Answer/La Respuesta* (The Feminist Press). Our critical edition and translation was the first to focus on the aspects of the famous 1691 essay that earned its author the title of the first feminist of the Americas.

Intense engagement with the arts and with the urgent political issues of the times has always accompanied my scholarly work. During what I call my first life, I was a prima ballerina with the early Joffrey Company. My play, *This Life Within Me Won't Keep Still,* based on the lives and work of two seventeenth-century poets, Anne Bradstreet of Massachusetts and Sor Juana Inés de la Cruz of Mexico, was previewed at the Modern Language Association convention of 1979 and premiered in 1980 at San Francisco's

Fort Mason Foundation. As a specialist in colonial literature and women's monastic culture, I coauthored two other books: *Untold Sisters: Hispanic Nuns in Their Own Works;* and *Cultura conventual femenina. Obras completas de Sor Marcela de San Félix, de la hija de Lope de Vega* (Women's Convent Culture: Complete Works of S.M. de S.F., Daughter of L. de V). I have begun a new play, related to my current research supported by the Rockefeller Foundation's U.S.-Mexico Cultural Fund, for a book and CD-ROM on a triumphal arch that Sor Juana both designed and wrote the text for in 1680.

"*What* Women Writers?"
Plotting Women's Studies in New York

In a field of positions, a passionate
position is held like fire.
. . . [In] some mythographies the past is construed
to be ahead, where it's visible, and the future
behind us, since it can't be seen.

HEATHER McHUGH, *BROKEN ENGLISH: POETRY AND PARTIALITY*

I.

Perhaps in part because my Mexican *abuelita,* Electa, told me when I was about seven to remember, always, that I was descended from Concepción Arenal, the nineteenth-century Spanish lawyer, prison reformer, feminist, and socialist—to whom Abraham Lincoln had given a medal—I grew up thinking that I had been born red-diapered and red-stockinged. In my heritage, *pan y tierra* (bread and land) melded with *bread and roses.* My Jewish mother, Rose, was an early member of the New York Teachers' Union. Born into Yiddish on a shtetl in Russia-Poland, raised and radicalized at the Educational Alliance and in the streets of Manhattan's Lower East Side, she went in the mid-1930s to a Congress of Anti-Fascist Writers and Artists in Mexico, where she met and married my father, Luis. From the double legacy, I learned that we were many, and mostly anonymous, that the struggles were continuous, unending. *El pueblo unido* ("the people united") sometimes won and sometimes lost.

I had just entered my thirties when the women's liberation movement hit New York in the last years of the 1960s. I remember the exact moment when I first heard the expression because of the dramatic backdrop: the Manhattan skyline etched by the Statue of Liberty, the New Jersey coastline, largely green, and the skyscrapers of the Wall Street district surrounding a clutch of students and faculty from Richmond College (a new upper-division branch of the City University of New York [CUNY]). Engaged in an animated conversation as we returned on the ferry from Staten Island, one woman spoke excitedly of a meeting she'd attended, at which women were witnessing their awakening, their rejection of silence, of subordination, of relegation to powerlessness. "It's called the women's liberation movement," another said. From what did women need liberation? was my first response. What did they have to complain of, compared with exploited farmers of what were then called the banana republics—the United Fruit—owned plantations throughout Central America—the miners of Chile and Bolivia, or the miserably poor students and teachers and poets throughout the hemisphere?

Having grown up in a family run by women, always thinking about what I'd do with my life rather than about whom I'd marry; having gone to a women's college; having had mother's helpers and housekeepers, and my own mother's help for child care, as well as sharing some of it with an artist husband, I seemed to have "made it in a man's world." And I also liked being an exception. My own internalized sexism was hidden from me. Sexism was to be shrugged off.

If I thought I'd been born a feminist as well as a revolutionary, still, I associated liberation movements with Latin America and other national struggles for self-determination and emancipation from imperialism and capitalism. As a child I marched in May Day parades and sang, "Put my name down, brother / Where shall I sign? / I'm going to join the fight for peace / All down the line." It was a song about the Stockholm Peace Appeal, a petition signed by hundreds of thousands of people around the globe that became a target of the House Un-American Activities Committee in the early 1950s. In my teens I'd read pamphlets on "the woman question" and books on the suffrage movement. My family had gotten a copy of *The Second Sex* as soon as it was translated into English (1952).

It was not until later that I understood the connectedness of the issues, how the women's movement and the establishment of women's studies were developments that evolved out of other movements of which I was a part: the peace movement, the civil rights movement, and the student movement. And I was prepared for a life in women's studies by many influences, including my background in dance, in Latin American art, and in the Spanish department of Barnard College, where Spanish was reputed to be a way of life.

The discipline and detail of ballet training developed endurance and attentiveness; my seasons with the early Joffrey Company taught lessons about the performance of sex roles. Exposure to my father's work as a lithographer and sculptor, and my uncle's as a muralist—art work in which women were depicted in socially significant roles, as teachers and as symbols of the new global democracy that was to follow the defeat of fascism—taught dedication and inspired utopian dreams. The Spanish department of Barnard, where I studied with three powerful women, immersed all its students in the culture of Spain and the Spanish-speaking Americas by drenching us in language and literature, as well as art and architecture, theater, history, and humor.

Barnard College had a feminist past, which it nodded to with genteel disregard. Nevertheless, when I think back on the subjects I chose to write papers about during my four years as a student there—medieval women in Chaucer and the Archpriest of Hita; Renaissance women in Cervantes, Renaissance women writers, St. Teresa of Avila and Sor Juana Inés de la Cruz, nineteenth-century Ibsen's Nora (for a course titled Man and His World!), and Concepción Arenal's work *La mujer del porvenir* (Woman of the Future)—I realize that we were given room at Barnard to pursue topics off limits to students in coeducational institutions. And my instincts and interests were all leading to a more conscious feminism.

The Spanish department of Barnard appointed me to an instructorship in 1960. By 1963, with a first baby and a full-time teaching schedule, the only way that I could get to read nonscholarly publications I was interested in was to assign them. I chose Betty Friedan's book *The Feminine Mystique* (1963) for discussion in my Spanish conversation course. Most of those particular students hated the book. Many of the students in the first-year Spanish and the literature survey courses were shocked to see me put the final exam questions on the board with my baby son peering at them from the sack on my back. Years later, some wrote to me about what an influence that had been on their lives: the example of a woman out in the world, adapting child care to her needs. And I'd wager that most of the Spanish conversation students eventually reconsidered their initial reactions to *The Feminine Mystique*.

II.

Richmond College, an experimental upper-division branch of City University of New York, opened in 1967. Its predominantly young, radical faculty were dynamic and divisive. I joined their ranks in 1968, and soon—because I remained nonaligned in local battles—became a bridge between factions.

The warfare between the straight Marxist women and the lesbian radical feminists was verbally ferocious. Excess—sometimes creative and productive, other times stifling and emptily explosive—characterized the founding seasons of women's studies. Pent-up, justified anger led to the formation of support groups; community action; the production of broadsheets, periodicals, and polemical treatises; street theater; and weekends of uninterrupted consciousness raising. The socialist feminists were highly homophobic; they focused on antiwar activities, and discovered that psychology oppressed women and that "fat was a feminist issue." The lesbian radical feminists mistrusted those who refused to accept the need for separateness and for open recognition of their sexual preference. They abhorred the absence of acknowledgment of the early and consistent contributions of lesbians to social struggles. Many of them were also involved in the antiwar movement. Some of them looked askance at those who slept with the enemy (men); a few didn't want to tolerate them in their classes. Some had to be convinced by Dean Dorothy McCormick to stop carrying baseball bats in self-defense and as assurance against political incorrectness.

Carol Alpert, a friend and librarian at the New York University (NYU) law library,[1] reminisced with me about her own student days at Richmond in its early years (1967–71), where she was among a group of women who got independent study credit for setting up a women's center. The center staff members helped women get safe abortions before *Roe v. Wade* and even after, accompanying women to the first Westchester clinics. The center had a library, and poets such as Judy Grahn gave readings and talked about their work. Carol recalled Richmond as an extremely progressive place, where the students lived their studies, and where in addition to (or despite) all the sex, drugs, and rock 'n' roll, they got an unforgettable education. "We would not be who we are today," she said of her friend Terry Lawler and herself, both active in organization such as Astraea and SAGE, "if we had not spent hours and hours back then discussing issues of race and class."[2] Only a few of their group of lesbian feminists actually took women's studies courses, although they avidly read and discussed feminist books and periodicals among themselves as soon as they appeared.

One of the women in my course on Pablo Neruda (I don't remember which faction she belonged to) stalked out of my class one day after lambasting the Chilean poet's exploitation/objectification of women's bodies as landscape. After Kate Millett's unmasking of the institutional foundations of male domination, such literary sexism was to be boycotted. Women's passionate attempts to put their actions where their ideas were led to a lot of acting out at Richmond College.

With the early flowering of consciousness-raising groups, collective political formations flowered as well.[3] There was no question of divorcing theory from strategy: they were intertwined and fed efforts to combat the many obstacles facing women. Words of Simone de Beauvoir ("Women are not born, they are made"); of Sojourner Truth ("I have ploughed, and planted, and gathered into barns, and no man could head me! And ain't I a woman?"); of Mary Wollstonecraft ("the consciousness of always being female which degrades our sex"); and of Sor Juana Inés de la Cruz ("Had Aristotle cooked, he would have written a great deal more") were taken as slogans and epigraphs. Letters were signed "In sisterhood." Women became more and more imaginatively confrontational. Their self-confidence and hope surged as they experienced their own transformation and watched others being transformed.

Ironically, at the end of the 1960s, some (educated, middle-class) women were not especially sympathetic to the term *mother*. We were rebelling against compulsory motherhood, against the dismissal of women who were not mothers, and against the disparagement of those who were. We began to analyze the hypocritical idealization of mothers that allowed for the building of monuments, the better to manipulate half the population in wartime. Our own mothers we criticized for their submission to sexism and domesticity. For a while, the mother was tossed out with the dishwater.

Those of us who were mothers were caught in many binds. When I confided in my poet neighbor and friend Jean Valentine about the difficulties of the mother-professor-activist-translator-researcher (not to mention lover) juggling act, she replied that I must speak to Adrienne Rich, who was staying at her place while working on a book titled *Of Woman Born*. Mothering and motherhood were becoming scholarly, theoretical, and literary, as well as consciousness-raising group topics. I turned my thinking to the Latin American, Spanish, and Latina context, especially as I undertook study of the convent *Madres,* of Sor Juana Inés de la Cruz's reclaiming of the "mother tongue," and of the strategic use of Marianism, the veneration of the Virgin, and the ambivalent space within religious orders to affirm women's right to interpretive power.

III.

If I am considered a pioneer, it is as a feminist Sor Juana scholar and, concurrently, for having explored the field of monastic women's culture in a new way, for introducing the work of Central American poets Claribel Alegría and Gioconda Belli to the North American women's studies community, and perhaps for contributing to intellectual rediscovery by the English- and Spanish-speaking Americas with my play, *This Life Within Me Won't Keep Still,* which is based on the lives and work of seventeenth-century poets Sor Juana Inés de la Cruz and Anne Bradstreet.

In part because of my multiculturalism *(avant la lettre),* the contributions I've made to the field of women's studies refuse compartmentalization in time or space. I can plot the sites where I have been a migrant women's studies worker in New York, France, Mexico, Cuba, Massachusetts, New Hampshire, Delaware, Hawaii, and Norway across more than two decades.

Sessions of the historic Sarah Lawrence College interdisciplinary seminar organized in the early 1970s by Gerda Lerner—and Sherry Ortner, Joan Kelly, Eva Kollish, and others—complemented the new perspectives I had garnered from books. Seeing me in the throes of my first great passion for a woman (writer and translator), a good friend gave me the book that caused my sea change: *Woman in Sexist Society: Studies in Power and Powerlessness* (twenty-seven essays, two plays, and an oral quartet), collected and introduced by Vivian Gornick and Barbara K. Moran.[4] The contents poured through me and took easily to my bloodstream, as they shed light on how knowledge has been constructed to our detriment.[5] It was no longer difficult to understand the mission of the women's liberation movement or to declare myself disloyal to a civilization that wanted me *virgen o puta,* temptress, goddess, or child improved. The ferry back and forth from Richmond became a reading room. *Woman in Sexist Society* and dozens of books—and articles, poems, pamphlets, fliers, and periodicals—redirected my spirit, inspired what

Hortense Spillers called "the release of the passionate dance of thought."

Minority status—or, I might say, my hybrid background—both marginalized and privileged me. Catharine Stimpson invited me to be the Latina representative among a group of African American women on a panel that looked at the Academy and the Ivory Tower. During an organizing meeting for the first Barnard College The Scholar and the Feminist Conference, called by Jane Gould, Louise Bernikow (who had studied Spanish and become interested in writing nuns) recommended me as a speaker. The essay written for that historic event eventually became a selection in Beth Miller's ground-breaking book *Women in Hispanic Literature: Icons and Fallen Idols.* Miller portrayed me, in her introduction, as a far-out feminist. The planning committee of Columbia University's *Casa Hispánica,* emboldened by the recognition I'd received from the Barnard Women's Center, invited me to give a talk. I titled it *"La nueva cuestión palpitante"* (The New Urgent Question), after a novel by Emilia Pardo Bazán, and attempted a sweeping revision of Hispanic literatures from a feminist viewpoint. Margarita Ucelay, one of my former Barnard professors, came up to me at the end of the lecture and said, "Electa, keep going" in a tone of voice I had not heard from her before.

The inspiration to do so is what pertains most to this volume: it came in the form of the course Marcia Welles and I devised called Women Writers of Spain and Latin America, one of the first of its kind in the United States and probably the world.

IV.

I'd known that official stories were skewed in favor of the winners. I'd learned that as a child going to school both north and south of the border. In New York the history of the Southwest was taught as the chronicle of purchase and treaty: Pancho Villa was labeled a bandit; *rebozos* (Mexican shawls) were associated with peasant mothers and picturesque scenes. In Mexico the history of its northwestern territories were a chronicle of invasion and treachery: Villa, along with Zapata, was a hero of the Mexican Revolution; *abuelita* proudly wore *rebozos* to keep warm, and explained to me that each region had its own style and patterns, which it took great skill to weave.

Native American, and Latina, and African American, and some white women were breadwinners, spiritual guides, medical experts, and leaders in their communities. Where were they in the printed record? If they were there, how were they presented? Why were the plots of history and literature, of all the disciplines, so wrong? Why, in the theater of the Golden Age, for instance, were rebellious women always tamed or defeated?

In 1971, when I approached the chair of the Division of Humanities at Richmond College with the idea for Women Writers of Spain and Latin America, he retorted, "*What* women writers?" Marcia Welles (who'd been my student at Barnard and now taught there) and I got together to discuss the new intellectual developments linked to the women's movement and the recalcitrance of members of our field, generally, to change. By the end of our meeting, we relished having become plotting women. We'd decided to join forces, designing a course fully, putting a reader together, and presenting the course description, syllabus, and reader to the respective committees at Richmond and Barnard at the same time, each mentioning the other as a way of encouraging competitive men to be in the vanguard of curriculum development.

We spent hours in the library reviewing literary histories and anthologies. Many didn't include women. Those put together by three people who had been my professors at Barnard and Columbia did, but they characterized them in sexist ways: "feminine," "exceptional," "unfeminine," "smart as men," and "soft and sentimental." In some books the poets were grouped separately as "the women poets" rather than integrated with others of their generation.

We approached the canonical writers we already knew differently, asking many new questions, and we (re)discovered dozens of authors who'd been active in every period and then ignored, erased, and forgotten. Our review of the literary histories and criticism we'd read as undergraduates and graduate students revealed much appalling condescension and antagonism we had not detected before. Martin de Riquer, a kind scholar and well-known medievalist, answered a friend's inquiry by claiming that there had been no women troubadours. That friend, Magda [Meg] Bogin, a senior at Sarah Lawrence, studying Joan Kelly, was soon to prove otherwise with a bilingual, English-Provençal anthology, *The Women Troubadours.*

When I mentioned our search for Spanish-language women writers to another friend, Randolph Pope, who was writing his dissertation on Spanish autobiography, he told me about bibliographical listings of unpublished manuscripts at the Biblioteca Nacional in Madrid by women who'd worked with Teresa of Avila. This sixteenth-century mystic, reformer, convent founder, and writer, de Beauvoir claimed, exaggeratedly, in *The Second Sex*, was the only woman in history who had had the sky rather than a ceiling over her head. Later I learned to valorize women enclosed under rooftops in domestic and monastic spaces, too. But de Beauvoir's enthusiasm—and that of English and French writers—for the Saint of Avila (whose Jewish background the Spanish experts hesitated to mention, and almost no one else knew about) animated my search for other monastic women authors.

Marcia and I—and our students the first time we taught the course in the fall of 1974—combed the libraries, and pored over bibliographies, amassing batches of three-by-five-inch index cards with works and authors we were shocked not to have known about. We rethought the canonical writers, selecting works of theirs never presented in anthologies or courses. We reread the great men, the poet and translator Fray Luis de Léon, for instance, author of a prose work titled *La perfecta casada* (The Perfect Wife). Fray Luis's influential portrait of the wisely efficient, organized, silent, home-bound wife was seen as advanced when we were students: the husband was not to beat her; there was to be respect. Then, in the sixteenth century, and still now, in the twentieth, we understood, *natural* meant doing what was expected of a woman and *unnatural* meant refusing to. Some of the writings by women we uncovered proved that a significant number of women had succeeded in becoming uppity.

We learned to disaggregate, to contra/dict (clearer in Spanish, *contra/decir*, to counter/say). We adapted terms, such as *counterpoint*, to express a process in which a multiplicity of voices were to be heard, each accorded equal importance, heard sometimes singularly, other times synchronically, or in unity. We also learned to trust and to legitimize our different ways of knowing.

V.

I am ever cognizant that in the United States, as elsewhere, it was undergraduate and graduate students and recent Ph.D.'s who spearheaded the movement to legitimize the academic study of women: the experience of women; their exclusion from, and unacknowledged participation in, human culture; and also the reasons for their relative invisibility. It was they who provided the elbow grease and the initial thinking. Hundreds and thousands of women whose names will rarely appear in books, women from all walks of life, created the movement that spawned the discipline of women's studies.

As often happens, many of those who worked in the trenches were later overlooked. Sometimes professors who had joined the bandwagon late took the reins in the game after it was safe, after careers were charred or burnout turned to disillusionment. Some of them, those who built careers from women's studies, severing ties with the larger activist communities, in turn, rendered the real pioneers invisible. At this juncture, at the end of the twentieth century, I'd like to say *¡Presente!* (as Latin Americans do for those who've given their lives to the struggle for social justice) to the unsung women without whom women's studies could not have become the field it is.

Barbara Smith

I have been politically active since the 1960s, when I became involved in the civil rights movement as a high school student in Cleveland, Ohio. As an independent scholar, I have edited *Conditions: Five, The Black Women's Issue* (with Lorraine Bethel); *All the Women Are White, All the Blacks Are Men, But Some of Us Are Brave: Black Women's Studies* (with Akasha [Gloria] Hull and Patricia Bell-Scott); *Home Girls: A Black Feminist Anthology;* and *The Reader's Companion to U.S. Women's History* (with Wilma Mankiller, Gwendolyn Mink, Marysa Navarro, and Gloria Steinem). I am coauthor of *Yours in Struggle: Three Feminist Perspectives on Anti-Semitism and Racism* (with Elly Bulkin and Minnie Bruce Pratt). My most recent book is *The Truth That Never Hurts: Writings on Race, Gender, and Freedom.*

I was cofounder and publisher of Kitchen Table: Women of Color Press. I have been a Scholar-in-Residence at the Schomburg Center for Research in Black Culture, a fellow at the Bunting Institute of Radcliffe College, and a Rockefeller fellow in the humanities at the Center for Lesbian and Gay Studies at the City University of New York. Currently, I am writing a book about the history of African American lesbians and gays. I live in Albany, New York.

Building Black Women's Studies

The first time that I ever experienced racism was in a classroom. Up until that point I had been lucky to have Black teachers or white ones who treated me decently. When this white teacher was hostile to me, I didn't even know what was going on. I just knew that I hated going to her class. I was eight years old. I had been taught to have a great deal of respect for teachers and for education. If I came home and complained about something a teacher had done, my grandmother would say, "She's got hers, you've got to get yours." And that was the end of the discussion. There was no question of her or anyone else in my family going to the school to tell the teacher what to do, based upon something I did not like. I was a child, the teacher was an adult, case closed. I encountered the racist teacher in a special summer French course that my sister and I had been chosen to take at Western Reserve University. She did not teach at our own school. It is likely that I did not even realize she was being racist until long after the course ended. It was horrible to experience this kind of treatment in a setting where I had always excelled and felt at home.

I entered Mount Holyoke College in 1965, before the student movement had reached its height and curricula began to be transformed, before there were new understandings about student power and autonomy. I got a fairly traditional education in an atmosphere that was quite intimidating. Not only was the volume of work staggering, but I was among a handful of Black students who had begun the process of desegregating the college. Too often we got the message that we were not welcome and did not belong because of both our race and our class.

I went to graduate school at the University of Pittsburgh in 1969, right out of college. Some women graduate students at Pitt who were interested in trying to put together a list of books by women and a potential syllabus for studying about women asked me if I'd like to participate. Of course, they were white women. Nevertheless, I was interested, because I was interested in anything in print and I was becoming familiar with the concept of sexual politics. At Christmas I had been given a gift certificate to a bookstore by one of my family members, and

I bought Kate Millett's *Sexual Politics,* which I read and found extremely thought provoking. I knew there was a growing feminist movement, but it just wasn't clicking for me as a Black woman. Middle- and upper-class white women had so much privilege in contrast with Black women. But on the other hand, being an adult who was responsible for myself, I was seeing more and more how being a woman influenced and affected perceptions about me and also my opportunities. Despite my education, there was still pressure in some circles for me not to put so much emphasis on my career, not to take myself so seriously. To compound the situation, Black nationalists frequently advocated extremely traditional roles for women, so I found racial loyalty being placed in opposition to Black women being able to do whatever they desired. Getting involved with the National Black Feminist Organization in 1973 was a lifesaver. It became possible for me to say that I was a Black feminist because I was finally with a group of Black women who acknowledged the impact of sexism at the same time that they challenged racism.

In the fall of 1971, I transferred to the University of Connecticut to begin work on my Ph.D., and I took a seminar in women's literature (one of the first offered in the country). Of course, all the women were white. I had to take an incomplete in the course, because my aunt, who had raised me after my mother's death, died that same semester, so the next year I was still looking for a Black woman writer whose work could be a topic for my final paper. During the summer I read in *Ms.* magazine, which had just started publishing, that Alice Walker would be teaching a course on Black women writers at the University of Massachusetts in Boston, where I had recently moved. Fortunately, she let me audit her course. It was perfect timing. We read Zora Neale Hurston's *Their Eyes Were Watching God,* Margaret Walker's *Jubilee,* and, most important, Ann Petry's novel *The Street.* I ended up writing about Ann Petry's novels for my seminar paper. I was not teaching at the time, but I swore that the next time that I got a teaching job, no matter where it was, I was going to teach Black women writers, too. Sure enough, the very next academic year, the fall of 1973, I got a job in the English department at Emerson College, and that is when I started teaching Black women's literature. I went from not knowing very many Black women writers and having no exposure to them in my course work to just reading, reading, reading them and being very ready to teach a course.

I had gone to graduate school with the objective of teaching African

American literature. During that period, courses in Black literature were not being taught at most white institutions, and if Black writers were mentioned, the focus was on male authors, just as it was on male writers in white literary contexts. I was enough of a feminist to realize that Black women were being excluded from the definition of Black literature, just as Black authors were excluded from the canon of "American" literature. In only a few years, my consciousness had markedly changed. In college, I had done a major independent study of four Black writers during my senior year, and all four of the authors I chose were male: Ralph Ellison, Richard Wright, James Baldwin, and Amiri Baraka (LeRoi Jones). Discovering Black women writers and teaching Black women's literature was transforming. I felt as if I had found the Holy Grail.

Introducing Black women's literature to the classroom was some of the most exciting work I have ever done. A large number of Black students enrolled in my courses, although Emerson did not have a large population of Black students overall. White women were also drawn to the subject matter. There were fewer white men, but the ones who did choose these courses were also enthusiastic students.

Because of the political and emotional depth of what we were reading, and because we had a shared sense of adventure in exploring something new that had not been set in stone, class discussions were quite lively and many students were very open. I got to know a lot of them, and in the case of Black women students especially, I think they were very appreciative that finally they were studying material that directly reflected their experiences and concerns.

I usually did not lecture unless there was a topic I wanted to emphasize and get them to grasp without interruption. Generally, we would have discussions and students would also do presentations. I would call on people, and I also liked for people to volunteer comments. My classes were always civilized because of the sense of discipline I was raised with and my standards for how each person should treat others. I respected my students and I expected them to respect me, themselves, and one another. Those values helped very much in the classroom, and I remember those early classes as being delightful, particularly those in Black women's literature.

Even in the early 1970s, I tried to use an interdisciplinary approach. We primarily read fiction by writers such as Toni Morrison, Alice Walker, Margaret Walker, Ann Petry, and Zora Neale Hurston, but I also included poetry by Gwendolyn Brooks and Lucille Clifton, Maya Angelou's *I Know Why the Caged Bird Sings,* and Toni Cade Bambara's ground-breaking collection, *The Black Woman.* Because there were no Black feminist periodicals, I assigned an issue of the new feminist literary magazine *Aphra,* which contained an article about the battered women's movement in the United Kingdom. This was before there was a widespread battered women's movement in this country, and the article was a catalyst for one of our most dynamic and unsettling discussions, because students acknowledged that violence against women was a reality in their own lives and within Black communities. I invited guest speakers and brought in materials about other art forms, such as music and visual art. I wanted the students to be exposed to Black history, culture, and politics in myriad ways and also to begin to identify common themes and concerns that crossed various disciplines.

A hitherto undocumented chapter in the building of Black women's studies unfolded in Boston during this period. Many Black women graduate students who later became key to building Black women's studies were studying in the Boston area at that time: Nellie McKay, Claudia Tate, Cheryl Gilkes, Hortense Spillers, Linda Perkins, and others. Andrea Rushing had the brilliant idea of getting together women she knew so that we could get to know one another and talk about our work. I think we referred to our meetings as salons. That is how I met Nellie McKay. Nellie likes to tell the story of our going to that first meeting. We had ridden the same subway, and we were both walking up the hill from Dudley Station to Andrea's home in Roxbury. Nellie was a bit behind me and because the street was nearly empty, she was wondering if we were going to the same place. She sensed that we were, and when Nellie tells the story she emphasizes the metaphor: indeed, we were going to exactly the same place, not just literally, but in our work and in our lives. She goes on to say how at that first meeting I talked about Black women's studies. She had never heard the term before and, like many others, wondered if such a thing could exist. As time passed, the women in that room and many other women, including Nellie, built the discipline. I do not remember anyone else I knew using the term *Black women's studies* during the early 1970s, but I had a clear sense that that was, in fact, what we were creating.

The women who attended the salons were in a variety of disciplines. Some of us were in sociology, some of us were in history, and many of us were in literature. I remember there being as many as fifteen or twenty people sometimes. It was just very exciting. We were searching for some kind of reflection of ourselves in the academic work we were doing and also sought support outside of the often hostile environment of graduate school. This is a part of the hidden history of how Black women's studies became established. Who would imagine that in the early 1970s a group of women who later went on to become distinguished in their fields were already in dialogue with one another, without any institutional backing and with minimal support from white women?

The sanctions against Black feminists were very high. Most of the women who came to those meetings would not have called themselves feminists then. It took a number of years for most Black women academics to feel comfortable using the term feminist about their work. Black lesbian feminists like myself, who were activists and who were actually involved in the women's movement early on, were much more willing to look at things from an explicitly feminist perspective. Black lesbian feminists were critical to building a Black feminist movement in this country, without which Black women's studies could not have grown.

It was no accident that I was a member of the Combahee River Collective, which had originally been the Boston chapter of the National Black Feminist Organization and which did multi-issue Black feminist organizing in Boston from 1974 to 1980. We wrote the well-known "Combahee River Collective Statement" in 1977 for Zillah Eisenstein's book *Capitalist Patriarchy and the Case for Socialist Feminism.* Historian Robin D. G. Kelley, in a 1993 article, cites it as "the most sophisticated Black socialist-feminist articulation of the multiple dimensions of Black women's oppression to date."[1] The statement still serves as a basic outline of Black feminist issues and politics, and at the time was a theoretical bedrock on which Black women's studies could be built. It does not seem a coincidence that I wrote "Toward a Black Feminist Criticism," which began to define the field of Black women's literature, in 1977 as well. During those years I felt that my life pursuit and my work were absolutely integrated. Everything I was doing was really toward a single purpose, which was the discovery and exposure of the reality of Black women's experience in the United States: teaching Black literature and Black women's studies and organizing around Black feminist issues all contributed to defining Black feminism. It was incredibly good cross-pollination.

In 1974 Nancy Hoffman nominated me to become a member of the Modern Language Association's Commission on the Status of Women in the Profession. My involvement with the commission also played an important part in helping to build Black women's studies nationally. I became the first woman of color appointed to the commission and began my term in early 1975. I attended my first MLA convention in December 1974 in New York City, and it was there that I met my long-time colleague, coauthor, and friend Akasha (Gloria) Hull. There were only a handful of Black women among the thousands of people in attendance at the convention, and there were no papers delivered concerning Black women's literature in either women's studies or Black studies sessions.

As a new member of the commission, I was determined that there would be programming about Black women writers at the next MLA convention. At the 1975 convention in San Francisco, there were two sessions: Black Women Writers: Strategies for Criticism, which I chaired, and a seminar on Zora Neale Hurston, chaired by Hortense E. Thornton. The MLA commission played a critical role in helping to institutionalize women's studies, and I thought its resources should be available to Black women and other women of color. This was by no means an easy task. Like most white feminists, commission members had a theoretical commitment to being racially inclusive, but on a practical level, they were not always conscious of how they excluded our participation.

One of the activities that the commission was involved in was increasing opportunities for feminist academics to publish. Once we held a small conference in New York City to which publishing professionals were invited. I was, of course, concerned that other women of color participate, because I was still the only woman of color on the commission, and knew that women of color had even less access to publication than white women. Even though I made suggestions of women to contact, those coordinating the conference did not follow through, so the conference participants were, with one or two exceptions, entirely white. The next day when the commission met, the other members were quite pleased with how well the conference had gone, and when I raised my criticisms about the absence of women of color, I was met with a suprisingly negative response. I was so upset that I actually left the room in tears. In those days I usually made plans in advance to meet Black women friends of mine during the weekends when the commission met, and sometimes even had them come to some part of our meetings, so I would not be so isolated. Fortunately, I had invited Elaine Scott, whom I had met when we were both graduate students at the University of Pittsburgh, to this one. The next morning, I think, I asked Elaine to accompany me to the commission meeting, and I laid it on the line. I told the other members that unless at least one other woman of color was appointed to the commission, I would resign. They asked me for suggestions, and I suggested Akasha (Gloria) Hull.

Akasha was appointed to the commission in 1976, which made it a much more viable context in which to work. I had already begun an anthology about Black women's studies under the commission's sponsorship, and when Akasha joined the commission, the two of us worked on it together. Florence Howe of The Feminist Press expressed interest in publishing the book, and she introduced us to Patricia Bell-Scott, who became the third coeditor of *But Some of Us Are Brave.* Because both Akasha and I were in literature, Florence thought it was important to have an editor with a social science background. It became a wonderful collaboration among the three of us, and Akasha, Pat, and I have remained lifelong friends. It was extremely challenging to identify contributors to the first book who would approach Black women's studies as a specific and legitimate academic field. I think that we were able to do a remarkable job, especially when one considers that we were working on this project during the mid- to late 1970s.

Each of us had in mind subject matter that we wished were available to incorporate into the finished work that would have made it even stronger. I would have liked to see a more consistent Black feminist analysis throughout the book, but that was probably not a realistic goal during that period. I was actually coediting *Conditions: Five, The Black Women's Issue* at the same time, which was published in 1979, several years before *But Some of Us Are Brave.* Contributors to *Conditions,* who were not primarily academics and many of whom were Black lesbian feminists, were writing from an explicitly Black feminist perspective even then. Both anthologies, especially *But Some of Us Are Brave,* opened up a path for the continued building of Black women's studies.

Sometimes I am amazed at how (relatively) easy it is now to pursue academic interests in Black women's studies and Black feminism. This subject matter has actually become legitimate—although not immune to attack. It is sometimes difficult to convey to younger Black women scholars how hard it was to do what we did. We were usually in the midst of a white female majority when we did our professional work, not to mention having to function in white male–dominated institutions. We had to devise ways to survive. Any kind of contact with each other was affirming: to see each other, to hear a familiar voice on the telephone, to laugh at the same things. The jokes we told and the satirizing we did of the improbable and infuriating situations we encountered were just as useful as the theorizing and the analysis. Every so often, we needed to have a reality check. In order to get work done, you have to be emotionally functional, and I feel that having sisters as friends, as sounding boards, was very, very important.

One of the women whom I could rely upon most for this kind of support was Audre Lorde. I actually met Audre for the first time at the annual MLA convention in New York in 1976. The incredible panels and readings that the commission, the Women's Caucus, and the Gay Caucus organized during those years made our part of the convention seem like a lesbian/feminist cultural festival. Audre had been invited to be on a major plenary. I had known her work for some time because she was one of the many contemporary Black poets published by the visionary Broadside Press. But I had no idea that she was a lesbian until I saw her name on the masthead of an issue of *Amazon Quarterly*. I was so amazed and excited to discover that this important Black literary figure was a lesbian, too. Audre tells the story of our first meeting in the documentary film about her, *A Litany for Survival*. During the question-and-answer period following her panel, I asked if she thought it was possible to be an out Black lesbian *writer* and live to tell about it. I asked that question a lot in those days. It was both a rhetorical question, to get people to think about the potentially frightening consequences of writing honestly from these combined identities, and a real-life question, because I was wondering if I had any future as a writer, which was really all I wanted to be. I cannot repeat Audre's answer word for word, but I know that it gave me much reinforcement and hope. That is how we met, and Audre later told me that it was my question that made her begin to think about writing a prose work about growing up and coming out as a Black lesbian in the 1940s and 1950s, the work that became *Zami: A New Spelling of My Name*.

The work of building Black studies, women's studies, Black women's studies, and lesbian and gay studies, in which I have been fortunate to play a part, has transformed both the academy and U.S. culture during my lifetime. The ongoing right-wing attacks against this subject matter, motivated by racism, sexism, homophobia, and the desire to maintain white, male intellectual and political hegemony in a country that will soon have a majority population of people of color, indicates how effective our work has been. As an independent scholar and activist, I will not leave behind a significant material legacy; indeed, it is questionable whether I will have sufficient resources to retire. It is good to know that the legacy I will leave, Black women's studies and Black feminism, has made a difference and will last.

Nellie Y. McKay

I am not sure whether I chose this life or it chose me. For although I feel enormously fortunate to have had the chance to contribute to the overall recognition of women's lives and academic achievements over the past twenty years (especially to those of black women), I'd like to believe that had the choice been entirely my own, I would have given more consideration to the personal costs. Fickle fate handed me a life to love, but also one I often resent for its relentless demands on my time—my person. So, while I take joy and satisfaction in my role in the project to which many of us committed ourselves three decades ago, I yearn for less: for my own time to rest from the weariness of continuous overextension—the relentless demands on my time. Like others, I see wonderful achievements but only at the cost of extremely heavy tolls on the well-being of the self, on personal relationships and health.

My life with this project began in 1969 when I entered graduate school to study American literature in search of answers to my questions about the American literature of the 1960s. As a graduate student I "met" the already received masters of American literature but also many others: African American writers (women and men together, but really men); African American women writers in their own right; the writings of other women of color; and those of women across the boundaries of race and ethnicity. These unforeseen meetings opened up a world to me that I had never dreamed of, one in which my greatest satisfactions come from studying, teaching, and writing about the lives of African American women and men. The field (now well established) was new in the early 1970s. Thus, I had the good fortune to be one with its growth and development over these decades. The early years were especially exciting: new ground waiting to be tilled that has yielded much fruit. Looking back over time, I am grateful to have been there, to have been a partner among those who created and shaped this vibrant and exciting area of intellectual inquiry. We made it happen. Of that I will always be proud: a legacy of great worth. But the work is not over yet, and neither am I, yearning for less: a lesser cost to all of our personal lives.

Charting a Personal Journey
A Road to Women's Studies

In 1965 I went to Queens College, where I majored in English and received my B.A. in 1969. In my sophomore year I chose a career path in higher education: to become a Shakespearean. With no plans then to ever leave New York City, I anticipated a lifetime of teaching at one of the City University of New York (CUNY) campuses, where I imagined I would claim distinction as the first African American woman Shakespearean in that system. But when I entered Harvard University's English department in 1969, I was there to study American literature instead. As a result of the social upheaval that shook the country throughout the 1960s, and especially the events toward the close of that decade, I had changed my course. By then, I wanted to learn more about the United States and the meaning of its history through its literature.

Beyond giving me sound training in canonical literature (for which I have always been grateful), my Queens College experience was instructive in other ways, especially in the close-up view of racial politics I had when the school began its transformation in the late 1960s from an almost all white, middle-class student body to one that, within a decade, had a substantial minority population. As at most white-majority institutions of higher education undergoing such changes then, the transition was not smooth. In this case, although the number of minority (read black) students in the first racially integrated class was small, hostile confrontations between black and white students and an administrative power struggle (also along racial lines) for control of newly implemented special education programs for minority group students forced the institution to close its doors for brief periods. Even though I was not involved in revolutionary civil rights activities, by 1969 I was dismayed by the urgent need that kept nationwide civil unrest, campus disturbances, and a senseless violence that wiped out the lives of some of the most prominent and promising talents of both races firmly in place. I was angry at and frustrated by the world around me and could find no rational answers to such questions as, Why was our country so close to the border of social chaos? Where did a nation founded on the ideals of equality for all people (I thought) go wrong? And why did so many whites in the United States still believe that racial discrimination was right? How could a civilized people not recognize the human injustice such beliefs embodied? Perhaps, I thought, answers to those questions were hidden in the works of the "great" nineteenth-century American writers: in Hawthorne's gloom, or in Thoreau's rationale for civil disobedience, or even in the riddle of Melville's white whale. As an undergraduate, I had come late to American literature. I intended to make up for that in graduate school: in the place where men such as the renowned F. O. Mathiesson, Perry Miller, and Howard Mumford Jones had validated American literature.

However, in 1969 my heightened racial consciousness did not extend into gender awareness. I had lived with and grown up around strong black women all of my early life. Although they often commiserated with one another about what they had done or needed to do, they did not spend time deconstructing the pros and cons of their strength. Instead, they *acted*, assertively or quietly, as situations required, doing whatever they needed to do to save their own lives and the lives of their men, their children, and everyone else in their orbit. Years later I recognized their literary counterparts in Toni Morrison's women who are both ship and safe harbor, making a way for themselves and everyone else where previously there was none; and in Paule Marshall's immigrant domestic day workers who, in "this man's country," "for a few raw-mouth pennies" to keep soul and body together, scrubbed floors and absorbed insults from the white people they served, when in reality they were poets and political analysts who "talked endlessly, passionately, . . . and with impressive range" with "[n]o subject beyond them."[1] Gender issues did not absorb them, and at the beginning of the 1970s they did not absorb me either. For although it is also true that the idea never crossed my mind that an African American, or *any-*

one from another minority group, or *any* woman writer might have the keys to the doors I wanted to unlock, in those unself-critical days, politically, I saw myself as considerably less oppressed by gender than by race. Racial discrimination had kept most of the women and men around whom I grew up from becoming the full selves they might have been in the world, and it was my sense that although my place in life would be a great improvement on theirs, racial discrimination remained the enemy against which I would always need to struggle. So even after I realized that black men also marginalized African American women, I dismissed the significance of black intraracial gender oppression on the basis of an analysis that considered black men only in the context of their powerlessness in relationship to white patriarchy. Patronizingly, I denied the significance of their abuse of black women. It was more than a decade later before I fully realized that gender seriously affected all women's lives. By then, I had left the East Coast.

My graduate school experiences were very different from what I had imagined they would be. Unexpectedly, I found the university environment much more inhospitable than I was prepared for and was soon experiencing a sense of personal insecurity that lasted for a long time. White women represented roughly 50 percent of my class of roughly fifty students. At the same time, the small number of students of color (five in my class, two who had arrived the previous year, and one young man completing his last year of graduate work, for a total of eight) in the English department's graduate population of approximately five hundred, seemed a replay of my early college experience, although there were differences between them. Living in Cambridge, unlike living in Queens, New York, I felt far away: far from home, far from New York City, and far from family, friends, neighborhood, church, and the professors whom I knew and who knew me. In Cambridge, alone in my first apartment, surrounded on all sides by unfamiliarity, I was unprepared for the isolation I felt.

Later I realized that Harvard University was a "foreign" country for large numbers of students, especially graduate students (not only minority students), and that in this aspect of its nature, across race, gender, and even class sometimes, the university was an equal opportunity distributor of anxieties. I also later realized how much all women there were on the margins relative to white men. Yet most of those of us who experienced alienation braved our first years and achieved a level of familiarity with the institution, even though we still felt like out-siders. Before long, we created communities for ourselves inside and outside of its boundaries, we made lasting friendships, and as the clay feet of what once seemed a distant idol became apparent to us, it no longer intimidated us.

In my courses at Harvard, I read the authors I had gone there to pur-sue. I also learned a lot, from what was encoded in invisible ink on syl-labi and reading lists, or went unspoken in classrooms about the liter-ary erasure of the lives and experiences of minority group peoples and white women. I made close friends among the small group of African American students in English and other areas of study across the uni-versity and with a small number of white men in my department, but, interestingly, I developed no close ties with my white women colleagues. Early on, in the company of my black friends, I gained an introduction to the world of African American literature. I discovered such writers as W. E. B. Du Bois, Charles Chesnutt, and Sutton Griggs, who, until then, had been unknown to me. At home, for many years, I had read Langston Hughes' newspaper columns that featured his character Simple (Jesse B. Semple). I knew of Baldwin because he was closely involved with Martin Luther King Jr. and the civil rights movement. I knew that his fiery essays earned him the reputation of "the angry young man" from many journalists. Ralph Ellison and Richard Wright were not unknown names among many African Americans in the 1960s and early 1970s. Yet I had no historical context in black writing into which to place their works. Conversations and discussions of these writers with my friends took the place of the seminars in black literature we never had. We brought to this field the passion for knowledge that we subsequently used to organize our mission and launch our careers. My study of African American literature began then.

In 1972, after completing my program's residency requirements, in search of an academic home outside of Harvard, I temporarily left graduate school for a lecturer's position at Simmons College on the other side of the Charles River. There I taught American literature and the African American literature that was still new to me. Two years later, I was an assistant professor, with my department chair's promise of tenure as soon as I completed my dissertation. In 1974, while still teaching full-time at Simmons, I resumed graduate work, emotionally healthier and equal to the challenges of that undertaking. Everything about that small women's college was what I desperately *needed* between

1972 and 1978: its small size (2500 students); English department colleagues (all white men when I arrived; women came later) who went out
of their way to welcome me as a full person; classes with smart, self-
confident, eager white and black women students who did not display
the arrogant self-entitlement common among many Harvard undergraduates; and a comfortable and lively intellectual atmosphere of its
own. After Harvard, Simmons College was a place of healing for me.
There I learned to teach and to love teaching, and there I gained a
wholesome self-assuredness. Although in my time at Simmons College
men still held the positions of power—from having the majority among
the faculty and department chairs, to the major administrative jobs,
including that of president and provost of the college—I saw the school
as women's space. Perhaps that was because the absence of male students meant women were the constant majority presence in daily life.
In any event, that women's space restored my psychological equilib-
rium. In it, surrounded by women students eager to learn, I received
my baptism into and taught the first classes that included African
American women writers. At the same time, although I had many very
good white women friends inside and outside of the college, I declined
invitations to officially link my name to the women's studies program
(then in its infancy). I knew just enough about the history of white
women's racism in America, from slavery to the present, to keep white
women as a group and white feminism from becoming a top priority
on my political agenda.

Then, with a jolt, I came to another turn in the road. Race and gender together, intricately interrelated, entered my consciousness. Late
on a summer's evening, most likely in 1972, I joined a group of about a
dozen African American women graduate students (candidates for the
Ph.D. in literary studies teaching in the Boston area) for dinner at the
home of one of the group. Unknown to us at the time, we were participating in a historic moment, not peculiar to our lives, but present in
the lives of many of this generation of African American women in the
academy. At what first appeared only as a social occasion, the group
galvanized itself around the issue of the absence of black women writers
from among the recently rediscovered black writers whose works were
coming to light and beginning to shape the African American canon.
We talked together well into the night, and each of us left that gathering
with a clear understanding of a new mission. We had work to do. The
task was to make black women writers visible in the world of American

literature: to be talked about, written about, and taught in classroom was part of the larger struggle for black rights from which we could not permit women to be excluded. Our dinner group reconvened occasionally, was flexible enough to welcome new women who wanted to be included, and was to accommodate those who dropped out when their schedules did not allow them to join us. Always, it remained dynamic, a source of support, and a space of knowledge for the taking.

Subsequently, we learned that in the early 1970s, similar gatherings were taking place in many places across the country: African American women scholars in literature were interrogating the gender of black literature. They discussed recently recovered and newly published books by black women writers; they talked about their classes and their research projects. As a community, they maintained momentum and energy, for the work itself helped to generate their enthusiasm, and they worked hard to recover many lost or long-forgotten names of and writings by black women. The idea of black women's studies as a field most likely began to take shape in these groups, but I do not recall when or where I was when I became aware of it. Those of us who were teaching not only read the newly discovered writings with enormous excitement, but we also introduced them into our classrooms, where white and black women students in particular were eager to become acquainted with these unknown women writers. Because almost all of these books were out of print, we duplicated whatever we found and circulated copies among ourselves. My first copies of Hurston's *Their Eyes Were Watching God*, Nella Larsen's *Quicksand*, and Gwendolyn Brooks' *Maud Martha* were duplications of recovered texts that friends near and far gave me. I, in turn, duplicated the duplications for my students and other teaching friends. We copied and shared them with one another in this way until publishers, recognizing a lucrative new market, began paying attention.

Awakening to the presence and significance of black women writers in literature in the early 1970s, I began to include their works in my classes wherever I found a place to fit them in. I had also found a new direction for my research and writing in black literature. The first essay I wrote on the subject was on Gwendolyn Brooks' poetry, but I never submitted it for publication and I no longer have it. The work that most interested me revolved around the effects of race on the lives of African American women and men and the meaning of gender relative to black women. In the 1970s I learned and have never forgotten that any analysis of race and the black condition in the United States that does not include gender is incomplete. But although I had many white women friends who were feminists, I was not ready to consider the variables within race and gender that link all women together.

In 1977 I received a Harvard Ph.D., and tenure and a promotion to associate professor at Simmons College. At the end of the spring semester of 1978, I resigned from my appointment at Simmons College, and in August of that year I left the Boston area. That fall I was a new assistant professor at the University of Wisconsin, Madison, giving up a "job for life" in an excellent college to begin a new chapter of my life in a more challenging educational environment. In deciding to leave Simmons College a year after completing my dissertation, the only scholarship I had done so far, I was aware of my ineligibility for a tenured position in a major university. Long before we left graduate school, my colleagues and I had accepted the daunting idea that we would be the first scholars to train students for Ph.D.'s in black literature. Simmons College offered no Ph.D. programs. Thus, if I were to fulfill that part of my educational mission, I had to leave Simmons and spend several years beyond my Ph.D. in a probationary position at a Ph.D.-granting institution, hoping I would produce the scholarship necessary to achieve tenure there. But while that part of planning for my future career was realistically in place, I overlooked how depressed the job market for new Ph.D.'s with degrees in English and other humanities disciplines was in the late 1970s and early 1980s. Naïvely, I expected to easily find a position to my liking in a place of my choice. That did not happen. I also overlooked the state of black studies in the white academy at the time, for by then, many such programs that came about in the 1960s were floundering or already extinct. This, too, lowered the necessity for a large number of newly trained faculty in various areas of the field. These realizations, not initially a part of my thinking, shocked me at a time when I did not want to break away from well-known and by then well-loved friends and community. However, I accepted the inevitable with reluctance, and only because my inner self told me that it was time for me to leave the comfortable nest that Simmons College and I together had built for me. To disregard that voice was to risk creating limitations to my future as a scholar and a teacher. Now I believe that 1978 was not only the right time for me to leave Simmons College but also time for me leave the cocoon of the East Coast.

In Madison, among other issues, the size of the university over-
whelmed me, and for almost two years I was very unhappy. I was lone-
lier than I had ever been before and that loneliness took over. But not
everything about the place was negative. I was situated in the Afro-
American studies department, which was exactly what I wanted. The
department, established in the late 1960s, was making an energetic
effort to recover from its first less-than-sterling decade, and I entered
with a mandate to design a literature curriculum for the program from
the ground up. I loved the responsibility and the many challenges the
assignment presented me. More than anything, it offered me the
opportunity to be at the starting gate of a project I could identify with:
institutionalizing black studies in this university. At that time I was the
only literature professor in the department, and the enrollment in my
first course was seven students. Two years later the department
recruited a second professor to teach in the area to accommodate frustrated students (who numbered in the hundreds each semester) unable
to get into my courses. By then, the departmental effort to reverse its
failing reputation was moving forward satisfactorily, and my contributions to that movement earned me professional respect from my colleagues. It felt good, too, to be in a department with faculty conscious
of and committed to the program and the future of the new field. I felt
good as a valued player on this team. So my professional life was off to a
running start.

But, unhappily, my achievements in building the Afro-American
studies department did not reach into my personal life. In a reverse of
the temporary sense of displacement I experienced in Cambridge,
where my personal life had adjusted itself in a timely manner, in
Madison I seemed to have ongoing difficulties defining a home community. For many months I was very lonely for what was not in my life,
and I refused to be comforted. Nor did it help that most of my colleagues were men and the few other women in the department had
other pressing personal obligations that left them little time to share
with me. I saw much more of the men than the women. They were
respectful and helpful professionally but could not fill the empty space.
Long telephone calls to the East Coast offered only temporary solace
but no adequate solution to the problem. I cried a lot from loneliness
during that first winter, which I maintain was the most severe of all the
winters I have lived through in Wisconsin. However, I know better than
to trust my judgment on the accuracy of that conclusion. What I am

sure of is that I felt very lost, and in that state of lostness, peers in the women's studies program found and rescued me.

None of my Afro-American Studies women colleagues were members of the women's studies program, and my inquiries of them regarding the program gave me information that discouraged me from trying to make that contact myself. Then, in my third semester at the university, a woman professor with appointments in the English department and the women's studies program invited me into a group of faculty women from the English department. Most of the women were, like me, untenured. All of the untenured ones, like me, were anxious about the process and feeling vulnerable. Some were associated with the women's studies program, others were not. The periodic meetings of this group, where women articulated fears and anxieties in the safe space of one another's company, was a welcome opening to new relationships with women, even if there were no women of color among them. Next I was drawn into the women's studies program through my friend with the appointments in the English department and the women's studies program, who introduced me to other faculty in the program. These overtures of friendship worked quickly, and my life began turning around. Reflecting on that period from a distance of twenty years, I realize that there were interesting events that created a symmetry to my life in the 1970s. At the beginning of that decade, members of the English department at Simmons College and the school's high-spirited young women opened a space for me to gather together the fragmented parts of my life as I attempted to build an academic career. At its close, women colleagues in the women's studies program in Madison, Wisconsin, did likewise. In these two institutions, dramatically different from each other, I moved my life forward, in directions I had not dreamed of. The gift of a copy of *Incidents in the Life of a Slave Girl, Written by Herself* by Linda Brent, from one of my new friends, marked the beginning of what my women's studies life has meant to me. Until I received that volume, I had not even heard of the book. Its theme of a black woman's search for freedom from chattel slavery and the happiness of a home for herself and her children was appropriate to the occasion. I like to believe that in the early days of my relationship with women's studies in Madison, my colleagues and I together planted seeds that yielded the rewards of women learning to work together across many differences, learning respect for and sharing knowledge with one another.

If my journey to women's studies and a fully developed sense of myself as a feminist took a long time, I was an enthusiastic latecomer. Although I've neither designed nor taught foundation courses in our program, by serving on the Curriculum Committee very early, I helped to shape the program's academic structure. For a long time, I taught women's studies through the courses that I taught in the Afro-American studies and English departments (by then I had an appointment in the latter unit also), offering students the only full courses then available to them on the writings of black and multicultural women. At the same time, through my presence and participation in policy making, in general program meetings, and on a variety of committees, and through my willingness to share in the many tasks that new programs must engage, I did my part to strengthen the work my colleagues began before I arrived.

In my early years with women's studies, I learned a lot about women as a group across the many divisions that separate us. At the beginning of the 1980s, there was a great deal of work to be done between white women and women of color. As the only woman of color in the program when I joined it, I was very aware of the difficulties in this area of our work. I give great credit to those of my white colleagues who, by recognizing how much they needed to learn about their own conscious and unconscious racism, helped to ease the situation for all of us. Across differences we could not ignore or alter, we consciously worked to debunk myths, preconceptions, and misconceptions as we eased our way through to new paths of respect for and a new understanding of each other. The journey was not always easy, but goodwill among many prevailed, and the successes of the program stand as a monument to those struggles. In that time, I learned about the marginalization of women in Western culture and their accomplishments through the centuries. My knowledge of black women and other women of color expanded through reading and, more significantly, through conversations with other black women like me in other parts of the country. And I gained greater appreciation for women like those I had grown up around and known as friends in New York until 1969. Across generations, these women, without fanfare, had done their part to subvert the white patriarchal order in the United States for almost two hundred years. In my association with women's studies, I learned to take nuanced approaches to black studies and women's studies, to evaluate them critically rather than to romanticize them. In women's studies I spearheaded events that brought black women scholars to campus for lectures and meetings with students and faculty. My life moved quickly forward, recovering from its previous state of displacement and fragmentation.

I came to Madison in 1978 to make a career for myself as a specialist in American and African American literature, and to help establish a permanent place for black studies in the American academy. Along the way, I discovered that racial identification alone is not enough to make a whole self: each of us lives in many worlds at the same time. Women's studies at large, and my women's studies colleagues in Madison in particular, helped me to clarify the meaning of inhabiting multiple spaces simultaneously and to define my identity in relationship to those spaces. Now I work to bring all of myself, together and whole, to everything that I do wherever I find myself.

Beverly Guy-Sheftall

I have been a faculty member at Spelman College since 1971, and involved with the national women's studies movement since its inception. In 1981 I worked to establish the first women's studies minor at a historically black college. In 1997, this minor became a major. At Spelman I am the founding director of the Women's Research and Resource Center as well as Anna Julia Cooper professor of women's studies. In 1983, I was also the founding coeditor of *Sage: A Scholarly Journal on Black Women*.

My publications include the following anthologies: *Words of Fire: An Anthology of African American Feminist Thought*, *Sturdy Black Bridges: Visions of Black Women in Literature* (edited with Roseann P. Bell and Bettye J. Parker), *Double Stitch: Black Women Write about Mothers and Daughters* (edited with the Sage Editorial Group), and *Traps: African American Men on Gender and Sexuality* (edited with Rudolph Byrd). My thesis was published in 1991 under the title *Daughters of Sorrow: Attitudes toward Black Women, 1880–1920*. Also in the early 1990s, I completed a report for the Ford Foundation, released (in collaboration with Susan Heath) as *Women's Studies: A Retrospective*.

I enjoy teaching and continue to invent new courses on comparative women's studies, global feminisms, and the experience of women of African descent throughout the diaspora—both at Spelman College and at the Institute for Women's Studies, which offers a doctorate in women's studies.

Other Mothers of Women's Studies

The founders of women's studies were largely white women.
MARILYN BOXER, *WHEN WOMEN ASK THE QUESTIONS:*
CREATING WOMEN'S STUDIES IN AMERICA, 1998

Women's Studies must divest itself of white-skin privilege, racism, and the feminist insistence on the primacy of gender.
JOHNNELLA E. BUTLER, *TRANSFORMING THE CURRICULUM:*
ETHNIC STUDIES AND WOMEN'S STUDIES, 1991

Since most Women's Studies programs fail to be inclusive in ways that radically subvert and challenge racism and racial hierarchies, the development of Black Women's Studies is a necessary corrective.
BELL HOOKS, "FEMINISM AND BLACK WOMEN'S STUDIES," 1989

My long journey as a committed feminist educator began in a southern urban community with other black women who weren't in spaces where white women's concerns were the major priority, though we were sometimes perceived within the African American community to be disloyal to the race and antimale. I want to describe what propelled me to women's studies at the age of twenty-two and what has kept me there for another thirty years. More important, I want to write a narrative that captures the voices and vision of a small group of African American women who have been crucial to the development of women's studies, but who remain largely outside the history of one of the most important challenges to the U.S. academy.[1] Unlike many black women academics, my first contact with women's studies pioneers in the 1970s was with other black women, so I never associated the development of women's studies with white women only.

When I think of the beginnings of women's studies, not necessarily academic feminism or the founders of women's studies programs, I think of Toni Cade Bambara, Audre Lorde, Alice Walker, Barbara Smith, Roseann Bell, Patricia Bell-Scott, Gloria T. Hull, Johnnella Butler, Mary Helen Washington, bell hooks, and many other black women whom I knew in the 1970s. Frustrated with the priorities of the new women's movement, which was emerging by the time she wrote the preface to her now-classic book *The Black Woman* in 1970, Toni Cade asserted, "In the whole bibliography of feminist literature, literature directly relevant to us wouldn't fill a page" (11). By "us," she meant black and other Third World women, for example, sisters in Vietnam, Guatemala, Algeria, and Ghana. Rather than simply complaining, she advocated a radical agenda for women's studies and the women's movement (inseparable, from her vantage point), which if it had been taken seriously (or even noticed), would have altered the course of "second wave feminism" within and without the academy:

> set up a comparative study of the woman's role as she saw it in all the Third World Nations; examine the public school system and blueprint some viable alternatives; explore ourselves and set the record straight on the matriarch and the evil Black bitch; delve into history and pay tribute to all our warriors from the ancient times to the slave trade to Harriet Tubman to Fannie Lou Hamer to the woman of this morning . . . interview the migrant workers, the quilting bee mothers, the grandmothers of the UNIA; analyze the Freedom Budget and design ways to implement it; outline the work that has been done in the area of consumer education and cooperative economics. . . provide a forum of opinion from the YWCA to the Black Women Enraged; get into the whole area of sensuality, sex; chart the steps necessary for forming a working alliance with all non-white women of the world for the formation of, among other things, a clearing house for the exchange of information.[2]

Commenting on the profound impact of Toni Cade's groundbreaking anthology on her own "revolutionary feminism many years later," bell hooks also captures the significance of *The Black Woman* for other black women like me who, in the early 1970s, were claiming feminism as a legitimate vehicle for understanding black life, and who were working within the academy to transform it:

> Singlehandedly, *The Black Woman* placed black women at the center of various feminist debates. "On the Issue of Roles". . . was one of the first essays on feminist theory that looked at the interlock-

ing relations between race, sex, and class. It legitimized looking at black life from a feminist perspective . . . it helped to create an intellectual climate where feminist theory focusing on black experience could emerge. Without the publication of this anthology, later feminist works focusing on black life might never have been written.[3]

Like bell hooks, whom I was to first meet at the National Women's Studies Association's meeting in 1980 in Storrs, Connecticut, where she was attempting to promote her soon-to-be published first book, *Ain't I a Woman: Black Women and Feminism* (South End Press, 1981), Toni Cade Bambara would also have a profound impact on my career as a feminist scholar and activist.

My own involvement with women's studies actually began, however, in 1968, while I was pursuing a master's degree in English at Atlanta University. Long and lonely days and nights in the library, trying to figure out how to write a master's thesis on William Faulkner's treatment of women, black and white, in his major novels forced me to immerse myself in what were the beginnings of feminist literary criticism. Though the black studies movement and African American scholarship had called attention to ways of analyzing images of blacks, especially racist stereotypes in literary texts, the idea of feminist literary criticism, which was to borrow heavily from the early work of black literary scholars, was only in its embryonic phase. As a graduate student I read, on my own, Katherine Rogers' *Troublesome Helpmate: A History of Misogyny in Literature* (1966), Aileen Kraditor's *Ideas of the Woman Suffrage Movement* (1965), Mary Ellman's *Thinking About Women* (1968), and Eleanor Flexner's *Century of Struggle: The Woman's Rights Movement in the United States* (1966). After I began teaching English, I read Kate Millett's *Sexual Politics* (1970); Sheila Tobias's first series of women's studies course syllabi, *Female Studies 1,* published by KNOW (1970); and Florence Howe's *Female Studies 2* (1970).

Though I had graduated from Spelman College in 1966 as a liberally educated English major, I began to realize while doing research on Faulkner's women and as I began my first teaching job at Alabama State University, how male-focused my education had been. Rereading my thesis (submitted in August 1969, the year before the first women's studies program was founded at San Diego University) for the first time in years, in preparation for writing this essay, I remembered several important things about my own feminist intellectual journey, which surely began while I was a young graduate student, alone, with no one to share my excitement and difficulties. Like most graduate students in English in the late 1960s, I studied mostly male writers, even in the few African American literature courses I was privileged to take. In 1967, the year before I entered the master's program in English at Atlanta University, I did a fifth year of study at Wellesley College and took a course called Women in Drama, which was taught by Patricia Spacks. It was the first woman-focused course I'd ever taken, though the focus was the treatment of women in canonical literature by males. Though I didn't realize the significance of this shift, I also began, for the first time, to focus on women in my assigned papers in class, which I had not done in the countless papers I wrote for my literature classes at Spelman. It is now clear to me that my graduate project on Faulkner's treatment of women was related to my new interest in gender issues, which began in earnest while I was at Wellesley. Moreover, in trying to understand Faulkner's women, I discovered my passion for unraveling the complex intersections between history and literature in constructions of black and white womanhood, especially in the South, the place of my birth and where I still feel most at home. It also sparked my interest in interdisciplinary inquiry, which remains the focus of my feminist scholarship. I began to realize, as well, that it was impossible to understand the complexity of U.S. history and cultures, which drew me to Faulkner in the first place, without probing deeply the connections between race and gender.

When my teaching career began a year later at Alabama State University in Montgomery, there was no women's studies movement to speak of; there were few, if any, critical works on women writers; there were no histories of African American women; there was profound silence about the existence of black lesbians; there were no biographies of black women writers; and there was no acknowledgement of a rich feminist tradition in African American intellectual and literary history. Like most beginning English professors, I was teaching the required freshman English and sophomore world literature classes, and I put on hold the work I'd been doing in American literature for my master's thesis.

When I returned to Spelman to teach primarily freshman English and world literature two years later in the fall of 1971, I was not aware of the extent of my commitment to feminism nor of a field about to emerge called black women's studies.[4] I do recall, after teaching for a

few years, being frustrated by my black female students' lack of familiarity with black women's literature or black women intellectuals, a
frustration that was shared by my colleague and friend Roseann Bell,
who was also teaching English. This frustration would lead to the publication of *Sturdy Black Bridges,* the first anthology of black women in literature; it included works about the African diaspora. We decided rather
abruptly during 1973 that we would assemble a collection of literary
readings that would include positive images of black women and that we
would make this collection available to our students, who, we believed,
were in desperate need of literary role models and stories about themselves. This was long before writers such as Zora Neale Hurston, Toni
Morrison, Paule Marshall, and Alice Walker were available to large
numbers of college students.

After a cursory review of the literature about black women writers,
which revealed very little, we decided to undertake a more ambitious
project, which was the compilation of an anthology that would include
critical essays on black women writers, interviews, and short literary
selections of fiction and poetry that included positive, complex images
of black women. After leaving Spelman and joining the faculty at
Cornell University, Roseann encouraged Bettye Parker to join the editorial group. After five years of hard work and a lot of rejection notices
from publishers, Marie Brown, a black woman editor at Doubleday,
said yes to *Sturdy Black Bridges,* which was published in 1979, two years after
the founding convention of the National Women's Studies Association
(NWSA) met in Lawrence, Kansas. This would be the first anthology of
black women's literature published in the United States. It would also
become a foundational text in the emerging field of black women's
studies. By this time, the women's movement was in full swing, and I
had begun to immerse myself in feminist theory, women's history, and
women's studies. During the publishing process I also enrolled in an
interdisciplinary doctoral program in American studies at Emory
University, and was on leave from Spelman for a year. I chose the
American studies program rather than English so that I could pursue
my interest in both women's studies and black studies.

Among the important linkages to the emergence of contemporary
black feminism included in *Sturdy Black Bridges* was an interview with Toni
Cade Bambara, which I conducted in her home in Atlanta in 1974.[5]
Because of the historical significance of *The Black Woman*[6] and her important work as a writer, feminist critic, and community worker, the interview with Toni was critical to our vision of *Sturdy Black Bridges.* Even today,

I believe it is highly important, because it enables readers to see the visionary thinking of early black feminist scholars and educators, which had a powerful impact on younger women like myself. When I asked Toni about the possibility of black and other Third World women forming political alliances around the eradication of both race and gender oppression, she revealed her involvement in what we would now call a global women's movement. She believed that feminist movements should not be narrowly focused on women but instead focused on eliminating oppression for all, including the colonized Third World and poor people in the United States:

> I was in Cuba in 1973 and had the occasion not only to meet with the Federation of Cuban women but sisters in the factories, on the land, in the street, in the parks, in lines, or whatever, and the fact that they were able to resolve a great many class conflicts as well as color conflicts and organize a mass organization says a great deal about the possibilities here. I was in Vietnam in the summer of 1975 as a guest of the Women's Union and again was very struck by the women's ability to break through traditional roles, traditional expectations, reactionary agenda for women, and come together again in a mass organization that is programmatic and takes on a great deal of responsibility for the running of the nation.[7]

Barbara Smith, a "founding mother" of black women's studies, essentially gave the same message to the audience of mostly white women at the closing session of the first NWSA conference in 1977 in Lawrence, Kansas.[8]

Toni Cade Bambara also bemoaned in the *Sturdy Black Bridges* interview a missed moment in the early 1960s when what she called a national black women's movement could have been multicultural if black women had joined Puerto Rican women and Chicanas "who shared not only a common condition but also I think a common vision about the future". In her usual prophetic fashion, she also anticipated that in the last quarter of the twentieth century, blacks would begin to forge critical ties with other communities of color, which, she believed, was also critical for U.S. women involved in the women's liberation struggle. When I asked her whether it was a dilemma for her to be both a feminist and a warrior in the race struggle, which for some black women and men was an oxymoron, she asserted unequivocably, "I don't find any basic contradiction or any tension between being a feminist, being a pan-Africanist, being a black nationalist, being an internationalist, being a socialist, and being a woman in North America". This was precisely the message many of us young black feminists needed as we found ourselves increasingly under suspicion with respect to our race loyalty. She also pointed us in new directions as she envisioned an updated version of *The Black Woman,* which would include position papers from the Women's Caucus of the Student Nonviolent Coordinating Committee (SNCC), the Women's Caucus of the Black Panthers, and the Third World Women's Alliance; there would also be writings from "the campus forces, the prison forces, tenants' groups, and most especially from southern rural women's voices, particularly from the migrant workers and sharecroppers of the Deep South". Clearly, her vision of women's studies was sensitive to class; she was also aware of the perils of exclusion and warned against the marginalization of women whom she knew were critical to an understanding of the female condition and the history of women organizing.

While completing *Sturdy Black Bridges* in 1973, I taught my first women's studies course, Images of Women in Literature; four years later I taught Images of Women in the Media before I started the doctoral program at Emory. These two courses were the first women's studies courses in the English department, and they remained in the Spelman curriculum (though they are now taught by other professors in the English department), as electives for the women's studies minor, which began in 1981, and the comparative women's studies major, which was approved in 1997. I also taught two mini-courses in the English department on a trial basis in the 1970s—Black Women Novelists and Black Women's Autobiographies—as alternatives to the two-semester world literature course that all sophomores were required to take. I was motivated in large part by my desire to teach about an important black female literary tradition that was missing from the mainstream literary canon. Designing and teaching these four courses were also critical to the introduction of women's studies into the Spelman curriculum.

I am reminded that bell hooks first taught Black Women in America in the 1970s in what she describes as an emerging, progressive black studies program because women's studies was not interested in the course. Having written the first draft of *Ain't I a Woman* while she was an undergraduate at Stanford University and a "fiery initiate into radical feminist politics," this ground-breaking black feminist text emerged because of her frustration with women's studies courses "in which Black women were never mentioned."[9] Assessing the impact of foundational texts, such as *The Black Woman; The Afro-American Woman: Struggles and Images; Sturdy Black Bridges; Black Macho and the Myth of the Superwoman; All the Women Are White, All the Blacks Are Men, But Some of Us Are Brave: Black Women's Studies* (and I would include hooks's *Ain't I a Woman* and *Feminist Theory: From Margin to Center,* 1984), hooks assesses the importance of the work of black feminist scholars to the evolution of women's studies as a field:

> Our collective work, though different in perspective and content, made it possible for individuals active in the feminist movement to demand that women's studies courses acknowledge that they claimed to be talking and teaching about women, when the actual subjects of study were white women. Thus this was an important breakthrough which has had and continues to have a profound impact on the feminist movement and feminist scholarship in the United States.[10]

In 1976, while still teaching at Spelman, completing *Sturdy Black Bridges* and pursuing the doctorate at Emory, my life was altered in significant ways because of a trip to New England. Judy Gebre-Hiwet and I, both of us from Spelman's English department, traveled to the Boston area to examine several women's studies programs that were in an embryonic state at this juncture. This trip became a major turning point in my own professional development. Most of the women with whom we met were African American. Among this group was Barbara Smith, coeditor of *But Some of Us Are Brave* (1982), who was teaching literature at Emerson College. I had met Barbara at the 1974 Modern Language Association convention in New York City, where I learned that she was the first black woman appointed to the MLA Commission on the Status of Women in the Profession, which was very involved in the development of women's studies in the academy. A small group of black women literature professors, among whom were Nellie McKay, Hortense Spillers, and Gloria Hull, also attended MLA conventions and commission meetings. Barbara Smith was instrumental in organizing two sessions on black women writers at the 1975 meeting in San Francisco. While we visited her at Emerson College, Smith shared with us her course syllabi, as well as Alice Walker's course syllabus for Black Women Writers, which she had taught at Wellesley College in the early 1970s. I didn't know it at the time, but it now seems clear that Walker had designed and taught the first course in the academy on black women writers. A little-known fact is that Toni Cade Bambara, in her capacity as a visiting professor at Spelman during the mid-1970s, attempted to teach a course called Black Women Writers but was prohibited from doing so by the English department. Not to be deterred, however, Toni offered the course at her home: students took the course for no credit! In our reconstruction of the history of women's studies, we must include the pioneering work and vision of Alice Walker (and Toni Cade Bambara), who initiated courses that have become staples within women's studies and many English departments. Walker's course syllabus certainly influenced my own thinking about the literary canon and the possibilities for curriculum reform within English departments.

Unlike most feminist women of color committed, from the beginning, to women's studies and its transformation, I have been located at black colleges throughout my teaching career, except for part-time teaching for Emory's women's studies program. However, because of the traditional nature of Spelman College, where I've done my most important work, it was not easy in those early years to advance a black feminist educational agenda. For example, despite the intent of several black women faculty in the 1970s to start a Women's Research and Resource Center, we were "allowed" to write a proposal for the establishment of a center only after the male president learned about the possibility that such a center might be established at nearby Atlanta University. At that time, whatever the president's views on the curriculum were, they prevailed. Ironically, therefore, the tiny group of black women on the campus who were committed to "feminizing" the Spelman environment benefited, in this particular case, from an empowered black male. At the same time, at his direction, the English department eliminated the alternative mini-courses (among which were my two courses on black women writers) for world literature. Had he been opposed to the Women's Research and Resource Center, it would have been almost impossible to prevail, no matter how intellectually sound our arguments. When there was a brief discussion and vote within the Humanities Division about the approval of the women's studies minor in 1982, it was ironic that two white female faculty voted against it. There was no black male opposition. There were also, during this early period, at least two feminist white women committed to women's studies (one a philosopher and the other a sociologist), who were always allies with black women faculty. We also experienced some indifference and mild suspicion from a few black women.[11]

Despite a few skirmishes, I felt that I was, in the final analysis, left alone to do the work of establishing women's studies at Spelman. I was assisted in the early years mainly by my friend and departmental colleague Jacqueline Jones Royster, who became a founding member of the SAGE editorial group (which also included founding coeditor Patricia Bell-Scott, Janet Sims Wood, and Miriam DeCosta-Willis). In the 1980s the Spelman group expanded to include Professors Gloria Wade-Gayles and Mona Phillips, Provost Barbara Carter, and, after 1987, President Johnnetta B. Cole, and Provost Ruth Simmons, who is now president of Smith College, and, finally, a Women's Studies Steering Committee. My off-campus support network in the early years—a righteous band of feminists of color, mostly black women, and white feminists—was too large to delineate, but without them, my work at Spelman would have been nearly impossible.

After thirty years of involvement with women's studies and eighteen years directing Spelman's women's studies program, I am as committed to the field and its continued transformation as I was when I took my first women's studies course as a doctoral student at Emory University in 1976 with Professor Darlene Roth. I continue to engage in interdisciplinary feminist scholarship, mostly now about the history of black feminisms, and expect to complete a biography of Anna Julia Cooper before I retire. For many reasons, including the presence of a women's center and women's studies, Spelman is not the institution it was when I left at age nineteen in 1966 or returned in 1971 to teach English and world literature. Perhaps more important, I am as passionate about teaching women's studies as I was when I taught my first women's studies course, Images of Women in Literature, in 1973 in a department in which I recall having read only a few women writers as an undergraduate English major. I am also still convinced that teaching antiracist, cross-cultural women's studies courses to undergraduates is still the most important and fulfilling work that I do. Perhaps it is even the most radical work in which I am still engaged.

PART V

Building
Women's Studies
Programs

No Easy Task

Anywhere

Marilyn Jacoby Boxer

B orn in Kansas City, Missouri, I attended Wellesley College but completed my education in California, receiving my bachelor's degree—with three children in attendance—at the University of Redlands and my Ph.D. in history at the University of California, Riverside. Commencing doctoral studies concurrently with the revival of feminism in 1970, I wrote a dissertation on the relationship between French socialism and feminism in the formative period of both sociopolitical movements, began teaching women's history in 1971, and chaired the nation's first women's studies program at San Diego State University from 1974 to 1980. I later became dean of the College of Arts and Letters there; this was followed by seven years as academic vice president at San Francisco State University (SFSU). I am currently an affiliated scholar at Stanford University's Institute for Research on Women and Gender and teach modern European history at SFSU. I am author, coauthor, or coeditor of books on socialism and feminism in European history, on European women in modern history, and on the development of women's studies in U.S. higher education, including *When Women Ask the Questions: Creating Women's Studies in America* (1998).

Modern Woman Not Lost

Shall I start with the shock of hearing the word *pregnant* spoken aloud by my uncle's new wife when I was fifteen, or, twenty-five years later, the equally surprising proclamation "I am a feminist," which I overheard at a student party before guests of both sexes? Can any who are younger than my generation appreciate the importance to the birth of women's studies of the repressive environment that surrounded the women who grew up in the United States in the 1930s and 1940s—the G.I.'s sisters? Also their wives and ex-wives? We were, I believe, the first generation of U.S. women educated through high school and college alongside those boys. Raised by mothers who voted, we were encouraged by "coeducation" to expect equal opportunities; then we were sent home to produce the baby boom and fancy Jell-O molds. We also helped to create women's studies.

It was not maternalism that brought us to women's studies, however, but a drive to recreate ourselves. When I was preparing my first women's history courses in the early 1970s, I was surprised to find data that showed higher percentages of women in selected European countries occupying positions as doctors, dentists, lawyers, and even—in the U.S.S.R—engineering than in the United States. Only later, aided by the new feminist history, did I learn to appreciate the importance of generational analysis, and realize that the dismal figures for our country's women in my generation reflected the success of our brothers, with government subsidy, in achieving upward mobility.

Meanwhile, "modern women," we read, had lost their way. Described in a popular postwar book, *Modern Women: The Lost Sex*, as "a problem to themselves, to their children and families, to each other, to society as a whole," women had forfeited their traditional roles in the home to transformations wrought by the Industrial Revolution. We had, moreover, been seduced by the women's movement. Like Mary Wollstonecraft, we were said to suffer from "penis envy," and to reject our assigned role as the "second sex."

For the experts who at midcentury dominated education, social work, psychology, medicine, and the professoriat, women's woes were not caused by an unequal, unjust distribution of power, but by personal flaws. Virtually everything I read in contemporary literature, from Freud to Hemingway, reinforced the view that women were secondary to men, intended to serve their interests. More interested in books than babies, I believed that I was a neurotic freak. Nevertheless—or perhaps because of this ideology—by the beginning of the 1950s, I was a pregnant teenager; by the mid-1960s I was in my second marriage and a mother of three, living in suburban comfort. I had many of the makings of a June Cleaver. But I also had an interrupted education, including some years at a women's college; and I had a great unfulfilled capacity for learning and for acting in the world. Daring to apply to myself the then-popular concept of self-actualization, I put myself into a double bind: bad if I did, bad if I didn't, seek to fulfill my needs.

Simone de Beauvoir, whose *Second Sex* I had read in the mid-1950s, helped me keep my intellectual flame aglow through these years. She had demonstrated to me that a woman's mind is capable of sustained, serious work in history and philosophy. A decade later, Betty Friedan also spoke to me with her best-selling book. I had returned to college to complete a bachelor's degree a year after *The Feminine Mystique* appeared, the same year that my youngest child entered first grade and freed me for enough hours to permit me to undertake full-time study, which was then required by most colleges. It was 1964; the term *re-entry woman,* (later *non-traditional student*) had not yet appeared. I had to meet with a dean to plead my case for (re)admittance as an undergraduate at the advanced age of thirty-four.

Fast forward six years. Happily for me, one serendipitous effect of my not starting doctoral studies until 1970 was that I caught a swelling wave of feminism. As I was recently divorced, my financial situation was precarious, but I benefited from the opportunity to select a field of study of interest and relevance to my current life. Among the limited choices of advisers I had at the small, nearby research university I decided to attend (so as not to dislocate my children) was one who worked on French socialism. Having heard discussion of dialectics at one of the first women's liberation group meetings I had attended, I chose socialist history instead of agricultural economic history (suggested by another potential adviser) and soon placed over my desk two large signs that reflected my situation. One, borrowed from Marx, read, "I refuse to let bourgeois society turn me into a money-making machine." The other, of my own invention, stated, "You can borrow money but you can't borrow time."

The first question asked of me two years later during my Ph.D. oral exam was, "What is Marx's concept of alienation?" Perhaps every survivor of a doctoral program remembers the opening words of that decisive event. For me, however, it held special meaning because of the circumstances that brought me to the examination room. Five years after attaining my long-delayed bachelor's degree, and one month after attaining tenure as a high school teacher, already forty and a single mother of three, I had great unmet intellectual needs. Rather than settle for the life that my early motherhood prefigured, I quit my job and returned to school. I believe that in this regard I exemplified the "founding mothers" of women's studies. We created women's studies, and it flourished beyond our dreams, because it offered (and offers) a means to fulfill a great need through the pursuit of nonalienated labor. Research and teaching in women's studies connects the work of our minds to the rest of our lives.

It has been commonplace since the 1960s to note the importance of linking learning to (the rest of) life. *Relevance* as a term of description for curricular content designed to attract students has been advocated, mocked, trivialized, and ignored—but it has not ceased to be effective. I have learned much from men and women of all times and types. But I have also failed to learn when the questions addressed, whether by dead authors or living teachers, ignored the realities of my life; and some of those omissions damaged me. Sometimes, when I was permitted myself to ask questions of my own devising, I inchoately invented my own "women's studies." In 1964, as an undergraduate history major, I found my way to an original copy of Mercy Otis Warren's three-volume history of the American Revolution, and wrote about her life. In 1966, as a master's degree student, I researched the origins and effects of a 1920s experiment in federal child and maternal health care, termed the Sheppard-Towner Act. I did women's studies before it existed, and I suspect that many other mothers of women's studies did likewise. Women's studies was germinating in the lives we often partially educated, intellectual women had lived for half a century before 1970.

I paid only peripheral attention to the developing women's movement until 1970, when Kate Millett's appearance on the cover of *Time* magazine alongside the words "Sexual Politics" sparked the transformation of my consciousness. It also created a new channel directed toward action—the intellectual action that became women's studies. I promptly bought and read Millett's book, all the while revisiting years of painful experience as a subject subordinated because of my sex. While living as a girl, woman, wife, mother, divorcée, undereducated worker in numerous jobs (paper cutter, supply clerk, waitress, engineer's assistant), student, and teacher, it had never occurred to me that it was men, posing the questions about women as well as virtually everything else, and providing the answers, who had determined my understanding of myself in the world. I had not noticed that, from early on, I had read as a boy, later as a man; that I had identified with male heroes, not their female subordinates—yet had laid on myself the burdens the authors placed on the women they created. Kate Millett's selections, mostly from literature I had already read, made this clear.

I would call 1970 the first year of my self-definition. When I heard about a regional meeting of the National Organization for Women (NOW), which was being held in Los Angeles, I traveled there with a small group to attend my first-ever organized feminist gathering. I was impressed by several things: the large number in attendance (probably four hundred to five hundred), which showed me that I was not alone in my dissatisfaction; the apparent diversity among the presumed feminists present in class interest and style; and the audacity, previously unimaginable to me, displayed by the group when it prohibited a male photographer from covering the proceedings.

At that meeting I collected from display tables a number of the early writings that became classics of the era, including an eighty-cent pamphlet copy called *Our Bodies, Ourselves.* I heard presentations about lawsuits waged, often successfully, for equal employment opportunities and against unequal application of laws in matters ranging from education to prostitution. The most important lesson I learned in 1970 was that women constituted a group or class or collectivity of some sort, to which I belonged, and that we were worthy of our own attention and of assertive action on our behalf.

In the fall of 1970 I started doctoral studies. My first course as a "women's studies" instructor was called Women in History and offered in 1971 under the rubric of Interdisciplinary Studies at San Bernardino Valley College, where I taught part-time while also serving as a teaching assistant at the University of California, Riverside (UCR). This course stretched a syllabus across the centuries, from Hesiod's *Theogony* and the Hebrew Bible (from which I photocopied excerpts) to the contemporary women's liberation movement (which appeared in selections from my NOW meeting acquisitions). Having written a seminar paper called "Marxian Socialism and the Woman Question," I also included readings from Bebel's *Woman under Socialism;* among them some pages in which he quoted the church fathers on the evils of womankind as well as discussed his hopes for a socialist solution to the oppression of both women and workers. I was intrigued enough by the socialist fathers that I went off to Europe in 1972 to spend fifteen months researching the relationship between socialism and feminism in France during the formative years of both sociopolitical movements.

During the academic year 1973–74 I began to write about my findings—results that rendered me a confirmed feminist and a skeptic about socialism. I also taught seminars to first-year students at UCR on Emma Goldman and Rosa Luxemburg. In 1974 I was hired to teach women's history at San Diego State University (SDSU). Too ignorant of university structures, and too deeply indebted and needy of employment, even to question the institutional location of the one-year lectureship I had happily accepted, I found myself, surprisingly, appointed not to the history department but to the women's studies program. More than that, soon after taking up my new position as its chair—a position offered by telephone as an additional duty at a time when I could only accept—I learned that the program was notorious, embattled both on campus and off. In 1973 a group from the San Diego program had played a central role in the conflict that tore apart a women's studies conference in Sacramento. Program faculty had likewise engaged in confrontations with students and other faculty in our university halls.

While I had been reading in the socialist and feminist archives of Amsterdam and Paris, women's studies at SDSU had undergone tumultuous change. Instituted in 1970 as the first integrated program of women's studies in the United States, the SDSU program in its first four years had suffered almost continual conflict, internal and external, surviving ultimately both the mass resignation of its faculty in the face of a new dean's demand for regularized personnel proceedings, and a recent vote by the administration on whether to terminate its existence or to try again. Unbeknownst to me, I had been hired, along with one other full-time and several part-time lecturers, as the "try-again" crew. I later learned that I had been a third-choice candidate for the job. Others had turned it down, at least partially because of the university's commitment of minimal, tentative resources to the program.

What was to be done? The first thing that I did on my first day on the job was to order pencils and paper. The only tangible goods remaining from the original program was one small box containing copies of a few documents from past campus proceedings and clippings from newspapers about the previous faculty's exit. I also began that day to hear stories, from faculty, staff, students, and community activists, about the program's strife-filled history. I began to worry about possible confrontations ahead. But nothing bad happened; the worst moment was probably when someone, knowing—as I had not—about the previous faculty's fight with the administration, asked me—a scholar of the French working-class movement—if I felt "like a scab." Ignorance had protected me.

As chair of the program, I was also the only full-time faculty member often present at the university. Not only was I responsible for all the student-related, curricular, personnel, financial, and other activities of an academic program, I was the focus of all the questions that anyone, on campus or off, might ask about women, any women, from any disciplinary perspective. That first year I talked to everyone I could engage, in committee meetings, faculty offices, or the lunchroom; and I read everything I could find on women in fields that included language and literature, political theory, philosophy, religious studies, anthropology, economics, sexuality, and sociology. Thanks to my colleagues and students, I discovered Ti-Grace Atkinson, Jessie Bernard, Ester Boserup, Shulamith Firestone, Zora Neale Hurston, Jill Johnston, Joyce Ladner, Eleanor Maccoby, Jean Baker Miller, Tillie Olsen, Sylvia Plath, Adrienne Rich, Michelle Rosaldo, Barbara Smith, Tish Sommers, Alice Walker, and many others. In 1975 *Signs* first appeared, and I soon furthered my education in feminist scholarship across the disciplines through its review essays. History I shelved until summer, when I intended to finish my dissertation.

As I read the new scholarship, I enjoyed a kind of re-education, escaping the socialization of my generation to meet women of different ages, places, races, and cultures. I also had a women's studies program to represent and to rebuild. Five principles controlled my approach to this task. First, I brought to SDSU from UCR some knowledge about other new programs that had been instituted to conduct and convey scholarship of a nontraditional, politically sensitive nature. Before moving to San Diego, I had asked Carlos Cortes, then professor of Latin American history and chair of Chicano studies at the Riverside campus, for advice. Carlos had recently conducted a study of the Mexican-American/Chicano studies programs founded in the 1960s and early 1970s. His survey showed that only those programs integrated into the academic structures of their universities had survived the founding years. His message was clear. As a personal survivor, I would not forget this lesson in professional persistence.

Personal advice also accounts for a second important lesson I tried to apply in women's studies and throughout my administrative career, sometimes to my own detriment if counted in friends or factions won and lost. This came from Joyce Appleby, then serving as associate dean of the College of Arts and Letters, where women's studies was located at SDSU. Joyce was on the committee that hired me, and she served as my mentor in academic administration. The day I started my new job as program chair, Joyce cautioned me to "avoid cronyism." I learned from her the importance of separating—for some purposes—personal relationships and professional needs. This is a tough and complex issue in women's studies, one of whose strengths is integrating personal and professional interests. But this awareness helped me to make difficult decisions in favor of what seemed to me the larger, longer-run welfare of women's studies (and later in my career, other programs).

A third principle that I applied came to me by way of doctoral research. Again and again, as I had followed my dissertation subjects' development through late nineteenth- and early twentieth-century politics, I encountered the gap between their ideology and their practice. The hypocrisy of the socialists of the Second International as they reneged on pledges about war, religion, women's rights, and other issues prepared me to observe myself and faculty colleagues, feminist and nonfeminist alike, critically. Sometimes this awareness has helped me to resist rhetoric and moral judgment in favor of a more realistic assessment and potentially more productive resolution of a problem. It has, on occasion, bolstered my backbone.

At other times, the conflict between ideal and real has led me to accept mixed motives. Inclined to pragmatism, perhaps by my origins in middle-class Missouri (the "show-me" state), perhaps by my early initiation into motherhood, I was clear in my own mind that first year that women's studies at SDSU had to prosper under my leadership, because I needed the job for two years. This was my fourth concern: my younger son, then a sixteen-year-old high school junior, had just started in his fourth high school, and I wanted desperately not to uproot him again before he graduated. Along with family cares, I had many constituencies to satisfy: students, women's studies colleagues, other faculty, administrators, and community feminists, including, in several of these categories, some people associated with the earlier program who now came to look us over. I set aside my dissertation and prospects as a historian in favor of motherhood and women's studies.

But finally, notwithstanding the importance of all these concerns, the fifth principle underlying my work in women's studies has always been my desire to be a scholar. I have always asserted with absolute conviction my belief in the integrity of academic feminism, because I am both feminist and scholar. I never doubted the validity of the movement toward feminist scholarship. Although I have questioned some work done in its name, it has been the lapse in realization rather than intention that I have criticized. Unfortunately, in the case of women's studies, critics sometimes impute flaws to the feminism rather than the scholarship. Every field suffers its imperfections. In my years as department chair, dean, and academic vice president, I gained good grounds for this argument.

The validity of women's studies as a field of scholarship began early and, of course, persists today, although it is still denied by some opponents of change. (Perhaps the only question from the beginning that one hears no longer is, "Is there enough material for a whole course?") The first day on the job, in August 1974, I was asked, "Where are the men's studies?" Even friends on the faculty, people sympathetic to feminism whose goodwill greeted the new women's studies lecturers and whose support grew as we demonstrated our scholarly credentials and ambitions, did not yet recognize that bias pervaded *their* fields as well. A myth of objectivity, of curricular neutrality, was pervasive. Similarly, many held a belief in disciplinary purity that made women's studies, with its multiple approaches, appear unfit for membership in the academic club. Two incidents from the mid- to late 1970s exemplify the opposition based on these false assumptions about the nature of academic pursuits.

Between fall semester 1974 and spring semester 1975, even as we revised the curriculum to strengthen academic content and course requirements, and the overall level of grades awarded dropped (in itself in some eyes a measure of increased academic rigor), enrollment in women's studies at SDSU rose 40 percent. As these increases continued, a college dean, pressed to compensate for drastic declines in other areas of the humanities and social sciences, invested greater resources in women's studies, and we rapidly grew in size. Faculty positions that numbered 2.4 in 1974 became 8.1 (including seven tenure lines) by spring term 1980. Enrollment increased by 300 percent. Dominated numerically by majors in business, psychology, and liberal studies (preteaching), our students constituted a cross section of the female student body (perhaps ten percent were male); but a striking number were older, returning students not altogether unlike ourselves in their intellectual quest. Like us, they were eager to read everything, to ask all the questions never before broached.

From the beginning, the students who flocked to our courses complained that they could count their hard-earned women's studies units only for elective credit. Why couldn't they use women's studies courses to fulfill requirements in a major when the coursework matched their field? Why didn't women's studies count for general education (GE) requirements? In response to their concerns, we naïvely assumed that it would be easy to gain admittance to this broadly inclusive enterprise. Instead, we ended up in deep intellectual debate on the floor of the university senate, a debate we won by using the master's tools effectively.

The collaborative ethos of women's studies may well reflect pragmatic as much as philosophical considerations. We had proposed a course, Sexism and the Social Sciences, to satisfy a criterion of breadth; the course engaged all of us, and we made certain that it met all other criteria as well. However, after gaining committee approval, which usually brought automatic passage by the whole senate, our course was challenged on grounds of bias. The leading adversary was an influential, long-time faculty leader from the anthropology department. Contending that our course did not constitute an introduction to a discipline, as did similar GE courses, but was merely a critique of disciplines from one perspective, he distinguished between his field, with its "objective" lens on various societies, and ours, with its "biased" approach. Drawing on a store of knowledge about nineteenth-century social science with its mission to repair social class strife, and early twentieth-century anthropology with its commitment to demonstrate cultural relativism, a feminist analysis easily demonstrated that our critic stood on fault-ridden ground. Our course was approved (unanimously save one), and others soon followed. By the end of 1977–78, the GE program included eight women's studies courses.

Next, we set out to support a student who asked for approval of an individualized, interdisciplinary major that included women's studies along with literature and dance. Her petition was denied, on grounds that women's studies was already multidisciplinary and hence unsuitable as part of a major that was intended to combine three disciplines. We overcame this challenge by showing change throughout time, the fluidity of disciplinary definitions, and the confusion between *discipline* and *department* in the university lexicon. If students could include such truly multidisciplinary or interdisciplinary fields as anthropology, classics, and religious studies (each of which had for some years constituted a department) in our university in an individualized, interdisciplinary major, then why not women's studies? This battle, too, we won.

We learned in those years that arbitrary distinctions and conventional practices often governed academic policies and university procedures. We learned to deploy the master's tools to gain our ends. But we also invented new tools. We created an ethos of what David Damrosch (in *We Scholars: Changing the Culture of the University*) calls "intellectual sociability," which enabled us, despite our separate institutional locations, to avoid isolation. Women's studies at SDSU was, and to a large degree still is, different from most women's studies programs. Established originally with 1.5 faculty lines allocated by a dean exclusively for the use of women's studies, a course rubric of its own, a small operating budget (supplemented the first year by a one-time foundation grant), faculty and program offices, and a part-time clerical staff, its chair reported directly to a college dean (after an initial experiment in university-level reporting). When I assumed the chair's role in 1974, freshly catapulted out of graduate school (still ABD), I became a member of the dean's council. Only yesterday a student, I found myself endowed with voting power, if not institutional presence, equal to the chairs of the School of Literature and the Department of History.

Thanks to a feminist-oriented dean, grateful that unlike our immediate predecessors we newly minted 1974 faculty answered his memos, met his deadlines, and engaged in neither anti-institutional resistance nor intersororal conflict—and thanks to the burgeoning enrollments we produced—the program enjoyed remarkable growth. This was not a period of overall expansion in college resources: we absorbed faculty budget lines taken from departments with shrinking enrollments. We ourselves became a department in name as well as practice thanks to my audacity and the dean's complicity. One day when we were running short on letterhead, I simply asked our secretary to order new stationery inscribed "Department of Women's Studies." I formally asked the dean to "regularize" our anomalous status in my annual report for the 1976–77 academic year; the following year, when we went public under the new name, he supported us against the one small protest that our action elicited.

The situation and structure provided perfectly the potential for women's studies at SDSU to become the feminist ghetto of dire prediction. That this did not happen reflects, I believe, two factors. One is the supportive role of the faculty advisory committee that was constituted to fulfill for women's studies the personnel functions reserved by university policy to tenured faculty. It met infrequently but its members stood ready to provide counsel if requested and to promote our work among their peers. This carefully chosen group of sympathetic, well-regarded senior women was dissolved in 1980 when women's studies had achieved tenure for three of our own. Secondly, there is the philosophy we adopted. Desiring to avoid the problems that had beset our forerunners, we endeavored to become an integral part of the academic structure of the college and university; and we chose, as we grew, to hire people with diverse approaches to feminist education. Within four years we had among our full-time faculty women with liberal, radical, socialist, and lesbian feminist perspectives. We recruited women of color from the African American studies and American Indian studies faculty to teach women's studies courses in 1976 and 1979, although ethnic diversity on the tenure track came only in the 1980s.

Along with breadth in our faculty and curriculum, we sought open lines of communication with all factions among community activists. Following our individual predilections, we became involved in a wide spectrum of feminist groups in San Diego. Reaching out similarly on campus, within a few years our faculty served on, and sometimes chaired, major committees throughout the college and university, sometimes through administrative appointment, sometimes through election by faculty peers. All this, of course, constituted activity supplemental to running our own department. It came to be expected that each faculty member would serve at all levels. The benefits were clear: we got to know "them" (and learn how things really worked), and they got to know us (and appreciate our abilities and contributions). Furthermore, we gained the opportunity to influence the institution.

In addition to intellectual sociability, we brought to the university— before it became fashionable—a new emphasis on interdisciplinarity.

There is probably some linkage between these tendencies, for disciplinarity, in its common departmental guise, tends toward what Damrosch identifies as a kind of "nationalism," encouraging separation, even "aggression," on the part of one department vis-à-vis other curricular units. This grows out of and in turn perpetuates, in Damrosch's view, an academic culture that selects, at the graduate school level, for people predisposed to solitary intellectual endeavor.

We were different. We talked with one another, across the disciplinary lines of our individual training. We learned from one another what other fields had to say about our own topics of interest, often developing ideas for enriching our teaching and occasionally for collaborative scholarly projects. We lectured in one another's classrooms and widened our bibliographic knowledge. Some of us sought close ties with colleagues in the campus departments where, in most other institutional settings, our own appointments would lie. (Despite a fierce loyalty to the goals of women's studies, some of us even admitted to one another our regret at not having at least a joint appointment.) We tried, repeatedly throughout the years, to cross-list our courses for credit in other departments; even where they were willing, we were stopped by a bureaucratic ruling against this practice, which in most institutions undergirds the cross-departmental structure of the women's studies program. Our reaching out was not essential to our survival, for we were protected by our independent status, which ensured that we were appointed, evaluated, and tenured or terminated, based entirely on our teaching, scholarship, and service in women's studies.

Like others in women's studies, we wanted to do more than survive: we wanted to transform the academy. Through continuous service outside the department, we took our work to many other places. We also sponsored a broadly conceived weekly lecture series, in which other faculty were invited to share their work. We constantly invited them to academic feminist events. Although too busy running a department to undertake formal "mainstreaming" projects, we spread feminist thought across campus.

As first I, and then two others of us, moved from departmental to college leadership, becoming dean or associate dean of the college, we applied our predilection for interdisciplinarity to a larger canvas. New academic programs we inspired included an interdisciplinary graduate liberal arts degree program; an undergraduate degree program in international business that required extensive cultural studies; an experimental teaching credential; and annual, college-sponsored seminars in which faculty from across the university worked with a visiting scholar on issues of race, gender, sexuality, or class. Women's studies faculty now collaborate across department lines in border studies, gay and lesbian studies, and service learning. They provide graduate courses for other departments, consult on their hiring decisions, and occasionally also teach their courses in other departments. Faculty from other departments sometimes teach in women's studies. Through myriad associations in teaching, scholarship, and service to the university and community, women's studies faculty demonstrate that feminist education constitutes "connected learning."

The case of women's studies at SDSU is extraordinary. It is, I suspect, impossible to sort out the factors of institutional structure and history, feminist commitment, political trends, psychological tendencies, personal ambitions, and considerations of self-preservation, in determining outcomes. My own contribution, I think, lay in the catholicity of my interests and breadth of my perspective as a historian and woman who has lived many female roles. I believe that women's studies belongs everywhere, as an integral part of the academy. Women's studies, in my view, constitutes an effort to devote women's intellect, infused variously with anger, compassion, and wisdom, to improving the world. The questions that women's studies asks grow out of women's lives in their own times. Initially, they were heavily weighted toward the concerns of a particular generation seeking a kind of redemption from our personal history. Through time they have come to encompass the interests of a larger, more diverse group of seekers of knowledge. But the answers offer new meanings and, I believe, hope, to all.

Personally, recognizing that Bonnie Zimmerman, whom we hired at SDSU in 1978, was born only three years before my daughter, I feel more like a grandmother than a mother of women's studies. My thoughts of grandparenthood are stimulated as well by an analogy that comes to mind between my granddaughter, born in August 1996 at a very fragile three pounds, five ounces, and women's studies: they both began very small and brought into my life mingled joy and fear for their future, but mostly a desire to see them survive and grow to their full potential in the world. Jenny, eighteen months as I write, now weighs in at more than twenty-three pounds, walks, talks, and is fiercely independent. I dedicate this essay to her.

Elizabeth
Lapovsky Kennedy

I am currently professor and head of the Women's Studies Department at the University of Arizona. I began this position in July 1998, after having been an active participant in the women's studies program and American studies department at the State University of New York, Buffalo, for twenty-nine years. I feel very privileged to have survived those years with enough energy and creativity to still be an active contributor to women's studies. I was born in Brooklyn, New York, to a Russian-Jewish family in 1939. Thanks to my parents, I had a protected childhood and a good education. For the longest time I have dreamed of a socially just world, where all humans treat one another with dignity, and have tried to live according to that dream, while working toward it.

I was trained as a social anthropologist at the University of Cambridge in England and did two years of fieldwork with the Waunan in Colombia, South America. Throughout the past thirty years, I have worked to build the field of women's studies and coauthored, with Ellen Carol DuBois, Gail Paradise Kelly, Carolyn W. Korsmeyer, and Lillian S. Robinson, *Feminist Scholarship: Kindling in the Groves of Academe* (University of Illinois Press, 1985). I have pioneered the study of lesbian history, writing *Boots of Leather, Slippers of Gold: The History of a Lesbian Community* (New York: Routledge, Chapman and Hall, 1993) (with Madeline Davis) and numerous articles. I also am a committed teacher and activist. I'm searching for the magic that will let me do all this, and still have time for my family and friends, my beloved Bobbi, and my dog, Sachi, not to mention traveling, walking in the country, gardening, cooking, and whatever else strikes my fancy and ambition.

Dreams of Social Justice
Building Women's Studies at the
State University of New York, Buffalo

The women's studies program at SUNY, Buffalo, as one of the first programs in the country, pioneered the direction and shape of the field. The founders were guided by a passionate concern to learn about women's history and culture and to improve conditions for women in the university and the world. The university administration, like most, was not welcoming. It reviewed the program five times between 1972 and 1978, a pattern that suggests not only hostility but systematic harassment.[1] In 1969 the initiative for women's studies, therefore, did not come from the top, but rather from a powerful social movement. The collective energy and intellectual prowess of a large number of activists—primarily students but also some faculty—burst onto campus, building a home for women's studies in whatever units were the most friendly and then producing the substantial research, courses, and arguments that validated its existence.

Women's studies not only changed the university, it changed my life. I was challenged by the new concepts that illuminated women's lives, promising gender equality. I was excited by the opportunity to create for women students a better educational experience than my own. I was supported for the first time in my life by a community whose interests were similar to mine. From being a shy and modest junior faculty member, who could barely believe that I had found a job, I became a leader of an educational movement. This history of women's studies in the 1970s is, therefore, a complex story, interweaving the hard daily work of institution building, the magic of individual growth and transformation, the subtlety of intellectual discovery, and the defiance of a grass-roots movement for change.

In 1969 I had minimal feminist consciousness. Some women comrades in England had tried to discuss Betty Friedan's book, *The Feminine*

Mystique, and other more radical treatises with me, but I was not sympathetic. I thought that women had choices: if they were not happy, it was their own fault. I had acted to maximize my choices, and expected others to do the same. I had a stubborn and proud side that led me to insist on taking shop instead of home economics in high school. With the support of my parents I won this right for myself, but not for all women students. Throughout college and graduate school, I never openly challenged sexism, except to endure and gain my degree. The idea that women's choices were more limited than men's was beyond me. I was oblivious to the pain that discrimination caused, and the emotional scars it left, and I had no sense of my connection to other women.

With this individualist yet rebellious consciousness, I could not have initiated women's studies, but I was ripe for being organized by graduate students to see its importance. In the fall of 1969, at an antiwar meeting, a colleague from the history department, Tom Rainey, asked me to be the faculty sponsor for an experimental course that graduate students were designing called Women in Contemporary Society. At first I turned him down, but curiosity and collegiality finally led me to agree to attend their meetings.

The meetings transformed my life. This group of graduate students, about thirty women and one man, were committed to social movements for change.[2] Some members were sectarian leftists, some were independent leftists, and some had already become part of the independent women's movement. Most were strong on socialist analyses of women's oppression, placing women's oppression in the context of class society and capitalism. But some had also begun to look at patriarchy or male supremacy and the cultural determinants of women's oppression. Although I'm sure that the tensions among the different tendencies were high, they didn't make a lasting impression on me. I was busy learning from everyone about woman's place in society.[3] For me, participating in the weekly meetings of this group was a consciousness-raising experience. Problems that I had faced and dismissed as rooted in individual character suddenly were illuminated as social patterns. In a flash I understood that I had not caused the hostility directed toward me in graduate school and that my unpleasant experiences were part of the same problem that caused few women to achieve the rank of full professor. The analysis also helped to illuminate some of the dynamics in my marriage such as the endless struggles about housework. I firmly backed the course and slowly joined the women's liberation movement in Buffalo.

The course was a tremendous success. It had approximately fifteen sections of about twenty undergraduate students each. Each section followed more or less the same syllabus, and the instructors met once a week to discuss how their classes were going and to support one another in this ground-breaking endeavor. I don't remember the course encountering any particular university hostility; by definition, it was an experimental course, and therefore not scrutinized carefully. But more important, there was so much radical activity on campus that semester that it would have been hard for the administration to single out this one course—its method or content—for disapproval. For example, at the same time that I was the faculty sponsor for this course on women in contemporary society, I was also the faculty supervisor, along with two others, Charles Haynie and Chip Planck, of a large course, Social Change in America, which consisted of thirty-three autonomous sections, each with its own critique of United States society.[4]

The excitement of that semester is hard to convey today, thirty years later, when the university has become committed to mimicking corporate commercial culture. In spring 1970, when the United States invaded Cambodia, universities around the country had massive anti-war rallies on campus, and Buffalo was no exception. The campus was shut down in May 1970 due to police occupation. As I went through my papers for this period, the thing that impressed me the most was the volume of different kinds of activities, the multitudes of concerns: meetings with a delegation of women from South Vietnam, meetings about support of the Black Panthers, demonstrations against the war in Southeast Asia, meetings to establish a child-care center. Campus activists were making connections among various forms of social and political oppression. Learning was connected to activism, to building a movement for change, to challenging the state. Most important, faculty, students, staff, and community members had the idea that their action would make a difference. This liberating atmosphere shaped the activist and scholar I was to become.

From its beginnings as a high-energy, innovative course in the spring of 1970, women's studies at SUNY, Buffalo, hurtled into the future. In a remarkably short period of time, women's studies was established. At first it was not difficult to find homes for our innovative work in the small progressive pockets of the university. We moved the successful experimental course into American studies, my home department, thereby beginning what was to become a long and fruitful institutional connection between American studies and feminist scholarship. The women graduate students and I developed the Women's Caucus in American studies, which evolved into the women's studies component, paralleling the newly formed Native American studies and Puerto Rican studies components. Together we forged an extraordinary governance model for American studies that assumed both autonomy and cooperation. Each component met separately to make decisions and then gave its recommendations to the department. When disagreement emerged, we worked toward consensus. As a component of a friendly department, women's studies could hire faculty, admit graduate students, and therefore set its own direction. In 1972 we hired Lillian Robinson as a full-time faculty member in women's studies/American studies, and we hired Ellen DuBois jointly with the history department. American studies also gave us a generous number of teaching assistants. By 1974 women's studies had a thriving M.A. through American studies.

In 1970–71, while some of us were building women's studies in American studies, graduate students who had been involved in the experimental course and their friends began to design new courses that focused on exploring issues of women and gender in their own disciplines. We listed these together in a mimeographed catalogue and called them a women's studies program. But we were unsure how to proceed. We were engaged in a national or at least regional dialogue about what to do with our burgeoning collection of women's studies courses. Should we set up a school outside of the university? Should we merely organize an informal collection of courses? Did we want to become an institutionalized program?

Some students argued that women's studies should leave the university and set up an alternative school. They thought that the university would never be supportive of the education of women and would always compromise our goals. They were concerned that success in the university would necessarily separate women's studies from the women's liberation movement, and co-opt women's studies, making it the province of professional women. I was too much of a pragmatist to be attracted to this way of thinking. Where would the funds come from for an alternative institution? From my perspective, I was a taxpayer and I didn't see why my tax dollars couldn't support a better education for all women. Rather than withdraw for fear of being co-opted, I thought it was better to work to transform the university. After this position won, we considered the institutional form of women's studies. I thought that we were most useful as gadflies, with faculty and graduate students located in different departments. Others made strong arguments that we would be more effective if we were called women's studies and gained independent funding. This was the path we chose, aiming to maximize resources and visibility. However, the issues were never completely resolved and would reappear often in the future.

An easy path for institutionalization was available to us. As a result of the student movements of the 1960s, this was an open and radical moment in higher education, particularly at SUNY, Buffalo. The university was building a division of experimental and interdisciplinary programs, called the Collegiate System, composed of small colleges, some of which were residential, designed to group faculty and students around thematic foci. In 1971 we decided to become the Women's Studies College.[5] The Collegiate System had a farsighted dean, Konrad Von Moltke, who was truly interested in educational change and welcomed the women's studies proposal, giving us a building and a small start-up budget with which to hire graduate student and community instructors. Becoming the Women's Studies College did not interfere with developing the women's studies component of American studies. The former was the locus for undergraduate education, and the latter for graduate education. Together they formed the women's studies program.

Students' desire for women's studies was irrepressible. The Women's Studies College, with only an ad hoc Steering Committee in 1971–72, taught 1400 students in about sixty courses.[6] Those first few years were times of construction, using the tools from our own lives, and also from all the liberation movements of the time, particularly the women's liberation movement: its newspapers, magazines, organizations, and cultural work. Buoyed by these movements, we boldly envisioned ourselves as constructing the Women's Studies College as an alternative program in the midst of the traditional university. We developed the structures for a governing body to set policy and for committees to design curriculum, monitor quality, and meet with administrators. We acted as if we were a mini-university and took pride in offering as good an education as the university, if not better. This period was one of endless meetings, not because of perversity, but because we were setting up a completely new unit without the professional structures of the university. These meetings not only planned and carried out policy, but also served as support and validation for people who were pioneering new ways of education and taking on completely new responsibilities.

As a faculty member in this student-run and movement-oriented program, I was simply one among many participants. I had no particular authority except that which I gained through expertise in a particular area, such as the functioning of the university bureaucracy or the scholarship on women in anthropology. My original experience with the first course—as a "student" rather than as a "teacher"—facilitated this status. Nevertheless, I took my responsibilities very seriously and gave endless time and energy to educating students. I was comfortable with this view of an educator: someone who recognizes what students bring to the university and then supports them to develop their goals. This mode of education drew on my strong skills as an anthropological field worker. It also was close to models of radical pedagogy, which interested me. In addition, it had strains of a maternal role, the developing of a young person's talents, that I found satisfying.

This period of high energy and creativity caused a great deal of uneasiness in the university, making confrontation inevitable. In the fall of 1970, Robert Ketter had been appointed president of the university to bring law and order to the campus following the student strikes and demonstrations that spring. He did not approve of the educational reforms set in motion by his predecessor, Martin Meyerson. Early on, Ketter set a repressive and bullying tone. Inside the Collegiate System, tension mounted, because our extraordinary size entitled us to more resources. In light of its thriving curriculum, the women's studies program developed a grandiose plan for hiring six jointly appointed faculty, which we presented to President Ketter. His negative response was based not on a lack of resources but on his dissatisfaction with women's studies. These early meetings with the president set the negative tone that was to characterize the women's studies program's relations with higher administration throughout the 1970s and thereafter. In the first meeting the president spent the entire time discussing the typographical errors in our letter, trivializing us and the issues we raised.

By the mid-1970s, the administration and the Faculty Senate decided to limit the radical education offered in the Collegiate System in general, and the Women's Studies College in particular, by having more direct faculty oversight of the programs. Every college was required to write a new charter, demonstrating its academic integrity. These would be reviewed by a Chartering Committee established by the Faculty Senate, and the Faculty Senate would make its recommendations to the president for final approval. The Women's Studies College, still concerned with being co-opted, debated whether we should go through the chartering process. In keeping with our activist politics, we decided to use the process as a way of educating the entire university about the principles and politics of women's studies. The goal was to have the chartering process transform the university by legitimating the women's studies approach to education. Amazingly, we partially achieved this.

What was it that worried the university administration? Why was it resistant to women's studies? The expressed concerns were about the political nature of women's studies: we were creating an academic area that was committed to critiquing male bias in research, and to teaching and improving the situation of women at all levels of society, thereby compromising objectivity in scholarship. Another articulated concern was that if it allowed women's studies, it would have to allow Jewish studies, and other programs, leading to the fragmentation of the university. In addition, faculty and administrators were concerned with issues of academic standards and with lines of responsibility. Did the instructors have adequate credentials? Who was in charge of this collectively run program? These issues were major and are worth serious discussion even today and certainly back then. But such discussion never happened: instead, most of the conflict seemed to be driven by personal prejudice about women and apparent discomfort with women taking leadership. We developed creative strategies to deal with the irrational dimension of the conflict. When necessary, we held rallies and demonstrations. Sometimes we used spectacle—moments of theater—other times, humor and songs. But we never gave up on the rigorous preparation of coherent argument.

We turned the public hearing on our charter into a rejuvenating spectacle. When more than three hundred people attended the hearing in fall 1974, even we were surprised. We had carefully planned our presentation of women's studies' goals and scholarship, aiming to take the offensive and speak to the audience's hopes and dreams for a more just world. We were more than successful. Each speaker received thunderous applause. In this process, faculty had primarily a supportive role. Even though this was a presentation to a faculty committee, women's studies voted not to have me or any of the other faculty as one of the four main speakers. Angela Keil, a replacement faculty, and I were assigned to answer some of the committee's questions later, after the formal presentation. The poise and intelligence of the recent and current undergraduates made a most convincing case for women's studies.

The effectiveness of our presentations moved the Chartering Committee and the new dean of the Collegiate System, Irving Spitzberg, to recommend us for rechartering to the president. Our tactics had broken through the wall of prejudice against women's studies. Still, the president was not convinced that we should be supported. He was particularly concerned that we did not welcome men in the program. As evidence, he offered that we used *woman* instead of *man* as the generic throughout the chartering document; he also cited our having some classes for women only. The approval of the charter became dependent on our changing its language. We had chosen this language as a humorous way of raising consciousness, but now it had become a major stumbling block. At first, we added a footnote explaining our usage, but that was not enough. Then we marked each time *woman* was used as the generic with an asterisk, thus indicating unambiguously when it was the generic and when it referred to female humans. The negotiations were lengthy and the coverage in the campus newspapers was an ideal opportunity for educating the university community about the contested nature of patriarchal language. Finally, with the help of Dean Spitzberg, we were able to solve this particular conflict, by adding the university's statement about being a nondiscriminatory institution.

Our successful rechartering had important effects nationally. We could now serve as an example of a women's studies program that had won a legitimate place on campus. But locally, in retrospect, perhaps we had won the battle and lost the war. For we continued to be harassed with repeated reviews and reprimands. Part of our energy had to be directed toward defense, taking time from what we had dreamed of accomplishing. I think we all underestimated how vindictive the male ego can be once it is ruffled. This is an error that I have made repeatedly in my career.

The nature and direction of the women's studies program remained contested throughout the 1970s, defined by skirmishes over the appropriate content and form of higher education. The grass-roots women's studies program challenged university customs by practicing collective governance, training undergraduate teachers, offering a course in auto mechanics, demonstrating self-help, changing the curriculum to include women of color, and reserving a few courses for women students. The administration responded by using its power to reject these innovations. The skirmish over having some courses for women only, which emerged during chartering and lasted for another two years before the women's studies program was forced to capitulate, demonstrated vividly that, even though women's studies had won a place at SUNY, Buffalo, the administration had only minimum respect for the ideas and practice of feminist educators.

By the time of chartering, women's studies participants were divided about the value of women-only classes for the education of women. From the beginning, most introductory course instructors and students wanted the course to be for women only, with a comparable course for men. They argued that the opportunity for women to discuss their experiences with other women helped develop theories based on women's experiences. They also noted that women's conversations changed with men's presence, either due to men's active work to draw the attention to themselves, or due to women's long habits of deference. Other instructors, including most of the full-time faculty, and students disagreed. They believed that the women's studies mission included the education of men about issues of gender and that teachers needed to create a women-centered atmosphere in a mixed class. Despite the division, most participants in women's studies came together to support the struggle for some women-only courses, because they saw it as an issue of control. The women's studies program organized marches and rallies in support of their right to determine what was good education for women. A verse from one of the rallying songs, portraying the university's attitude toward women's studies, captures the energy and defiance behind self-determination:

You're illegal, well not really,
But you're wrong, it's plain to see
For your students are really learning
and THAT'S against our policy[7]

Because no one knew then, or knows now, the best way to educate women, a rational response by the administration would have been to encourage multiple models of education that could be evaluated over time. However, women claiming the right to decide the shape of their education triggered an emotional response that substituted for educational philosophy. To force capitulation, the administration threatened to name the women's studies program—not the sports team, not the School of Engineering—as being in violation of Title IX.

I came to understand during those years that the university was a deeply conservative institution with a strong commitment to blocking change, and that rarely was success gained on the basis of the merit of an idea. To achieve my goals, I had to learn to think strategically and tactically, building allies among faculty and administrators. I liked the challenge of taking charge of my life through changing the nature of my workplace. It didn't occur to me, however, to give up or to become completely cynical, because I had witnessed the process through which students, community women, and faculty had created women's studies. I knew that the effort made new courses available and placed new research on the agenda.

Women's studies' origins in a social movement for change profoundly shaped the form and content of our curriculum at SUNY, Buffalo. Rather than starting from the learned scholarship of faculty, women's studies curriculum grew out of the needs and demands of students and, to a lesser extent, community women. The astonishing growth in the number of courses, from several in 1970 to almost sixty courses in 1971–72, concisely conveys the explosion of curricular energy. It was as if the floodgates had opened, and women's intellectual curiosity rushed out to scrutinize and query the world.

Surprisingly, the kinds of courses offered in the 1970s were not that different from those offered today, indicating the intense creativity of that moment. The curriculum was organized around five kinds of courses: 1) introductory courses, including a general course as well as introductions to specific groups, such as Black and Female or Lesbianism: A Cultural, Political and Personal View; 2) theoretical and analytical courses, such as Feminist Theory or The Family as an Institution; 3) fieldwork courses, such as Women and Prisons or internships; 4) skills courses, such as Women's Poetry Workshop or Auto Mechanics; and 5) courses that offered feminist approaches to traditional disciplines, such as The Social History of Women.

There are two big differences between the curriculum of the 1970s and today. First, many instructors were not full-time university faculty.

Most courses were taught by graduate students or community instructors. Selected undergraduates also taught in introductory courses. We justified the use of community and student instructors because the university had so few faculty trained in feminist scholarship. Second, only a few of the courses were located in traditional disciplines. The curriculum had an interdisciplinary emphasis, defined by the questions of a social movement, not by a disciplinary method.

The women's studies curriculum at SUNY, Buffalo, did pioneering work in connecting antiracist and feminist issues. I want to emphasize this because the history of the 1970s women's movement is often told as if the only concern of activist women was gender.[8] In my experience of this period in Buffalo, it was not so much that antiracist work was not part of women's studies, but that it did not have long-term effects in challenging the racial hierarchies in higher education. Moving toward an antiracist feminism was particularly important to my own intellectual growth. When I entered the university, having completed my fieldwork with the Waunan of the Choco province, Colombia, I was painfully aware of four hundred years of genocide against Native Americans and was committed to slowing down imperialism. I was not unique. Other founders of the women's studies program at Buffalo had been involved in the anti-imperialist movement or the civil rights movement, and had a genuine commitment to doing antiracist work. In the early 1970s a number of women of color actively participated in the Women's Studies College. Wanda Edwards, an African American undergraduate, provided exceptional leadership for an antiracist feminism. She was helped by Lucy Burney, a community woman who designed and taught Black and Female and by Verdia Jenkins, who designed and taught Black Child in America. Marilyn Schindler, a Native American community woman, and Eileen Williams, a Native American graduate student, designed and taught Savage Women. A few years later Bonita Hampton joined them in providing leadership to make antiracism part of feminism. The work of all these women affected the curriculum.

One of the many distinctive and innovative aspects of American Studies/Women's Studies 213, Women in Contemporary Society, was its attempt to be inclusive of all women, both through encouraging discussion of different women's lives and through providing a framework that was antiracist and anticapitalist. From 1971, and perhaps even earlier, the syllabus opened with a section called "Who are the women of America?" which introduced women of color, working-class women, and lesbians, and, from the mid-1980s, Jewish women. By making it explicit that the women's liberation movement included more than white, middle-class Christian women, the course challenged students to think about the effects of social hierarchies on lives other than their own. This was definitely controversial, generating complaints that the Women's Studies College did not focus enough on the successful "normal woman." As instructors wrestled to teach "Who are the women of America?" issues of creating an inclusive curriculum were necessarily at the forefront of our thinking. Because we gave presentations at national conferences, we were catalysts for raising these issues outside of Buffalo as well.

The Curriculum Committee also engaged in antiracist work, looking for courses relevant to "Third World women," the term used at the time. In addition, as early as 1973, the Curriculum Committee began the practice of examining new course proposals to see if they were inclusive of all women, and sent back for revision courses that lacked material on women of color. For a student-run committee to ask a faculty member for revisions was very risky, more than likely helping the administration's attempt to marginalize women's studies as a bunch of crazy radicals. One of our first faculty allies from another department, Gail Paradise Kelly, was outraged by having her course sent back for revision; however, her love for women's studies and her forward-looking vision led her to add material on women of color to her course, and thereafter to her research. But some other faculty left rather than contemplate issues of racism.

Despite this active work to develop an inclusive curriculum, the program made, as women of color repeatedly pointed out, very little progress. Women of color did not hold positions of authority, and their history and culture remained marginal to most courses. Nevertheless, I would argue that these early attempts to create a more inclusive curriculum need to be recorded, because they give visibility to activists who are women of color and to the connections between the women's liberation movement and the civil rights movement, while clarifying the long-term nature of the struggle against racism. In my mind, the preliminary work in the 1970s created a little more space for the development of intellectuals who are women of color and, in the long run, led to the more lasting structural changes of the 1980s, particularly the hiring of faculty who are women of color.

Although most of our course proposals, after careful preparation by the Curriculum Committee, were approved, some of our courses were harassed by regular review for years. Courses taught by full-time faculty members, in traditional formats but including feminist ideas, were accepted more easily than those taught by students or community women, or those that in practice challenged the hierarchical relationships of society and the university. My favorite course skirmish was over Auto Mechanics, because it revealed clearly the patriarchal and class components of the university's judgment of what was an acceptable course.

Auto Mechanics became a part of the Women's Studies College curriculum in the early 1970s, because women students felt that learning to take care of their own cars was a pathway to independence and an example of newfound competence. Taught by community instructors, the course had good evaluations and was always full, but some members of the university were very uncomfortable with it. In particular, a physicist, Jonathan Reichert, who had taken an active role in the chartering process of the colleges, brought this course forward for repeated public scrutiny. The first round of complaints was that the course was open only to women, and in time we bowed to the pressure and allowed men. The university's concern then became: Was it appropriate to have an auto mechanics class that taught skills at a research university? We defended the course by showing that the instructors did not just teach skills, but taught the theory behind the combustion engine, and also by pointing out that the university offered other courses that were primarily skills courses, such as courses in the Management School on buying and selling stocks and in accounting.

When we became a B.A.-granting program, we were ordered to terminate Auto Mechanics. The peremptory nature of the administrative decisions on Auto Mechanics is brought into focus today, when the university is attempting to increase the numbers of women in science. Ironically, at a meeting I attended on this subject, a woman engineer said that the best thing the university could do to increase the numbers of women in engineering was to offer opportunities for women to familiarize themselves with tools through building and repairing things. Of course, she did not know the tale of the endless attacks on the Auto Mechanics course fifteen years earlier. From her perspective, no one had ever tried this. How could she know that ordinary women empowered by the women's liberation movement had once implemented such a learning opportunity? The skirmish around Auto Mechanics suggests the immense possibility for change at a university as well as the depth of a university's resistance. It also highlights the foolishness of seeing the goals of women's studies as completely harmonious with those of the traditional university.

Equally as important as the innovations in curriculum content were those in form. As early as 1969, women's studies was particularly creative in its forms of pedagogy, learning more from social movements than traditional education. The course, Women in Contemporary Society, used distinctive teaching methods that aimed to decenter authority in the classroom, to develop the voices of students, and to encourage students to take control over their education. Women were fed up with the classrooms, not to mention the world, that had silenced them. They intended to do everything possible to disrupt the forces of oppression. Because many women's liberationists had been involved in the civil rights and antiwar movements, thinking about education for freedom was not new. The roots of the new pedagogy were eclectic, some coming from consciousness-raising groups in the women's liberation movement, some from Chinese and Vietnamese struggles for liberation, some from Mississippi Freedom Schools, and some, a little later, from Paulo Freire's *Pedagogy of the Oppressed.*

Instructors advocated small course sections, run as seminars rather than lectures, each team-taught, to help develop knowledge in this new field, and also to decenter the focus on a single authority. The course used the technique of a rotating chair: the teacher no longer called on the students; instead, the last person to speak called on the next person. The idea was to give everyone a chance to speak, not just those who were the most aggressive or most vocal. In order to encourage students to take more responsibility for their education, we developed the technique of student initiators, in which two students were responsible for developing discussion questions and then leading the class. The course also asked students and instructors to share brief life stories, what we called personal histories, to help students appreciate the similarities and differences among women's lives and to help facilitate their moving between the personal and the political in their analyses. I was very impressed with the ideas of process that informed the founding graduate students' teaching techniques. They were conscious of having been silenced, but aware of developing alternative understandings of the world through consciousness raising, education, and activism. They understood that undergraduate students were just beginning this process for themselves, and therefore were deserving of patience and respect. "Criticism, self-criticism" was a technique used at the end of each class to encourage growth, through students and instructors reflecting on the progress of the hour and their own learning. As part of the emphasis on process, instructors avoided using arbitrary authority. If they wanted to convince students of the correctness of an argument, then they aimed to do it through reason, not power.

The effects of these varied teaching techniques were dramatic. Students insisted that the course had changed their lives. Women students broke patterns of passivity and began to take responsibility for their education. Their new confidence opened up opportunities that they had never dreamed of before: graduate education, professional schools, administration, and social change activism. They worked enthusiastically to create women's studies: witness the numbers who came to the public chartering hearing and who defended our courses against repeated attacks. Many faculty outside of the women's studies program noted that there was something special about our students, that they more actively pursued their education and were therefore a pleasure to have in class. This helped us win friends and support for the program. The activism of our students even stood out nationally, because of the numbers of students we took to conferences.

These feminist forms that empowered students were also used in governing the Women's Studies College, which was run by a staff collective, composed of two coordinators and part-time and full-time paid staff, all of whom were students or had just graduated. The staff were assisted by committees of students, faculty, and some community women. The final policy-making body was Governance, a regular meeting of participants in women's studies that occurred every Wednesday night.[9] The staff collective, Governance, and the committees used many of the same techniques as the introductory course, such as a rotating chair and criticism, self-criticism. The collective forms were crucial in maintaining this student-run program, because they offered support and training to newcomers, encouraging their development as capable human beings and as leaders in women's studies. The regular meetings—whether they were for teaching groups, committees, or Governance—provided a structure in which participants could report on their work and others could comment on it. As new projects were started, their success needed to be quickly evaluated and plans for modification developed and implemented. Sometimes the criticisms were painfully personal and unfair. But most people put up with them because they were gaining so much. For students and community women, who had limited, if any, training as professional educators and who were fighting a lifetime of messages about women's incompetence, the regular schedule, the immediate evaluation, and the explicit loops of communication built confidence and motivation. Looking back, I am still impressed by the ways in which students, staff, and community women, with the help of a few faculty, struggled to hammer out policy for a women's studies program that would serve the many constituencies of the women's liberation movement.

The Women's Studies College also had clearly marked pathways for leadership. Students who were active in Governance and had served on committees could apply for a part-time paid staff position. Then, as they learned the job and graduated, they could become full-time staff and, finally, co-coordinators. They might hold each position for a year or two before moving on. The selection of the staff people was taken very seriously, with the final decision made by Governance.[10] Women's studies expected its staff to be Renaissance women, knowing how to design university curriculum, support community activism, and administer a complex program. The coordinators were special women, bravely coming forward to head a student-run program. They had tremendous talent and a strong commitment to a better world for women.[11] Most of the coordinators have continued to be feminists and activists. The bad parts of the job were typical of all movement jobs: low pay, lack of job stability, and no career track for future work. The good part was that the staff learned to think critically and strategically, in a situation where what they did mattered; they could use these skills to succeed in whatever else they did.

By choosing leaders who were excellent students and brilliant activists, the women's studies program affirmed its connections to an activist social movement. But structurally, the program could not help but to conflict with the interests of faculty. Though they might have the same political interests, the faculty had another set of priorities, including the production of valuable scholarship, the training of future scholars, and the furthering of their own careers in the university. The path to transforming the university was not going to be easy.

The democratic and participatory forms of women's studies were long-lived at SUNY, Buffalo, because the program also achieved academic excellence. While one group was working to establish the Women's Studies College, another group was working to improve the status of women on campus through the hiring and promotion of women faculty and staff. I was a member of that group as well. In the early 1970s, it was given some affirmative action budget lines to bring excellent women faculty to campus. I worked as hard as I could to make sure some of these hires would be interested in feminist scholarship, and could become part of our incipient women's studies program. On the committee were several feminists, including Bernice Poss and Daphne Hare, who were favorable to this sort of hire. When, in spring 1972, American studies hired Ellen DuBois and Lillian Robinson, these pioneering feminist scholars made it possible for women's studies to become a dynamic force in feminist scholarship nationally, and for me to become a serious feminist scholar.

DuBois and Robinson knew what it was to bring feminist scholarship to the disciplines and to consider the benefits and problems of inter-disciplinary work, because their dissertations were feminist projects. Unquestionably, they added substance to the academic focus of the program. Although I had always been concerned with quality scholarship, I was just beginning feminist research and writing and did not yet have a strong voice. In addition to being serious scholars, DuBois and Robinson were also firmly rooted in the politics of the women's liberation movement. DuBois had been connected to the Chicago Women's Liberation Union, and Robinson had been part of the first Bread and Roses group. Their political inclinations were very different from each other's, and from mine, but nevertheless we all fell into the general tendency of socialist feminism.

Their first few years at SUNY, Buffalo, were difficult. Although they liked the excitement of the student activism, they also wanted more time to do their own scholarship. The students' activism had a streak of anti-intellectualism, judging scholarship as elitist, and something faculty did only to further their careers. They did not see the contradiction between loving the feminist articles they read in courses but not giving their own faculty time to write feminist articles. Though hurt by the students and overburdened by the demands of the job, DuBois and Robinson couldn't look to the administration for support, because of its hostility to women's studies and feminism. They also couldn't seek support from a network of feminist faculty, because we didn't yet have one. The new faculty recognized that to keep the women's studies program vital, they needed the students.

The amount of time that everybody—the staff, the faculty, and the students—put into women's studies was, objectively, a problem. It consumed people's lives. We lived, breathed, and ate women's studies. Between teaching and program building, faculty had very little time for their own research, not to mention personal lives. But the conflicts between students and faculty were caused by more than lack of time. The students were opposed to the professionalized values and forms of the university and had set up new structures responsible to a movement. Even though DuBois and Robinson were critical of some parts of university culture, they also appreciated the professional structures that would support them in achieving their goals as professors. To survive, we had to begin hammering out various compromises.[12]

I was pulled in two directions. I recognized that my colleagues were correct in valuing scholarship: one of the important reasons to set up women's studies was to further the life of the mind. They were also correct in believing that not everything could be a matter of political principle requiring a long meeting, because, if it were, how would faculty ever do research and writing? At the same time, I thought that students were correct to want to create a less repressive educational institution, not to mention a new world. These pressures, plus two good fellowships and the birth of her son, led Robinson to decide to leave in 1979. Robinson's departure was a sobering reminder of the tremendous toll that women's studies took on some faculty careers. Despite the fact that she has remained a productive scholar, she did not find a permanent job teaching graduate students at a research university. DuBois stayed for ten more years, and then left for a position at the University of California, Los Angeles. While in Buffalo she took the lead in insisting that women's studies foster excellent scholarship, so that students might become the next generation of faculty. She was helped by a series of fellowships that allowed her to be away enough to further her own scholarship, which, in turn, helped her to develop the strength to influence women's studies to respect her research and writing. It was not easy, because this approach did not endear her to many students at first, but by the 1980s all of women's studies had come to value scholarship as much as, if not more than, activism.

The presence of DuBois and Robinson allowed me to survive thirty years in women's studies. Their concerns about the position of faculty raised questions about what I was doing to my career. All the work was consuming me and I was not writing. Although they both felt that scholarship and writing were paramount, they never belittled me for building women's studies. They, too, were committed to institutional change. Rather, they helped me understand my strengths as an architect of women's studies. Their respect for my knowledge of the university and the possibilities of feminist scholarship allowed me to become a serious writer, a great gift that only feminist faculty could give. They gave me the kind of mentoring that I did not receive in graduate school.

Throughout the 1970s some participants in the women's studies program at SUNY, Buffalo, buoyed by the active women's liberation movement, regularly asked whether women's studies should continue to pursue institutionalization at the university; they feared that this path would inevitably lead to co-optation. Today, when the feminist movement in the United States is fragmented and underdeveloped nationally, participants in women's studies are debating the reverse question: Should women's studies sever its ties with the feminist movement in order to better pursue institutional legitimacy? The history of the founding and establishing of women's studies at SUNY, Buffalo, suggests that such polarized questions are faulty. Women's studies' successful existence has been forged from striking appropriate compromises between university tradition and movement innovation.

Although the founding of women's studies at SUNY, Buffalo, is a story of tremendous success, it is also a story of loss, of conflict, of harassment, and of compromise. The founders' dreams of social justice have yet to be fully realized. The university administration has offered serious resistance, holding back change and cutting short the careers of faculty and graduate students. The skirmishes about such issues as single-sex sites of education, about Auto Mechanics, and about curriculum transformation, not to mention the many other fights that I did not have the space to include, demonstrate the university's unwillingness to encourage serious discussion about what constitutes the best education for and about women. Many ideas have been foreclosed before being put into practice. Despite this hostility, the women's studies program at SUNY, Buffalo, has continued to grow and influence the university. Its feminist scholars excel by even the most traditional standards. When professional culture began to support this new scholarship, it increased the tension within women's studies between the scholars and the activists. To accomplish what it has in the past thirty years, women's studies at SUNY, Buffalo, has met professional standards, but has also incorporated student voices and developed connections with communities outside the university to pursue social change, searching for ways to combine these various tendencies. Nationally, women's studies has come ever closer to being a legitimate part of the contemporary university, with some programs achieving departmental status and offering doctoral degrees. Although it is tempting in this situation to jettison connections to a feminist movement for change, I would argue that such a solution is shortsighted. To put it simply, neither women's studies nor the women's movement has yet made a significant impact on the prestige structures of the university. The most money still goes to male-dominated fields, while departments with mainly women receive the least money and are the most likely to be cut. In addition, gender, race, and class hierarchies continue to have material effects in society at large, disempowering the majority of women and people of color, while an elite few become more privileged. Only a social movement can shift these hierarchies. To accomplish such change, women's studies needs to continue fostering connections with community activists and current manifestations of the feminist movement. We also need to continue letting students and instructors influence the direction of women's studies, ensuring that there are ways for new ideas to come from the bottom as well as the top. These alternatives to professionalized structures will help women's studies continue to push the university to consider new ideas, to reconsider connections between theory and practice, and to explore new pedagogies and methods, while still functioning within accepted guidelines for research and teaching. Our history suggests that women's studies should always pursue legitimacy, taking whatever institutional form is useful and meaningful, but it should always remain in creative tension with the university, keeping as its goal long-term institutional change.

Tucker Pamella Farley

I began doing what was to become women's studies in the community in the 1960s and by 1970 was developing women's studies for trade union women as well as for the academy. This included founding the New York Women's Labor Project, being active in the Workers Education Local 189 of the American Federation of Teachers (AFT) and starting its Women's Caucus, participating in the early days of the Coalition of Labor Union Women, and establishing a women's studies program, a Women's Center, and a program for returning women at the City University of New York. By the mid-1970s I was concentrating on developing women's studies as a field, first regionally, and then nationally. I was instrumental in founding and governing the National Women's Studies Association and its New York regional association, NYWSA, as well as the NWSA Lesbian Caucus, during their first decade, and I served on the editorial board of the *NWSA Journal*. I have been a member of organizations for progressive scholars and activists, including Marxist-Feminist Group I (MF-I), New University Conference (NUC), and Socialist Feminist Philosophers Association (Sofphia); in the Modern Language Association I chaired the Job Market Advisory Commission and served as liaison from the Gay and Lesbian Caucus to the Commission on the Status of Women in the Profession. Most of the time since the 1960s I have belonged to a women's group; each group has meant a great deal to me. Teaching graduate and undergraduate courses at the City University of New York, Brooklyn College, my courses, all taught from a feminist perspective, now range from a premed and honors seminar called Discourse, Objectivity and Science to Modernism in Crisis; from Contemporary American Writing to Graduate Feminist Literary Theory. My work has been published in *The Future of Difference, Women in Search of Utopia, 20th Century Women Writers of the U.S.: A Critical, Bio-Bibliographic* *Source Book, Women's Review of Books,* and *Lesbian Review of Books,* among others. I enjoy sailing, and dance West Coast Swing on the champion team, "Dance Manhattan," as the first woman to dance what used to be called the "the man's part" in national competition: a sign the times are changing.

Changing Signs

The first public meeting of my women's liberation group in the mid-1960s was held in the "Ladies Room" of the Pennsylvania State University (PSU) student union building. I was a radical and an activist, teaching and earning a graduate degree at PSU after teaching in rural Appalachia. Isolated and ineffective in my efforts as a white woman to make some changes there, I had returned to school to learn to write textbooks that included the black children I had taught in my classes. In the movement at PSU, I learned to organize. And when Cindy, another woman in Students for a Democratic Society (SDS), told me she had heard of women meeting in Berkeley and daring to call themselves the Women's Liberation Front, it became possible to organize not only for civil rights and against poverty and the war in Vietnam: participatory democracy meant women's oppression should be changed, too. When the university denied us a meeting room, we marched down the hall, crossed out "Ladies," put up "Women," propped open the door, and proceeded to have our meeting in the outer restroom area. With little support from the left and no response from the university, the women's group ended up with its own house in town,[1] the Women's Liberation House, where women and men lived, held meetings, and published a newspaper. We meant to change the world. That meant organizing and working in public institutions, where the people were.[2]

In 1970 I took a job at the City University of New York (CUNY). Its open admissions policy made it one of the nation's cutting-edge public universities, graduating students of distinction. Brooklyn College's famed night school, which produced the ranks of professionals in New York City, afforded higher educational opportunities for a very widely diverse, working-class population. Thanks to CUNY student activists of the 1960s, I was hired at CUNY, Brooklyn College, to teach women's studies as well as American literature. I was one of few that year to be offered jobs, for the bottom had dropped out of the job market in English; that very disaster and my active response to it in the Modern Language Association (MLA) made me chair of the Job Market Advisory Commission as a graduate student.[3] Activism informed my professional work in several ways: I had a broad vision and an imperative for equity and change; I developed leadership and organizing skills useful in challenging institutional practices; I had an understanding of the political nature of cultural practices and an optimism that generated alternatives as much a part of life as breathing. I worked simultaneously on the left, in unions, and in the academy,[4] and each arena was informed by the others. So when I developed my first women's studies course, it was designed to challenge students to question not only the position of women but "the system" that produced subordination.

I began developing women's studies in the English department, but when the School of Humanities canceled a course suddenly, I went to the School of Social Sciences where Dean Thomas Birkenhead scheduled a women's studies course for me, and I taught in both schools. Because I took inspiration, practices, and materials from different progressive movements, including the women's liberation movement,[5] with its flourishing culture of poetry, theater, consciousness-raising groups, and radical democracy, everyone was encouraged to participate. We often broke down into small groups, met where possible in a circle, rotated the chair, voted and made contracts and agreements about course procedures, used journaling and student experiences (in more than one course, mother-daughter teams signed up), and brought in women from the community to teach aspects of the courses.[6] Toni Cade came and introduced us to Zora Neale Hurston and *Their Eyes Were Watching God* when the book was still out of print.

The material was interdisciplinary: I would use material from literature and the arts, the media, advertising and sex manuals, economic and political analyses, and anthropology and other disciplinary texts to make connections and raise the consciousness of students. It worked. They produced bold, innovative, and first-rate scholarship; the classes

were enormous; and the demand grew. When my own department neg-
lected, for its first women's studies course, to put a cap on class size and
ninety registered the first morning alone, the department began to
enjoy the budgetary benefits of large women's studies electives. I was
making up the courses as I went along, drawing heavily on my own self-
education in numerous study groups.[7]

Although many feminists were active in New York, much early
organized feminist activism in the academy was centered at Brooklyn
College. The Brooklyn Women's Organization devolved into several
groupings, almost as though we had divided up tasks. Lelia Melani, a
lecturer in the English department working in coalition with women
from other CUNY campuses in the CUNY Women's Coalition
(CWC), filed a class action suit against CUNY for sex discrimination,
which historian Renate Bridenthal and others joined.[8] A dedicated
group worked for many years to establish and run a child-care center.
Jackie Eubanks in the library organized book fairs. My focus was on
institutional change and the development of programmatic resources
for women. In all these arenas, activist students were the backbone of
the movement, among them Hope Singer, Debby Cherry, and Rosella
Mocerino.

For curriculum development, it made sense to build from strength
in the two of the five schools at Brooklyn College where we were already
teaching: humanities and social sciences.[9] A group of scholar-activists
and students constituted ourselves as a planning group for a women's
studies program, leveraging support from social sciences dean Birkenhead to get official committees appointed. Psychology's Evelyn Raskin
chaired the Social Sciences Planning Committee, and in humanities,
Dean Ethyl Wolfe appointed a committee chaired by Kay Rogers from
English, a senior professor we invited to join us, thinking she could
help shepherd the proposal through official channels. Dean
Birkenhead appointed me as liaison between the two committees to
coordinate efforts and produce a coherent joint program proposal. I
sat on the humanities committee as well; the Planning Committee
members were active feminists, and Raskin, as a chair, supported our
vision and our work.

Brooklyn College already had a Puerto Rican studies department, an
Africana studies department, and a Judaic studies department. The
question we debated as feminist scholars was whether it made sense to
try for departmental status, with the dangers of ghettoization and

isolation in relation to other departments but with the advantage of a small power base. Or should we try for program status, which would force us to fight for our budget and disperse our institutional power base, but would allow us broad interdisciplinary relations and cost the university less up front? In 1972 the latter was the strategy we chose.

We began with a small number of course offerings in departments. I had fought for and won a Women and Literature course as a permanent offering in English. Psychology offered a multisection course, which was very popular. The senior faculty tended to stigmatize feminist education as "political" and oppose it to "scholarly" academic work. Gradually, however, the courses became popular not only with the students but with some of the faculty. Within a few short years, many wanted to teach women's studies courses, including my own course. In those days while women's studies was generally considered to be a fad, special topics courses in women's studies constituted the fastest-growing means of increasing profitable departmental student enrollment, and women were the largest future population of the university as a whole.

We planned three tiers of courses. The first tier was an introductory, team-taught interdisciplinary women's studies program (WSP) course in each of the two schools (humanities and social sciences) to start with. In the second tier, students could take electives in any school, offered out of departments and cross-listed with women's studies, a design that necessitated—and facilitated—negotiations with departments and faculty concerning course offerings, instructors, prerequisites, evaluation procedures for courses and instructors, and long-term planning. In the third tier was a WSP seminar that called for the development of interdisciplinarity—spanning humanities and social sciences material in one seminar. The WSP also offered independent study and special topics courses. We negotiated the courses and the program through the channels successfully, and began teaching them, so that in 1974, when Albany approved the program and we began our official existence we were offering thirty-four courses, team-taught in the first tier.

By 1974 we had an office, a small budget, a staff member, courses to offer, and people to teach and take them. We had a feminist collective, and we had allies, some warm, some cool, with whom we had shepherded the program through its many-layered hurdles. We were successful enough to generate a backlash, even within our own ranks.

Birkenhead was gone. Provost Marilyn Gittel, new to Brooklyn College and our efforts, was persuaded by Rogers to appoint a woman unfamiliar with feminist studies or feminism to chair an appointed governance committee. As the planners, we were surprised and offended. That committee (I was not appointed) met for several weeks, apparently without being able to engage in governance issues or program planning, until their floundering became so painful that the committee called on us to go with them to the provost to determine a new structure. We came away with cocoordinators (Bridenthal and myself) from the two schools; an elected student, faculty, and staff Coordinating Committee; and a general Policy-Making Committee of the whole. This was the structure that governed the women's studies program for many years. Each year we elected its coordinators and coordinating council, and we were very content to have as staff the extremely able Pat Quercia, work-study students, and volunteers. Students operated as integral members of the program; one summer, to staff the office when we were offering summer courses, Carol Lafazan and Davida Mayan acted as student cocoordinators. Our radical practice was cheaper for the university, as well as consistent with our collective governance. Working this way gave us strength, helped us be effective in the university at large, and kept us aligned with other progressive forces on and off campus. It also allowed us to survive and grow amid massive cutbacks threatening on the horizon.

To support nonacademic feminist activities and programs on campus and to supplement the curricular offerings, we needed a Women's Center. A Women's Center would help ensure that the radical visions of feminism were actively present on campus, would sponsor political and cultural events, would provide support services for women of all backgrounds, and would open up the educational resources of the university to community women. The Women's Center was my special project. It had a broad-based, diverse constituency, consisting of older and younger women, black, Puerto Rican, Jewish, and white women; and day and night school students. They were from traditional, nontraditional, and continuing education programs, and they were from the community. They were staff women, faculty, secretarial staff, lesbians, straight women, and representatives from the CUNY Women's Coalition and our three unions. We made an appointment with President John Kneller, who agreed to meet with our group to hear our proposal for a Women's Center.

When the day came, I was told that he was canceling the meeting. With an enormous number of women arriving for the scheduled appointment, and with the press invited as well, I went in to advise him that it would be wiser to meet with us. The CWC had a class action suit against CUNY, and in Albany he, as president, had praised our accomplishments at Brooklyn in leading the way in the development of women's studies. He agreed to look at the proposal, and we went over it page by page. By the time the press arrived, together we joined the large crowd outside waiting for our appointment. The Women's Center Planning Committee came out of the meeting with a one-year commitment to a Women's Center, the first that we knew of on an academic campus. We had a year to make the center self-supporting.[10]

In those days, I remember feeling the strength and confidence that came from being part of large numbers of women united for a purpose. Even walking down Brooklyn streets, late at night, after staying overtime to write reports and proposals and to deal with the myriad details that made for good communication on a large campus with many points of contact with the women's studies program—a young white woman alone on midnight streets—I felt powerful. I would walk right on, moving among groups of men instead of crossing to the other side or going down a side street, because I had the feeling that an army of women walked with me.

That trial year I won a three-year grant for women returning to school, linking the women's studies program and the Women's Center.[11] Envisioning this grant, I had used my own experience, remembering the daunting prospect of leaving the ordinary world of work and trying the waters of academe. I had not known whether I could do graduate school work. I had had to mend my life after a divorce, take courses at two universities on a provisional basis, and move and live alone in order to go back to school.[12] In one late-night session as we put pieces of the proposal together with the assistance of Fran Gottfried from Provost Gittel's office, I generated great hilarity with my impassioned rhetoric for the introduction. I laughed, too—but I really did believe we would have "unrest in the land" were we not to serve the needs of these women! [13]

The grant proposal, "Alternatives for Women: The Return to School," designed an innovative program to reach out to women in poor communities in Brooklyn and to change institutional practices to meet the special needs caused by their returning to college as adult women who also led family, work, and community lives. Demonstration education projects, for remediation and re-entry, would help to bridge the gap between the communities and the school. Interdisciplinary academic modules would integrate theory with the practices of these women. We would also offer workshops, courses, and internships, both on campus and in communities, in order to improve skills that could lead women into college degree programs, employment opportunities, and participation in community affairs at all levels.

The Fund for the Improvement of Postsecondary Education (FIPSE) awarded us a three-year contract. We went into the poorer communities of Brooklyn with Project Chance, did outreach, took college courses to the women, and brought women to the college. I taught in church basements and at other community sites. Some of the women were beaten by their husbands, boyfriends, or fathers for attending those classes. We included a counseling component, offering crisis intervention, family counseling, a mini–services referral network, and individual and group, peer and professional counseling. The project increased the number of women who returned to—and graduated from—college, on the principle of the multiplier effect: women who received training returned to their communities and jobs as educational resources themselves. Project Chance provided a replicable public model for changing institutional practices to serve returning women.

With a degree-granting program, a center, and an outreach project, Brooklyn College, in the forefront in the academy during the early 1970s, was part of the great movement of women during that era. Yet our existence was not secure in the academy. Women's studies was established in New York at a time of great upheaval, including massive cutbacks in the city. The backlash against CUNY's successful open admissions policy was exacerbated by the fiscal crisis of the city. New York City was taken over at the brink of bankruptcy in 1974 by a cartel of financiers, who suspended city government and ran the city for a period. Health, education, and welfare were the hardest hit.[14] Even as the university was forced into massive restructuring, women's studies was growing—and being threatened—on all fronts simultaneously. We needed to build the field and establish it as a regular part of the academy.

In 1974 I began to organize a regional conference, Strategies for Survival, composed of several tracks, so that participants—who came from far and near, Maine to Georgia, Long Island to Pennsylvania—could discuss not only course materials and plans, controversies in their fields, working in an interdisciplinary mode, and developing feminist pedagogy; but also learn how to start and expand a program or a center, and debate the need for a women's studies association. For more than a year before the conference in 1975, we held meetings attended by women from several states to research, debate, and plan specific sessions on the forming of a professional association, which we initially thought of as a regional organization. SUNY, Buffalo, argued strongly that we needed to build the grass roots before attempting a national association, which was also being discussed as a possibility. The regional conference planners corresponded with women in California also proposing a national association, and offered critiques and suggestions for a more democratic and participatory convening.[15]

At the opening session I spoke about the contradictions in our situation: we were growing fast, functioning very successfully, and doing exciting educational and scholarly work; at the same time we were under attack, driven to defend ourselves, and struggling to survive. It was a complex moment. We emerged from the conference in 1975 with a great deal accomplished. We had organized a large regional network for a future National Women's Studies Association and a regional New York Women's Studies Association, and we had established an autonomous regional association for women's studies in the interim. The Northeast Regional Women's Studies Association held a conference in May 1976 at the University of Maryland. Many of these feminists helped to form regional bases for the subsequent National Women's Studies Association (NWSA), founded in 1977.

In January 1977 I represented New York at the founding conference of NWSA.[16] I helped to shape NWSA's vision and governance during its first decade. In order to carry on struggles for equity, the association represented constituencies as well as regions, a form of organization that survived, with structural representation for women of color, lesbians, Jewish women, working-class women, students, and disabled women, among others, for nearly two decades. Flying back to New York after helping to found NWSA and, in the process, a national lesbian caucus,[17] on the plane I recall reading about work for endangered species—and identifying intensely.

As cocoordinator of the first women's studies program at CUNY, I was headed for difficulty surviving myself: I was fighting for tenure. The entire city was in crisis, attacks came from reactionary faculty, support was withheld more than granted by liberal faculty, and these

positions did not know gender. During one particularly tense procedure, a member of the Personnel and Budget Committee accosted me
in the hall and expressed his disappointment that I had so flagrantly
destroyed my case for promotion. What had I done? I was accused of
refusing to allow men in my classes, of refusing to teach anything that
mentioned marriage, of giving all women students A's, of wearing
leather pants, and of having a lesbian around to light my cigarettes. I
am grateful to the man who expressed his surprised disappointment in
me, for I was able to invite him into the women's studies office, introduce him to program committee members and staff, turn over the
records to him, and leave. He examined syllabi; student and course
records, including grade sheets and bibliographies; and whatever else
he wanted. He talked with other women's studies faculty, staff, and
students. He discovered that, as a member of the Personnel and
Budget Committee, he had been lied to. The chair of the English
department, Jules Gelernt, had invited this testimony from two
women faculty members before the committee in secret (and illegiti-
mate) hearings. He took the case back to the committee. When the
department chair (who had dissented from the favorable departmental
committee recommendation) objected, the committee went over his
head to Dean Ethyle Wolfe.

Much of the controversy regarding feminism was structured by
homophobia. The trick was to turn opposition into assistance. When
I was called before the university Promotions Committee, a colleague
from Judaic studies regarded me with some hostility and gave me the
opening I needed to explain my work by demanding, "How can you,
as a lesbian, claim to do research?" I spoke for half an hour in reply
and by the end had shown that we both did work in the face of slanted
history; I defended his right to call his work scholarship and claimed
the same for myself. Members of the committee applauded. But I had
challenged the basic tenet of objectivity by showing that knowledge is
produced from standpoints. A colleague during these years of tenure
testing confided in me that he thought my work was excellent, but
that there was some fear among the faculty about "you-know." What
was "you know"? Oh, you know. No, I didn't know: What were they
afraid of? Oh, that I would make some Steinian gesture. And what
would be a Steinian gesture? Oh, you know, putting your feet up on
your desk. Separately, another colleague told me that the department
was having difficulty because "We already have one." Internal WSP

divisions were painful. At Brooklyn, the WSP had been forced by a recalcitrant Curriculum Planning Council to spend weeks fighting for our proposed literature course[18] while our history course passed immediately; just the proposal of this course generated the familiar charge that lesbians were taking over. Freddie Wachsberger of the art and archaeology department, Lucille Goodman of the music and performing arts department, and Pat Lander of the anthropology department courageously came out of the closet in defense of the program's course at Brooklyn. At Barnard, where I was also teaching a lesbian course, the students defended it amid ongoing resistance among the faculty.

I came up for tenure and promotion at the height of CUNY's fiscal crisis and the downsizing of the university. I hadn't been trying to build my presence in an established field: I had been building and establishing a field, working as an untenured assistant professor. In the process, of course, I jeopardized my job. But at the same time, I had established the basis of my defense. By the time that I came up for tenure and promotion decisions throughout a three-year period, people all over the country knew my work. In November 1977, the week before the presidential decision was due on my case, the NYWSA and the Brooklyn College WSP held a massive public forum, Frontier or Backwater? Can Feminism Survive in the University? and invited people representing different constituencies to speak. Anne Sutherland Harris, curator with Linda Nochlin of the pathbreaking "Women Artists: 1550–1950" show at the Brooklyn Museum in 1976, spoke about the dangers of doing nontraditional work in an institution before having job security. She had been let go after putting on that exhibition. Contingents of women's studies people came from all over the state and testified about these issues, for the forum was held as a strategy to defend my job as one of the first coordinators of an early women's studies program and one of the first such cases. Some, such as Elly Bulkin of the Brooklyn College Women's Center, spoke about the impossibility of being able to do really radical work in the institution, advocating working "outside the system" to retain the fire and purity of a women's studies vision. Dean Barbara Gerber from the State University of New York (SUNY), Oswego, chaired the session and defended my work. I spoke passionately about what it was like to love women and work for women in a culture designed to keep us down, and went on to outline what I saw as the basic structures of knowledge that were repressive and yet constituted the basis of our disciplines, our understanding of reality, and our educational system.

In my critique I said that, to the extent that I had been a dutiful daughter, I had taken "medicine" when I hurt. The more I hurt, and the more medicine I took, the sicker I got—for that medicine was poison. What I had been taught was good for me, was bad for me. With the provost sitting directly in front of me in the audience, and my job on the line, I said in public many things that I had not yet heard spoken before; I was afraid of being perceived in that listening space as "beyond the pale"—but I already was. I spoke of my sense that Western knowledge was structured to maintain power, authority, and control by what was white, male, and "rational" over what was dark, female (and of the body), and different (or "irrational"). I saw the same hierarchical structures of opposition in language, politics, history, psychology—and science, which denies that knowledge is shaped by power and justifies its practices as objective descriptions of reality. Education functioned to induce neurosis, I said, like caged rats trained to press a bar for food, only to find when they went to the bar that they stood on a grill that was electrically charged, shocking them each time they tried to feed themselves. The rats would become paralyzed. As a woman who loves women in a society built on our oppression, I had to work to shift our culture and the way it becomes embodied in us.

The symposium went on all day; from the floor as well as the platform, the women spoke movingly. Though I was not promoted, I did win tenure. Nationwide, faculty and administrators who knew my work in the National Women's Studies Association wrote fine letters of support.[19] I work for everyone; but I am indebted to them.

Annette Kolodny

In 1975 I began to publish a series of articles, which included "Some Notes on Defining a 'Feminist Literary Criticism'" (1975), "Dancing through the Minefield: Some Observations on the Theory, Practice, and Politics of a Feminist Literary Criticism" (1980), and "Map for Rereading: Gender and the Interpretation of Literary Texts" (1980). *The Lay of the Land: Metaphor as Experience and History in American Life and Letters,* my study of the male-centered cultural mythology of the U.S. frontiers, also appeared in 1975. That same year, the English department of the University of New Hampshire voted against my promotion and tenure. I sued, charging the university with sex discrimination and anti-Semitism. The case settled out of court in 1980. I used part of the financial award to establish the Legal Fund of the Task Force on Academic Discrimination within the National Women's Studies Association; and I wrote about the experience in "I Dreamt Again That I Was Drowning" (1989). Continuing my scholarly work, in 1984 I published an analysis of women's responses to frontier landscapes, *The Land Before Her: Fantasy and Experience of the American Frontiers, 1630–1860.* I left New Hampshire for the University of Maryland and then moved to Rensselaer Polytechnic Institute. From 1988 until 1993, when crippling rheumatoid arthritis forced me to step down, I served as dean of the College of Humanities at the University of Arizona, Tucson, where I am currently a professor in the interdisciplinary graduate program in comparative cultural and literary studies. My latest book, *Failing the Future: A Dean Looks at Higher Education in the Twenty-first Century* (1998), derives from my years in academic administration and from my work as a consultant in higher education policy.

The full version of this essay appeared in the *NWSA Journal* 12.1 (Spring 2000). Because I am telling a story that belongs as much to others as to me, I am deeply grateful to former colleagues and students who, with enormous generosity, shared materials and reminiscences: Rob Chapman, Helga E. Jacobson, Meredith Kimball, Deborah Parker, Sheryl Perey, Teresa Plowright, Audrey Samson, Leslee Silverman, and Dorothy E. Smith. I also owe thanks to Jo Hinchliffe, administrator for the Centre for Research in Women's Studies and Gender Relations as well as administrator for the undergraduate women's studies program at the University of British Columbia, who provided me with material about the current women's studies program at that university. Finally, I owe a debt of gratitude to my research assistants, Jodi Kelber and James Lilley, who helped check footnotes and prepare the manuscript for publication under impossible deadlines.

A Sense of Discovery, Mixed with a Sense of Justice

I.

Our shared opposition to the war in Vietnam and the fact that my husband was about to be drafted into that war propelled us across the border into Canada in the summer of 1970.[1] Before leaving the United States, I had accepted an assistant professorship in the English department at the University of British Columbia (UBC) in Vancouver; my husband had been granted a fellowship for graduate study in that same department. During those first weeks in Vancouver, before classes began, I feared that I would be isolated. I feared the loss of the engaged political life that I had known during my years in graduate school at the University of California, Berkeley, and, most of all, I feared the absence of a sustaining feminist community. I did not yet know that Vancouver was alive with feminist projects, nor did I know that UBC was home to the Women's Office Collective, an assembly of determined student activists.

When I first arrived at UBC in the fall, the Women's Office, housed in the student union building, was run by students who were also community activists and who saw those roles as mutually reinforcing. Despite repeated difficulties in securing adequate financial support from student government, the Women's Office Collective nonetheless developed education and outreach programs that served women both on and off campus. The group's most ambitious goal, however, was to launch women's studies at UBC. To be successful, the collective would have to challenge the habitual conservatism of a university attached, on principle, to maintaining clear separation among the disciplines; a university with no mechanism for promoting inter- or cross-disciplinary cooperation; and a university where a few of the faculty, trained at Cambridge or Oxford, regularly wore their academic robes to class, in the manner of British dons. And the collective would have to change fundamentally the culture of a campus where one of my senior English department colleagues deemed it his duty to chide me for encouraging my students to speak in class. As he pronounced with obvious distaste, I was guilty of "invading their privacy."

But in 1970, the energy and enthusiasm of feminism was international and infectious. Nothing, it seemed, was impossible. Thus the Women's Office Collective joined forces with a handful of sympathetic faculty and key community organizers to obtain a provincial Opportunities for Youth grant. That grant funded the planning and implementation of a noncredit women's studies course entitled The Canadian Woman: Our Story. This first, noncredit course began in 1971–72, organized around twenty weekly evening presentations given by faculty and by women from the nonacademic community. For those who were interested, the lectures were often supplemented by small-group seminars facilitated by faculty and by volunteer student teaching assistants. There was no charge for any of it. In the first year alone, attendance at the noncredit evening course averaged more than four hundred each week.

At the same time that they began putting together the evening course, members of the Women's Office Collective also initiated plans to establish an academically credited, multicourse women's studies program taught by regular faculty. The students wanted rigorous, in-depth treatment of topics that the evening course could treat only superficially; and they wanted opportunities for concentrated research on women and women's issues. With that in mind, Jeanette Auger—an undergraduate sociology major and a leader in the collective—began to identify faculty members who might want to teach in such a program.

She easily persuaded me and a group of about ten faculty members from different departments to constitute ourselves as the Ad Hoc Committee on Women's Studies and, with the students, to submit to the Faculty Senate a student-generated forty-nine-page proposal for a credited multicourse program. The program was to involve a number of disciplines from the Faculty of Arts, and—as faculty member Lorraine Weir later recalled—its courses were to cover "the history of women in Western civilization, the socialization of the girl child, the psychology of women, the images of women in literature, the position of women in the family, and the treatment of women under the law." Lorraine also remembered that the proposal called for "a discussion of the present status of women in Canada and the history of the women's movement."[2] The outline for the noncredit evening course The Canadian Woman: Our Story was appended to the proposal.

The decision to send the proposal directly to the Senate, thereby bypassing both individual departments and the dean of the Faculty of Arts, was prompted by our commitment to inter- and cross-disciplinarity. We hoped that the Senate's New Programmes Committee would approve the concept in principle and recommend that the dean name faculty members from different departments to a committee charged with developing a specific curriculum. This was a recommendation that no department would make on its own; and it was a step we feared the dean would be reluctant to take without some clear signal of faculty support. To the proposal the students attached the lecture schedule for The Canadian Woman: Our Story—both to indicate the range of possible course topics and to remind faculty senators of the overwhelming interest already demonstrated in the noncredit course. Both decisions proved to be major blunders.

Unwilling even to consider a proposal that had not come to them through the established department-based curriculum review process, the officers of the Faculty Senate forwarded the forty-nine-page document to the dean of the Faculty of Arts. He in turn referred the matter to the Curriculum Committee of the Faculty of Arts, which circulated the proposal to a number of departments that might conceivably be asked to contribute faculty to a multicourse women's studies program. Within months, the curriculum committees of all these departments buried the proposal through one procedural maneuver or another, and the comments passed on to the ad hoc committee were almost uniformly negative.

The questions most often raised, it turned out, were whether men would be allowed to teach in the program or be enrolled as students. This took us by surprise, because several male faculty were listed as lecturers in the evening course, and we had made it clear that men regularly attended that course. Another set of repeated questions revolved around whether those who taught the courses would be required to hold Ph.D. degrees and what would constitute their expertise to teach this subject matter. These questions, we surmised, derived from the fact that some of the presenters in the evening course came from the nonacademic community and did not possess graduate degrees. But the questions that completely surprised us came from departmental curriculum committees, who asked whether there was any subject matter available to teach. In their view, women were already included in all the disciplines, so anything called women's studies could only be redundant.

The nastiest comments, however, focused on the outline for the student-sponsored noncredit evening course. Those pages were mistaken by some professors as the intended curriculum for the credited program. In that confusion, professors bristled at what they took to be an overture that faculty would teach a course designed by students. The clear message was that students were not to be a part of the academic governing process, and that faculty resented their attempts to bring into the university any outside political agenda.

I remember Jeanette Auger fuming at what seemed to her an impenetrable bureaucracy. But although the students in the Women's Office Collective and the faculty members on the Ad Hoc Committee on Women's Studies were all disappointed, no one was willing to give up. We needed to find a different strategy. That strategy, we decided, was to use the normal process of curriculum development and course approval—and force it to serve *our* purposes. In consequence, four faculty members from the ad hoc committee volunteered to work together to develop a new proposal and a set of detailed course syllabi that we ourselves would be prepared to teach. The four included Helga E. Jacobson (tenured associate professor of anthropology), Meredith Kimball (untenured assistant professor of psychology), Dorothy E. Smith (tenured associate professor of sociology), and me (untenured assistant professor of English). The defeat of the student-generated proposal thus turned into an extraordinary collaboration in the summer of 1972.

The ad hoc committee persuaded the dean of the Faculty of Arts to secure for the four of us a seminar room in the lower level of the Faculty Club and to allow us to have exclusive use of the room during June, July, and August. We also received a small budget with which to purchase books and monographs, because the library's holdings in women's studies were slim, at best. In a pointed gesture of support, the dean even provided us with free coffee.

Our meeting room had a medium-sized seminar table at its center. Throughout the course of the summer, we piled on that table all the books, articles, and journal issues we could find dealing with the new field of women's studies. Given the enormous body of feminist scholarship available today, it hardly seems possible that in 1972 we could have loaded it all onto a single table and read it through in one impassioned summer. But as Dorothy reminded me recently, "When we started, there was very little that could be called a body of literature in any of our fields, and we drew on whatever we could find."[3] From June through August, each of us went through every item on the table and, against the background hum of male voices and the clicking from the billiards room down the hall, we talked and talked about what we were reading. As Dorothy put it so well, "We were all learning and discovering together."[4] In essence, we taught one another how to read critically across the disciplines and, by the end of the summer, none of us could engage our disciplinary practices in quite the same ways that we had been taught them in graduate school.

By August, we were ready to prepare a formal proposal. Our goal was to devise a program that would cross discipline boundaries and interrogate discipline-based assumptions about women's lives and work, and human sexuality. In effect, we wanted to reformulate the existing discipline-based ordering of knowledge.[5] But our radically interdisciplinary aspirations collided with the university's hidebound departmental and discipline-based structure. Our solution was to propose a six-credit, year-long central interdisciplinary lecture course (Women's Studies/WMST 222, An Introduction to Women's Studies) and four six-credit, year-long complementary seminars in each of our disciplines. The four of us were to teach the lecture course together. Then, each week, we would take up the topic of the lecture course and examine it in depth within the disciplinary context of our individual seminars. Students were required to register for both the lecture course and for one of the seminars. In retrospect, Dorothy called our solution "both ingenious and effective. . . . Our idea was both to open up women's studies and also to introduce to students the scholarly constraints of the disciplines which we represented."[6]

Having learned valuable lessons from the responses to the earlier, student-generated women's studies proposal, we carefully framed our proposal to anticipate objections. To begin with, we promised "a systematic and academically rigorous approach." In order to establish the legitimacy of women's studies, we cited "the very large body of material which is now being published in a variety of fields." Our opening paragraph ended by noting that "many major North American universities are now offering major programmes in women's studies at the undergraduate level; at least two are offering graduate degrees.[7] Finally, we concluded the narrative portion of our proposal by "recommend[ing] that the design of this programme be treated as experimental and that in this form it be given a two or three year trial."[8] We even suggested a format for reviewing the program at the end of the trial period. Our hope was thereby to win over those who would not otherwise support anything so unfamiliar.

The last three pages of our proposal contained a reading list and a detailed topic outline for the six-credit interdisciplinary lecture course WMST 222. To forestall objections that women's studies was just another faddish import from the United States (in a period when many Canadians wore buttons reading "Nixon drinks Canada dry"),[9] we included significant material by Canadian scholars and novelists. To blunt the assertion that we were simply exploiting anecdotal complaints about the local situation of women in Canada, we included the latest anthropological and ethnographic studies of women in Africa and Asia. In our view, we had been persuasive, we had been succinct (our entire proposal ran only six pages), and when we forwarded the document to the dean, we believed that our job was done. But as it turned out, in order to keep the proposal moving through the pipeline, and in order to answer the questions that kept getting asked at every level, we four were on constant call.

At the end of May 1973, with the curriculum approval process finally completed, Helga read a paper at the annual meeting of the Canadian Sociology and Anthropology Association. In that paper, she described what we had encountered. In brief, we personally had to shepherd our document through "eleven different committees."[10] Although this was the standard process for approving new courses at UBC, as Helga noted, what struck her "repeatedly as differentiating the Women's Studies course from others going through the same process were the terms in which justification was required of us. . . . The focus of interest was not on what was to be taught but on who had the right to teach and learn, e.g. would men be allowed to teach and take it . . . and whether or not we had Ph.D.'s."[11] In short, the same questions that had killed the initial student-generated women's studies proposal were also raised about our document. What perhaps saved our proposal was that every time it appeared on any committee's meeting agenda, "we were required to be there to present our case."[12] After the first few meetings, it became almost routine—especially because, as we soon realized, the various committees weren't communicating with one another, and "basically the same questions were raised at every committee meeting."[13]

There were other problems, too. The department heads and the curriculum committees of the anthropology and sociology departments and the psychology department were not supportive of women's studies. Only reluctantly did they approve and credit the year-long seminars attached to the lecture course. But although they counted the seminars as part of the regular teaching load, both departments balked at giving faculty release time for the team-taught interdisciplinary lecture course. As a result, Helga, Dorothy, and Meredith ended up receiving only a semester's course release for the year-long lecture course. Like so many other women's studies faculty in those early years, they were teaching an overload.

In the English department, although the department head was generally supportive, the overwhelming majority of those on the Curriculum Committee were not. I was wholly unprepared for the self-righteous vehemence of those who insisted that Edith Wharton was not as good as her contemporary Henry James. No one recognized Kate Chopin's 1899 novel, *The Awakening.* "If Kate Chopin were really good," one of my Oxford-trained colleagues kept lecturing me, "she'd have lasted—like Shakespeare.[14] For a time, our multicourse program looked as though it might have no literature seminar. In the end, with the help of the head of the English department and the dean of the Faculty of Arts, a compromise was struck. The seminar Women in Literature became WMST 224—rather than an English department course—and carried service (or general education) literature credit in the Faculty of Arts. This compromise required another two committees, thus bringing the total number from eleven to thirteen.[15]

The ugliest moments of the approval process took place at the general meeting of the Faculty of Arts. Faculty of Arts meetings were usually sparsely attended; most votes were uncontested and pro forma. On this occasion, by contrast, the large auditorium was packed and the atmosphere was charged. The press was in prominent attendance, and students—male and female—lined the walls or sat on the stairs. Both were unprecedented. Unfortunately, faculty members entering the auditorium had to squeeze past the double rows of students along the walls, and some professors experienced this as a threatening gauntlet. What the faculty members did not know was that the chair of the meeting had ordered the students to stand in the back or along the stairs; anticipating a large turnout, he was concerned that there might not be enough seats for all the faculty. Adding to the tension in the room was the fact that the vote on women's studies had been scheduled just days before the long-anticipated release of the "Report on the Status of Women at UBC." This one hundred—page analysis, complete with statistical data, was then being finalized by the Women's Action Group, an informal, ad hoc gathering of faculty, staff, and students. As everyone on campus knew, that report was about to document systemic discrimination against women "at every level of the University."[16]

The meeting dragged on for three hours. Repeatedly, Meredith, Helga, Dorothy, or I—or one of our many faculty supporters—rose to respond to questions that we had answered dozens of times before. Until, that is, one particularly eminent senior professor took the floor. His was a voice that always carried weight, both because of his elegantly turned sentences and because he was rumored to have served in the British Office of Special Services (OSS) during World War II.[17] He was very tall, slender, ruggedly handsome with beautifully groomed graying hair, silver-white at the temples, and he wore an expensive tweed jacket. He rose to speak and then turned slowly to point to the students hugging the walls or sitting on the auditorium stairs. In a deep and commanding voice, he compared those students to the brown shirt brigades of Nazi youth, invading a campus in order to intimidate and force conformity to a false ideology. He then pointed to the four of us and compared us to Nazis, too. We were the ones guilty of discrimination, he intoned, because women's studies would separate and segregate women, as the Nazis had once separated out and segregated Jews.

Did he know that Helga and I were Jewish and that Helga still had vivid memories of fleeing with her family across Europe? Did he hold the students in such utter contempt that he could not even contemplate their presence as anything other than intimidating? I shall never know. But for several minutes, as this man calmly proceeded, it appeared that our proposal was dead. Meredith, the most junior of the four and uncomfortable with public debate, whispered that she could not respond. Dorothy, the most senior of the four and our best strategist, was too enraged to speak. Given the experience of her family in leaving Germany, Helga was appalled and chose not to speak. Dorothy urged me to raise my hand. After all these years, I have only an imprecise notion of what I said. I quoted Helga's frequent observation that the university had courses in Canadian studies and in Asian studies, yet no one saw these as discriminatory.[18] And I think I challenged the charge of political dogma by quoting from the proposal our determination to "equip students with sound critical approaches."[19] What I do remember clearly is that I rejected his grievous misuse of Holocaust associations, and I pointed to the utter obscenity of his comparisons. I was angry and I allowed my anger to fuel every word.

The vote was close, but the proposal was approved. In relatively quick succession, the Faculty Senate approved the proposal during the closing week of January 1973 and, soon thereafter, the Board of Governors did the same. The courses were scheduled to begin in the fall. Thus, even as the administration scrambled to respond to the devastating revelations of the "Report on the Status of Women at UBC," it could simultaneously boast of "the first courses of women's studies ever to be offered for credit by the University."[20] *UBC Reports,* the faculty-staff newspaper and the official on-campus information arm of the university, characterized the students who would be enrolling in our courses as "pioneers on a discipline that has only recently been explored in the academic world."[21]

With the unflagging help of students, both female and male, and the ongoing support of many colleagues, we had finally succeeded. Yet the entire process, as Dorothy later noted, proved to be "radically disillusioning." Naïvely, she said, we had "taken for granted that the university was conducted in accordance with rational principles and that decisions were reached after discussion, in which reasoning and evidence played the major roles." But, as Dorothy put it, "In trying to get the women's studies course in place . . . we came up against levels of prejudice, anger, perhaps fear, that overrode commitments to rational process. Whatever might be the case in other areas, when it came to . . . admitting women to full intellectual and professional equality in the university, the deepest springs of irrationality came to the surface ."[22]

With the approval battles behind us, Dorothy, Helga, Meredith, and I devoted all our spare time to refining our courses for the fall 1973 semester. One of our main concerns was to avoid the construction of "women" as a hegemonic category. For us, heterosexuality was never a given because one of us was a lesbian, two were straight, and the fourth was beginning to experiment with her sexuality. Moreover, although faculty could not risk identifying as lesbian in those days on that ultra-conservative campus, the organized feminist community in Vancouver—of which we were a part—was decidedly mixed in terms of ethnicity, race, class, and sexual preference. Many of the students in the Women's Office Collective who helped plan and advocate for women's studies were out lesbians. Thus from the beginning, the subject of women's diverse sexualities and their socialization into gender roles was very much a part of our interdisciplinary lecture course.

So, too, were issues of class, because this was one of Dorothy's major research areas. In the fall, she offered several presentations on the construction of women's work under capitalism. And because Helga was an anthropologist with comparativist theoretical interests, the lecture course attended in some depth to the varying roles and experiences of women in different societies. All of February, for example, was given over to eight lectures in a series called Women in Other Cultures. For us, the "women" in women's studies represented a vast umbrella under which we expected to analyze both commonalities and differences. It had also served as a grammatical convenience for establishing a collective subject where our colleagues claimed none existed.

Finally getting into the classroom, however, made all the battles seem worthwhile. As Meredith recalled, "the excitement of teaching women's studies for the first time was intoxicating. The feeling of being pioneers, of doing it for the first time, of putting it all together from scraps of information and our own critique was one of the most exciting academic endeavors of my life."[23] Former students say they shared that excitement. Those who composed brief reminiscences for me all echoed the sentiments of one woman who declared, unequivocally, that women's studies "permanently transformed me."[24]

II.

We had no budget for books or supplies, but cadged what we could from our respective departments and paid for the rest out of our own pockets. We had no clerical budget, but depended on the goodwill of departmental secretaries and ended up doing most of the typing and mimeographing of course handouts ourselves. Except for our individual faculty offices, we had no space that we could designate as belonging to women's studies. Still, nothing could dampen our enthusiasm. Throughout the 1973–74 academic year, for three hours each week, the four of us taught the eighty students enrolled in the interdisciplinary lecture series, and then for another three hours each week, we taught the students in our separate seminars. In the lecture course, we experimented with interdisciplinarity. Frequently, two of us paired to offer a joint lecture—as when, for example, Meredith and Dorothy together discussed the development of women's movements in England and North America; or when Meredith and I offered both psychological and stylistic analyses of women's work narratives. I am reminded also of the guest lecturers from other disciplines who joined us periodically: Jean Elder from the history department, whose lecture was "Women in the Middle Ages," or Marvin Lazerson from the education department, whose talk was "Industrialization and the Ideal Woman."

Because the lecture course met for two hours on Wednesdays and one hour on Fridays, on Wednesdays especially we enjoyed ample time, not only for the lectures themselves but, just as important, for active discussion among the four of us and between us and the students. The goal was to allow our different disciplinary frames of reference to play off of, elaborate on, or even refute one another. Meredith recalls with pride that the students "saw faculty arguing with and correcting each other. They saw disagreements, discussion, and the construction of knowledge in ways that were unimaginable in any of their other courses."[25] One of the former students from my literature seminar remembers that "suddenly women's literature was no longer a thing apart but discussed in an inter-disciplinary context." For the first time in her educational experience, this student had been "given the lenses of psychology and sociology to illuminate poetry and novels and, conversely, to begin to see how literature informed the other systems of describing reality." To her, "this was academic Nirvana."[26]

Dorothy compares the four of us working together in the interdisciplinary lecture course to "the Pied Piper who led the children of Hamlin out of the city and through a door in the mountain into another and glorious world of light." Twice weekly, in her memory, "we went through a door in the mountain and into that other university in which teachers and students alike were deeply engaged and wanted to know; where discussion was open and urgent, and all of us cared about the questions we were discovering how to ask and the answers we did not yet know how to make. Here was the real university hidden within the mountain."[27]

The seminars offered a more intimate environment than did the large lecture class, and, as I look back on WMST 224, my seminar called Women in Literature, I remember exchanges that were always spirited and sometimes passionate. Former students still speak fondly of the "intellectual liberation" made possible by "a small class . . . the only class of that size that I had at the time."[28] And although, as one of these students remarked in the summer of 1998, "we all read so many women [writers] these days that it's hard to even imagine a time when their voices did not have validity,[29] in 1973–74 the fifteen women and four men enrolled in the literature seminar found the intensive study of women writers "awakening."[30] Given the themes of Chopin's novel, it strikes me as no accident that the reading most often mentioned by former seminar students is, ironically, the very text that English department colleagues condemned as unimportant. "One of the books we discussed in our seminar was *The Awakening,*" wrote one woman, "an apt title for my year in women's studies at UBC. So many assumptions of mine were turned on their heads so rapidly, so much was confirmed that I had suspected, but never had the ammunition to articulate previously."[31] Another student "summed up" her experience of first encountering women's literary traditions as "a sense of discovery, mixed with a sense of justice—doors that had been wrongly kept shut were opening."[32]

At the end of the spring term, when I composed the course evaluation that was required by the dean, I easily boasted that the combined lecture course and seminar format had "proven a great success for all involved." I concluded that "the Women's Studies Program is the most successfully innovative experiment to be launched at U.B.C. . . . and . . . I speak both for myself and for my students when I say that it ought to be supported, encouraged, and enlarged."[33]

III.

Individual departmental colleagues kept questioning our course content and academic rigor. A few faculty members continued vocally to protest our existence. And despite solid enrollments and outstanding reviews from students, the original constituent departments—anthropology and sociology, english, and psychology—continued to resist assigning faculty time to women's studies. Even so, the program received final approval from the Faculty of Arts in 1976, and women's studies became a permanent feature of the university catalogue. But the design that we initiated did not long survive.

In our original program, students registered in any of the designated departmental seminars were required to take the interdisciplinary lecture course. And students in the lecture course were required to sign up for one of the four designated seminars. Over time, however, departments insisted that the seminars be open to any student, resulting in a dilution of the linkages between interdisciplinary lecture course and discipline-based seminar. Moreover, although we four taught the lecture course collaboratively, by 1976 only two faculty members were permitted to share that responsibility—a concession to budget constraints and a further diluting of our original interdisciplinary intentions. In 1977 the format was changed altogether. A single faculty member was designated as a women's studies coordinator. She arranged a series of guest presentations (from different departments) for the lecture course, while assuming sole responsibility for that course's assignments, examinations, and grades. When this proved to be unworkable, in 1979 a single instructor was assigned to teach An Introduction to Women's Studies. Individual departments continued to offer courses on discipline-based women's studies topics—and, in fact, such courses proliferated throughout the 1980s in response to increased student demand and growing faculty interest. But departmental courses were no longer formally linked to any interdisciplinary offering. By 1978, the original year-long, twelve-credit program, which integrated a truly interdisciplinary lecture course with discipline-based seminars, had virtually disappeared.

The truth is, there was simply no institutional support. No dean or vice president was interested in taking either financial or administrative responsibility for women's studies, thus leaving the program vulnerable to the vagaries of departmental patronage. And those of us who had worked so hard to get women's studies established were paying too high a price in our home departments. Promotions did not come when they should have, salary increases were minimal, relations with colleagues or department heads were strained, and Meredith was denied both promotion and tenure. By 1980, three of the four original faculty members were gone, including me.[34]

Despite the loss of three of the four founding faculty members, and despite the lack of a coherent or integrated program, student enrollments never flagged, and more courses with a focus on women and gender issues were added to the university catalogue. Ironically, however, by the end of that decade, the university that had mounted the first credited multicourse women's studies program in Canada was now one of the very few Canadian campuses without either a major or a minor in the field. Frustrated and fed up, the Advisory Committee on Women's Studies compiled a detailed report and, in March 1989, presented it to the university's president. In sum, the report concluded that "the programme, such as it is, has survived thanks to the efforts of a few dedicated faculty members, but voluntary work and charitable good will are not sufficient for it to thrive and grow."[35]

The report had an impact. In spite of continuing staffing problems and chronic underfunding, women's studies at UBC today is housed in a wheelchair-accessible building central to campus, where it shares space and support staff with the Centre for Research in Women's Studies and Gender Relations. Undergraduates are offered both a major and a minor; and beginning in 1998–99, graduate-level courses were offered through the University of British Columbia Interdisciplinary Studies Programme. I note with unabashed pleasure that the course that I originated, WMST 224: Women in Literature, is still in the catalog for six credits, remains in high demand, and is taught regularly.

Myra Dinnerstein

I was the founding director of women's studies at the University of Arizona, remaining in that position from 1975 to 1989. In 1992, I published a book on married women who returned to work after staying home with children entitled *Women between Two Worlds: Midlife Reflections on Work and Family*, which was published in 1992. More recently, I have been focusing on women's relationships with their bodies. I teach a course called Women and the Body and I am writing a book on the impact of being fat on the lives of professional women, tentatively called *Fat Matters: The Lives and Careers of Successful Professional Women from Girlhood to Adulthood*. Currently, I am research professor of women's studies at the University of Arizona. I also am chair of the University of Arizona's Commission on the Status of Women.

A Political Education

I became the first director of women's studies at the University of Arizona by default, an illustration of the way that my career has been marked by both serendipity and politics. When the university agreed to establish a program in 1975, I was the only one in the group who had lobbied for the program who had a doctorate, experience in teaching women's studies, and, most significant perhaps, no full-time job. Other potential directors, women on tenure track, were warned by their department heads not to become too closely involved with a maverick program lest that association deal a blow to their academic careers. I, on the other hand, had little to lose. I had followed my husband to the University of Arizona in 1970, and found myself for the first time in my adult life without a full-time job. I was desperate. I taught any and all classes I could in the history department, and it was there that I introduced A History of Women, simply because I had friends who were doing it at other schools and I was looking for more courses to teach.

It was in that women's history classroom that, along with my students, I first experienced feminist consciousness. Not only did I become aware for the first time of the social structures that influenced women's lives but, in true consciousness-raising style, I realized how my own life had been affected, why I had unthinkingly followed my husband to Tucson without any prospects of a job, and why I had then become depressed. As one of my students remarked, "This class educated my rage." It did the same for me. That same student gave me an enlarged copy of that well-known photo of the sitting Elizabeth Cady Stanton with Susan B. Anthony peering over her shoulder, a picture that hangs on my office wall today, reminding me now, as it did then, that women can effect change. That first women's studies course was a powerful, life-transforming experience and began my passion for feminism and for women's studies as an avenue to change.

The establishment of our program in 1975 was preceded by three years of struggle to persuade a disbelieving university administration of the need to initiate women's studies on our campus. The political nature of our struggles was reflected in the very origin of our program as a part of the Committee on the Status of University Women

(CSUW), designed to improve the status of women faculty, staff, and students, an organization that would never have been formed without the inspiration of the women's movement. Soon after the founding of CSUW in 1972, Kate Cloud, a nontenured faculty member in the College of Education, hearing of women's studies programs at other universities, formed a subcommittee of CSUW to explore the possibilities of such a program at the university. For the next three years, a group of full-time and part-time faculty, students, staff, and community members worked together to develop a proposal, lobby administrators, and develop support among students and faculty on campus. Graduate students were already interested; in fact, the first women's studies course, in sociology, was organized in the early 1970s because of the demands of these students. Our group realized that the interest was there; all we needed to do was develop the courses.

For most of us in the group, feminist politics was a driving force. Some of us had been involved in other movements, but for us the women's movement was the watershed moment, the time that marked a leap in consciousness. At this stage, when we were all involved in professional careers, the university became the site of our activity. Establishing a feminist program, creating a curriculum, and offering students a new way of thinking about the world was our political work. This political commitment to activism motivated tenure-track faculty, whose careers were just beginning and who had much to lose by associating themselves with a marginalized program. Only the heady conviction that we were doing something important for women and that we had right on our side in our battles with the university kept us going during those years.

The political power of working as a group became clear to all of us. Students, community activists, and part-time faculty worked feverishly over commandeered photocopy machines and through late-night meetings, plotting and planning our next moves. Among the faculty, Sidonie Smith, English department, Mary Thornberry, political science department, Eliana Rivero, Spanish and Portuguese department, Susan Philips, anthropology department, and later Karen Anderson, history department, and Susan Aiken, English department, and Sherry O'Donnell, a graduate student in the English department, whom we often hired on projects, were an extraordinary cross-departmental group: all of them were willing to give time that their careers could ill afford to what they considered a political cause. I remember Kate

Cloud sneaking office supplies over to our tiny office because we had no money to buy them, and I could never forget sitting with Sidonie Smith in her backyard, creating a final proposal for the establishment of our program that was half realistic and half fantasy. Most of all, I remember the energy and exhilaration of those years. What courage we all had in taking on the university and trying to make it change—or what naïveté.

During the three years that we fought for a program we accrued an education, not only in feminist politics, but in university politics, becoming aware that understanding how to make our way through the system would be a necessary prerequisite to our success, not only in establishing the program but in its continued success. Though learning the politics of the university seems an obvious strategy, most of us were new to the academy in any capacity other than students and were just discovering its political nature. We came to realize also that the conservatism of the state affected all institutions that were beholden to the legislature, and that university administrators, whether conservative or liberal themselves, were sensitive to these concerns. We learned that if we were to challenge the university establishment, we had to do it in terms that the university administrators would not find too difficult to defend. Most of all we found out how to maneuver within the bounds of what was possible in our state and university to get as much as we could of what we wanted and needed.

This approach, we believed, would work best in our conservative state and in our university, a research university in transition, striving to raise its academic reputation. As a result, we decided early on that we should stress the merits of feminist scholarship which we believed in— rather than our political aims to change the university and inspire a feminist consciousness in our students. What administrators didn't realize, of course, was that it was almost impossible to take a women's studies class, as scholarly as it might be, without developing a feminist consciousness, or at least a new way of thinking about women's issues, as our course evaluations continue to attest. Although our emphasis on academics might not seem radical, at that particular historical moment, establishing a women's studies program in a state as conservative as Arizona was in itself as revolutionary as a determination to challenge patriarchal institutions and ideas.

One of our strongest allies in getting the program established was Janelle Krueger, a professor of nursing, one of the few female profes-

sors on campus. She was the token woman on many university committees and so had the access we lacked to deans and vice presidents. Her
intelligence and her agreeable manner made her well respected by
administrators. Although she was a fierce tiger in defense of women
and was totally committed to the establishment of a women's studies
program, she decided that the way to succeed was to work the system in
a style that was not antagonistic or threatening. Because of her, a group
of otherwise marginal and powerless women could present our cause as
a respectable academic enterprise. What I personally learned from her
was that you can be forthright about what you want and even aggressive,
but whether you win or lose, there will be another day, another battle,
and that it is best to maintain connections, even when you are aching to
shout and rage.

Women's studies, once established, continued to participate in
broader political issues affecting all women faculty. After the demise of
the Committee on the Status of University Women (CSUW) in 1978,
our program remained the only active pro-woman center on campus.
It is not surprising, therefore, that, when women began to recognize
the salary disparities between men and women faculty, they turned to
women's studies for leadership. In 1982, when I invited a group of
feminist faculty to lunch to discuss the formation of a new organization
to replace CSUW, the Association for Women Faculty (AWF) was born,
an organization dedicated to improving the status of faculty women,
dealing with such issues as salary, tenure decisions, and overload.[1]

Our proposal for a women's studies program was finally accepted in
1975. I would like to think that we had made our case and made administrators realize that to be in the forefront of education they had to
include women's studies. Our proposal and our persistence certainly
played a part in our victory, but I think it had as much to do with the
university being under pressure from a variety of vocal community
groups to establish Mexican American and black studies programs. The
fact that all of our programs were established at the same time and given
few resources made us think that, to the university, all these "minority"
groups could be taken care of in one fell swoop by offering them some
kind of recognition but few resources.

As with the other programs, we received official university acceptance, but of the most minimal kind. The dean gave me the weird title
of counselor (I think he must have thought of me as a quasi dean of
women), a minuscule budget of a few hundred dollars, a salary equiva-

lent to an assistant professor's, and a ten-hour-a-week student worker. Then he left me alone. For the first three months, I traveled with a boxful of files from desk to desk of vacationing staff until the dean's secretary, one of the many women staffers who covertly supported our efforts, found me a tiny office. I now realize that the greatest gift the dean gave us was benign neglect. Nobody told us what to do or seemed to care, and that turned out to be a favor, although we didn't know it at the time.

The struggle to establish the program had been protracted, and something of a cliff-hanger, which meant that I had had little time to think about what the job would entail. I remember my husband asking me, "What will you do all day?" I didn't have an answer, but I soon found one. Our first order of business was to begin to act as though we were an academic program. So I renamed myself director, listed the few women's studies courses offered by departments, called them a program, and advertised it in a flier and in our campus newspaper. I later found out that that "let's pretend" technique was followed by programs throughout the country, although some programs, such as the one at the State University of New York, Buffalo, which had started earlier, were already offering a full panoply of courses.

From the beginning we thought that it was important to find ways to legitimize ourselves to the upper administration, which controlled resources, and to the wider campus, which controlled important committees, such as the Curriculum Committee. But first, as a representative of the program, I had to go through my own personal political education and feel legitimate myself. In the same spirit that we advertised our (nonexistent) program, I tried to behave as though I were an administrator of a program, even though it barely existed. As our program was starting, our dean was leaving, and the first official meeting that I was invited to was his farewell luncheon. I realized that everyone at the lunch was a head or director of a department, and although I was the only woman there, it was clear that someone, somewhere, thought I belonged in this group. This was further confirmed when I was invited to attend the heads and directors meeting, although I always wondered whether it was the dean's supportive secretary who put me on the list! Further, when I called up department heads or deans and said that I was the director of women's studies and wanted to meet with them, they responded as though I were someone with legitimate business, no matter what their personal opinions of our program. As a result of these encounters, I began to feel like an administrator who could speak up, voice opinions, and make claims.

My full-time status in women's studies turned out to be an important advantage to the program, although it is odd, I now realize, that I was given a full-time position when throughout the country other programs were forced to make do with part-time directors. In our proposal, we had asked for a full-time position and the university, probably without much thought and without the need to spend much money, acceded. Having a full-time position in women's studies meant that I could dedicate myself to the work of institution building with no obligations to any other department. I also had an anomalous university status that made it possible for me to be so single-minded. I was not on a tenure track, although others reacted to me, I realize as I look back, as though I were a fully tenured faculty member. I decided on my own, foolishly, perhaps, for a career in academe, that my major responsibility should be the administration of the program and not research. I found that organizing and running the program left little time to do anything else except teach whenever it was possible.

My personal situation also allowed me to spend enormous amounts of time on the program. Although I had small children, I also had an academic husband who was willing to do more than his share of child care, and so I was free to work on nights and weekends. The result of all these factors was that I was able to work night and day to build the program into a substantial presence on campus and in the community, a luxury that most other women's studies programs did not have.

When I think about the politics of our program, I can only label early governance as informal but consultative. When I heard about more formal committee structures at other universities, I worried that I was not consulting enough, but I soon realized that faculty and others interested in women's studies were in constant contact and interaction with one another and with me. I rarely made a decision, no matter how small, without hashing it over with my colleagues on the phone or at lunch. I particularly consulted with the people who emerged as the core group. They were totally committed to the program and many of them were also responsible for its establishment. They were Sidonie Smith, English department, Mary Thornberry, political science department, Eliana Rivero, Spanish and Portuguese department, Susan Aiken, English department, Susan Philips, anthropology department, Patricia MacCorquodale, sociology department, Karen Anderson, history

department, Laurel Wilkening, lunar and planetary sciences department, Chris Tanz, psychology department, Ruth Dickstein, our invaluable women's studies reference librarian, and Sherry O'Donnell, then
a graduate student in the English department. I also shared every bit of
university information and news I heard with this group, as they did
with me and one another. Knowledge *is* power, and knowing what was
happening on campus was crucial to all of our empowerment. I used to
say that as members of an interdisciplinary program, we had the advantage of hearing multidisciplinary rumors. There was no doubt that that
was an advantage. Members of the core group also worked closely
together on a number of women's studies projects, funded by grants
described later, which brought us all into close connection with one
another. After a few years, the arrival of more feminist faculty, the
development of a still larger women's studies community, and the
desire to be inclusive led to the establishment of a formal structure with
Executive and Curriculum Committees. Because I was still the only one
who was working full-time in women's studies, I would often leave these
meetings reeling with the amount of work that needed to be done to
implement the many decisions that had been made.

Group coherence was fostered, even when the faculty expanded, by
the many community-building activities we did together. For all faculty
interested in any way in women's scholarship, the women's studies program was the place where they, often bruised by a lack of appreciation
in their departments, could find a welcoming and understanding
reception. Many of us recall with fondness the annual weekend retreats
at a university-owned ranch in the Chiracaua Mountains, where we
made policy decisions and shared meals and hikes.[2]

Another important community event, still continued today, was our
annual fall luncheon, where faculty with any interest in women's scholarship and teaching gathered and reported on their current work and
courses. We always left those luncheons energized by the growing number who attended and the elation of feeling part of an expanding community. The luncheon also offered an opportunity to discover women
with similar research interests around campus, important particularly
in the early days, when there were often only one or two feminists in
each department. Our monthly feminist theory meetings, held in the
evenings, were a place to discuss the exciting new books that were being
published and to learn from one another about scholarship outside of
our specific disciplines. Visits from scholars outside the university were

occasions for parties and another opportunity to meet together. Our office staff, particularly Jo Ann Troutman and Maureen Roen, wrote songs and skits for all our special occasions. All of these activities made us think of ourselves as a community, bound together by our feminist politics, our scholarly interests, and our enjoyment of one another's company.

The lessons we learned about university politics during the years we were trying to establish the women's studies program continued during the first years of the program. I worked sometimes by intuition and often by observing other successful administrators and getting their advice. As director of a program with few resources, learning how to work the system to get what we wanted was imperative. Eventually, I am somewhat chagrined to say, I came to love the political game. I enjoyed the challenge of trying to get deans and vice presidents to see it our way by thinking up strategies to win their support. Of particular interest were the conservatives who held many of the top positions. We found that we were more likely appeal to them best if they had daughters, particularly if the daughters were professional women.

One important strategy that we developed early on was to form a network of influential allies all over campus. This was a very deliberate policy, motivated by our recognition of our outsider status and the need to find support wherever we could. We were fortunate that a highly respected gray eminence on campus, a former professor of our president, was very interested in us because of his commitment to interdisciplinary programs. He saw us as a prototype of interdisciplinarity and, as a father of a professional daughter, gave us a great deal of excellent advice. There were others who, if you were willing to disregard their paternalism, were also helpful. Cultivating these administrators and faculty could often be hard, discouraging work. It meant spending hours listening politely to uninformed views on how women's studies should be run. It was sometimes difficult during these conversations to hold on to the thought that the goal was to establish goodwill that we could draw on another time. I am amazed that I had the patience, a quality I am not known for, for these endless encounters. I can only attribute it to my fervor for the cause, and a kind of bullheaded determination that I would sit through anything if it would help our program. These men were often the necessary legitimators of our enterprise. [3]

In another attempt to expand our curriculum, I made it a point to meet with department heads, telling them about courses at other universities that they might offer at Arizona, and trying to persuade them —as much as is possible for someone with no standing in her department—to hire more women's studies scholars. I still remember an early experience of meeting with the head of a department in the business school and one of his faculty members—a man whose daughter was a feminist scholar. I often thought of it as the day I lost my innocence. I had proposed to the professor that he teach a course on women, and he and I went to discuss it with the head of his department. I am not sure when, in my enthusiastic recital of the importance of the course for business students, I realized that the head was staring at me with what I can only describe as hate-filled eyes. He eventually approved the course—the faculty member was a respected member of the department—but I will never forget that moment when I realized how much personal enmity I would encounter as I pushed for more courses on women, and how it was necessary to continue anyhow.

The enmity we sometimes experienced became even clearer as our program embarked on a series of projects intended to integrate new scholarship on women into the universitywide curriculum, an experience that we have already chronicled in an article in *Signs,* in a book entitled *Changing Our Minds,* and in other publications.[4] Our curriculum transformation projects arose as part of the nationwide determination on the part of feminist scholars to spread feminist scholarship throughout the departments and disciplines, not only women's studies courses. We also hoped that our colleagues would find the scholarship relevant and become more interested in feminist work being done in their departments. Dealing with mostly male faculty, we learned just how resistant some of them could be to expanding their knowledge base to include women and how hard we had to work to make the slightest dent.[5]

Despite our willingness to work the university system, whether in making friends with influentials or working with faculty on curriculum projects, we thought it important never to forget that as women's studies faculty we were outsiders in academe. It was that status that gave us the perspective and the strength we needed to challenge the academy, and it was that status that I, for one, never wanted to relinquish. Such a critical stance was tricky to maintain because we had, after all, chosen to work within the institution. So at the same time that we worked hard to get accepted within the university, I always felt it crucial to maintain a sense of alienation from the institution. The university, of course, helped us maintain that stance because of their disparate treatment of male and female faculty and because, although there eventually was a degree of acceptance of women's studies, we never achieved the same respect as the longer-established disciplines.

From almost the beginning, our minimal financial support from the university dictated that we look elsewhere for resources for specific activities that we wanted to undertake. Although we never made a decision to make getting grants a centerpiece of our program, one proposal led to another and we found that obtaining grants became an essential part of our program.

For example, because we were a new program and a new field, we felt that it was important to let the campus know that women's studies was a serious field by bringing in scholars with established reputations as speakers. But we had no funds. Someone told me that the Arizona Humanities Council gave funds for conferences that would be accessible to a community audience, and so only a few months after the program was established in June 1975, we were off and running to write the first of many grant proposals. Together, numbers of the women's studies program designed a conference, one that we thought would have general appeal, called Can Women's Liberation Be Men's Liberation? None of us had ever written a grant proposal before, but we learned how to do it together and, in the process, developed skills that continue to be useful to this day. The preparation of the proposal established a collaborative pattern. A member of the women's studies program would write a draft, drawing on the specific knowledge of other members for particular sections. Then the proposal would be written and rewritten by the members involved. Sidonie Smith, one of the founders of our program and now director of women's studies at the University of Michigan, thinks that the collaboration we did provided a useful and effective model for those in the group who went on to administrative careers. That first successful proposal taught us an early lesson: if you want to do something, write a grant proposal to support it. Having found the usefulness of grants, I began a deliberate policy to enhance our resources through grants.

Pursuing a grants strategy was a balancing act between knowing what grant money was available and seeing whether it fit in with the general, vague mission our women's studies program. Often I would hear about a new grant and ask specific women's studies members if they were interested in undertaking such a project. Being asked to participate in a project sometimes shaped the careers of the untenured faculty who took advantage of a grant to start a new research agenda. For the administration, however, winning grants competitively in the national arena, as the vice president of research told me often, was the real indicator of value.

The grants strategy that we pursued would not have been as successful as it was without the ideas and support that we garnered from our national networking. When the program was first established, I, a provincial New Yorker, felt isolated working at a university that was in the middle of the desert. My impulse was to reach out to national leaders in women's studies and to programs throughout the country, both to feel ourselves a part of a national movement and to learn more about developing our own program. When Elsa Greene at the University of Pennsylvania wrote in the *Women's Studies Newsletter* in 1975 about the possibility of forming a national women's studies association, I was overjoyed and bombarded her with phone calls and letters supporting the idea. Once the Ford Foundation decided to fund a planning meeting in 1976 to organize the National Women's Studies Association, I was evidently the only name anyone knew in the West, so they invited me to attend, asking me to represent an area that included Kansas and Oklahoma, an indication that territory beyond the East remained a mystery. It was at that meeting that I met a number of women who were to play a significant role in the development of our program: Florence Howe, Catharine Stimpson, then at Barnard and the founder of *Signs;* Alison Bernstein at the federal funding agency FIPSE (Fund for the Improvement of Post-Secondary Education); and Mariam Chamberlain at the Ford Foundation.

During our third year, we invited Florence Howe to come to Arizona to evaluate our program. We decided that it would be a good political move to have an important person from outside the university—a former president of the Modern Language Association—visit our campus as a way of increasing our legitimacy with university administrators. Howe was able to impress upon them the importance of women's studies as a field. Her visit also gave us a chance to get advice on our program from someone who had recently evaluated women's studies programs around the country. Like so many of the early developments in women's studies, her visit led to unexpected and beneficial results for our program. Howe met with our faculty and liked what she saw, and in her travels around the country and her encounters with funding agencies, she sang our praises, preparing the way for a number of our visits to private foundations.

One of the women Howe told about our program was Mariam Chamberlain at the Ford Foundation. This introduction led to funding of our Southwest Institute for Research of Women (SIROW) in 1979, a regional research institute attached to our women's studies program.[6] That Ford had selected us as one of only a small number of universities to establish a feminist research institute gave us enormous visibility at the university, in the Southwest region, and nationally.[7]

All of us thought of ourselves as activists, animated by the women's movement, and we were happy to do activist work when it came our way, moving beyond the university to work on community projects. As the representative of women's studies, I became the unofficial university ambassador to the women in the community, attending as many meetings and talks involving feminist issues as I could. We all participated as speakers at various events.

Many of these activities were shaped by new feminist scholarship that established that girls and women needed support in such areas as science, mathematics, and engineering. Some of those projects connected us to women scientists on campus and led us to establish an ongoing program, the Women in Science and Engineering program (WISE), led for many years by Laurel Wilkening, a feminist scientist in the lunar and planetary sciences department. Under the aegis of WISE, we developed mentoring for precollege girls and workshops for undergraduates and graduate students, and worked with David Gay in the mathematics department to establish institutes for precollege teachers of math to make them sensitive to the needs of girls and minorities.

To ensure that girls would be introduced to women's studies at an early age, we devised precollege teachers' institutes for teachers in grades 1–12, for rural teachers in the Southwest region, and for high school teachers of English and history. We also undertook other community projects as diverse as offering career education to American Indian women who were clerical workers and writing research reports in support of the Arizona Women's Town Hall. One of my last organizational efforts before stepping down as director was to establish a community support group for women's studies at Arizona, the Women's Studies Advisory Council (WOSAC), modeled after a similar group at Stanford. WOSAC has made important financial contributions to grants for students and faculty and has provided us with political support at the university.

After fourteen years as director, I decided that enough was enough. I was proud of our achievements, but years of intense, sometimes frantic, work had left little time for either the teaching I loved or for finishing a book on midlife women. By 1989, the year I stepped down, the women's studies program at Arizona appeared to be firmly established.[8] On our campus, outstanding scholarship by the increasing numbers of feminist scholars in almost every department and the growing number of courses and students made it clear that women's studies would be a permanent presence on campus. The grants strategy also had paid off: by the time I stepped down, SIROW and women's studies had garnered more than $4.5 million in grants.

Despite our very real accomplishments, we are often reminded that the fight for legitimacy is far from finished. The struggles to establish an M.A. program and get departmental status were just that: struggles. Karen Anderson pursued departmental status for the five years of her tenure as director (1989–1994), a fight that was continued by Judy Temple, director from 1994 to 1998. We were turned down repeatedly at the highest levels by some administrators who, puzzled by interdisciplinarity, couldn't quite see women's studies as a field worthy of departmental status. It was only in 1997 that we finally became a department after mounting the kind of political campaign that we have always had to wage: talking endlessly with administrators and regents, and deploying people, such as former regents and an acquaintance of the most unwilling regent, to argue our case.[9]

The experience of establishing a program affected all of our lives, giving many of us new directions in our research and teaching, and giving us a chance to develop skills that we have continued to use. Personally, I loved almost every minute of the job, despite the frustrations and problems. I felt that the work enabled me to use whatever personality, talents, and energy I had to the fullest. I was thrilled that I had the rare opportunity to be able to combine work and feminist politics: head and heart. What I liked particularly was the sense of camaraderie, the exhilaration of working with like-minded women, and the fun. Who could ever forget the deep-bellied laughter of feminists plotting their next move or discussing the foibles of those with whom we had to contend? A friend and I used to joke about how often we arrived at a school or a job where everyone talked nostalgically about the golden years, long past. We knew that, for once, we were living right in the middle of the first, but certainly not the last, of the golden years of women's studies at the University of Arizona.

Sue-Ellen Jacobs

My appointment as the first tenure-line director of women's studies at the University of Washington began in fall 1974, six years after the pioneers began their work to start a program there. I may not have been one of the pioneers in women's studies, but during the past twenty-five years, I have been central to its advancement to its certain survival well beyond 2000. Beginning with my first new course at the University of Washington in 1975, Anthropological Studies of Women, I developed eight courses, all still being taught in our women's studies department. I teach only one of these now, and occasional graduate courses for our Ph.D. and M.A. students. My research has included women in commercial fishing; women and international human rights conventions; and Native American women's health. My central research remains based on my association with friends in San Juan Pueblo, New Mexico, where my work (begun in 1972) has covered many topics. Current research includes ethnohistorical studies of women's and men's changing roles and lives; Tewa language preservation; and rights to land and water.

In 1982, after an internal search at the University of Washington, Sydney Kaplan (professor of English) was chosen as the new director of women's studies. I was then able to devote more time to research and teaching. My work continued as a faculty member. In subsequent shifts in the management of our Department of Women Studies, accomplished under the leadership of Professor Susan Jeffords (now associate dean for social sciences, College of Arts and Sciences), Shirley Yee became the departmental chair, and I the director of undergraduate women's studies. I was the first faculty member to be promoted to associate professor, then full professor, in women's studies. By fall 1999, we had three full professors, five associate professors, two assistant professors, one permanent full-time lecturer, and six part-time lecturers. I am glad that I was part of this evolution.

Has It Really Been Thirty Years?

As a graduate student in anthropology at the University of Colorado in the 1960s, I was scolded by two professors for expressing interest in women's lives cross-culturally; I was told that if I persisted in this interest, I would not be taken seriously, and of course would never get a job in academia. But one wise professor told me to bide my time, saying that once I had my degree and a job, I could begin asking questions based on my own interests.

I went from graduate school at the University of Colorado to Sacramento State College (SSC) in 1968, where I brought a quiet determination not to let anything stand in my way as I used the knowledge I had gained from civil rights and antiwar activism to inform my increasing feminist consciousness. Because tenure and promotion had to be accomplished before I could be totally brash about my politics, I kept my involvement in the Sacramento Women's Liberation Front (SWLF) a private matter. At meetings of the SWLF, I made no mention of my teaching job at SSC for the first year (1968–69), until the fateful evening when the closet faculty were challenged by community women to develop courses that would help articulate women's contributions to art, science, literature, development—in short, to life. In a burst of enthusiasm I spoke up, saying that I would ask the chair of anthropology about introducing a course called Women Cross-Culturally. Others joined this call to make our teaching relevant to the needs of women in the community, and to our students' needs and interests. Even though I was only in my first year of teaching and still had the dissertation to write, I could no longer hold back. With the chair's approval and encouragement, I began the research necessary to teach the course in 1969. The bibliography I developed that year would not be finalized until I was at the University of Illinois (1971–74), where it was published as my first book: *Women in Perspective: A Guide for Cross-Cultural Studies.*[1]

In the meantime, I became more involved in campus politics and was asked to speak publicly about women's liberation, to compare women's lives in cultures that anthropologists had studied, to comment on women's lives in the United States, and to discuss prospects for improvement in educational and occupational equity, on and off campuses. Some of those speeches were published in underground magazines, fliers, and newsletters. As the women faculty became more public in their rhetoric, students strongly encouraged the faculty to form a women's studies program at the college. After only a few months of planning, with a statement of purpose and a budget in hand, about thirty of us kept an appointment with the new African American college president, James Bond. We were prepared for a sit-in, if necessary. President Bond greeted us cordially and invited several faculty and students into his inner office, asking the others to wait outside. In his office we presented a brief overview of our case, answered his few questions, and were astonished to hear him say, "I see no problems here. You can begin as soon as you are ready." Consequently, in the spring semester of 1970, we began one of the first academic women's studies programs in the United States, with faculty teaching course overloads in order to add a course about women to our respective departmental curricula, no staff, a broom closet converted into an office for administrative purposes, a nominal head of the program, and a lot of volunteers.

In 1971 I moved to the Department of Urban and Regional Planning at the University of Illinois for postdoctoral work and teaching about community development. As an applied anthropologist I focused my work on reducing infant and maternal mortality rates in the local African American community.[2] My interest in women's studies was sustained by this work, and by my participation in various feminist collectives within my professional associations, including the American Anthropological Association.[3] In 1973 I accepted the offer from the dean of the College of Arts and Sciences at the University of Washington to become director of women studies and assistant professor of anthropology, but deferred moving there until a replacement could be found for me in the community project.

I moved to the University of Washington in fall 1974 as the first tenure-line faculty member directing the women studies program, with an untenured joint appointment in the extremely misogynist anthropology department. Still believing that it was only a matter of time before reason would prevail and studies of and by women would be integrated into the core curriculum of all the disciplines, I also thought that it would not take long before tenure would be granted to me in anthropology.

Although I was not present in 1973 when the students' demands for relevant instruction broke on the University of Washington campus, I have learned secondhand that some of the strongest support for my appointment came from three very active graduate students in anthropology.[4] Although these students wanted me to be hired, a contingent headed by radical women activists in Seattle was more interested in other candidates. The Women Studies Advisory Committee (made up of students, staff, and faculty from various departments) ranked at least one other person above me, and offered the position to her. She turned it down, saying that the work load was unreasonable; research and teaching support were absent, as was an autonomous budget and direct line to the college dean; and the salary was paltry. I accepted those conditions because Donna Gerstenberger (the assistant dean in charge of general and interdisciplinary studies, in which women studies was located) told me that she was confident that my request for fiscal autonomy could be met right away, and that in time structural autonomy could be achieved. I knew that the women studies program was merely a collection of courses that had begun in 1970 with a spring quarter course, Women 200: Introduction to Women Studies, taught by graduate students and peer tutors under the General Studies Division of the College of Arts and Sciences. Although I had two offers in hand to go elsewhere, my belief in Gerstenberger's implied promises and her support of my dream of a women studies graduate program someday led to my acceptance of this job.

My faith in future possibilities was, in largest part, due to Florence Howe. I had been in touch with Howe while I was at the University of Illinois, as had many of us who were dreaming of how our new discipline would be shaped. But we at our respective institutions were only vaguely aware of how many women studies programs were coming into being each year. Florence Howe had a pretty good idea because she was traveling around the country, following up on leads about new programs (or at least courses of study). She knew that feminist teachers and organizers on campuses needed a focal point for two reasons: so we would not feel as though we were alone in our efforts; and so we could bring the numbers of us to bear on administrators who were reluctant to "waste" faculty positions (and offices) on this "new fad." Those administrators could not have imagined how deep and wide would be the effect of the new academic paradigm they were trying to hold back. Feminist theory would carve out revolutionary theoretical stances for most disciplines by the early 1990s, interestingly, without the full consent of all women studies founders, especially those schooled in the community activism models of the 1960s and 1970s.

By the mid-1970s, I was part of an enormous force of women liberationists from all walks of life in the Pacific Northwest. Our Women Studies Advisory Committee was made up of students, staff, community members, and faculty—each with an equal vote and voice in the (sometimes very rowdy) meetings. We talked with our counterparts throughout the state and the region, and all agreed to have a regional meeting where we would discuss the possibility of forming a regional women's studies association. At that meeting, we agreed on a constitution, sliding-scale membership dues, our name (the Northwest Women Studies Association, or NWWSA), and other matters. I knew that the National Women's Studies Association (NWSA) was about to form because I was on an early steering committee for NWSA, so our regional group tried to imagine how our Northwest regional needs, goals, structure, and membership might be consistent with the national group. With thoughtful consideration of emerging programs in various regions, the national agenda and structure looked to the larger goal of providing a forum and structure for shaping the content of the new discipline, while keeping community needs in mind. As time passed, trying to serve the growing needs of both academic and nonacademic sources of study led to difficult (and sometimes unresolvable) tensions at all levels (NWSA, NWWSA, and the University of Washington).

At the University of Washington, one of the structural issues we faced was also the principal fiscal problem. In 1974 I began as the first tenure-line director of women studies; I did not have full budget authority, nor could I decree what courses we would offer, because these all had to go through the General and Interdisciplinary Studies Program (GIS). I could not hire whomever we had chosen in our open searches for the few part-time courses we were offering, without approval from that office. So one of the first challenges was to get the budget into the hands of the women studies administrator, to create a line-item budget over which we would have full authority. While we were at it, we thought also to separate the courses from GIS listings and begin the *women* listings. It took some serious consultations set up by senior tenured faculty women with the male administration, throughout the course of two years, to achieve the separation.

In 1978, with support from a new college dean, I gave up my joint appointment in the anthropology department, because it was too difficult to administer a growing program and try to meet the demands put on a junior faculty member by the senior faculty.[5] Now we were ready to think about how we were going to expand our program with tenure-line faculty appointed full-time in women studies. We hired physiological psychologist Nancy Kenney with a joint appointment, two years after I was hired. We next hired a historian full-time, someone who would also take on teaching three academic quarters of Women 200, which now had enrollments of more than two hundred undergraduate students each quarter—and an average of nine peer tutors who held quiz or discussion sessions one period a week. The historian was also expected to teach two history courses, publish, and serve on committees. She came to the University of Washington without tenure, and was not able to produce the publishing necessary to advance to tenure. This failure was felt by all of us in women studies: we overworked her (as we did ourselves) and could not fix the problems because we discovered them too late.[6] Throughout the course of the next twenty years, we would be given permission to hire five additional full-time tenure-line faculty members, and one jointly appointed faculty member. We also expanded our roster of adjunct faculty from five to sixty,[7] developed our own cadre of research faculty,[8] and have supported assistant professors' advancement to associate professor with tenure, and associate professors' advancement to full professor. Others are well on their way up the ladder.

In 1974 I would not have believed anyone who told me that we would become so numerous and diverse as feminists in our extracurricular communities (while fighting a continuous battle against antifeminists, who seemed also to grow in number), and as feminists in the academy. That we have become diverse ethnically and racially is a wondrous achievement, given that (irrespective of our racial, ethnic, class, or national origin) we behave more and more like the establishment we sought to change, or even dismantle, rebuilding in other images. We behave more like that establishment in our conduct of departmental business, which includes setting and following strict criteria for tenure and promotion, exercising conservative approaches to incorporating

312 ✳ SUE-ELLEN JACOBS

new ideas from "outside sources," (feminist organizations outside academia), and defending the need to operate within the institutional structures. In the early years, we felt camaraderie and love for one another, in spite of all the glorious shouting matches, crying sessions, and make-up sessions. Our close relationships were facilitated by hopeful and determined rap sessions and by retreats (usually in some safe outdoor space away from town or at least away from campus), where we hammered out manifestos and challenged the hierarchical ordering of ourselves and our colleagues. The implicit assumption was usually that we were all in this together, and our goal was to achieve the long-term gains necessary for all women to have educational and occupational parity. We thought that we would be a different kind of academic study: cooperative, communal, and collaborative in teaching, research, and service. But the institution more often rewards evidence of singular achievement: the independent scholar who makes it on her own. We have had to adjust to these circumstances.

We became a department in order to offer an autonomous B.A. in women's studies. This was the first step in our plan to become a graduate degree—offering department. It took us fifteen years from the time we began the formal institutional processes to the time of approval for the M.A./Ph.D. programs. In order to evaluate faculty for promotion, in 1978 the university administration created the Women Studies Standing Committee. The committee is made up of full professors from outside of women studies, who agree to advise the chair on policy matters, as well as serve as the executive committee for the department. All hiring, retention, promotion, and tenure decisions made by tenured faculty are put before the standing committee, who make a final vote that is then passed to the chair. Once there are enough senior faculty (full professors) in the women studies department, there will no longer be a need for the standing committee—but even today (with only two full-time full professors, three associate professors, and two assistant professors), we have some distance to go before we reach critical mass at either the junior or senior level.

One of our early goals was to increase the academic and ethnic diversity in our program. Working with Marilyn Bentz of American Indian studies, Artee Young of black studies, James Morishima of Asian American studies, and Gary Trujillo of Chicano studies in the 1970s, I sought to ensure that we kept our attention on diversity in our teaching and hiring practices. From the beginning we have required that our courses contain content on race, class, gender, and sexuality. When the National Endowment for the Humanities made a three-year grant for the Washington Women's Heritage Project to the University of Washington, Washington State University, and Western Washington University (to be jointly carried out by all three), the directors of the ethnic studies program and I were part of the original Advisory Committee. We also had volunteer and paid community members, such as Dorothy Cordova, a Filipina who helped us develop one of the most successful oral history projects to be conducted in any state. When the Ford Foundation chose our university in 1981 to be a Center for Research on Women (CROW) site, troubles began. The university administration decided that the Northwest Center for Research on Women (NCROW) would be located in the Graduate School with de facto administration by the Graduate School associate dean for research. I proposed the same group of people for the Advisory Board, as the ones who formed the Advisory Committee for the heritage project. This proposal was summarily turned down by the upper-level administrators, who instead formed an Advisory Board made up of select deans from several different schools and a vice president from the medical school, who was publicly adamant that NCROW should have no connection to the women studies program. As NCROW began to be shaped, and the meetings became blisteringly unpleasant, I had no choice but to refuse to continue sitting in on what I perceived to be a misogynist mission—especially because my role as director of the women studies program did not even give me a vote on the committee! Fortunately, by 1992 a new Advisory Committee (and a new, supportive dean of the College of Arts and Sciences) allowed Angela Ginorio, the director of NCROW, to bring NCROW to women studies when she became part of our tenure-line faculty.

We were collaborative dreamers, in spite of what is said by the naysayers of today who were not there.[9] For some of us, our dreams of a better world for women came from sources that we would not or could—in that time and in that place—name. Even in our rap groups in those early days, we rarely talked about women and violence except in hushed voices—and never about our own experiences; lesbianism was a dangerous topic, legally and socially; and the special status, problems, and needs of immigrant women and women in prisons were not part of our concerns. There were many things that we did not talk about, nor envision teaching in our women studies courses. Today we teach courses entitled Women and Violence; Women and Human Rights Abuses; Lesbian Lives and Culture; Race, Class, and Gender; and Ideologies and Technologies of Motherhood: Race, Class, and Sexuality; as well as many other courses dealing with other harsh realities of everyday life. In these courses we use textbooks and other writings in feminist studies that show clearly the inequities among and between women in our own towns and around the world. We have learned to read new texts, available because of courageous publishers who continue to support the writings by scholars in American Indian studies, American ethnic studies, and women studies.[10] Today there are theoretical, empirical, and expository studies numbering in the thousands, rather than the few dozen we all relied upon in the 1970s and 1980s—some of which remain as salient today as they were originally.[11]

In 1998 I interviewed a graduate student who began her Ph.D. work in our department in that same year. The shining joy in her eyes, in the radiance of her skin, and in her voice, as she explained that she had been waiting for more than ten years for this day, had me close to tears. She was enthralled that the first step was now possible for pursuing her dream of becoming a professor in women's studies at a university. In 1999, we admitted to our Ph.D. program a Native American woman who had been waiting nearly thirty years for this opportunity. The amazing thing is that she was part of the community of local radical women who fought to establish women studies at the University of Washington in the late 1960s and early 1970s. They are on the edge of the future, the ones who will help shape the next generation of feminist scholars. They may be on the market in the same year that I retire, giving up (in 2001) a coveted professorial position for a member of the next generation. These new students give me joy in their enthusiasm for shaping a new feminism to match their needs, drawing from me every ounce of memory and insight I might have about the past and the future.[12] They ask wonderful questions in class, and they challenge me with new ways of seeing and thinking. They dream of futures impossible for me to imagine, yet I do try.

My mother's mother was born in 1875; she died at 104 in 1979. She used to tell me and my siblings stories about growing up in the late 1800s and about all the wondrous things that she had seen come to pass in the 1900s. We listened in awe to her stories, including those about her travels, first by horse and buggy, later by train, still later by "the Greyhound" (bus), and her last trips by jet airplane. Today I feel blessed to have a connection to the world of my parents' parents, and to other elders[13] whose lives I have been privileged to share. It is very humbling to realize that within my own memories are the memories of those who came before me, not in diaries, not in books, some in letters, though most didn't write about their lives and some were only nominally literate (if at all). It's the stories they told that connect me to their past and my own stories. These stories also provide a link for my students who dream a world of possibilities. I have known some truly remarkable women in my travels as a professional anthropologist and as a feminist. And I expect to meet more.

Yolanda T. Moses

I am a feminist cultural anthropologist with a research and scholarly focus on women and economic development in the United States, in the Caribbean, and in Africa; the origins of inequality; and anthropological perspectives on the American university in the late twentieth century. I am a product of public higher education in California, and I have spent my academic career teaching, doing research, and holding administrative and leadership positions in public higher educational institutions in an effort to give back what I got: a quality education at an affordable price.

As an administrator, I have always been motivated to create the kind of institution where all students can be successful; where faculty can push the envelope with their creative ideas; and where administrators are empowered to imagine new structures and ways of conceptualizing and organizing the academy to be more inclusive, and to value inclusion. As a faculty member who has taught anthropology, women's studies, and ethnic studies throughout the past twenty-five years, I can attest firsthand to the importance of teaching students two things above all else. The first is to critically question everything. The second is that knowledge has no boundaries. For twenty-five years, I have been working to blur those distinctions between bodies of knowledge by promoting structures that encourage interdisciplinary collaboration.

One of my major contributions to women's studies has been to promote its link and connection to ethnic studies and to show how race/ethnicity, gender, and class are all part of a women's studies

knowledge continuum. The following article chronicles how I came to
help establish one of the few of ethnic and women's studies departments in the United States.

Linking Ethnic Studies
to Women's Studies

I came of age in a household where it was expected that women would
take care of themselves as well as everyone else. My mother, my aunts,
and my grandmother were my first feminist role models. I did not
know it at the time, but my early years in the company of three generations of working-class African American women helped to shape my
notions of womanhood.

I went to San Jose State University as a freshman in 1964. There I
immediately began to work with the Student Nonviolent Coordinating
Committee (SNCC). The civil rights and women's rights movements
were coming of age, and students across the country were involved.
When I took a sociology course in which the instructor talked about
women's issues and about race relations, the white women in the class
did not see the connections of sexism to racism, and the men of color
in the class did not see the connections of racism to sexism. The other
women of color and I saw both connections immediately, but as a
freshman I had no idea how to express my vision. Thirty-four years
later, I am still grappling with how to express the impact of these systems of oppression on women of color everywhere.

In the summer of 1965, I moved closer to home in Southern California to attend San Bernardino Valley College, a community college.
When I joined the campus Black Student Union in 1966, I saw my
leadership talents thwarted when the men of the organization continued to make all the decisions. Though I had declared my major as sociology, a galvanizing experience planted the seed that would lead me to
anthropology one day.

The humanities program at San Bernardino Valley College brought
Margaret Mead as a distinguished speaker to the campus. I had heard of
her, but I was still ignorant about anthropology as a field of study. In a
memorable talk, Mead explained why young people in U.S. society were

alienated from adult expectations of appropriate behavior and purpose. She saw this alienation as dysfunctional for our culture. In the
question-and-answer period, I asked her what she thought of the new
black power movement. Did she see it as a positive or negative development? Mead responded that she thought it was positive that blacks had
taken a negative concept, co-opted the negative use of the word *black,*
and turned it on its head to make it a positive, powerful concept. She
said that she thought it was healthy. Immediately, I liked this woman
who could think unconventionally about race in U.S. society. Later,
when I read her book *Coming of Age in Samoa,* I found that she could also
think unconventionally about gender. The premise of Mead's study was
that gender roles are culturally, not biologically, determined. Her
findings actually upset the thinking of the psychologists in the late
1920s, who were still very much steeped in theories of innate gender
behavior. So, I thought, anthropology is a field I want to know more
about. Still, sociology seemed a bit more relevant to me.

From 1966 to 1968, I was a student at the newly established San
Bernardino State College. With an enrollment of five hundred students, it was dubbed the Dartmouth of the West. There I got a fine liberal arts education. I also had one memorably betraying experience in
the Sociology of the Family, a course required of all sociology majors.
We had just read Daniel P. Moynihan's account of why the black family
was in trouble. Moynihan said it was the fault of black women! I could
scarcely believe what I was reading. The discussion in class was quite
lively, because everybody but me seemed to accept this explanation. Not
only did Moynihan describe the black family as negative, he also called
it deviant. I came from a female-centered family, and I knew many
other black folks who did, too. I had never before thought of my working-
class black family life as abnormal, and I said so that day in class. The
professor became defensive and I could feel my classmates lining up on
his side. Though my term paper in that course was a refutation of
Moynihan's theories, and I got a good grade, the experience left a bad
taste in my mouth.

From 1968 to 1970, I worked as a vocational rehabilitation counselor in Los Angeles. Thanks to my mother[1] and to a new program at
the Ford Foundation,[2] in the fall of 1970, I began graduate studies in
anthropology at the University of California, Riverside (UCR), where I
was finally free to explore the issues of class, race, and gender in comparative perspectives. At UCR I soon began to form ties with women

graduate students both inside and outside of the department. I began to attend the activities sponsored by the Women's Center at UCR, and helped to form a feminist group within the department. We organized a seminar in the spring of 1971 called Women in Cross-Cultural Perspective. Most of the speakers were female professors and graduate students, all of whom knew the ground-breaking readings in the new book by Michelle Zimbalist Rosaldo and Louise Lamphere, *Woman, Culture and Society*.[3] This was the book that opened the feminist scholarship movement within anthropology.

It was soon apparent that sexism was alive and well across racial and ethnic boundaries. In the department, our women's group was met by hostility on the part of many male graduate students, and by indifference and ambivalence on the part of the faculty, who, with one exception, were men. I was surprised that these anthropologists did not see the focus on gender as an opportunity to empower their graduate students to create new knowledge for the field of anthropology. Instead, they misunderstood women's studies, characterizing it as only political, ignoring it as an academic area of study.

Though I was actively involved with the women in the Department of Anthropology, I had also formed a friendship with one of the few African American male faculty on campus—in the political science department. I used to enjoy talking with him about issues of critical race theory, and about black/white political issues. I even considered him to be a mentor of sorts. When I was asked to write a piece for the special women's studies issue of the university newspaper, I wrote about the similarities between racism and sexism, and how black women and other women of color suffered from both "isms." I thought that it was a well-thought-out piece that was breaking new ground. My mentor was unhappy when he read it. He said to me, "Why are you wasting your time with those feminist white women? They do not have your interests at heart, nor do they really care about you. Besides, they are 'male bashers.'" I was shocked. I had no idea that he felt that way. Needless to say, this was my introduction to the kind of cold shoulder that I would get throughout the years from ethnic studies faculty, especially men, when they found out I was a feminist.

In the spring of 1972, I married a white man, despite the disapproval of some of my friends, both black and white. In 1973 I passed my orals, was advanced to candidacy for my Ph.D., and went to Montserrat, a small island in the British West Indies, to do my fieldwork. When

I decided to do my research on the women of the island, one member of my dissertation committee said, "I can understand how you would want to devote a chapter to women's issues, but can you write a whole dissertation?" "Female Status and Male Dominance in a West Indian Community" was a study of the economic choices of working-class and middle-class women that controlled whether they chose to marry in order to create better lives for themselves and, ultimately, for their families. My thesis concluded that working-class women chose *not* to marry in order to maximize their strategic economic advantages, and middle-class women chose to marry in order to achieve the same end. Mine was one of the first research studies to focus on class differences among black women in the Caribbean. When I returned to the university to write up my work in 1974, I saw my thesis as an opportunity for me to introduce a group of senior white male faculty to the writings of women anthropologists.

I was hired in the fall of 1975 as a part-time instructor at California State Polytechnic University (Cal-Poly) in Pomona, thirty-six miles east of Los Angeles. Later that year, Dr. Joan Greenway, the first woman department chair in the Division of Social Sciences and Humanities, convinced the dean that I should be appointed on a tenure-track line while I wrote my dissertation. I was also pregnant during the 1975–76 academic year, in which I taught full-time, commuted seventy-two miles three times a week, and wrote my dissertation. In June of 1976 I graduated with honors, the first in my class, and on July 7, 1976, I had my first daughter, Shana.

During my first few years at Cal-Poly, I taught in the anthropology department. In the summer of 1978, I received a fellowship to attend a summer seminar called Biological Differences and Social Equality at the Center for Advanced Studies in the Behavioral Sciences at Stanford University. This summer fellowship program brought people together from various disciplines to exchange perspectives and share information about sociobiology, issues of race and intelligence, and the meaning of the newly decided *Bakke* decision. As an anthropologist, I focused on issues of race and intelligence as they intersected with gender and inequality. Many of the participants attended the seminars on race and intelligence, but far fewer (and almost no men) attended the seminars on gender issues. The women participants persuaded Michelle Rosaldo, who was in the anthropology department at Stanford, to talk to our entire group. Even then, the men in the group (of all ethnicities) were not interested. I was surprised by how difficult it was, at the time, for men of color to see the links between institutional racism and sexism.

In 1980, when I received early tenure, I inquired about teaching a new course that I had developed on women in cross-cultural perspective in the women's studies program. I learned that there was no organized program, only some courses taught within the ethnic studies department. I was really surprised to find that women's studies courses were taught under the umbrella of the ethnic studies department. Both were marginalized programs in this polytechnic environment of science, engineering, business, architecture, agriculture, and education programs. Although the campus also had a large liberal arts division (that I eventually became dean of), in the late 1970s, women's studies and ethnic studies were considered irrelevant to and superfluous in a highly technical and professional environment.

Thus, women's studies and ethnic studies banded together to survive. But they had never thought through a coherent, intellectually based program that maximized the juxtaposition of race and gender. I found it very exciting to work with a group of faculty to create our interdisciplinary curriculum, and tried not to worry about jeopardizing my promising career as an anthropologist. Despite warnings from colleagues, I first taught a cross-listed women's studies course in anthropology in the ethnic studies department. In 1980, when the chair of that department, Dr. Charles Irby, went on a sabbatical leave and the dean asked me to step in as acting chair, I did so despite the objections of my anthropology colleagues. I spent the next two years developing what has come to be one of the most unique ethnic and women's studies departments in the United States.

I was lucky in that I began this curricular work without having to argue for departmental status for the ethnic studies programs. That battle had been fought before I got to Cal-Poly. The four ethnic studies programs, black studies, Chicano studies, Asian American studies, and American Indian studies, had been separate programs whose faculty had decided to merge to gain departmental status so they could compete for resources in the manner of the traditional academic units on campus. The few women's studies courses that were taught in the department were not integrated in any intellectual way. The faculty did not interact across the great divide of race or gender. But my tenure was to change all that.

First the vision: we seized the opportunity to design a cohesive, cutting-edge curriculum that integrated issues of race and gender throughout, and to market it as an attractive program for students. For this vision to become a reality, most of the faculty in all of the programs would have to accept the interdisciplinary nature of the program, and would have to work on substantive curriculum revision. Approximately 80 percent of the faculty in ethnic studies and in women's studies embraced the model. Because there was relatively little resistance to the development of minors, we worked first on these in all four of the ethnic studies areas. In the late 1970s, it was not clear to students in that polytechnic university what good an ethnic studies or women's studies major would be in the workplace. It was a lot easier to convince the professional majors how appropriate an ethnic studies or women's studies minor would be for the multicultural, multiethnic workplaces of California.

We then had to decide how to revamp existing courses and create new ones for the integrated parts of our curriculum. At the introductory level, for example, we planted reinforcing themes in the introductory courses. Introduction to Ethnic Studies and Introduction to Women's Studies both included within a U.S. worldview the historical roots of race and gender oppression. It was also important for male faculty (both Euro-American and faculty of color) to understand gender issues, especially as they related to women of color. It was equally important for Euro-American women to understand the impact of the double oppression of race and gender bias on women of color. Needless to say, the faculty in our department argued endlessly before agreeing about what we wanted our students to learn.

In the upper-division levels, we supplemented our own core courses with courses cross-listed with other programs and departments in the university. These courses were selected by our departmental Curriculum Committee through an established review process. These courses complemented the core we had designed. For ethnic studies, we developed courses that explored the themes of family, religion, education, economics, race, and gender. The course called The Family and Ethnicity, for example, could be taught with an integrative or comparative approach, or it could be taught with a focus on one ethnic group.

For women's studies, we developed a series of traditional women's studies courses, including Ethnic Women. Although we had a feminist theory course, we also developed a course, Racism and Sexism, that students minoring in both ethnic studies and women's studies had to take. Often it was team-taught, with a faculty member from each area. As was true of the program, not all courses were immediately popular outside of the department.

Within the department, it took about a year's worth of retreats, seminars, and meetings to educate ourselves about the theory, content, and intellectual assumptions of one another's areas. Once we developed a coherent interdisciplinary curriculum within the department, we had to consider how to get our courses into the university's distribution list for general education. Because I had been a faculty member of the Senate Educational Policies Committee, I understood the curriculum politics of general education. I had also been in a special administrative program in 1978–79, when I worked as an assistant dean at the California State University, Long Beach. This experience gave me the opportunity to see the larger, universitywide picture of how policies and practices are adopted or implemented. I was able to put those administrative skills to use at Cal-Poly.

Before the time came for the ethnic and women's studies department to present the curriculum to the Educational Policies Committee for approval, I talked to the members of the Senate committee one-on-one behind the scenes. Once the curriculum was approved, the lower-division courses (the introductory courses and the 100- and 200-level courses) appeared in the catalogue. At that point I began to feel a backlash from other departments in the Division of Social Sciences and Humanities, who saw our courses as being in direct competition with their courses. Our response was to boast that we team-taught our courses in an interdisciplinary manner unique to the campus.

The program flourished for two years while I was the acting chair of the department. When I became acting dean and then the new dean of the College of Liberal Arts, I appointed Lillian Jones as acting chair of the department. As she implemented the department's vision from the inside, I worked to keep it funded and in the mainstream of campus curriculum, academic, and governance issues. I encouraged the members of the department to get involved in campus governance and leadership activities, so they could take part in any policy-making that would affect the department's strength. For example, the faculty in the ethnic and women's studies department taught in an award-winning interdisciplinary general education program designed to provide social sciences and humanities content to all engineering students on campus. Faculty who taught in this program were generally recognized as faculty leaders, and were called upon to serve on Senate committees.

It now seems clear to me that my commitment to women's studies and ethnic studies drew me into university administration. Had I not been the dean of the College of Liberal Arts at Cal-Poly, the ethnic and women's studies department might not have continued to grow and flourish. The lesson to be learned from all this is that it takes committed people at all levels of the university to make women's studies successful.

When I became dean in 1982, I felt that the College of Liberal Arts needed a cultural pluralism course requirement. We worked for almost five years to make that happen. When I became a provost of the California State University, Dominguez Hills, in 1988, I worked to help model for the whole university what an institutionalized academic commitment to diversity might look like. Under the leadership of the women's studies, ethnic studies, and anthropology faculty, the university created an environment that valued diversity. When the opportunity came for me to go to the City College of New York in 1993 as its president, I knew that it was a chance for me to model what a total institutional commitment to diversity could look like. Again, women's studies and ethnic studies faculty have been leaders in this effort. As we move into the next millennium, we need to look back and celebrate the achievements of the past thirty years, and look to a future with a new generation of feminist scholars and teachers who will lift our understanding of women's studies and ethnic studies to even greater heights.

PART VI

Looking
Back

Cups Half Empty
or Half Full?

Johnnetta B. Cole

I graduated from Oberlin College and earned my master's and doctorate in anthropology at Northwestern University. I recall the pride and excitement I felt when I first learned of the work of a sister anthropologist, Zora Neale Hurston.

My decision to leave a teaching post for an administrative post in 1987 was deeply affected by the fact that I was standing for the presidency of Spelman College as its first African American woman president. My ten years in that job were profoundly rewarding. During those years, approximately a third of Spelman's graduates majored in mathematics, physics, chemistry, biology, computer science, and a dual degree in engineering. When *U.S. News & World Report* named Spelman the number one liberal arts college in the South, it became the first historically Black college to receive a number-one rating in the magazine's annual college issue. During my years at the college we completed a major capital campaign that raised $113.8 million, the largest sum ever raised by a historically Black college or university.

My appointment to the presidency of Spelman College opened up appointments to corporate boards; I was the first women or the first African American woman to serve on several of them. As I work on various boards, I continue to call for greater inclusion of all women and men of color, not only on boards but throughout institutions.

I am proud of the hard work I do on a national and local level in Atlanta, and I am grateful for the recognition I have received for such work. I am especially pleased that women's colleges and historically Black colleges and universities are among those institutions awarding me 43 honorary degrees.

I have published two textbooks, *All American Women* and *Anthropology for the Nineties*, and two volumes of essays, *Conversations: Straight Talk with America's Sister President* and *Dream the Boldest Dreams and Other Lessons of Life*. I now hold an endowed professorship at Emory University that engages all three of my intellectual interests and passions, anthropology, African American studies, and women's studies.

The Long Road Through Gendered Questions

While growing up, I developed a far deeper consciousness of racism than of sexism. As a youngster, my vocabulary did not include the word *class*, but I knew that my nuclear family was not poor: I heard again and again that the man I ever so respectfully and affectionately called Fa-Fa—my maternal great-grandfather—was the richest Black man in all of Jacksonville, Florida. The relative weight of race, gender, and class in my hometown as I grew up in the 1940s was such that all of my great-grandfather's money was not and never could be sufficient to "buy" me out of all of the lines that so clearly determined the access that Black people had to institutions and resources, to privileges and simple courtesies that even the poorest white person had as a birthright.

In 1960, when I was twenty-four years old, personal and professional circumstances propelled me toward a critical examination of the intersections of race, gender, and class. As a graduate student in anthropology in an interracial marriage, I was living in Liberia, West Africa, where for the first time in my life, I was in the racial majority. There, I pondered questions that I would never have raised were I living in my own society.

In Liberia, it mattered greatly to which group of Black people one belonged: the privileged Americo-Liberians, who were the descendants of U.S. slaves who had been sent back to Africa, or the native people, who were the descendants of one of the twenty-two so-called tribal groups who had never been enslaved and sent to the United States. Here I first learned the bitter lesson that being a victim of oppression does not give one an immunity to oppressing others. Here I also raised questions about gender, for in Liberia, it was clearer to me than in my own country just how disproportionately women labored, both in the fields and in child care. The practice of polygamy raised yet other questions. Still, I could only observe, query, and feel discomfort. I had no developed feminist lens through which to analyze my feelings and observations.

Following the prevailing [...] 1960s among married academics, on returning from [...] th-old son, we moved to where my husb[...] Washington State University in Pull[...] fter, I, too, was offered a job in the a[...] iversity.

As a young African A[...] ask why there were so few Black stude[...] rofessors and staff. Why, in the tellir[...] tes, were there so few references to folks who look[...] s there so little in the academy that seemed to have a direct relati[...] ip to what people were experiencing in their everyday lives? In short, I was asking the very questions that fueled the Black studies movement as it was being organized on various college and university campuses. I was very much a part of the movement of students and faculty who demanded a Black studies program at Washington State University, and I became the director of the program, one of the first such programs in the United States.

[handwritten note: Lack of representation]

This was also the time when there was, across campuses in the United States, an anti–Vietnam war movement. I came to feel deeply about the war in Vietnam, and to believe that it was fundamentally wrong. I also became very conscious of connections between the questions that I was raising about my own people and the large presence of African American soldiers in Vietnam. A line spoken by a Black U.S. soldier was repeated throughout Black communities and on college and university campuses: "No Vietnamese ever called me nigger."

The 1960s were very exciting times for me. As a freshly minted instructor of anthropology who was the director of a Black studies program, I was not only deeply engaged in teaching, I was also politically active, participating in sit-ins and marches. On one occasion, I went to jail with members of the Black Student Union, an organization for which I was the faculty adviser. It was all reminiscent of the 1950s. At Fisk University, where I was an early entrance student, faculty, students, and staff challenged the outrageousness of Jim Crow segregation in public facilities and in businesses, such as lunch counters. And at Oberlin College, where I completed my undergraduate studies, I was again in an academic environment where intellectualism and activism lived comfortably with each other.

Of course, no single event galvanized activism in African American communities and on college campuses like the assassination of Dr. Martin Luther King Jr. in 1968. There was a direct correlation between that tragedy and a positive response to the call for increased numbers of Black students on college campuses and a second wave of Black studies programs.

Although I remained deeply involved throughout the 1960s in efforts to counter racism in the academy, it was not until the 1970s that I fully came to grips with the reality that sexism was very much alive in the academic world. And yet I did have enough consciousness while at Washington State University to teach a course on Black women. It was the lack of readily available material for that course that prompted me, a few years later, to do the research that led to the publication in *The Black Scholar* of one of the first annotated bibliographies on Black women in the United States.

My course Black Women in America, one of the earliest such courses, would today be evaluated as woefully lacking in sophistication. In those days, there was a tendency in all Black studies courses to do what I used to call the Wheaties approach, that is, to identify the great figures in Black history and ask, in essence, why they were not on the front of a cereal box as were the white heroes. Of course, the candidates were overwhelmingly men. Hence, out of a desire to balance matters, I looked for great Black women in history. I remember challenging myself to focus on far more African American "sheroes" than Sojourner Truth and Harriet Tubman. Discovering the writing of Anna Julia Cooper was particularly important to me, for she captured in words the duality of African American women that I was confronting: that we are characterized by both the race problem and the woman question.

In that early course on Black women, I was also advancing notions about myself and my sisters that were grounded in characteristics that I had seen portrayed and had not challenged. For example, it took years before I could say with conviction that not every Black woman, indeed not every woman, wants to be a mother. It took me years also before I could truly understand the degree to which patriarchy affects women and men in African American communities, just as it does white and folks of all racial and ethnic groups.

During those early days in Black studies, I also debated with so my students and colleagues in Black studies about the lives and responsibilities of women in African societies. Many Black nationalists of that period romanticized women in traditional African societies. Myths about their roles and status were then superimposed on the African American reality as Black men began to address Black women as "my African queen," even in situations where African American male chauvinism was obvious.

In 1970 I joined the faculty at the University of Massachusetts, Amherst, with an appointment in anthropology and African American studies, even as from across the disciplines women faculty began teaching courses in what would become women's studies. In the English department, several women were developing and teaching these courses: Margo Culley, Rayna Green, Arlyn Diamond, Lee Edwards, and Ann Jones. They met regularly and called themselves the Ladies' Tea and Mau Mau Society. Courses were also being taught by Ann Ferguson in philosophy and Sara Lenox in linguistics. African American studies professor Esther Terry and I were the only women of color affiliated with the program in women's studies in those early days. A few men on the faculty also supported this new interdisciplinary program. Notable among them was a historian in the University of Massachusetts Black studies department, Professor John Bracey.

Among the Five College (Smith, Amherst, Hampshire, Mount Holyoke, and the University of Massachusetts) faculties, the few African American women scholars continued to call for diversity in women's studies. Dr. Johnnella Butler was at Smith College, Professor Andrea Rushing was at Amherst College, and Professors Gloria Joseph and Fran White were at Hampshire College. Although there were two women's colleges, Mount Holyoke and Smith, within the Five College group, it is the case that generally in women's colleges across the country, women's studies did not have a strong early presence, just as Black studies was and is not particularly associated with historically Black colleges and universities.

In the 1960s, I often asked my male colleagues in Black studies, "Where are the women?" Then in the 1970s, I often asked my colleagues in women's studies, "Where are the Black folks and other people of color?" From time to time—most memorably during a course called Black Women in America, which I team-taught with Esther Terry—I was able to unite my love for anthropology, my commitment to African American studies, and my new interest in women's studies. Together, Professor Esther Terry and I could offer students both literary and social sciences perspectives on women and gender. One of the readings we assigned, Professor Angela Davis's essay "The Role of Women in the Community of Slaves," pushed my development as a feminist scholar more than any text I had encountered. Written while Professor Davis was still in prison, the essay provides a clear exposition of the social construction of gender, as well as an illustration of the interrelationships among gender, race, and class. In this essay Davis theorizes that female slaves were viewed not only in economic terms, as racial property, but also as women, who had to be dealt with through the violence of sexual exploitation and rape. It was very important to me and my students that this pioneering work had come from an activist scholar who was a Black woman, for it was rare in those days to find references to African American women as intellectuals.

One of the students in Black Women in America was Arlene Voski Avakian, a woman of Armenian descent who was a staff member in women's studies—and today is a member of the faculty. With a clear voice, Arlene Voski Avakian challenged her white sisters to confront their white skin privilege. She also was instrumental in helping our class to confront homophobia. Indeed, this was a time when I was dealing with my own heterosexism; and it was some time before I fully understood how sexuality—like race, ethnicity, religion, gender, age, and physical disability—is used as the basis of a system of inequality.

In 1982, I went to Hunter College, where my appointment was in the anthropology department; but I also had close ties with women's studies and the program in Black and Puerto Rican studies. Secretary of Health and Human Services Donna Shalala was the president of Hunter at that time, and her support of women's issues was a factor in the growth of women's studies at that institution. Perhaps it was because Hunter College students were so diverse that I felt compelled to find materials that reflected their realities. Most of the students that I taught in women's studies were enrolled in the college's returning women's program. My students in the returning women's program were older than most college students, had been out in the world of work, had fewer financial resources than most college students, and were the principal caretakers if they had children.

The anthology that I edited while at Hunter, *All American Women: Lines That Divide and Ties That Bind,* grew out of a course that I taught in the returning women's program. The central point of that anthology, and one that remains understated in words and actions in women's studies, is that, although all women are to some extent victimized by patriarchy, the specificities of any particular woman's oppression can be understood only in terms of the extent to which she is also subjected to other systems of inequality, such as racism, classism, heterosexism, ageism, and ableism.

In 1987 I left Hunter College to assume the presidency of Spelman College, a historically Black college for women where there was already in place a Women's Research and Resource Center. Founded in 1981, one hundred years after the college began, the center was the first of its kind to exist on the campus of a historically Black college or university.

Under the consistently creative and effective leadership of Dr. Beverly Guy-Sheftall, Spelman has continued to develop its women's center as a leading institution in the birth and maturing of Black women's studies. Today the Women's Research and Resource Center and the women's studies program focus on theorizing global Black feminisms. Giving support to these developments in the women's studies curriculum and to the expansion of outreach activities into women's communities in Atlanta and beyond was, in my view, one of the most important of my many tasks as the president of Spelman College.

Today, as a professor of anthropology, women's studies, and African American studies at Emory University, I feel no less committed to raising gendered questions, both in and outside of the academy. To do so is not an event but a journey.

Nona Glazer

My political consciousness grew from being a lower-middle-class urban Jew in Chicago, a city that was racist and anti-Semitic, in a family driven into poverty by the Depression, and broken by illness. My father lost his family in Lithuania during the Holocaust, and by the early 1940s I knew refugees from Europe: they were supervisors in the children's home I lived in after my family dissolved. After the war, other adults and children who survived the death camps came as supervisors and new residents. From age eight until nearly sixteen, I went to activities at Chicago's inner-West-side Jewish People's Institute (JPI), a working-class version of New York City's 92nd Street Y. Although my father was a racist who, to escape pogroms, had been sent to South Africa as a twelve-year-old, and whose attitudes toward blacks was not much different from his attitude toward white "goyim"—disparagement and distrust—the JPI, my much older siblings, and other adults to whom I was close had progressive politics.

Hence I remember being on a train going west when the Rosenbergs were executed in June 1953, as others may remember where they were when the United States landed a man on the moon. Although I had always hoped to be an artist, I was moving to Eugene, Oregon, to begin my junior year, where, to get through university rapidly, I majored in psychology. At the University of Oregon (UO), I connected quickly with radical students working to desegregate the dormitories for black women students, and to support professors against a possible visit by the House Un-American Activities Committee (HUAC). Several UO professors, such as

334

historian William Appleman Williams and sociologists Herbert Bisno and Ely Chertok, encouraged my critical perspective on our society in an era of McCarthyism. Chertok also led me to study at the London School of Economics and Political Science, a setting somewhat sympathetic to Marxist theory, where I went on a Fulbright scholarship in 1959.

The women's movement and feminist studies bolstered my sense of being as capable as my male colleagues of writing scholarly papers for publication and professional societies. I also did a lot of scut work in the university, the American Sociological Association (ASA), the Pacific Sociology Association, and, for a bit, the Eastern Sociological Association, to promote research by and about women. I helped local women's groups write grant proposals, and I gave lectures to women's caucuses and student groups. I chaired two sections (sex and gender, and the family) in the ASA, and served as president of Sociologists for Women in Society (SWS), hoping but failing to push SWS toward more left politics. Through all this activity, I was asked to write an article for *Signs* (1976); writing this article confirmed my interests in the division of labor, and so I committed myself to a long course of research on the invisibility of women's domestic labor and its contribution to capitalism, an interest that I continued to pursue to the end

of my career (*Women's Unpaid and Paid Labor,* Temple University Press, 1993).

I came to Portland State University (PSU) in 1964 after receiving a doctorate in sociology and anthropology from Cornell University, and stayed there except for a sabbatical abroad in 1971. After I decided I would be an active feminist scholar, I looked for better research facilities and a more intellectually interesting and supportive setting than PSU had. Hence, I left PSU as often as I could. From 1978 to 1990, I lived outside of Portland six or seven times, increasing my contacts with other feminist scholars. Starting especially with fifteen months in 1982–83 at Radcliffe's Murray Center (funded to do research at the Schlesinger Library), I began to gain a sense of my intellectual worth. The support I got—an earlier fellowship at the University of California, Berkeley (1982), and another one at Radcliffe, (1989–90), one at Wellesley (1983), one at the University of California, San Francisco (1984–85), and a summer fellowship at Tufts (1987)—was possible only because the women's movement forced a new willingness on foundations (Ford, Mellon, and the National Science Foundation) to fund feminist scholarship.

I had a supportive network, and I thank Chuck Bolton, Grant Farr, Bob Liebman, and Eric Lincoln, valued colleagues at PSU at one time or another; the late Jessie Bernard for modeling how to pair professional accomplishments with support for younger colleagues; and many students and sister sociologists for support, nagging questions, and feisty exchanges—especially Joan Acker, Arlene Daniels, Roz Feldberg, Rachel Kahn-Hut, Stephanie Limoncelli, and Judith Lorber. Nancy Porter and Jeanette Harvey helped me enormously in the writing of this essay.

Making a Place

When I first became conscious of the women's movement, the year was 1969, and I was in my thirties, teaching sociology at Portland State University (PSU), a recently tenured associate professor, and married to a professional with strong ties to the old left. At that time I believed that the civil rights movement was important, not actions for women, whom I saw as facing no serious problems.

The critical, galvanizing moment that pushed me to feminism was accidental. I was a radical sociologist. I had analyzed poverty, and I had worked for Head Start and written about poor kids, but I had never connected the poverty of children to sex discrimination against their moms. In 1969 I went to San Francisco for the annual American Sociological Association (ASA) meetings with my husband. The official meeting at the Hilton Hotel was incredibly boring, so my husband and I crossed the street to Glide Memorial Church and the Women's Caucus.

In my totally sexist way, I expected the women at the meeting to be frumpy, ugly, and complaining about the situation of women because they were unattractive and "not feminine." To my surprise, the women looked like me: young, attractive, happy, and confident. Three women were on the stage: Alice Rossi, whom I had always thought of as wearing invisible white gloves and who reminded me of Katharine Hepburn; a young woman with a brand new Ph.D., Barbara Laslett; and Marlene Dixon, who presented herself as a counterculture dyke, wearing overalls and talking about her work life at the University of Chicago demanding that she strap on a plastic penis each morning before going off to teach.

It was a wonderful tactic of the women's caucus to present three such very different women: one could alternately identify with, laugh at, or laugh with each of them. But what got my attention was not so much the tales as the laughter of recognition that swept through the audience as each woman spoke, laughter in which I joined easily. My experiences at PSU that I had thought a result of my character or my personality flaws, including especially my inability to get along with my male colleagues, were ones that I had in common with other women. I learned from that meeting to recognize a structure of male power, fear, and jealousy. No woman had to stand up and say, "Oh yeah, I had this experience, I had that experience." The laughter said it all, and I was struck, well, not dumb: I was *struck verbal*.

Experiences at Cornell (1960–64), where I earned my Ph.D., and at the University of Oregon (UO) (1953–57), where I had completed my bachelor's and master's degrees, now made sense as discrimination, not sweet reason. For example, at the UO, I had been denied a teaching assistantship in the sociology department because the then-chair had had a bad experience hiring a woman professor.[1]

The San Francisco meetings—and afterward my feelings of relief, joy, and anger, and my heightened awareness of men's entitlement and women's acquiescence—catapulted me into the women's movement, changing my professional and personal life. This second wave of feminism enabled me to survive and grow intellectually, despite a workplace then openly hostile to women scholars (as well as to Marxists), and a discipline that was, if not hostile, condescending and indifferent. Too many of my colleagues believed that the university was for men, with a male culture, that women did not belong, and that if they were (unfortunately) present, they should happily act like quasi wives (adoring, compliant, and sexually available): the same expectations men often had of women students.

Women's studies gave me support for the multiple-discipline approach of my intellectual style. Long before women's studies, I had been working collaboratively, and had been discipline based but not discipline bound.[2] I taught and wrote collaboratively with people from other disciplines, for example, with a Reed College social psychologist; and I team-taught at PSU with a political scientist and an economist. I had never believed that sociology had the sole perspective on understanding social life. But women's studies made me unapologetic about my multidisciplinary intellectual work. Feminism and other intellectual subversions of the 1960s and 1970s also changed my work toward more ethnographic-historical methods, away from the narrower enumeration analyses favored in sociology.[3] In part, I switched because I read feminist scholarship that respected women's daily experiences and valued biographies, autobiographies, and ethnographies of daily work and family life. The renewed emphasis on qualitative methods was also part of a much broader political stance and intellectual critique by historians, sociologists, and other scholars—perhaps even artists—who spoke for a bottom-up, inside view, not a top-down, outside one.

After the 1969 meeting in San Francisco, I began to teach feminist studies. I was asked by students to give a course on women, so I taught a couple of sections of Sociology of Women simultaneously as an over-load, and with the students, tried to work out reading assignments. At first I used a wide variety of texts. We read Simone de Beauvoir, Juliet Mitchell, Betty Friedan, and bits and pieces of articles from pamphlets and works that circulated through radical bookstores. But I moved rapidly to materials that were more research based. Working in 1971 on the reader *Woman in a Man-made World* with Helen Waehrer, an economist, made me rethink issues as well as made me aware of the vast amount of materials written about women, especially radical analyses from the 1930s. The collection that we edited drew on social psychology, anthropology, and history as well as sociology and economics.[4] There was a dearth of research-based collections for teaching at that time, although there were fine ones of personal narratives and political statements, emphasizing consciousness raising, so our reader was useful for the burgeoning courses on women.

My teaching itself was influenced by my class background and my own schooling, and, of course, the 1960s as well as women's studies perspectives. Given my background, I empathized with the (mostly) working-class or lower-middle-class employed students and working parents at PSU. I taught, selected readings, and assigned writing projects as nearly as I could as if I were teaching undergraduates at a first-class college for the American elite. As well as wanting students to see the value of intellectual work, I considered the practical consequences for PSU students: I knew that the university, as an upscale vocational school—churning out engineers or social workers or even teachers with only bachelor's degrees—would dump graduates into an unpredictable labor market in which employers seemed to cycle between reducing their costs of training newly hired recant college graduates on the job by demanding narrowly trained college graduates, and then, frustrated by the inflexibility of such training, wanting broadly trained liberal arts students. Therefore I saw a liberal education as students' vocational insurance, as well as a base for their political actions.

I worked very hard to help women's studies students see that they could use sociology and other social sciences to understand the organization of power, and to challenge and change social relations. Even in the early women's studies classes, I did not tolerate "whimpering" sessions. Instead, I helped students organize consciousness-raising meetings outside of class, and encouraged them to go to local women's studies conferences and take part in community-based women's groups. I also had no patience with mixing psychobabble with social analysis. I wanted desperately for students to grasp how social relations they never saw shaped their own lives, to jettison the American love of psychologizing social events. To help them to understand the social context of their lives, I asked them to examine their personal experiences in journals, trying out the analyses presented in C. Wright Mills' vision, Marx's vision, and feminists' visions recognizing the public creation of private worlds.

I had another agenda: to develop intellectual self-confidence in (especially) women students. I did this *not* by telling women how wonderful they were, how great feminine qualities were! Rather, I pressed them to work hard, to read and reread, to write summaries and to explain the articles to one another. I tried to help them to learn the process of reading and considering their assignments critically. I also encouraged peer support and peer teaching, drawing on Paolo Friere and my own learning as a student from critiques in art courses. I forced the students to write essays and journals, and I upset them sometimes, I suppose, with heavy and difficult reading assignments. But I wanted students to finish my courses feeling proud of themselves for having "cracked" difficult materials, and for developing new writing and thinking skills through their own hard work.

Often I thought I was fighting *with* (not *for*) students, going against the grain of feminists who embraced, it seemed to me, vacuous psychologizing about men and the ahistorical individualist interpretation that is the penultimate American disease. Students often complained in and about my classes. Throughout the years, however, former students said things such as, "Well, I really struggled through your class. I really hated it because I couldn't understand stuff. But I got out in the real world, and there it all was!" Or, "I was angry that you made us write and rewrite, but suddenly I realized that I knew how to write well!" The point of my teaching was not whether students "got it" in class, but whether, years later, what they had learned in class allowed them to make unfamiliar invisible social worlds visible.

I was also going against the grain when I attended local or regional women's studies conferences, as distinct from academic or policy ones. Perhaps there was a sub rosa struggle over knowledge—over who really could know what women's lives were. Women's studies conference-goers excelled in the breadth of their knowledge of the everyday lives of a wide range of women, but it seemed to me that they came up short in locating the sources of our misery. The conferences provided moral support and a chance to consider practical problems for activists concerned with rape centers, health clinics, battered women's shelters, and the like. Teachers and researchers seemed to be seen as rivals or "evil stepmothers"; we were rarely recognized as even having our own workplace struggles. We academics did often have more secure jobs and higher incomes than community activists, and looked perhaps invulnerable, too powerful. But also, many Americans have a peculiarly negative attitude about teaching and other intellectual activities.

One year after I began teaching a class about women, I joined Nancy Hoffman in an effort to start a women's studies program. With other faculty and students, we sponsored a lecture series on women's issues and conducted a campuswide survey to assess interest in women's studies. Aware of the difficulties of establishing new programs in the Oregon State System of Higher Education, we made a tactical decision to start an ad hoc women's studies program, one that remained ad hoc for five or six years.

After the program was more firmly established in the mid-1970s, I ceased much involvement as a planner or decision maker. I was impatient with long discussions of process and the then-popular consensus model of decision making. I considered the latter a tool of the verbally aggressive, a process some used to intimidate dissenters, and a process others used to avoid making difficult decisions.

But I always rejoined the program actively in times of crisis, such as the repeated budget crises of the 1970s and 1980s. We women faculty in academic departments—sparse in the social sciences and the hard sciences—divided our energies among our own departments, university-wide work, and so on, and the women's studies program. But the instructors hired by the women's studies program were themselves just the forerunners of the contingent labor force, the "academic gypsies" so common to universities by the late 1980s. They were marginal in all possible ways to the organization of the university. They could not serve on committees; they could not run for, vote for, or hold offices; and they usually taught for "wages" rather than a salary and received no benefits. As part-timers, they could not join the American Association of University Professors, the bargaining agent for the PSU faculty. Without formal power or responsibilities outside of the women's studies classroom or program, they had few chances to understand how the university functioned and were rarely around for the consequences of any decisions they made as members of the women's studies governance board. Most taught courses for a year or so, and then they were gone—off to graduate school or a job elsewhere.

Ultimately, there was no democratically organized governance of the women's studies program. There was a mix of myth and hope about the program in the belief that it had been developed and was run collectively by a volunteer board of faculty, students, and community activists that reached decisions by a democratic process of consensus, that it escaped the hierarchies and routines of PSU. This legend overlooked how programs were developed and survived in higher education; how power was exerted informally by bullying, secretiveness, and exclusion; and how power was exerted formally by the faculty, state legislators, and administrators. The program was initially "coordinated" by tenured or tenure-track faculty and student volunteers and run by the volunteer women's studies governance board, which made only temporary hires. PSU's president, advised by the board and university administrators, appointed the coordinator once the program was formally recognized. By 1981 the board was so "democratic" that students and community people showing up for a single meeting were bestowed the right to make decisions, even if this was a first and last attendance. I went to the meetings fairly regularly and concluded that the board process was destroying the program. This happened after the first full-time coordinator left and the president's choice of a new coordinator ended with bitterness on the part of a rejected job applicant. Women's studies board meetings revolved around open hostility and unresolved conflicts between the newly hired coordinator and the rejected applicant from the community and her lover, a part-time teacher in the program. The essential governance of the program virtually ceased. After several attempts to mediate failed, another professor and I asked the dean of the College of Social Science, where the program was housed, to disband the governing board. The dean did so, the coordinator quit, and we hired a new coordinator.

The program survived, but the result was regrettable for democratic governance. Dissolving the board dealt only with a momentary crisis. We women's studies faculty should have said to the dean, "We need to establish a new form of governance, for example, a board of faculty members who are elected or appointed, two people from the community, and three or so students from the program." For me, the irony and regret are that we went from at least the goal of an alliance among faculty, students, and the community to having one coordinator totally in charge—and for sixteen years. Despite the elimination of the board, the title "coordinator" was retained: women's studies had won the right, after a protracted battle with the administration, to use that rather than the name "director" or "chair," supposedly because these two suggested male-type centralized authority. Since no new formal structure was developed, however, that assured faculty, student, or community power, the coordinator position became, de facto, that of a director; it was something that was between a dean and a department chair: appointed for life like a dean, rather than elected by the faculty for a term like a chair, seeking advice like a dean rather than bound by faculty votes like a chair, and so on. (The coordinator continued all the budgetary, supervisory, and organizational responsibilities of a department chair.) The long-time coordinator, Johanna Brenner, has been very dedicated, and has done a good job meeting student needs, instituting outreach programs, and developing women's studies courses. But we went from an "ultrademocratic" system to one of authority resting in a single position—hardly a structure for teaching women students about democratic alternatives to "patriarchy." I don't know if we women's studies faculty were lazy or were overworked by obligations in our own departments. Perhaps in the 1980s the program succumbed to the isolation of "studies" programs, insulated from faculty and student pressure to democratize governance, pressure to which departments had had to respond in the 1970s.

Most sorrowfully to me, feminist scholarship has not yet produced an intellectual revolution, one that is integrated into the curriculum across disciplines. How much feminist scholarship has changed the disciplines has been debated: for example, some sociologists think that anthropology has undergone tremendous change because of feminist scholarship, but feminist anthropologists are skeptical.

I have been reluctant to see women's studies become permanent and institutionalized. In the early 1970s, most of us saw women's studies as separate from the academic disciplines only temporarily. Beginning in 1983, I had urged integrating feminist scholarship into the university curriculum, and did some workshops and writing on this. I did consistently integrate feminist scholarship into my graduate and undergraduate courses. I worry now that PSU's new women's studies major is a dedication to separateness and an abandonment of the hard task—the actually harder task—of challenging and reworking the disciplines. Studies programs have not been a successful strategy for integrating good analyses into the academic disciplines. The elite institutions exemplify the resistance. Harvard (where I spent more than two years at Radcliffe College) has finally enshrined (or entombed) black studies in the Du Bois Institute, and tipped its hat to women by joining an areawide women's studies consortium. In 1999, Radcliffe College itself was reduced to being an institute of Harvard. Harvard's School of Theology had been a haven for feminists—hardly a likely route for widely integrating feminist scholarship. I also believe—as I noted earlier—that undergraduate degrees in highly specific programs are an intellectual and practical disservice to working-class and lower-middle-class women and men, who are likely to be able to afford the time and money for undergraduate training only.

On the plus side, however, women's studies programs are great for women students: students learn about critical issues for women and get support for taking part in the university and the community. Yet I found many problems hard to consider well in my women's studies courses. I never worked through to my satisfaction how to talk or write cogently about gender, race, ethnicity, sexual orientation, and class simultaneously. Perhaps my dissatisfaction with the lack of a strong theoretical integration of these factors into sociological theory or feminist theory is why I believe that women's studies has its limits along with its strengths. "Adding on" gender and then race and so on is not sufficient. We learned that early on. Feminist scholarship has to change theory in the disciplines, or else a new field, broader than feminist studies—perhaps "people's studies"—has to be developed. By the time I retired in 1995, younger sociologists were recycling some of the analyses we had done in the 1970s. I have talked with colleagues in my generation of feminist scholars; some of them are more optimistic than I, but they agree that too often young scholars are redoing old stuff. To see young feminists affected by historical amnesia is disheartening, but it reinforces my belief that feminist scholars need to leave the intellectual ghetto to confront traditional disciplines and develop, perhaps, a people's studies.

Whatever my qualms, women's studies was my survival. The women's movement helped me to understand much about my life and gave me the courage to become an active intellectual, to work for a women's studies program, and to work for women sociologists' full participation in the discipline. The movement gave me the courage to teach for and about women, to apply for fellowships, to write and publish for women—and perhaps even to leave sociology to paint full-time, and hence fulfill the ambitions of my seventeen-year-old self.

Nancy Porter

I have been employed at Portland State University since 1968, though I am officially retired from teaching. A founder of the women's studies program at Portland State University, I have published on women's literature and feminist pedagogy, have edited *Women's Studies Quarterly*, and am completing *My Mother, Her Daughter: A Memoir*. Coordinator of graduate programs in English for the past seven years, I am currently working part-time for the dean of the College of Liberal Arts and Sciences on community relations and development.

One of the challenges I see in retirement is to change the relation I have to work. Not until I stopped did I realize how deeply rooted my identity has been in teaching. I feel fortunate to be able to bridge the classroom and "the world" by using what I learned about community building from my involvement in women's studies to get the largely untold stories of the quite excellent faculty and students at Portland State out to the Portland metropolitan area.

The Ground Revisited

The Women's Literature class met in the living room of Montgomery Court, a student residence hall on the edge of the Portland State University (PSU) campus. Three comfortable couches covered in worn green velvet, several overstuffed armchairs, and an assortment of Goodwill vintage pillows had been cajoled into the semblance of a circle. Twenty-five women, blue jeaned, for the most part, with plaid flannel shirts from J. C. Penney or oversized hand-knit sweaters, no makeup, and backpacks, had arranged themselves around the room. Two sat cross-legged on the faded Oriental carpet. They were the teachers.

I was the one in the tan suede jacket, with red-blonde hair down to my waist. The one who looked, as a Chicana student said, "like a brown Madonna," with black curly hair and an expressive face, was Nancy Hoffman. On that cool day in April 1972, we were beginning a discussion of Doris Lessing's *The Golden Notebook.*

Nancy and I read aloud the intense exchange between Anna and Molly, which opens the novel. Good friends that we were, we really got into it. Our voices rose. Anna and Molly, self-described free women, were discussing the men in their lives. The personal is the political, we had been telling the young women. We were discovering how swiftly political differences could turn personal. Soon the whole class was involved, talking sometimes at once, sometimes in turn; quoting Doris Lessing, quoting Shulamith Firestone; or quoting from a copy of *The Communist Manifesto,* which one of the students had found on a shelf in the back room of the Old Oregon Bookstore downtown.

We never knew, Nancy and I, where the main discussion would head, with its laughing, teary, and engaged side discussions in tow. That day, I believe, Lessing was left behind. But it hardly mattered, because we, students and faculty alike, felt that we were pioneering a different sort of classroom: nonhierarchical, collaborative, intellectual yet intimate, and, above all, woman centered. It was the kind of classroom that none of us had ever been in before, with a syllabus of women writers and theorists that Nancy and I had not encountered in our graduate school years, Nancy at the University of California, Berkeley, and I at Yale.

The course was offered through the English department, where Nancy and I were untenured assistant professors. It was also listed on a mimeographed sheet distributed by an agitprop women's studies program, which was housed in a male philosophy professor's office and operated on no budget.

The women's studies classroom—and, in our case, shadow women's studies program—did not develop in a vacuum. In the fall of 1970, Nancy Hoffman brought the word up from California, where she had taught, at the students' request, a women's literature course at the University of California, Santa Barbara. Nancy was also the youngest member on the newly formed Modern Language Association (MLA) Commission on the Status of Women in the Profession. PSU sociologist Nona Glazer contributed the concept of a women's research center. Together they called a meeting of interested faculty and students. Many of the students who showed up came from Glazer's Sociology of Women course, which she had first offered in 1969. I attended the meeting partly because a male colleague said he would go with me and partly because I had begun to respond to ideas set in motion by the women's liberation movement, to think of myself as a woman, a recently divorced woman, "free" or constrained—I was not sure which—to construct a new life and identity.

Out of this meeting emerged a lecture series on women's issues. Faculty, women and men both, proposed courses on women in a number of departments, including a pioneering course on the biochemistry of women. The high quality, courage, and commitment of the faculty were to prove an abiding strength of women's studies at Portland State.

Throughout the summer of 1971, faculty and students drafted a proposal for a certificate program, equivalent to a minor in women's studies. That fall the students, partly as the result of what they were learning in Amy Kesselman's course Styles of Women's Liberation, partly as a revolt against faculty arbitrariness in decision making, formed what they termed a seven-person collective to run the program.

As various commentators of the time noted, however, issues of power continued to haunt the revolution. The students had no sooner formed their collective—randomly selected but representative of the orientations and identifications of the women in the program (gay, straight, faculty, student, community, working class, middle class, mothers, and women of color)—when students not in the collective began to feel disenfranchised and charged their sisters with elitism.

Meanwhile, we had been written up in the *Oregonian* and in *Time*. What-ever our internal struggles might be, to the outside world we were beginning to sound established.

In June 1972 Nancy Hoffman moved to a new job at the Massachu-setts Institute of Technology. I agreed to fill in for her at a talk that she had been invited to give about organizing a grass-roots women's studies program at a Woman on the Move conference at the University of Ore-gon. Because I had lost my voice and pleasure in writing while milling out papers in graduate school—and had been blocked for almost a decade on finishing up my doctorate—I was terrified by the prospect. However, in the two days between the end of spring term and the beginning of the conference, I sat at the typewriter. Astonishingly, instead of agony and gray cotton wool, images, dialogue, and analysis inspired by our common life flowed out of my fingertips and onto the page. For the first time in years, I had a purpose in writing.

But was there an audience for what I had written? I tried not to think much about that as I took my place behind the lectern in an amphitheater classroom in the University of Oregon Law School. The room was already warm at nine o'clock in the morning. The seats were less than one-quarter filled. No matter. Seated at eye level and squarely in front of me, with her journal open and pen in hand, was Florence Howe. She was the perfect audience: focused, encouraging, and mag-netic. Her face completed the act of writing the paper. When she came up to me after the session to discuss publication, I thought that perhaps I could become a writer after all. That summer I cabined myself in a forest on the skirts of Mount Hood to write on Doris Lessing. I pre-sented the paper the following December at an MLA meeting. Again I was asked to submit an essay for publication. Later both articles appeared in volume 6 of *Female Studies*. I became part of the growing community of women's studies programs and feminist scholars.

The spring of 1975, another classroom, a seminar on Virginia Woolf, a writer rediscovered by feminist readers after many years of critical neg-lect. We met in the lounge of the Campus Ministry building (brown tweed carpet, black Naugahyde couches, low wooden coffee tables, and tall potted plants), closer to campus now, across the street from the Smith Center, where the women's studies program shared space with its vigorous younger sibling, the Women's Union.

The students looked pretty much as they had three years before, except women's studies courses were now attracting the occasional male. It was a warm evening in May, and many wore shorts or cut-off jeans and no socks with their Birkenstocks. A few of us were beginning to wear long skirts. We planned a dinner party à la Mrs. Ramsay to celebrate the end of the school year (an English graduate student, tired of our tuna noodle casserole and hard-boiled egg potlucks, offered to prepare enough *boeuf en daube* for the whole class), and argued whether Woolf's tilt toward androgyny at the end of *A Room of One's Own* meant that she had abandoned the (hoped for) "lesbian" vision of Chloe and Olivia. After I read the journals that the students had turned in that night, with the colors and textures of their own awakenings and dreams shining through their responses to the literature, I was deeply moved by the evidence that women's studies changed lives. A woman who had previously evinced no intellectual interests had made a serious effort to follow Woolf's logic in *Three Guineas.* Several women who had assumed that they would marry and stay home with their children were tentatively planning careers. Students were being trained as volunteers to work on hot lines and in shelters. One who said that she had never "run anything" before exulted in how well she had conducted a meeting. Inevitably, some of the young women revealed that they were trying out a different sexual orientation.

In 1971, at the beginning of my involvement with women's studies, I was still relating to men, in fact, was living with one. But he soon moved on and, with a creole of anger, desire, and logic, I began to identify as a lesbian. For the most part, the only lesbians I was aware of at the time were women's studies students. I had one torturous year-long affair with a student after she graduated and a brief, uneasy tryst with a graduate student before I met a woman older than I and from a similar background, but not involved with women's studies or Portland State, with whom I could build a life. I break my reticence to speak about the sexualizing of women faculty–student relationships because, as much as they are recognized today as abuses of power, violations of student trust, and—truth be known—exploitations of faculty vulnerability, these relations are also part of the historical record of a time when the world of women's studies was new. At places such as Portland State, faculty and students worked closely together, some of us not thinking of ourselves as faculty and of "them" as students, but thinking of all of us as women unified in a common cause, in varying degrees alienated from our respective peer groups, and wanting very much to believe that consensual relationships erased the fact that faculty always have power over students.

In the spring semester of 1975, with the support of a significant number of the women faculty at PSU and key administrators, the program passed through the Faculty Senate and was forwarded to the Oregon State Board of Higher Education for final authorization. The university was still in the expansive mood of the 1960s. We encountered, on the whole, much more willingness to go along with student-faculty initiatives than affronted resistance. The only condition that the administration attached to its support was conformity to departmental structure. We must have someone with academic rank to head the program and be accountable for curriculum and budget. Until we were authorized to search for a full-time salaried faculty coordinator, I added that responsibility to my teaching load in the English department.

In the spring of 1975, I received tenure, at least in part in recognition of my work for women's studies. The correlation, however, was not automatic. Despite my renaissance as a teacher-scholar through women's studies, I remained all-but-dissertation. My department, the dean, and the vice president for Academic Affairs, nonetheless, supported me for tenure. One morning in early June, I found myself in the president's office, mounting an argument for the equivalency of publications and program development with a terminal degree. The president asked me if I were willing to head the women's studies certificate program. Even knowing that his decision on my tenure might hang in the balance, I said no. I had done my part. The program would benefit most from the fresh perspective, energy, and additional faculty that an outside search and appointment would allow.

Throughout the years I have wondered about my decision to let go of the program that I loved and that, fairly literally, had saved my professional life. Why did I pass up the opportunity to work in administration, for which, as it turns out, I have vision, patience, and talent? I would say that all along I knew that women's studies could consume me, particularly its politics. Our efforts to work collectively and to be inclusive led to strains and power struggles between university and community, and between faculty and students. In the early 1970s, in many parts of the women's movement, powerful individuals were considered suspect, and individual leadership was anathema. On the one hand, I was not in the habit of thinking of myself as powerful—or as a leader. On the other hand, I had been working for five years in a program that believed that the welfare of the organization came before individual ego. Therefore, when power came along, what I had learned from women's studies was—indeed—to share it and any skills I had acquired with others. Although I would say that women's studies students and teachers today are less conflicted about power and leadership than we were in the 1970s, the principle and practice of empowering individuals to act on their own behalf and for the common welfare of women is still in place and has served the program and the university well under two extraordinarily gifted and dedicated coordinators—Meg O'Hara (1976–79) and Johanna Brenner (1982 to the present)—and through several generations of students.

The spring of 1998. I am a full professor, the director of graduate programs in English at Portland State, and teaching my last women's studies course before I retire. For the first time in many years, all forty of the students enrolled are women. Now that we offer a B.A. in women's studies, several are women's studies majors. Because women's studies is also a cluster in the reconfigured general education requirement, others have entered by that route. Some are just plain vanilla English majors and graduate students.

We meet in an ordinary, scruffy classroom right on campus. The chairs are arranged in rows each day when we enter. Many days they are still in rows when we leave. I stand in the front of the room and, upon occasion, lecture. Mostly, however, we talk or write, sharing our responses—sometimes in small groups, more often as a group of the whole. Except for those of us who have jobs that we need to dress for—and I now count myself as one who needs to look as though I am trying, at least once in a while—the attire is casual. There are, particularly among the younger members of the class, tattoos, body piercings, lipstick, nail polish, and a virtual rainbow of hair dyes. Many more of us claim Asian, Latin, African American, or Native American heritage than was true thirty years ago. Some of us are recent immigrants. More of us have children, some even grandchildren. One of us is blind. The syllabus, too, has changed: the course focuses on women's communities, and three-quarters of the texts we read are by women of color.

What has not changed is the power of women's writings to unlock their stories and of women's studies classes to change lives. Ours is not a particularly censored classroom. People say what they think and feel, and sometimes that is pretty raw. A lot of our differences play out as attacks or defenses of the books we are reading. But throughout the course of the term, respect for the books builds, people read again after class discussion, opinions modify, and the personal stories behind the perspectives emerge, as does the understanding of the connection between encouraging the individual voice and empowering women's communities. One more time a class learns that what may be unbearable alone—such as the spousal or boyfriend abuse a classmate has suffered or the problematic in a text—is less of a burden when shouldered by thirty-nine others. We share stories, thoughts, and annotated reading lists of our favorite authors.

On the last day of class, I bring cookies. Someone else surprises us with champagne. The students offer a toast to my retirement. I say what a wonderful class they have been and what a pleasure it has been to teach them. One more time I feel that we have had a class of our own.

Mariam K. Chamberlain

I was born and grew up in Chelsea, Massa-chusetts, an industrial suburb of Boston, and entered Radcliffe College in 1935. As an undergraduate during the Depression years, I majored in economics, and in 1939 I went on to graduate study at Harvard in the same field. My graduate study was inter-rupted during World War II by a tour of duty in Washington, D.C. as an economic analyst in the Office of Strategic Services, but I returned to complete my doctorate in 1950.

I then taught part-time in the Department of Economics at Connecticut College and after that at the Columbia University School of General Studies. From there I went to the Ford Foundation in 1956 for a position as assistant program officer in the Economic Development and Administration Program. In 1960 I moved to New Haven to accept a position as research associate at and execu-tive secretary of the Economic Growth Center. In 1967 I returned to the Ford Foundation as program officer in the Higher Education and Research Program, retiring in 1982. At that point I took up an appointment as a resident scholar at the Russell Sage Foundation. In that capacity I headed the Task Force on Women in Higher Education. The work of the task force extended throughout a period of four years and culminated in the volume *Women in the Academe,* which the Russell Sage Foundation published in 1988.

During the same period, I served as presi-dent of the National Council for Research on Women. The Russell Sage Foundation pro-vided a temporary home for the new organi-zation until we moved to our own quarters. I remained as president of the council until 1989. Since then I have stayed on as founding president and resident scholar to carry out special projects. I serve on the board of several feminist organizations, including The Feminist Press, the Institute for Women's Policy Research, the Network of East-West Women, and the Women's Interart Center.

There Were Godmothers, Too

When Florence Howe asked me to write a memoir for this volume on mothers of women's studies, I initially held back. I did not consider myself a mother of women's studies in the same sense as those who labored to establish it as a field of study on college and university campuses. On further reflection, however, not to mention Florence's subtle strategy of sharing some of the other papers with me, I came around to the idea that, if not a mother, I could at least write as a god-mother of women's studies. In fact, I am aware that I have sometimes been referred to as the fairy godmother of women's studies. That was largely the result of my work as program officer in higher education at the Ford Foundation during the 1970s, when a major program of support for women's studies was undertaken and many grants were made. That program continues to the present day with a new generation of program officers. How did this come about and how did it influence the field? That story is my contribution to this volume.

As the women's movement gained momentum in the late 1960s and early 1970s, women activists, both those inside and outside the foundation, pressed for support of efforts to overcome sex discrimination in society at large. The foundation was not unfamiliar with issues of inequality, having committed substantial funds since the 1960s to the civil rights movement. Until then, however, only sporadic grants had been made on behalf of women, mainly in the areas of legal rights, reproductive choice, employment needs such as day care, and access to educational opportunities. In the field of higher education, the foundation made grants during the 1960s to Radcliffe College for support of the Bunting Institute for independent study by women scholars and professionals and to Rutgers University for the advancement of women in science and engineering. Beginning in around 1970 the foundation established formal programs designed to help eliminate sex discrimination and advance opportunities for women along several fronts within its existing sphere of activity.[1] One of these areas was education. My own jurisdiction was higher education. My colleague Terry Saario carried the ball for girls and women in primary and secondary education.

Our program in higher education was a multifaceted one. It encompassed, in addition to women's studies, support of affirmative action efforts and litigation, training programs for the administrative advancement of academic women, support of women in professional associations and professional life, studies of the role of women's colleges, and research on public policy issues relating to the educational needs of women. Between 1971 and 1981, when I left the foundation as part of a major staff turnover to make way for a new regime, grants in this area totaled some $9.25 million. Well over half of that was devoted to women's studies: research, curriculum development, distribution of information, and mainstreaming.

How did the program evolve, and why the emphasis on women's studies in the overall higher education priorities? My own background was in economics, and prior to 1971 my position at the Ford Foundation was concerned with programs relating to graduate and professional education, particularly in the fields of economics and business administration. I had not been involved in the civil rights movement or the women's movement. I recall returning from a trip to Europe in connection with the foundation's management education program in the summer of 1970 and encountering the August 26 march for women's equality on Fifth Avenue. I had no idea what it was all about. I asked a spectator who was wearing a button with the slogan "Equality in Marriage" what that meant. I don't recall that I got a clear answer.[2]

I first became aware of sex discrimination in 1971, when Shirley McCune, then at the American Association of University Women, came to the foundation to discuss a proposal to deal with sex stereotyping in guidance counseling of adolescent girls. That was outside of my area of responsibility in higher education, but she made eminent sense to me and raised my awareness of sex discrimination, not only in education but in society at large. I referred the funding of the project to the foundation program concerned with the precollege age group, but they were not yet geared up to make grants of that kind. It was, however, the opening wedge, and Shirley subsequently received substantial support for her work from the foundation when she went on to serve as director of the Resource Center on Sex Roles in Education at the

National Foundation for the Improvement of Education under the auspices of the National Education Association. (Shirley McCune later joined the U.S. Department of Education as deputy assistant secretary for Equal Opportunity Programs.)

During 1971 advocates for women in higher education also came in with proposals for support. The earliest of these was Sheila Tobias, then associate provost at Wesleyan University, who was responsible for the concerns of women on campus. An active feminist, she had previously been instrumental in initiating women's studies at Cornell, and her ideas came to play an important role in the evolution of the foundation's higher education program.

At about the same time, Florence Howe, who headed The Feminist Press, then a newly established concern, also entered the picture. She made a persuasive case for women's studies at all levels of education, in schools as well as colleges and universities. She, too, went on from there to become a mainstay of the foundation's women's studies program.

With a green light from foundation officers to pursue possible lines of program activity, we continued our explorations by consulting other leading feminist scholars and educators in the New York area. We did not go farther afield because we did not yet have a budget on which to draw for travel expenses. "We," in this case, refers to me and Elinor Barber, a colleague in the International Division of the foundation, who graciously volunteered to help. Elinor's background was in history and sociology. Drawing on her contacts at Barnard College and Columbia University, we initially invited Patricia Albjerg Graham, then at Teachers College at Columbia and now president of the Spencer Foundation in Chicago. Graham had written a landmark article entitled "Women in Academe" that appeared in *Science* magazine in September 1970. In it she presented a cogent analysis of the inequalities confronting women as students, faculty, and administrators in higher education. The article made a lasting impression on foundation officers and staff members concerned with education. Another person whom we consulted was Cynthia Fuchs Epstein, then at Columbia and now Distinguished Professor of Sociology at the Graduate Center of the City University of New York. Cynthia's book *Woman's Place* provided the theoretical framework for the study of women in the professions and the rationale for the foundation's efforts on behalf of women in this field.

At the end of 1971, taking up a suggestion from Sheila Tobias, we convened a meeting at the Ford Foundation, bringing together those whom we had consulted and others to present their views and to discuss possibilities for action on behalf of women in higher education. We held the meeting in President McGeorge Bundy's conference room in the hope that he might sit in, at least at the start. He did more than that: he stayed throughout and participated in the discussion, as did Harold Howe, vice president of Education and Research, and Marshall Robinson, director of the Higher Education Program of the foundation. Alice Rossi, professor of sociology at the University of Massachusetts, Amherst, played a key role at the meeting with her opening remarks about the limits that society places on the aspirations of women. Other participants in the meeting included Bernice Sandler, director of the Project on the Status and Education of Women at the Association of American Colleges; Florence Howe of The Feminist Press; and Ruth Mandel, director of the Center for the American Woman and Politics at Rutgers University. The meeting turned out to be a strategic one. It achieved its intended purpose of giving leading women activists in higher education an opportunity to present their concerns. The upshot was the approval of the Women in Higher Education Program with an initial budget of $500,000.

With a budget in hand, we lost no time in getting the Women in Higher Education Program under way, and women's studies was at the forefront of the effort. We embarked on women's studies with a fellowship program for faculty and doctoral research, and in many ways that was natural for us. We had been in the fellowship business for a long time and had used it with great success to advance similar program objectives in management education. Moreover, an opportunity presented itself to launch the program without delay. In 1972 the Ford Foundation was planning to phase out its Sciences Fellowship Program for faculty research in political science, economics, and sociology. Awards were made on a competitive basis to candidates nominated by their institutions, more specifically, their departments. Rather than close down the program, we prevailed upon the foundation to let us use the administrative system that was in place for research in women's studies. Thus began the Ford Foundation's Faculty Fellowships for Research on the Role of Women in Society and Women's Studies Dissertation Fellowships. Throughout 1972 to 1975 we made 122 grants, totaling more than $1 million, for research in a wide range of disciplines.

The impact of this program went beyond anything we could have imagined. The recognition of women's studies by a major foundation gave legitimacy to a field in a crucial stage of its development. Feminist scholars were elated, some expressing the view that the recognition was at least as important as the money involved. Within the foundation, the range of scholarship and topics addressed in the applications that we received gave testimony to the potential of the field, and we used it as such. Another outcome of the program, which we had not fully anticipated, was the visibility it gave to women on campus. Although the fellowships were open to men as well as women, and a few awards were made to men, most women's studies scholars were women. The department chairs in the major research universities who had routinely submitted nominations under the previous faculty research program in social sciences were now hard put to find eligible candidates to sponsor. The institutional pattern of nominations and award recipients changed dramatically from what it had been. Clearly talented women faculty members were more likely to be found at that time in less well-known institutions, whether because of discrimination or deference to the employment location of a spouse.

On the negative side, we received a certain amount of flak from feminist scholars who did not have an institutional affiliation and who felt that they should have had an opportunity to apply. Although sympathetic to the problem, we had no way of handling an unlimited number of applications. In any event, other sources of funding for women's studies scholars began to become available during this period, and in 1975 the foundation phased out the fellowship program to move on to support for specific projects and for research institutes.

The establishment of a network of campus-based centers for research on women as part of a support system for women's studies began in 1974. At that time a few centers were already in existence. The Center for the American Woman and Politics, a unit of the Eagleton Institute of Politics at Rutgers University, was founded in 1971 to conduct research, develop educational programs, and provide information services relating to women's participation in the political process. The center was funded under the National Affairs Division of the foundation. Also funded under the National Affairs Division was the Center for Women Policy Studies, which was organized as an independent entity in Washington, D.C., in 1972. As the name indicates, its research focuses on issues of public policy relating to women.

On campus there were centers providing resources for research on women at Radcliffe College: the Schlesinger Library on the History of Women in America, established in 1943, and the Bunting Institute for independent study, established in 1960. The formation of two new centers in 1974 provided the models for the rapid expansion of the research centers that followed. The Wellesley Center for Research on Women, under its founding director, Carolyn Elliott, was the prototype for several of the campus-based centers. It was launched with support from the Carnegie Corporation. The Center for Research on Women at Stanford was established with an enabling grant from the Ford Foundation and from the beginning involved senior faculty members, men as well as women, from a broad spectrum of disciplines and professional schools.

Between 1974 and 1981, when I left the foundation, twelve new centers were established, and three existing centers, such as the Center for the Education of Women at the University of Michigan, received support for the research component of their work. One of the most notable of the new centers was the Southwest Institute for Research on Women (SIROW) at the University of Arizona under the leadership of Myra Dinnerstein. Established in 1979, its success paved the way for other grants supporting regional centers, such as the Center for Research on Women at Memphis State University for the Southern region and the Northwest Center for Research on Women at the University of Washington.

In 1981 these and other centers for research on women joined to form the National Council for Research on Women as an association to promote collaboration and exchange of information. The initiative for organizing the council was taken by Marjorie Lightman, at that time director of the Institute for Research in History, which was one of the research centers supported by the foundation. Marjorie and her colleagues at the institute organized a conference in November 1981, which brought the centers together to discuss common concerns and to explore the idea of forming a coalition to promote collaboration and to exchange information. The idea was enthusiastically received, and the council was born. Starting with twenty-eight founding centers, the council has since grown to more than seventy-five member institutions.

In 1976 Florence Howe brought to my attention the draft of a proposal, prepared by a group of scholars on the West Coast, to establish a national women's studies association. Florence and I agreed that the idea was a timely one, and I recommended support for the proposal. It called for $39,000 for a founding convention. I did not succeed in getting approval for the request as presented, but was permitted instead to provide $3515 to help plan such a convention. Accordingly, a grant in that amount was made to the University of Pennsylvania, where a planning group assembled. Planning documents were worked out, and the founding conference was duly held in San Franciso in 1977. With the late Shauna Adix ably presiding over the plenary assembly, the National Women's Studies Association was born. This grant became legendary in the foundation as an example of how much can be accomplished with a small sum.

Another small grant that made a significant contribution to the advancement of women's studies was a grant of less than $6000 to Barnard College in 1975 to release Catharine Stimpson from some of her teaching duties to found *Signs: The Journal of Women in Culture and Society*. None of us anticipated the widespread circulation and prestige that it would attain.

At least as important as the two examples I have cited is the small grant that was made to Princeton University in 1976 for a project on women in the college curriculum. A group of women faculty members had submitted a proposal to analyze the impact of women's studies on the liberal arts curriculum. The original proposal was an ambitious one, and I was again unable to get approval for full funding. However, we did provide $6000 for an experimental project to be carried out over the summer. The project was limited to an examination of the introductory courses in four disciplines that were the most active in women's studies. Lois Banner, the project director, collected and analyzed 355 syllabi from 172 departments in a variety of institutions. Supplementary information was gathered through questionnaires sent to department chairs, directors of women's studies programs, and publishers of textbooks. Not surprisingly, it was found that with few exceptions, little or nothing was being taught about women in these courses. Department heads reported that the presence of women in their departments and the existence of women's studies programs on campus were important factors in whether faculty members were taking heed of the new scholarship on women and incorporating it into their courses. On the basis of these findings, the report concluded that special efforts were called for to introduce faculty members to the new scholarship and its implications for the general curriculum.

Specifically, the report recommended the preparation of monographs or guides to relevant topics and source material to help faculty members incorporate issues relating to women in their courses. As a first step, it was recommended that the foundation, jointly with the American Historical Association, support such a guide for teachers of history to be prepared under the direction of Gerda Lerner. With yet another small grant in the $6000 range that was done, and the outcome was Lerner's *Teaching Women's History,* a monograph that was widely distributed by the association.

Further monographs in other disciplines were not forthcoming, in part for budgetary reasons and in part because of the departure of key members of the Princeton project. However, the idea of curriculum integration was not lost: other programs were initiated elsewhere. One of the first and most influential of these was the four-year cross-disciplinary project undertaken in 1981 at the University of Arizona with support from the National Endowment for the Humanities. Since that time there have been numerous integration or mainstreaming projects using a variety of approaches, which together constitute a veritable movement in the development of women's studies.

With the Ford Foundation as a platform, I was able to use several other strategies to advance women's studies. One was to show to visiting college and university presidents The Feminist Press 1974 volume, *Who's Who and Where in Women's Studies,* listing nearly 3000 faculty members and 4700 courses in 885 colleges and universities. The purpose was, of course, to impress them with how important and extensive the field already was.

Another kind of publication that I found useful during this period to spread the word about women's studies resulted from campuswide surveys of ongoing research on women. Specifically, I had reports or directories based on such surveys at the University of California, Berkeley, the University of Michigan, and the City University of New York. Their size and range was always a source of surprise. There were also a few other universities where such surveys were carried out, and where they did not exist, I suggested them to women's studies program heads as a strategy to give more visibility and acceptability to the subject on their campus.

As a further step in the strategy to promote women's studies, we supported and collaborated with the Association of American Colleges (now the Association of American Colleges and Universities) in a three-day conference held at the Wingspread Conference Center in

Racine, Wisconsin, in 1981 entitled Liberal Education and the New Scholarship on Women: Issues and Constraints in Institutional Change. The conference brought together fifty college and university presidents and other senior administrators and leading women's studies scholars. The featured speakers were Florence Howe, Elizabeth Minnich, and Gerda Lerner. This conference and the resulting report went a long way toward ensuring that serious attention be given to women's studies on campus.

My jurisdiction at the Ford Foundation was largely confined to the United States. We were active to a lesser extent in Canada and Western Europe, but programs elsewhere in the world—the developing countries and Eastern Europe—were the province of the International Division of the foundation, which did not have women's studies on its agenda. The United Nations Decade for Women, which began in Mexico City in 1975, was the galvanizing force that extended the global reach of women's studies. At the time of the Mid-Decade World Conference, which was held in Copenhagen in 1980, I urged Florence Howe to give some thought to doing a presentation of some kind on women's studies for the Forum of Non-Governmental Organizations, to be held in conjunction with the official conference. She was at first reluctant to do so, saying that she wasn't sure she was ready for such a step, but I persuaded her that this was an opportunity not to be missed, and that there wouldn't be another one until the end-of-decade conference five years later. Florence then proceeded to organize an international advisory group, which prepared an outstanding program of seminars and roundtables. Sessions on the subject of feminist theory, pedagogy, research, and public policy were held throughout a ten-day period and drew more than five hundred participants from fifty-five countries. Many of the women from developing countries learned about women's studies for the first time. It was indeed a historic occasion. A network known as Women's Studies International was formed, and five years later at the UN End-of-Decade Conference, which was held in Nairobi, there were more than one thousand participants in the women's studies sessions. Since then, Women's Studies International has continued to plan events at other international conferences, most notably the Fourth UN Conference on Women that was held in Beijing in 1995.

After leaving the Ford Foundation, I continued my involvement in women's studies as president and later founding president and resident scholar at the National Council for Research on Women. In that capacity I have served as director of two multicampus curriculum integration programs, both funded by the Ford Foundation. The first was a four-year effort launched by the foundation in 1988 to mainstream minority women's studies. Liza Fiol-Matta of the English department at LaGuardia Community College was appointed coordinator of the program. Liza and I edited a volume reporting on the program, which was published by The Feminist Press in 1994 under the title *Women of Color and the Multicultural Curriculum.* The second program, initiated in 1995, was designed to strengthen links between women's studies and international and area studies. The program facilitates exchange of information and experience to assist scholars working to internationalize the content of women's studies courses in the United States, to bring gender perspectives to international and area studies, and to foster collaboration between U.S. and international scholars and institutions, particularly in developing countries. For this program, the coordinator was Sarah Ashton, a consultant formerly with the Ford Foundation. A description of the project and a series of essays on the issues that have been addressed are featured in *Women's Studies Quarterly* 26, nos. 3 and 4 (Fall/Winter 1998).

My work in women's studies at the national council has also included administering a program of travel grants for women's studies scholars and practitioners from India, Nepal, and Sri Lanka. A similar program for Bangladesh was recently ended as the Ford Foundation closed its Bangladesh office. The India program has been based at the council since 1984 and is intended to promote international exchange and collaboration.

More recently, my work has focused heavily in two areas. One is women's studies in the context of the transitional countries of Eastern Europe and the former Soviet Union. In this area I have been active primarily through the Network of East-West Women (NEWW), of which I am a board member. The network was established in 1990 as an international communications and resource network for women advocates, researchers, professors, journalists, lawyers, and others concerned with ensuring equality for women. Gender research centers and women's studies programs are burgeoning throughout the region and are playing a key role in the development of a fledgling women's movement. There is a large cadre of educated women to build on, and they have shown themselves to be eager to catch up on developments in the

West throughout the past thirty years and to play a greater role in the international arena. At a meeting of the network members that was held in Warsaw at the end of 1998, it was clear that the flow of information was not only West to East but also East to West, unifying the group. There is much to share and to learn, and I anticipate greater involvement on my part, both through the network and through the national council.

The other area in which I have been active in recent years is feminist economics, combining my interests in economics and in women's studies. I am a founding member of the International Association for Feminist Economics (IAFFE), which was organized in 1992. IAFFE has dual aims: to advance feminist inquiry into economic issues, and to encourage the inclusion of the feminist perspective in the economics classroom. For girls and young women, there is the added objective of encouraging more interest in careers in economics, where women continue to be severely underrepresented. There is also a need to encourage greater participation of feminist economists in women's studies programs, where thus far they have been scarce. I have a particular interest in promoting economic literacy programs for women and girls. Economic literacy is, of course, important to an informed citizenry, and women need to understand and influence public policies that may affect them. In the international sphere, economic literacy is particularly important for critiquing policies affecting women in development. And for women in countries in transition from command economies to free market systems, it is important to understand the constraints as well as the opportunities involved.

At the start of this memoir, I allowed as how I considered myself to be more of a godmother than a mother of women's studies. At this point, I also see myself as a veteran.

Notes

Mari Jo Buhle

1 *PMLA Directory* 114 (September 1999): 899–906; Marilyn Jacoby Boxer, *When Women Ask the Questions: Creating Women's Studies in America* (Baltimore and London: The Johns Hopkins University Press, 1998), 240–42.

2 Florence Howe, *Seven Years Later: Women's Studies Programs in 1976*, Report of the National Advisory Council on Women's Educational Programs (Washington, D.C., The Department of Health, Education and Welfare, 1977), 15.

3 Florence Howe, "Women and the Power of Education," *American Association for Higher Educational Bulletin* 33 (1981): 13–14.

4 National Center for Education Statistics, *Digest of Education Statistics 1969* (Washington, D.C.: U.S. Government Printing Office, 1969), 74, table 99.

5 National Center for Education Statistics, *Digest of Education Statistics 1977–78* (Washington, D.C.: U.S. Government Printing Office, 1978), 108, table 110. See also Patricia Albjerg Graham, "Expansion and Exclusion: A History of Women in American Higher Education," *Signs* 3 (Summer 1978): 759–73.

6 National Center for Education Statistics, *Digest of Education Statistics 1973* (Washington, D.C.: U.S. Government Printing Office, 1973), 84, table 100; National Center for Education Statistics, *Digest of Education Statistics 1982* (Washington, D.C.: U.S. Government Printing Office, 1982), 117, table 108.

7 Jean Campbell, "Women Drop Back In: Educational Innovation in the Sixties," in *Academic Women on the Move*, ed. Alice S. Rossi and Ann Calderwood (New York: Russell Sage, 1973).

8 Susan Boslego Carter, "Academic Women Revisited: An Empirical Study of Changing Patterns in Women's Employment as College and University Faculty, 1890–1963," *Journal of Social History* 14 (Summer 1981): 675–700.

9 Lyde Cullen Sizer, "'A Place for a Good Woman': The Development of Women Faculty at Brown," in *The Search for Equity: Women at Brown University, 1891–1991*, ed. Polly Welts Kaufman (Hanover, N.H. and London: Brown University

Press/University Press of New England, 1991), 197–200.

10 William H. Exum, "Climbing the Crystal Stair: Values, Affirmative Action and Minority Faculty," *Social Problems* 30 (April 1983): 383–97.

11 Florence Howe, "A Report on Women and the Professions," *College English* 32 (May 1971): 847–54.

12 Hunter College Women's Studies Collective, *Women's Realities, Women's Choices: An Introduction to Women's Studies* (New York: Oxford University Press, 1983), 3. The women's studies program at Hunter College was formed in 1971.

13 Sara Evans, *Personal Politics: The Origin of Women's Liberation in Civil Rights and the New Left* (New York: Random House, 1979).

14 Florence Howe, *Seven Years Later,* 23.

15 Sheila Tobias, *Female Studies: An Immodest Proposal* (Ithaca, N.Y.: Cornell University, 1970).

16 Students for a Democratic Society, *The Port Huron Statement* (New York: Students for a Democratic Society, 1962), 6.

17 Florence Howe and Carol Ahlum, "Women's Studies and Social Change," in *Academic Women on the Move,* ed. Alice S. Rossi and Ann Calderwood (New York: Russell Sage, 1973), 396–98.

18 Quoted in ibid., 420.

19 The duality of feminist scholarship is well articulated in the early literature on women's studies. See Ellen Carol DuBois, Gail Paradise Kelly, Elizabeth Lapovsky Kennedy, Carolyn W.

Korsmeyer, and Lilian S. Robinson, *Feminist Scholarship: Kindling in the Groves of Academe* (Urbana: University of Illinois Press, 1985); and Gloria Bowles and Renate Duelli Klein, eds., *Theories of Women's Studies* (London: Routledge and Kegan Paul, 1983).

20 Florence Howe, "Women's Studies and Curricular Change," in *Women in Academe: Progress and Prospects,* ed. Mariam K. Chamberlain (New York: Russell Sage Foundation, 1988), 148. For recent trends, see Boxer, *When Women Ask the Questions,* 27.

21 See, for example, Joanna de Groot and Mary Maynard, "Facing the 1990s: Problems and Possibilities for Women's Studies," in *Women's Studies in the 1990s: Doing Things Differently?* ed. Joanna de Groot and Mary Maynard (New York: St. Martin's Press, 1993), 147–78.

Florence Howe

1 See my essay "Mississippi's Freedom Schools: The Politics of Education" for examples of students' writing as well as descriptions of the new pedagogy. I wrote the essay shortly after my return in the fall of 1964; it was published first in *Harvard Educational Review* (January 1965), and then republished six times, including in my own *Myths of Coeducation: Selected Essays* (Bloomington: Indiana University Press, 1984).

2 Often profoundly uneasy in middle-class or elite surroundings, and ashamed of my origins, I

first wrote openly about class in
"Is She My Mother, Am I Home?"
for Janet Zandy's remarkable
book *Liberating Memory: Our Work and
Our Working-Class Consciousness* (New
Brunswick, N.J.: Rutgers State
University Press, 1995). I owe to
Tillie and Jack Olsen the ability to
think and write about my origins.

3 Nor did I move swiftly toward
feminism. My political work
through this period continued to
be focused on Mississippi and
racism, both linked in the summer of 1965 to the effort to stop
the war in Vietnam and to integrate schools in Natchez, Mississippi. I never was part of a
consciousness-raising group, nor
had I any connections with the
early days of the National Organization for Women (NOW).

4 Malcolm Scully, "Teaching Consciousness," *The Chronicle of Higher
Education* 4, no. 18 (9 February
1970): 1, 2–4.

5 See Florence Howe, "Identity and
Expression," *College English,* May
1971. The essay was reprinted by
the National Council of Teachers
of English in a publication called
*A Case for Equity: Women in English
Departments,* also in 1971. By then,
Carol Ahlum, my work-study
assistant, and I had issued the first
of what were to be several stapled
pamphlets under the title "The
New Guide to Women's Studies,"
which listed information about
the faculty and courses they were
teaching about women.

6 Nor did my choice of topic win
accolades among the faculty, a few

of whom criticized me merely for
"wasting" Ellison's fine novel on
freshman students, and then
judged me privately for choosing
so "trivial" or "faddish" a topic as
"identity." Because I had tenure,
worked hard on committees, and
taught my literature courses in a
fairly traditional manner, I was
tolerated, though my activist work
and my missing dissertation
assured me a permanent place
among the assistant professors of
the world. Between 1968 and
1971, when I left Goucher, my
department chair nominated me
several times for a promotion,
citing my publications as well as
my work with the MLA, to no
avail.

7 The poetry project in the Baltimore schools was the first project
of what became the Teachers and
Writers Collaborative, begun in
the mid-1960s by a group of educators and writers in an inn on
Long Island. The group included
Herbert Kohl, Grace Paley, and
Anne Sexton. In the early 1970s, I
wrote about the project. See, for
example, "Untaught Teachers and
Improbable Poets," *Saturday Review,*
15 March 1969: 60–82; and "Why
Teach Poetry?—An Experiment,"
in *The Politics of Literature,* ed. Louis
Kampf and Paul Lauter, (New
York: Pantheon, 1972).

8 Two accounts of the history of
The Feminist Press (with photographs) are available from our
office, the first published on the
occasion of the fifteenth anniversary, the second on the occasion

of the twenty-fifth. They are not for sale, but we make them available to donors.

9 The Reprints Advisory Board of The Feminist Press between 1973 and 1983 included the following "feminist historians and literary scholars": Rosalyn Baxandall, Mari Jo Buhle, Ellen Cantarow, Blanche Wiesen Cook, Marsha Darling, Ellen DuBois, Moira Ferguson, Elaine Hedges, Onita Hicks, Florence Howe, Gloria Hull, Louis Kampf, Joan Kelly-Gadol, Alice Kessler-Harris, Paul Lauter, Dora Odarenko, Marilyn Richardson, Ellen Rosen, Michele Russell, Elaine Scott, Elaine Showalter, Catharine Stimpson, Amy Swerdlow, Rosalyn Terborg-Penn, Mary Helen Washington, and Marilyn Young.

10 Since leaving SUNY, Old Westbury, in 1985, I have refused to write about its politics, and write only reluctantly here, for much that may have pained me may have been good for students.

11 From the course syllabus.

12 These were first self-published as Glass Mountain Pamphlets, but then turned over to The Feminist Press, where they are still in print.

13 See Florence Howe, *Seven Years Later: Women's Studies Programs in 1976*, Report of the National Advisory Council on Women's Educational Programs (Washington, D.C.: The Department of Health, Education and Welfare, 1977).

14 Teaching guides were to accompany each volume, all to be field tested in schools across the country with very different kinds of populations. Six anthologies, including a literary anthology called *Women Working*, were to be multicultural—on art, agriculture, sports, social change, and teaching. Four were to be potentially multicultural texts, on employment, the law, sex roles, and the family. And two were to focus on specific minority populations: *Black Foremothers* and *Las Mujeres*.

15 By 1980, though I was looking for an Indian scholar who could search for lost Indian women writers, I could not have predicted that the two hundred Indian scholars who worked on *Women Writing in India: 600 B.C. to the Present* (in two volumes) from 1984 to 1989 would find six hundred lost Indian women writers, nor that the 1990s would find The Feminist Press engaged in a series called Women Writing Africa.

Nancy Hoffman

1 Sally Kempton, "Cutting Loose, " in *Liberation Now! Writings from the Women's Liberation Movement*, ed. Deborah Babcox and Madeline Belkin (New York: Dell-Laurel, 1971), 39–54.

2 I kept what I called a class chronicle. The chronicle begins on Halloween 1969, follows the development of the course and its first run-through in the winter quarter of 1970, and then provides a justification to the English department for the course to run again the following year, not with a "special topics" designation, but

as an upper-division departmental offering.

3 For a closer analysis of the Portland State University program and the sometimes contentious politics of maintaining the oxymoronic collectivist leadership we desired, see the essays by Nona Glazer and Nancy Porter in this volume.

4 From 1979 to 1981, I was program officer at the Fund for the Improvement of Postsecondary Education, U.S. Department of Education, Washington, D.C. I returned to CPCS after a delayed sabbatical in spring 1982.

5 See the essays of Mary Anne Ferguson and Barbara Smith in this volume.

Sheila Tobias

1 Charlotte Conable writes, "Yet the history of women at one institution, Cornell University, shows that the policies of the administration changed [over time] and were determined more by economic considerations and social pressures than by the founders' ideals. These changes differentiated the educational experience offered to women from that of men and resulted in dissimilar preparation or motivation for later endeavors." *Women at Cornell: The Myth of Coeducation* (Ithaca, N.Y.: Cornell University Press, 1977), 7–8.

2 Charlotte Conable, *Women at Cornell: The Myth of Coeducation.*

3 Sara Evans, *Personal Politics: The Roots of Women's Liberation in Civil Rights Politics and the New Left* (New York: Vin-

tage Press, 1980), as quoted in Sheila Tobias, *Faces of Feminism: An Activist's Reflections on the Women's Movement* (Boulder, Colo.: Westview Press, 1997), 77.

4 Mariam K. Chamberlain, "The Emergence and Growth of Women's Studies Programs," in *The American Woman: A Status Report, 1991,* ed. Sara E. Ritz (New York: W. W. Norton, 1991), 315 ff.

5 Sheila Tobias, *Female Studies: Vol. 1* (Pittsburgh: KNOW, 1970).

6 Judith Jacobs in women and mathematics; Jean Bethke Elshtain and Amy Swerdlow in women and war and in women and peace politics; Londa Schiebinger and Evelyn Fox Keller in women and science; and Kate Millett, Myra Dinnerstein, Florence Howe, Susan Koppelman, and Annette Kolodny in women and the biases inherent in male culture.

7 Such as my collaboration, beginning in 1976, with Wesleyan historian Donald Meyer (the biographer of Mary Baker Eddy) in teaching jointly Men and Women in Wartime: America in the Forties, featuring such topics as women's war work, the celebration of masculinity in popular culture, changes in marriage and divorce, postwar adjustments, and the baby boom.

Jean Walton

My story describes one beginning of the Claremont Colleges women's studies program, as it happened at Pomona College, where I was working. Faculty members at the other Claremont Colleges would describe other beginnings. I can tell only my own story. I wish to express my thanks to Sue Mansfield, history department at Claremont McKenna College, who shared with me her own research on the early days of our intercollegiate women's studies program.

1 The Claremont Colleges are five autonomous undergraduate colleges (Claremont McKenna, formerly Claremont Men's; Harvey Mudd; Pitzer; Pomona; and Scripps) and two graduate institutions on adjacent campuses, affiliated to broaden the intellectual, social, and cultural resources available to their students. The colleges jointly support certain central facilities, open their courses to one another's students, and cooperate in sponsoring special academic and extracurricular programs. (Description based on a statement in the 1998–99 Pomona College catalogue.)

2 The five coordinators have been Susan Seymour (anthropology department at Pitzer); Anne Bages (physical education department at Pomona); J'nan Sellery (literature department at Harvey Mudd); Sue Mansfield (history department at Claremont McKenna); and Jane O'Donnell (music department at Scripps).

3 Our primary interest was in the development of women's studies courses, but we were concerned also with the integration of women's studies materials into the traditional liberal arts curriculum. An early example of our efforts is the well-attended conference offered in February 1983, Traditions and Transitions: Women's Studies and a Balanced Curriculum.

Nancy Topping Bazin

1 Although *androgynous* was not properly defined in dictionaries, I claimed that it was a word that was "coming into being." In accord with my prophetic sense, in April 1973, my book appeared, along with Carolyn Heilbrun's *Toward the Recognition of Androgyny;* Adrienne Rich's poem "The Stranger" (from *Diving into the Wreck*) about the baby "androgyne;" and Mary Daly's *Beyond God the Father: Toward a Philosophy of Women's Liberation,* which focused on the ideal of "androgynous being." Androgyny was the topic of a major panel at the 1973 Modern Language Association Convention and a special 1974 issue of Wendy Martin's journal, *Women's Studies* 2, no. 2. In it, my coauthor, Alma Freeman, and I published an article titled "The Androgynous Vision" (185–215). In that same issue, I also published a long, annotated bibliography titled "The Concept of Androgyny: A Working Bibliography," (217–35). My inclusive philosophy developed from the concept of the androgynous vision; see Nancy Topping Bazin, "Emerging from Women's Studies: A New World View and a New Goal for

Educators," *The Journal of Curriculum Theorizing* 4, no. 2 (Summer 1982): 187–92; and Nancy Topping Bazin, "Integrating Third World Women into the Women's Studies Curriculum,"*Frontiers: A Journal of Women's Studies* 7, no. 2 (1983): 13–17.

2 Nancy Topping Bazin, *Virginia Woolf and the Autonomous Vision* (New Brunswick, N.J.: Rutgers University Press, 1973).

3 Several of the Rutgers College women faculty were in romance languages. Among the departments with no female faculty were art, history, music, and psychology. Nationwide, in art, those getting Ph.D.'s were 18 percent female; in history, 15 percent; and in English, 30 percent. As a response to a threat of having federal contracts withheld, Provost Kenneth Wheeler announced that faculties in departments should reflect these Ph.D. percentages. The Women's Equity Action League (WEAL) had lodged a complaint with the Department of Health, Education and Welfare. In an article about this in the May 10, 1971, *Rutgers Daily Targum,* a male professor was quoted as saying that the obvious discrimination against women was "as it should be." In addition, at that time faculty contracts provided "compensation of all diseases except those specifically related to women." Women staff members were fired in their seventh month of pregnancy and allowed to return only if their position were "still avail-

able." See Irene Ronciglione, "Discriminatory Employment Patterns Uncovered at R.U.," *Rutgers Daily Targum,* 10 May 1971: 3, 7.

4 Elaine Showalter, "Women and the Literary Curriculum," *College English* 32, no. 8 (May 1971): 855–62 (publication of the paper read at the MLA Forum on the Status of Women in the Profession, December 27, 1970); and Elaine Showalter, "Women Writers and the Female Experience," in *Notes from the Third Year: Women's Liberation,* ed. Anne Koedt and Shulamith Firestone (New York: Notes from the Third Year [P.O. Box AA, Old Chelsea Station, New York, N.Y. 10011], 1971), 134–41.

5 For the 1971 statistics on the actual number of women in the House of Representatives and in the Senate, see *Biographical Dictionary of the American Congress, 1774–1996,* ed. Joel Treese and Dorothy Countryman (Alexandria, Va.: CQ Staff Directories, 1997), 469–74; and Office of the Historian, U.S. House of Representatives, *Women in Congress, 1917–1990* (Washington, D.C.: U. S. Government Printing Office, 1991), 1–241 *passim.* In 1971, the cabinet consisted of fifteen members, none of whom were women. See Robert, Zobel, ed., *Biographical Dictionary of the U.S. Executive Branch, 1774–1977* (Westport, Conn.: Greenwood Press, 1977), 398–99.

6 Alicia Ostriker, "Once More Out of Darkness," in *Once More Out of*

Darkness and Other Poems (Berkeley: Berkeley Poets' Cooperative, 1974), 7–15.

7 See Melanie Janis Cooper, "'Resolved That I Should Be a Man': A Comprehensive Study of Coeducation at Rutgers College" (Henry Rutgers honors thesis submitted to the Department of History and the Department of American Studies, Rutgers University, 1997), 33–37 (available in Special Collections and University Archives, Rutgers University Libraries).

8 In 1974, when the first Rutgers College women's basketball team began playing, "'hostile spectators' chided the coaches and players with, 'Go back to the kitchen. Get out of our gym and go home. Whatever happened to motherhood?!'" (Jaynee LaVecchia and Beth Ludwig, "Women Add New Element to B-Ball Program," *Rutgers Daily Targum*, 5 December 1974, as quoted in Cooper, "Resolved," 100. Sexism existed, too, in certain classrooms. For example, on November 21, 1974, a female student published a letter in the student newspaper about "blatantly sexist film clips" shown as part of her biology teacher's "recent lecture on photosynthesis." The letter stated, "The woman hanging out of her bikini was offensive enough without having to take off her top, and finally her bikini bottom!" She asked, "Is this the only way you can make biology lectures more interesting—by spicing them up with *Penthouse* pic-

tures?" She concluded, "I can recall that last year many students complained to the biology department as well as the *Targum* that the lecture was offensive, yet nothing was done to change it. Why, gentlemen?" (Letters, *Rutgers Daily Targum*, 21 November 1974, as quoted in Cooper, "Resolved," 95). In response to the film clips, she and other women in that biology class had risen to their feet in protest and walked out.

9 At the other end of New Brunswick, Elaine Showalter and her colleagues were already teaching several women's studies courses at Douglass College, but at that time we had little direct contact. Kate Ellis in the Livingston College English department was interested in women's studies, too, but its development on that new campus had just begun. In working to develop women's studies, Ann Parelius in the sociology department at Rutgers College was a particularly supportive colleague. For acquiring women's studies books for the library, I had strong support from librarian Joan Walsh. Among administrators, Georgina Smith, Guida West, and Joyce Wadlington were active on several fronts.

10 Our other guests during that first year included artist Faith Ringgold; Cindy Nemser of the *Feminist Art Journal;* creative writers Doris Lessing, Adrienne Rich, Anaïs Nin, Diane Wakowski, Maxine Kumin, and Marge Piercy; biographer Nancy Milford; actor

Donna Wilshire; feminist writers Deirdre English, Florence Howe, and Robin Morgan; members of the Viola Farber Dance Company; members of the Barbara Lloyd Dance Company; and New York City Ballet dancer Violetta Verdy.

11 During an earlier evaluation, the first ploy of the department's power clique (usually three men) was to declare that they did not need a tenured faculty member in my field of twentieth-century British literature. Because I had been the only one teaching that course at Rutgers College and for the graduate program, I was able to reply quickly to that, and they never mentioned it again.

12 The next year at Rutgers College a young man was coming up for tenure, but he did not yet have a publisher for his book. The department's powers called unsuccessfully all over the country to help him find a publisher. Finally, they removed the name of a colleague from his acknowledgments and made this same colleague a reader (quickly, over the weekend) for Rutgers University Press. In this way his book was accepted for publication, and he was granted tenure.

13 When I left Rutgers College, the dean placed women's studies in the hands of a moderate feminist who had become his associate dean, thus putting the program where he could control it.

14 Old Dominion University had the first women's studies program in Virginia. It was initially funded by a 1977–78 pilot grant of $42,836 from the National Endowment for the Humanities. During the first year, under the leadership of Carolyn Rhodes, six courses were team taught. When the dean of arts and letters, Heinz Meier, decided to seek a permanent director to be hired in time for the fall 1978 semester, the post could be full-time in women's studies or half-time in women's studies and half-time in a department. Before my on-campus interview, the chair of the English department had decided not to have the women's studies director in his department. However, while on campus, I convinced him that he should be interested in adding this extra position. Thus he canceled a meeting of English faculty and had them attend my talk. He told someone that he became interested in hiring me "because I looked like a Southern lady." Luckily, I had not fit his image of a feminist!

15 One history professor predicted, "By the year 2000, the 'new freedom woman' will have dropped her hyphenated name and will have crawled out of her trousers and back into the security of her foundation and home. NOW will again become an adverb, and ERA a common noun." This prophecy appeared in a feature article by Patrick J. Rollins in the November 17, 1978, issue of *UNews*. The title of the article asked, "Feminist Consciousness Marks Collapse, Social Chaos?" Rollins fervently

answered yes to that question.

16 Nancy Topping Bazin, "Expanding the Concept of Affirmative Action to Include the Curriculum," *Women's Studies Newsletter* 4, no. 2 (Winter 1980): 10–11, 14–15; and Nancy Topping Bazin, "Transforming the Curriculum, the Mission Statement, the Strategic Goals: A Success Story," *Initiatives* (Journal of the National Association of Women in Education) 54, no. 1 (Spring 1991): 39–46.

Annis Pratt

1 See W. E. Cross, "Negro to Black Conversion Experience," *Black World* 20, no. 9 (1971): 13–27.

2 See Nancy E. Downing and Kristin L. Roush, "From Passive Acceptance to Active Commitment: A Model of Feminist Identity Development for Women," *The Counseling Psychologist* 13, no. 4 (October 1985): 695–709.

3 See Sarah Slavin and Jacqueline Macaulay, "Joan Roberts and the University," in *Rocking the Boat: Academic Women and Academic Processes,* ed. Gloria DeSole and Leonore Hoffmann (New York: The Modern Language Association of America, 1981), 37–49.

4 See Jacqueline Macaulay, "The Failure of Affirmative Action: One University's Experience," in *Rocking the Boat,* ed. DeSole and Hoffmann, 98–115.

5 During the Nazi era, Paul de Man, for example—the darling of the deconstructionists—wrote collaborationist journalism. See

Alice Kaplan, *French Lessons: A Memoir.* (Chicago: University of Chicago Press, 1993), 167–69.

Josephine Donovan

1 This was what I heard at the time. The apocryphal bra burning was actually alleged to have occurred at the Miss America pageant in Atlantic City, New Jersey.

2 Robin Morgan, "Goodbye to All That," *Rat,* January 1970, reprinted in Robin Morgan, *Going Too Far* (New York: Random, 1977), 121–30; see also Marge Piercy, "The Grand Coolie Damn," in *Sisterhood Is Powerful,* ed. Robin Morgan (New York: Vintage, 1970), 421–38; Anne Koedt, "Women and the Radical Movement" (an early version of which appeared in *Notes from the First Year* [1968]) in *Radical Feminism,* ed. Anne Koedt, Ellen Levine, and Anita Rapone (New York: Quadrangle, 1973), 318–21; and Thomas Powers, *Diana: The Making of a Terrorist* (New York: Bantam, 1971). The phrase "goodbye to all that" actually dates from World War I.

3 Elaine Reuben was then, I believe, an assistant professor in the English department at the UW. She later became the first coordinator of the National Women's Studies Association.

4 I might mention as a historical footnote that my first assignment as a teaching assistant was in the spring of 1967 under Cyrena Pondrom (Evelyn Beck was also a TA in that course, Masterpieces of

Western Literature). Of course, although both Cyrena and Evelyn later became active in women's studies, none of us had heard of it at the time.

5 Catalyzed primarily by Carol Gilligan's *In a Different Voice* (Cambridge: Harvard University Press, 1982), this direction is usually referred to as cultural feminism.

6 Ti-Grace Atkinson, *Amazon Odyssey* (New York: Links, 1974), ccliv. Atkinson is referring to the emergence of radical feminism in New York in 1968–70.

7 On this, *Three Guineas* has much to offer. Also very influential on me at the time was Barbara A. White's article "Up from the Podium: Feminist Revolution in the Classroom," in *Female Studies 4* (Pittsburgh: KNOW, 1972), 28–34. It called for egalitarian relationships between students and teachers. Barbara, whom I didn't then know, later became a close friend and colleague at arms at the University of New Hampshire.

8 The prevailing power relations in the American university reflect a military model. As Michael Ignatieff notes in a review of Barbara Ehrenreich's *Blood Rites* (1997), "War militarized the male and the male militarized the routines of factory, office, and school. As the military begins to recede as the most influential model for human organization, styles of management will emerge that depend less on command, more on cooperation" (*New York Review of Books,* 9 October 1997, p. 13).

9 The Tulsa Center for the Study of Women's Literature at the University of Tulsa (where I was a visiting scholar in 1982) had a similar house with kitchen facilities. I recall that in my interview for the position, Germaine Greer, who was then director of the center, asked me if I would mind fixing a pot of homemade soup for the students in my weekly seminar. I wasn't sure whether this was a condition of employment, so I answered somewhat noncommittally that I thought it was a nice idea. In fact, I did one time prepare a large pot of split pea soup for those students, who much appreciated the gesture.

10 (Lexington: University Press of Kentucky, 1975; rev. ed., 1989). Still in print, it remains one of the University Press of Kentucky's all-time best-sellers.

11 I wanted to complete two books that I had under way (which became *New England Local Color Literature* [1983] and *Feminist Theory: The Intellectual Traditions of American Feminism* [1985; rev. ed., 1992, 2000]), and I simply had to get away from the poisonous UNH atmosphere. I might mention that there was plenty of squabbling during this period among the women's studies faculty—much of it disgraceful—although we generally managed to put up a united front for the administration. But the untrustworthiness of several of the women's studies faculty made my position especially difficult. And being a lesbian with a partner

on the faculty didn't help either. In those days in academia, it wasn't chic to be gay—especially in a state controlled by Meldrin Thompson, a right-wing politician whose perhaps most memorable act as governor was to have the state flags hung at half-mast when China was admitted to the United Nations. There was, in fact, at the time a requirement of UNH faculty that they sign a loyalty oath to the state as a condition of employment. I refused to sign.

12 I recently edited my father's account of the war: William N. Donovan, *P.O.W. in the Pacific: Memoirs of an American Doctor in World War II* (Wilmington, Del.: Scholarly Resources, 1998). It includes a chapter by me, "The Home Front," about my mother's experience of the war.

13 Susan Sontag, "The Third World of Women," *Partisan Review* 60, no. 2 (1973): 192.

Inez Martinez

1 Ruth Herschberger, *Adam's Rib* (New York: Harper & Row, 1970), 213. First published in New York by Pellegrini and Cudahy in 1948. Herschberger cites Robert M. Yerkes, *Chimpanzees* (New Haven: Yale University Press, 1943), 176–77.

2 Since that time, women's studies at Kingsborough has flourished at a faster clip. In addition to traditional courses such as Women and Work (created by Norah Chase), Images of Women (created by Louise Jaffe), The Biology of Women (created by Dorothy Schweitzer), new courses in art (created by Janice Farley), in anthropology (created by Suzanne La Font), in the sociology of gender (created by Susan Farrell), in business (created by Amy Haas), and in U.S. women in the performing arts (created by Terry Trilling) have been developed.

Through a 1995 grant from the New Visions for Education Project of CUNY, sections of basic courses in mass media, sociology, English, music, and student counseling have been developed with a women's-issues focus. Professors Cliff Hesse, Bobby Laurenti, Barbara Walters, Isabella Caruso, Robert Singer, Lea Hamoui, Eleanor Cory, Estelle Miller, and Mary Dawson-Basoa are among those who have made this innovative approach to mainstreaming women's studies work. That same grant, written by Bonne August, enabled a seminar for women's studies faculty development to be held, under the direction of Hope Parisi. This seminar is now under the direction of Susan Farrell. Currently, Joe Muzio and Loretta Taras are preparing a laboratory portion of Women and Biology, so that the course may fulfill the science distribution requirement for students in career programs such as early childhood education and mental health. A concentration in women's studies under the liberal arts degree has been approved by Kingsborough's college council and CUNY's board of trustees. An articulation agreement enabling the smooth transfer of credits has been worked out with Hunter College for Kingsborough students wanting to transfer to a four-year college and to major in women's studies. A demographic survey taken in spring 1999 indicates that almost two-thirds of all students taking women's studies courses are people of color, and almost one-fifth are male.

Mimi Reisel Gladstein

1 Mimi R. Gladstein, "Ayn Rand and Feminism: An Unlikely Alliance," *College English* 39, no. 6 (February 1978): 680–85.
2 Billie Jean King, "Interview," *Playboy*, March 1976: 194–96.
3 Edith de Rham, *The Love Fraud: A Direct Attack on the Staggering Waste of Education and Talent among American Women* (New York: Pegasus, 1965).

Kathryn Kish Sklar

1 I am especially indebted to conversations with Gayle Rubin and to her printed interview with Karen Miller, "Revisioning Ann Arbor's Radical Past: An Interview with Gayle S. Rubin," *Michigan Feminist Studies* 12 (1997–98): 91–108. This essay also draws on insights that Lynn Weiner and I generated in our coauthored introduction to Ruth Bordin, *Women at Michigan: The "Dangerous Experiment," 1870s to the Present* (Ann Arbor: University of Michigan Press, 1999), xvii–xxv.

2 On this point I am grateful to conversations with Linda Gordon, Jacquelyn Dowd Hall, Mary Beth Norton, and Ruth Rosen at Longford Lake, Brackney, Pennsylvania, June 6–8, 1999.
3 See Todd Gitlin, *The Sixties: Years of Hope, Days of Rage* (New York: Bantam, 1987), 187.
4 For BAM and antiwar campus activism in this era, see Zelda Gamson, "Michigan Muddles Through: Luck, Nimbleness, and Resilience in Crisis," *Academic Transformation: Seventeen Institutions Under Pressure*, ed. David Riesman and Verne A. Stadtman (New York: McGraw-Hill, 1973), 173–97.
5 Lynn Weiner, "Women Disrupt 'U' Teach-In," *Michigan Daily*, 13 October 1970.
6 Bordin, *Women at Michigan*, 78–80.
7 Gerda Lerner, *The Creation of Feminist Consciousness: From the Middle Ages to Eighteen-seventy* (New York: Oxford University Press, 1993), 10–11.
8 Marilyn Jacoby Boxer, *When Women Ask the Questions: Creating Women's Studies in America* (Baltimore: Johns Hopkins University Press, 1998), 7–10.
9 Sara Fitzgerald, "Fleming Meets Unit on 'U' Sex Discrimination," *Michigan Daily*, 9 December 1971; and Virginia Nordin, "Defending Women's Commission," *Michigan Daily*, 9 December 1971.

Gloria Bowles

Thanks to Florence Howe and to Christine Colasurdo and Robert Wazeka of my writing group for

comments on earlier drafts of this
essay.

1 Marsha Hudson first organized a
salon, which met for two years at
her apartment to discover and
discuss women writers. From
those gatherings emerged the
energy and knowledge to create a
women's caucus and demand a
course.

2 *The Other Voice: Twentieth Century
Women's Poetry in Translation* was published by Norton with an introduction by Adrienne Rich (New
York: W. W. Norton & Co.,
1976). Participants in the translation workshop would go on to
publish several more anthologies
of women poets.

3 Statistics are from Sheila
O'Rourke of the Office of Academic Compliance at the University
of California, Berkeley. See also
Natalie Angier's interview with
Virginia Valian about her book
Why So Slow? The Advancement of Women
(MIT) in the New York Times, 25
August 1998, sec. B, p. 10. At
Berkeley now, my toiling friends
are among the 249 tenured
women in a total faculty of 1457, a
number all the more disappoint-
ing now that affirmative action is
illegal.

4 Conversation between the author
and Marilyn Boxer, May 1997.

5 Gloria Bowles and Renate
Duelli-Klein, eds., *Theories of
Women's Studies* (New York: Routledge and Kegan Paul, 1983).
For further elaboration of ideas
of autonomous women's studies
and mainstreaming, see *Strategies*

for Women's Studies in the Eighties,
(Elmsford, N.Y.: Pergamon,
1984).

Margaret Strobel

For their comments on this essay,
I thank Emily Abel, Bill Barclay,
Jessica Barclay-Strobel, Sandra
Bartky, Marilyn Carlander, Judy
Gardiner, Florence Howe, Cheryl
Johnson-Odim, Stephanie Riger,
Mary Todd, and Lynn Weiner.

1 I was gone from Los Angeles for
two years, from 1971 to 1973,
when other graduate students and
faculty began to develop the
women's studies program; during
those years I taught history at
Middlebury College and then did
my field research in Mombasa,
Kenya. See Margaret Strobel,
"Drop by Drop the Bottle Fills,"
in *Voices of Women Historians,* ed.
Nupur Chaudhuri and Eileen
Boris (Bloomington: Indiana
University Press, 1999), 174–88,
for a discussion of the development of my political consciousness and my ideas as a historian of
Africa and of women.

2 NAM was a New Left–derived
national organization founded in
1972. In 1982, it merged with
Michael Harrington's Democratic
Socialist Organizing Committee
to form Democratic Socialists of
America. NAM's Socialist Community School was modeled after
the Liberation School of the
Chicago Women's Liberation
Union.

3 This is the title of one of the sessions that Emily Abel, Debby

Rosenfelt, and I put together as program organizers for the First National Conference of the National Women's Studies Association in 1979; see later in this essay.

4 Our efforts to share ideas about the new field of women's studies are discussed in Yolanda T. Moses, "A Short History of the Pacific Southwest Women's Studies Association: Bridging the Gap between Academy and Community," in *Re-Membering: National Women's Studies Association, 1977–87,* 2d ed., comp. Kathryn Towns with Caroline Cupo and Phyllis Hageman (College Park, Md.: National Women's Studies Association, 1994), 27–36.

5 Now the Western Association of Women Historians. See other chapters in Chaudhuri and Boris, *Voices of Women Historians;* as well as Marguerite Renner, ed., *Histories of the Western Association of Women Historians, 1969–94* (n.p.: WAWH, 1994); and Hilda Smith, Nupur Chaudhuri, Gerda Lerner, and Berenice A. Carroll, *A History of the Coordinating Committee on Women in the Historical Profession/Conference Group on Women's History,* 2d ed. (Chicago: CCWHP-CGWH, 1994).

6 In the three years that I taught Women's Studies 100 at UCLA, I assigned Michelle Rosaldo and Louise Lamphere's *Woman, Culture, and Society* (1974); Barbara Deckard's *The Women's Movement* (1975); Agnes Smedley's *Daughter of Earth* (1929, reprinted 1973); Ousmane Sembene's novel *God's*

Bits of Wood (1962); Studs Terkel's *Working* (1972); Sheila Rowbotham's *Women, Resistance, and Revolution* (1972); Jo Freeman's *Women: A Feminist Perspective* (1975); Ester Boserup's *Woman's Role in Economic Development* (1970); a pamphlet from the North American Congress on Latin America, *Women's Labor* (1975); Rudolfo Anaya's novel *Bless Me, Ultima* (1972); Delia Davin's *Woman-Work: Women and the Party in Revolutionary China* (1976); Linda Gordon's *Birth Control in America: Woman's Body, Woman's Right* (1976); Florence Howe's *Women and the Power to Change* (1975); Juanita Kreps' *Sex in the Marketplace* (1971); Agnes Smedley's *Portraits of Chinese Women in Revolution* (1976); and editors Rosaura Sanchez and Rose Martinez Cruz's *Essays on La Mujer* (1977), published by UCLA's Chicano Studies Center.

7 See Strobel, "Drop by Drop," 178, for a discussion of this question. I believed, and still believe, that the appropriate political response is to work to counter the inequalities from which the absence of Third World women's voices stems, to make known the research by these women, and to be self-critical. In this spirit, I coedited a special issue of *Signs* (16, no. 4, Summer 1991) on African women, with Bolanle Awe, Susan Geiger, Nina Mba, Marjorie Mbilinyi, and Ruth Meena. In addition, one aspect of my research deals with white women in the European empires of the nineteenth and twentieth

centuries and with issues of gender, race, and empire; see Strobel, "Drop by Drop," 185–86.

8 In "Fighting Two Colonialisms: Thoughts of a White Feminist Teaching about Third World Women," *The Radical Teacher* 6 (December 1977): 20–23, I compared the teaching of that course with teaching a course on African women at UCLA.

9 The Feminist Press published the screenplay, with Debby's commentary, in 1978. In the late 1960s, when there were far fewer feminist films available, such groups as the Chicago Women's Liberation Union showed *Salt of the Earth* to celebrate International Women's Day.

10 UIC was formed in 1982 from the merger of the University of Illinois Medical Center with the newer (founded in 1965) University of Illinois at Chicago Circle (UICC). For simplicity's sake, I will refer to the institution as UIC, even when I am writing about the UICC period.

11 Judith Kegan Gardiner, "A Short History of Women's Studies at UIC," [UIC] *Women's Studies Program* [newsletter] (Fall 1993): 4–5.

12 The Liberation School is discussed in Margaret Strobel, "Consciousness and Action: Historical Agency in the Chicago Women's Liberation Union," in *Provoking Agents,* ed. Judith Kegan Gardiner (Urbana and Chicago: University of Illinois Press, 1995), 52–68.

13 Jennifer Knauss, interview by author, Chicago, 6 April 1986.

14 Ellen DuBois, interview by author, Buffalo, New York, 25 April 1986.

15 Material on the work of Circle Women's Liberation comes from my group interview with Holly Graff, Jo Patton, Marilyn Carlander, Sandra Bartky, and Judith Kegan Gardiner, Chicago, 18 March 1986.

16 The term *socialist feminist* was not yet in use. Its first use, I believe, came with a paper by the Hyde Park chapter of the CWLU: "Socialist Feminism: A Strategy for the Women's Movement," self-published in Chicago in 1972. Available in the CWLU archives at the Chicago Historical Society, box 1, file 7, the document was widely circulated in women's liberation circles in the early 1970s. Women who identified as socialist feminists tended to value Marxism as an analytical method, while being critical of Marxism for its weakness in explaining sexism. They took seriously issues of oppression based upon class and race, not only gender and sexual orientation. They were opposed to imperialism, both in its historical form (colonialism) and the ongoing U.S. war in Southeast Asia, and hence paid attention to women's participation in revolutionary, anti-imperialist movements.

17 Holly Graff, interview by author, Chicago, 18 March 1986.

18 The process of criticism and self-criticism was borrowed from various sources, including the labor

movement's "good and welfare" sessions and what we understood to be a process developed in the People's Republic of China. Participants in the meeting were expected to evaluate their own and their sisters' contributions in a constructive manner. When used effectively, the process prevented small objections and grievances from smoldering and thus promoted the companion process of decision making by consensus.

19 Sandra Bartky, interview by author, Chicago, 18 March 1986. The "Circle" in Circle Women's Liberation refers to the then-name of the campus, University of Illinois at Chicago Circle; see note 10.

20 Jo Patton, interview by author, Chicago, 18 March 1986.

21 The use of the now-suspect term "other" should not obscure the fact that the women's studies program, in the early 1970s, devoted one-third of its core curriculum to women outside the United States.

22 *Muslim Women in Mombasa, 1890–1975* (New Haven, Conn.: Yale University Press, 1979).

23 See note 8.

24 For a brief report of this struggle and victory, see Peg Strobel, "News from the University of Illinois at Chicago," *NWSA Newsletter* 2, no. 4 (Fall 1984): 60–61.

25 Reports include Carol Lee Sanchez, "Multicultural Women's Summer Institute," *NWSA Newsletter* 2, no. 1 (Winter 1983): 1–2; Peg Strobel, n.t., *Women's Studies*

Quarterly 13, no. 2 (Summer 1985): 19–20.

26 I am on the editorial board of *Women Building Chicago, 1790–1990: A Biographical Dictionary,* edited by Rima Lunin Schultz and Adele Hast (Bloomington: Indiana University Press, forthcoming) *Women Building Chicago* is itself a model of feminist collaboration across the university and community. It began in the early 1990s as a volunteer project of members of the Chicago Area Women's History Conference. Members included activists, public intellectuals, unaffiliated scholars, and faculty from postsecondary institutions. A grant would provide some reimbursement for project members, and UIC's new Center for Research on Women and Gender (CRWG) wanted to support research in the humanities. Hence I invited the group to submit a proposal, which was funded on the first attempt, to the National Endowment for the Humanities through the CRWG, thereby using the bureaucratic structure and legitimacy of the university.

27 Information about this course and the larger initiative of which it is a part are available in Margaret Strobel, "The 'Don't Throw It Away!' Project at the University of Illinois," *NWSA Journal,* forthcoming in 2000. The text of a booklet *Don't Throw It Away! Documenting and Preserving Organizational History* is available at www.uic.edu/depts/lib/collections/dont/.

28 Our present women's studies program director, Stephanie Riger,
hired in 1990, has written on the
conflicts that arise in feminist
organizations with a collectivist
orientation as growth forces
changes. See "Challenges of Success: Stages of Growth in Feminist
Organizations," *Feminist Studies* 20,
no. 1 (Summer 1994): 275–300.

Mary Anne Ferguson

1 We met once a quarter for three
days in New York, and each member contributed one day a week to
commission business. At the 1970
MLA meeting, at which we had
our first forum—a major program
with satellite workshops—I led a
panel titled The Job Market: A
Department Chairman's View (I
wasn't a chairman!), and in 1971
one called Affirmative Action:
How It Works. I also represented
the commission on the new MLA
Job Commission, which was trying to adjust to the reality of the
growing depression in our field.

In order to encourage the
growth of the Women's Caucus, a
grass-roots organization that
helped the commission to lobby
the administration of the MLA, I
answered letters from women isolated in their positions and long-
ing for the kind of comradeship I
was experiencing not only in our
commission meetings but now
more widely in women's groups at
my university, at meetings of the
regional MLA, and eventually in
the National Women's Studies
Association. In 1972 at a Radcliffe
College meeting called Women as
Resources for Society—billed as
the first international meeting on
women's studies—Catharine
Stimpson and I led a small group
to overcome the conference
administrators' reluctance to send
a resolution to Congress about
the invasion of Cambodia, news
of which came during the meeting. They insisted that women's
studies was not political, but those
of us who realized that it was in
essence political prevailed: we
outwaited those who had to leave
early and won the final vote.

2 Florence Howe, ed., *Female Studies 2*
(Pittsburgh: KNOW, 1970).

3 My search led me first to discuss
the issue with a colleague in psychology, but her discipline at that
time (1971) offered no theoretical
perspective. Mary Ellman's *Thinking
about Women* (1961) influenced my
thinking greatly.

4 I chose Houghton Mifflin because
of its prestige in Boston, and
because they promised to keep the
price low and to market the
anthology vigorously. I did not
anticipate having a best-seller in
its field, but the time was ripe
(four editions followed, through
1991; translations of parts into
Swedish and Japanese appeared).
In order to beat the secondhand
market, I had to re-edit the book
every four years, which required
one-third new material. I was able
to make use of the proliferation of
works by contemporary authors. I
realized by the third edition that I
was in a position of power and

could introduce new authors; Houghton Mifflin never censored me. I also kept up with feminist theory and debate, going to major meetings; I changed my introductions and added extensive bibliographies to take account of new works. It was gratifying to read the list of adoptions, widely scattered throughout the country and usually *not* at prestigious research institutions; I learned from the comments of users, whom Houghton Mifflin solicited. My editor discovered that even at Harvard some of my material was infiltrating standard courses, and I was particularly pleased when my daughter introduced the first edition into a student-chosen course at Yale.

While still on the commission I envied Elaine Showalter and Carol Ohmann, because they had specialized in nineteenth-century women writers; Carol was already publishing her insights into the difficulties of the Brontës. Elaine, in one of our discussions, told a story that helped me see how a woman's perspective could, in fact, change one's view of the world. At her Ph.D. finals at Bryn Mawr, she was asked what she thought to be the most important discovery of the nineteenth century. "The vulcanization of rubber," she calmly replied, to the committee's astonishment: enabling women to practice contraception she saw as more important than the steam engine or the cotton gin. Focusing on women,

she made me see, changed one's perception of history. I began to feel that my course Images of Women in Literature might be revolutionary enough to change more than the English curriculum.

5 Linda Gordon taught one on the history of women, and Nina Alonso taught Women Poets in the English department. Nina could not continue, however: she did not get tenure. And Linda, though tenured, could not expand: hired to teach Russian history, she found the history department unreceptive to her announcement that she now considered herself a historian of women. (Her book on the history of birth control was acclaimed elsewhere, and eventually she moved to become a distinguished professor at the University of Wisconsin.)

6 In 1979, when I was acting chair of the English department, I was particularly happy to be able to negotiate the hiring of Mary Helen Washington. We had met when we were both fellows at the Wellesley Center for Research on Women. The dean wanted to hire her without tenure and at a much lower salary than he eventually agreed to. In 1980 I became the first woman to be elected chair of the English department. Because of the success of our program, I was often asked to write letters for faculty at other institutions and was gratified that many women I wrote for were successful in gain-

ing tenure. The look of my profession began to change: it took
many years, but eventually even at
prestigious universities larger
proportions of women faculty
achieved tenure and promotion.
Feminists, including Florence
Howe, Carolyn Heilbrun (whose
book had initiated heated discussion about androgyny as a goal of
feminism), and Elaine Showalter,
a member of the original commission, even became presidents
of the MLA!

Electa Arenal

1 Carol Alpert, telephone conversation with author, 7 March
1999.

2 Astraea is the only national fund-
raising organization for lesbians,
and SAGE stands for Senior
Action in a Gay Environment. It
is also a national organization.

3 Fewer members of the (white)
women's studies field than should
be are aware of the early contributions of African American
women to the effervescence. See,
for instance, Paule Marshall's
1970 essay, "The Liberation of
Black Women," in *Words of Fire: An
Anthology of African American Feminist
Thought*, Beverly Guy-Sheftall
(New York: The New Press,
1995), 185–97.

4 I spoke of this book's impact on
me in a five-minute talk at a
Chicago MLA convention in
1990, as part of a session organized by Florence Howe called
"Books That Changed Our
Lives." See *Women's Studies Quarterly*

25, nos. 1 and 2 (Spring/Summer
1997): 329–22.

5 New York: Basic Books, 1971.

Barbara Smith

1 Robin D. G. Kelly, "The Left," in
*Black Women in America: An Historical
Encyclopedia,* ed. Darlene Clark
Hine et al. (Brooklyn, N.Y.:
Carlson Publishing, 1993), 713.

Nellie Y. McKay

1 Paule Marshall, "The Making of a
Writer: From the Poets in the
Kitchen," in *Reena and Other Stories*
(New York: The Feminist Press,
1983), 4–5.

Beverly Guy-Sheftall

As is my frequent reaction to
projects attempting to provide a
retrospective on the development
of anything related to the history
of the second wave women's
movement, I was ambivalent about
agreeing to become a contributor
to this volume on mothers of
women's studies. I was wary about
joining a collection of writings
where, yet again, most of the
women would no doubt be white.
(See *The Feminist Memoir Project: Voices
from Women's Liberation,* ed. Rachel
Blau DuPlessis and Ann Snitow
[New York: Three Rivers Press,
1998], which includes a short
essay by me entitled "Sisters in
Struggle: A Belated Response,"
and essays by four black women:
Barbara Smith, Michele
Wallace, Barbara Omolade, and
Barbara Emerson.) I also felt that
I had written, in some detail in

various places, about the history of my involvement in women's studies and the founding of the Women's Research and Resource Center at Spelman College, as well as the evolution of black women's studies, and didn't have much new to say; so I won't be repeating the early history of the evolution of the women's studies program for which I have assumed the major responsibility since 1981 at Spelman, the first historically black college to have an undergraduate women's studies program. See *Women's Studies: A Retrospective*, a report to the Ford Foundation (June 1995), for my assessment of women's studies as a field, which includes a discussion of the evolution of black women's studies. See also my essay "A Black Feminist Perspective on Transforming the Academy: The Case of Spelman College," in *Theorizing Black Feminisms: The Visionary Pragmatism of Black Women*, ed. Stanlie M. James and Abena P. A. Busia (London and New York: Routledge, 1993), 77—89, which provides a history of the development of women's studies at Spelman. I have also written about my own feminist pedagogy in "Transforming the Academy: A Black Feminist Perspective," in *Changing Classroom Practices: Resources for Literary and Cultural Studies*, ed. David B. Downing (Urbana, Ill.: NCTE, 1994), 263—74. A shorter version appeared as "Practicing What You Preach," *Liberal Education* 77, no. 1 (January/February 1991): 27—29.

In any case, I agreed to become a contributor because, like Florence Howe, I believe it is important to hear from a variety of program founders who were active in the 1970s in the development of women's studies even if women of color were atypical.

1 An important exception to the invisibility of women of color in scholarship about the evolution of women's studies is *Transforming the Curriculum: Ethnic Studies and Women's Studies*, ed. Johnnella E. Butler and John C. Walter (Albany, N.Y.: State University of New York Press, 1991).

2 Toni Cade, ed., *The Black Woman: An Anthology* (New York: Penguin, 1970), 11.

3 bell hooks, "Writer to Writer: Remembering Toni Cade Bambara," *Remembered Rapture: The Writer at Work* (New York: Henry Holt and Company, 1999), 230—32.

4 See the ground-breaking anthology *All the Women Are White, All the Blacks Are Men, But Some of Us Are Brave: Black Women's Studies*, ed. Gloria T. Hull, Patricia Bell-Scott, and Barbara Smith (Old Westbury, N.Y.: The Feminist Press, 1982).

5 Toni Cade had recently moved to Atlanta, and her anthology *The Black Woman* had been in print for three years. In fact, Toni was also one of the first people with whom Roseann Bell and I consulted when we began talking about our anthology six years earlier.

6 In *Women's Studies: A Retrospective*, I argue that *The Black Woman* was the first critical publication in the

newly emerging field of black women's studies, and was important in the development of women's studies, though Toni Cade Bambara's work has rarely been seen in this context by white feminists writing the history of women's studies or the contemporary women's movement (10). It preceded by two years Gerda Lerner's 1972 documentary history *Black Women in White America,* which is often erroneously cited as having ushered in black women's studies. The *Black Woman* is also critically important for an understanding of the emergence of black feminist thought in the 1960s. It is significant, as well, because of the value it attached to hearing the distinct voices of black women, arguing that their experiences were different from both black men and white women.

7 Roseann P. Bell, Bettye J. Parker, and Beverly Guy-Sheftall, eds., *Sturdy Black Bridges: Visions of Black Women in Literature* (New York: Doubleday, 1979), 238–240.

8 See "Racism and Women's Studies," in Barbara Smith, *The Truth That Never Hurts: Writings on Race, Gender, and Freedom* (New Brunswick, N.J.: Rutgers University Press, 1999), 84–98. See also *But Some of Us Are Brave* (1982), which she coedited with Gloria T. Hull and Patricia Bell-Scott, and which is the pioneering black women's studies text.

9 bell hooks, "Feminism and Black Women's Studies," *SAGE: A Scholarly Journal on Black Women* 6 no. 1 (Summer 1989): 54.

10 bell hooks, "Feminism," 54.

11 This was particularly the case when I invited Barbara Smith, an out lesbian scholar and activist, to be one of the first speakers at the center; apparently, a few students complained and a black woman professor warned me about the possibility of the center being perceived early on as a haven for lesbians and therefore doomed to failure.

Elizabeth Lapovsky Kennedy

Dedicated to the memory of Gail Paradise Kelly and in the memory of Wanda Edwards, who, despite their untimely deaths, had a lasting effect on me and on women's studies at SUNY, Buffalo. I want to thank my Tucson writing group—Myra Dinnerstein, Pat MacCorquodale, Susan Philips, and Sheila Slaughter—for reading and discussing two early drafts of this essay. Thanks also to Susan Cahn for her insightful comments at this early stage. A number of people who were intimately involved in building the Women's Studies Program at SUNY, Buffalo, read the middle draft and offered brilliant comments. Ellen DuBois, Lillian Robinson, and Angela Keil gave the kind of thorough reading that only the best of colleagues provide. In terms of big ideas, they challenged my thinking, but they also paid attention to the details and the subtlety of the prose. Margaret Small made important suggestions for improving the section with which she was most familiar. Carolyn Korsmeyer offered general reactions to the whole essay, allowing me to work on its overall effect. Margaret Randall, who had no involvement in building women's studies in the United States, offered her insights as a long-term activist and personal friend. Thanks to Florence Howe for working with me to cut the original 107-page manuscript to an acceptable length for this book.

1 Barbara Shircliffe, *The History of a Student-Run Women's Studies Program, 1971–1985,* Dissertation, State University of New York at Buffalo, October, 1996, 243.

2 The group included Margaret Small, Bonnie Zimmerman, Susan Cohen, Fran Dolinsky, Fran Zucker, Carol Twigg, Carol Olicker, Alison Jagger, and Don Sabo. I have kept in touch with the first two, both of whom have remained committed to teaching and educational change.

3 Alice Echols characterizes radical women of the late 1960s as dividing between two political tendencies, the politicos and the feminists (*Daring to Be Bad: Radical Feminism in America, 1967–75* [Minneapolis: University of Minnesota Press, 1989], 51–102).

4 This course grew directly out of my antiwar activism and initiated my thirty-year involvement in institutional struggle. It was attacked by the local press, and investigated by a grand jury looking to determine the causes of campus unrest.

5 As we moved forward to establish the Women's Studies College, we learned that others had made an unsuccessful attempt before us. This first application was submitted by Ann Scott, a professor in the English department; Bernice Poss, an administrator; Daphne Hare, a medical school professor; and Peter Gessner and Theresa Gessner from the School of Pharmacology, all of whom were associated with the National Organization for Women (NOW). In hindsight, I think that the reason their application was rejected and ours was accepted was simply the power that we gained from being directly associated with the women's liberation movement. Their use of reason could not change the prejudice that was deeply rooted in the university. We contacted those who had previously expressed interest in a Women's Studies College, and they graciously supported our proposal.

6 Barbara Shircliffe, *History of a Student-Run Women's Studies Program,* 94.

7 This song is quoted in full in Shircliffe, *History,* 176–77. Shircliffe offers a detailed description of the fight for women-only classes.

8 In *Daring to Be Bad,* Echols suggests that radical feminists concern with race was minimal (106–107). Janet Jakobson, in her book *Working Alliances and the Politics of Difference: Diversity and Feminist Ethics* (Bloom-

ington: University of Indiana, 1998), suggests that this cast of 1970s feminism as a time that did not deal with racism is a tale that allows feminists to buy into a narrative of progress without making any change in their paradigms about racial hierarchy. Thus the women of color who struggled actively in the early second wave of feminism are obliterated from history, and the good white feminists who learned something in the 1980s can now right the problems. But meanwhile no real change has taken place.

9 See Shircliffe, *History*, 117–130, for a discussion of changing Governance forms.

10 The selection process was public and frank, trying to mesh a person's past work with the needs of the college. A talented young woman was turned down for the coordinator position because she tended to get angry at people quickly and didn't have the patience to facilitate the working together of the many different constituencies of the women's liberation movement. She was told why she didn't get the job and was expected to work on these traits. She did and went on to be an excellent coordinator the following year.

11 The first few years the coordinator was Val Eastman, then Theresa Epstein and Marge Cramer, Kathy McDermott and Ann Williams, Sherri Darrow, Rena Patterson, Elene Krystyk, Diane Carr, Nancy Savoy, and Linda

Sudano took their turns. All of these women, except one, had simply a B.A. when they became coordinator, although some went on to become M.A. students in American studies during or after their tenure.

12 For the sake of simplicity, I identify the conflict as occurring between students and faculty. But, in fact, some graduate students were fully sympathetic to the faculty, as were a few undergraduates. In a personal communication from Bonnie Zimmerman, I learned that she experienced the lack of support for intellectual work just as the faculty did.

Tucker Pamella Farley

1 Feminist education took place in our meetings and programs unsanctioned by the university, whose standard response to radical pressure—and feminists were an important part of the movements—was to call out the armed National Guard. I learned leadership in these struggles. See Kenneth J. Heineman, *Campus Wars: The Peace Movement at American State Universities in the Vietnam Era* (New York: New York University Press, 1993).

2 I learned organizing with the mixed left, and later applied it in my workplace. I headed the English Graduate Organization at PSU, an early graduate student union. As a labor educator, I was a member of Workers Education Local 189 of the American Federation of Teachers, where I formed the Women's Caucus; we labor

union women were making our own movement, and when I moved to New York, I was active after 1970 in the early Coalition of Labor Union Women (CLUW). Two types of struggles were particularly educational for me: those of unorganized women—the farm workers and Dolores Huerta, the National Welfare Rights Organization, and the domestic workers—and the organizing drives affiliated with unrecognized unions, especially the Women Office Workers.

3 As part of a small group of women at the MLA who organized for a Commission on the Status of Women in the Profession, I suggested that Florence Howe present our proposal. She was a colleague in the New University Conference (NUC), a successor to SDS, but was not known as a wild-eyed feminist. She became chair of the Commission on the Status of Women in the Profession and then president of the Modern Language Association.

4 I began teaching women's studies courses both in unions and in academic classrooms around the same time. I organized the New York Women's Labor Project, which developed a course and taught it to women in the trade unions in the tri-state area, forming the basis of the trade union women's studies program by 1974 at the New York State School of Industrial and Labor Relations at Cornell University, where I taught labor education

courses. See New York Women's Labor Project Collective, "Women in the Work Force: A Course for Trade Union Women," *Women: A Journal of Liberation* 2 (Spring 1973): 26–28.

5 For one perspective on the development of lesbian voices in this era of intense feminist creativity, see Tucker Pamella Farley, "Reality and Difference: De-Constructing the Absolute," introductory chapter in *Contemporary Lesbian Writers of the U.S.: A Critical Bio-Bibliographical Critical Source Book*, ed. Sandra Pollack and Denise Knight (Westport, Conn.: Greenwood Press, 1993).

6 Joan Critchlow moved for one semester from State College, Pennsylvania (the town where PSU was located), to Brooklyn to teach with me unofficially (she was paid out of my salary rather than the college payroll) and provided the strong voice of an experienced community activist and mother.

7 In the early 1970s two independent groups were especially important to me: Marxist-Feminist Group One, in the northeast region, and in the city, Alice Kessler-Harris and I formed a Marxism study group with Joan Kelly-Gadol, Renate Bridenthal, Marilyn Arthur, and later Blanche Wiesen Cook, among others. After the gay-straight splits, I formed a lesbian study group on race. From that period I particularly appreciate the support of Audrey Ewart, Rena Patterson, and Susan Cayleff.

8 A decade later the suit was settled
in favor of the women on the
matter of discrimination in
wages; unfortunately, as Melani
pointed out to me, the settlement
money was distributed by the same
people who had been found guilty
of discrimination.

9 Although I began teaching by
myself (and I had never heard of
another academic women's studies
course for credit), I moved into
team-teaching in the School of
Social Sciences with a lecturer
from the history department,
Renate Bridenthal, and in the
School of Humanities with Marilyn Arthur from the classics
department and Freddie Wachsberger from the art and archaeology department.

10 The Women's Center was
designed to be run by cocoordinators, but because of the university's contractual requirements
for nonacademic office budget
lines, we ended up nominally
and, unfortunately for collective
work, then in fact, with a director
and an assistant director. Shotsy
Faust provided vision and energy
to the center for that year, and
when she left we were unable to
get a replacement budget line.
Barbara Gaines remained with the
center until she was able to retire.
Thanks to the work of students
such as Patti Gaier, the center
developed a model peer counseling program; put on bilingual
health fairs, conferences, and
workshops; brought in films,
speakers, concerts, and theater;
and did projects in coalition with
other groups.

11 The Project for Returning
Women had a principal investiga-
tor (a rotating faculty position), a
project coordinator, and various
staff throughout the years. It was
directed by the late Luvenia Pin-
son, who also represented the
project at the first NWSA convention, and played some role in the
(uneasy) relationship between the
Women of Color Caucus and the
Coordinating Council. Wilmette
Brown and Digna Sanchez were
research assistants, and Ann
Williams was staff, assisted by Elly
Bulkin and Batya Weinbaum of
the center. In the context of continuous retrenchment since 1974,
we have been able to retain very
little of what became Project
Chance as a coherent program,
although many of its practices
have been integrated into the university; in addition, we have gotten grants for specific programs
for girls and mentoring, and for
internship programs. Nancy
Romer from the psychology
department has been particularly
effective, as was Alice Cook, our
late Women's Center director. We
are still, years later, struggling to
replace her budget line and to
keep the center open some of the
time.

12 In the process I had left small-
town Appalachia, and my two best
friends there. They did not fare so
well: it is my understanding—for
my letters were returned
"addressee unknown"—that one

friend was institutionalized by her husband, and that the other tried to commit suicide. This proposal was for them.

13 Two studies were helpful in documenting that the university did not properly serve its female constituents: Suzanne Paul, Jolly Robinson, and Gloria Smith, *Project Second Start: A Study of the Experience of a Group of Low-Income Women in Adult Programs at Brooklyn College* (New York: The John Hay Whitney Foundation, 1973); and *Second-Start Revisited: A Follow-Up*, (1978), appeared five years later with new material included.

14 In the mid-1970s, progressive and liberal people were engaged in institutional struggle at every turn. There were massive firings, and hospitals and child-care centers were closed. More than half the workers in New York City were women even after the layoffs, which targeted women primarily. Several CUNY campuses were closed. A memo written by Newt Davidson, head of the Rockefeller Commission, to Governor Rockefeller, leaked by an office worker and used in the CUNY-wide struggle against cutbacks, noted the need for "businesslike standards of efficiency and accountability," which had been tried in 1961, and again from 1970 to 1973:

> Our main obstacle to date has been the CUNY faculty, who defend their traditional and outmoded prerogatives with the rhetoric of "quality educa-

tion" and an emphasis upon non-productive "liberal arts" curricula. We are agreed, however, that arguing with such an articulate segment of the community would be counterproductive. Our aim, therefore, has been to encourage faculty preoccupation with "bread and butter" issues, while at the same time restructuring the teaching staff from within.

These policies generated tremendous pressures to eliminate women's studies and reinforced conservatives' labeling the new field a "fad."

15 The letter was answered by Sybil Weir with apologies for her language and thanks for practical and democratic suggestions. The position papers and that correspondence were distributed, to allow people to discuss them at their campuses before coming to the conference, and were available there.

16 The idea of supplementing selective founders by running a regional lottery had been accepted in California, and I was accompanied by Jo Gilliken from the College of Staten Island, who won the draw in New York. Our region was so well developed already that New York by itself became one region of the new national association.

17 The NWSA Lesbian Caucus was formed out of meeting about an issue; we decided to present to the body an appeal for recognition and representation of our diverse

constituency (of students, staff, faculty, and women of color) as lesbians. Susan Cayleff and I read the statement from the podium, asking those who could—realizing the risk to jobs and friendships—to rise, to show the body the diversity of lesbian lives. First, there was silence. Gradually, one by one, and then in increasing numbers, women began to stand, until there was a tide of women rising in that large room. It was a galvanizing moment for many. See the video *A Call to Rise,* Tucker Farley and Sandra Pollack, producers; Tucker Farley, director; 90 min. (Tucker Communications, Box 148, Manomet, MA 02345), 1998.

18 So challenging did members of the Curriculum Planning Council find the proposed lesbian literature course that, at the height of the fiscal crisis, the council spent weeks debating the course, violated and redid its own governance rules, went into secret ballot, and retains to this day an elaborate structure by which a single special topics course offering by a department must be approved on a collegewide basis.

19 Gloria DeSole wrote a sharply detailed analysis of the legal status of tenure fights for women's studies faculty in the academy; Paul Lauter presented an erudite and lucid account of the historical context for the case; Florence Howe brilliantly surveyed the situation of women's studies as a growing field and discussed the importance of my work within it; Louis Kampf praised my work in the Modern Language Association as chair of the Job Market Advisory Commission. For these and other letters of support, I remain grateful.

Annette Kolodny

1 See Daniel Peters' novel, *Border Crossings* (New York: Harper and Row, 1978), a fictional account of events leading to our flight to Canada.

2 These 1980 recollections of the original document come from professor of English and former coordinator of women's studies, Lorraine Weir, and are quoted in "Report of the Women's Studies Programme," University of British Columbia, 20 November 1996, 28.

3 Dorothy E. Smith, letter to author, 23 July 1998.

4 Ibid.

5 In the early 1970s, many Canadian universities had credited courses on women's studies topics located within traditional departments. To the best of our knowledge, ours was the first attempt at an integrated interdisciplinary program of courses.

6 Smith, letter to author.

7 "Proposal for an Inter-Disciplinary Women's Studies Course," University of British Columbia [1972], 1.

8 Ibid.

9 This was an expression of Canadian disdain for the increasing impact of United States culture

on Canada and a comment on economic relations that benefited U.S. corporations at the expense of Canada.

10 Helga E. Jacobson, "Organizing Women's Studies at the University of British Columbia," *Canadian Newsletter of Research on Women* 11, no. 3 (October 1973): 20.

11 Ibid.

12 Ibid.

13 Ibid.

14 I discussed the implications of this episode for feminist theory in my "Dancing through the Minefield: Some Observations on the Theory, Practice, and Politics of a Feminist Literary Criticism" (*Feminist Studies* 6, no. 1 [Spring 1980]: 1–25), most recently reprinted in *Feminisms: An Anthology of Literary Theory and Criticism,* rev. ed., ed. Robyn R. Warhol and Diane Price Herndl (New Brunswick, N.J.: Rutgers University Press, 1997), 171–90.

15 The positive outcome was that the head of the English department saw to it that I did not take on a teaching overload. He was persuaded by my argument that instruction in the interdisciplinary lecture course demanded even more preparation than a single-discipline course, and he counted the lecture course as part of my regular six courses per year assignment.

16 See "Women's Status Report—Recommendations and Equality Guidelines," *UBC Reports,* 8 February 1973, 3.

17 From a variety of secret locations in and around London, the Office of Special Services (best known as the OSS) coordinated intelligence operations—including spying and code-breaking—for the British government. Its activities were instrumental in the eventual Allied victory.

18 The following exchange between Helga and newspaper reporter Leslie Peterson appeared in "The Last Academic Frontier—Women: Courses Finally Get Official Seal," *Vancouver Sun,* 10 February 1973, 40: "To charges that women's studies programs discriminate against women by segregating them, she replies: 'If you have courses in Canadian or Asian studies you're not discriminating against them, are you? There is a legitimate discipline that can set about analyzing and adding to the full knowledge of this material, this is what we are doing.'"

19 "Proposal," 1. (See note 7.)

20 One-page news release from UBC Information Services, 26 January 1973.

21 "Breaking New Ground," *UBC Reports,* 8 February 1973, 1.

22 Smith, letter to author.

23 Meredith Kimball, letter to author, 20 July 1998.

24 Sheryl Perey, letter to author, 20 July 1998.

25 Kimball, letter to author.

26 Leslee Silverman, letter to author, 17 August 1998.

27 Smith, letter to author.

28 Perey, letter to author.

29 Audrey Samson, letter to author, 11 August 1998.

30 Teresa Plowright, letter to author, 5 August 1998.

31 Silverman, letter to author.

32 Plowright, letter to author.

33 Annette Kolodny, "For the Women's Studies Coordinating Committee: Course Evaluation, 1973–1974," University of British Columbia [1974].

34 I was the first to leave, because the laws governing Conscientious Objector status in the United States changed in 1973. As a result, my husband belatedly received CO status and was then reclassified as "currently not eligible for processing for induction." He wanted to go home. I accepted a position in the English department at the University of New Hampshire. Arriving there in the fall of 1974, I tried to reconstitute the experience of UBC and encouraged other interested faculty women to work with me on developing that school's first women's studies program. We succeeded, but almost immediately, I was denied promotion and tenure. I sued the university under Title VII of the Civil Rights Act; see Annette Kolodny, "I Dreamt Again That I Was Drowning," in *Women's Writing in Exile,* ed. Mary Lynn Broe and Angela Ingram (Chapel Hill: University of North Carolina Press, 1989), 170–78. In later years, what I had learned at UBC about bureaucracy and institutional intransigence proved invaluable when I worked to develop interdisciplinary pro-

grams as dean of the College of Humanities at the University of Arizona; see Annette Kolodny, *Failing the Future: A Dean Looks at Higher Education in the Twenty-first Century* (Durham, N.C.: Duke University Press, 1998). Dorothy left UBC to become a full professor at the Ontario Institute for Studies in Education (OISE). When Meredith was denied promotion and tenure, she found herself recruited immediately for a joint appointment in women's studies and psychology at Simon Fraser University in nearby Burnaby, British Columbia, where she is today a full professor. Of the original four, only Helga remained. For the rest of her career at UBC, she continued to teach women's studies courses and to support the program's existence.

35 "Report," 31. (See note 2.)

Myra Dinnerstein

1 The establishment of AWF allowed women's studies to maintain the fiction that women's studies was not directly involved in contentious faculty demands, even though for many years almost all of its officers were women's studies faculty and our faculty were some of the most vigorous participants.

2 Interestingly, although I still remember the complaints about the full agenda and the policy decisions that had to be made, the memories we share when we get together are of the fun we had

spending time with one another and of the hilarious feminist charades we played in the evenings, acting out the titles of the newest feminist books.

3 I remember attending a university Curriculum Committee meeting at which our major was being considered. We had asked some of these prominent men to attend and, as galling as it was to have to be authenticated by these men, I have no doubt that it was their presence and verbal support that carried the day with that unwilling committee. We felt that we had to be politically astute as well because, as a program without its own faculty, we had to depend on other departments for the development of our curriculum.

4 Susan Aiken, Karen Anderson, Judy Lensink, Myra Dinnerstein, and Patricia MacCorquodale, "Trying Transformations: Curriculum Integration and the Problem of Resistance," *Signs,* 12, no. 2, (Winter 1987): 255–75; Susan Aiken, Karen Anderson, Judy Lensink, Myra Dinnerstein, and Patricia MacCorquodale, eds., *Changing Our Minds: Feminist Transformations of Knowledge,* (SUNY Press, 1988); Patricia Mac-Corquodale and Judy Lensink, "Integrating Women into the Curriculum: Multiple Motives and Mixed Emotions," in *Women's Higher Education in Comparative Perspective,* ed. G. P. Kelly & S. Slaughter (Boston and London: Dordrecht, 1990), 297–314.

5 Our commitment to this enterprise is indicated by the fact that in the first of these projects, funded by the National Endowment for the Humanities in 1981, only one women's studies faculty member got paid to lead the seminar each semester, even though all of the women's studies faculty attended each seminar for three years, working with a different group of faculty each semester. In contrast, each of the faculty we worked with received a stipend the semester that they attended a seminar.

6 SIROW also provided an enormous boost for our faculty. As my women's studies colleagues Susan Philips and Patricia MacCorquodale recall, the establishment of SIROW was a milestone event in our program's history: it was a confirmation that we would continue to flourish. One crucial mark of the university's approval, due in no small measure to SIROW's success in obtaining grants under the leadership of Janice Monk, its executive director, was the university's willingness to support SIROW with state funds when the six-year Ford funding ran out.

We designed SIROW as a regional center because of the relative isolation of the women's studies programs in the Southwest region and in other areas, and because it would make our proposal distinctive. SIROW has connected scholars in the region and has made us attractive to funding agencies eager to support projects that have an impact on more than one campus. Our decision to make SIROW a part of women's studies (other programs most often set up separate feminist research institutes) also had positive and far-reaching consequences. The grants that SIROW garnered made it possible not only to extend the range of our program's research and activist projects, but resulted in a large number of books and articles. Funds from the grants made it possible to augment the financial resources of the women's studies program, an important benefit. These funds have contributed to the running of the office and program, including basic necessities, such as supplies and equipment; they also contribute to women's studies events and faculty travel.

7 The connection that we established with Ford, which continues to this day, meant that we were asked to help organize and become a charter member of a new organization, the National Council for Research on Women, an organization that helped us to expand our national contacts. These national connections made us more appreciated on our own campus, particularly when they led to grants.

8 The expanding space of women's studies also reflected our changing status, as Sidonie Smith, now director of women's studies at the University of Michigan, has pointed out. In 1975 we started out with no office; a few months later we moved into a tiny office in the corridor of the Russian department. The increasing number of staff we hired for each grant project meant pressure for more space, so in three succeeding moves we acquired more and more space; at the end of 1996, women's studies had moved to more spacious and well-decorated offices in a building where there should be room for further expansion.

9 The fight to establish our M.A. program was another reminder that, despite our successes, there remained a good deal of resistance. Our strength lay in the support we received from the provost, nudged along by a feminist vice provost. That support showed that we had managed to make some headway with the administration and also reflected the impact of having more feminist women in positions of power. Despite that backing, however, the Graduate College turned down our proposal, not once but twice. At a time when resources were scarce, many saw us as competitors that were not as worthy as established departments. The Faculty Senate eventually overruled the University Graduate Committee, but even that was a heart-stopper: it looked for a while as if those wanting to table our proposal would carry the day.

Sue-Ellen Jacobs
Professor Emerita Dorothea V.

Kaschube, my chief mentor and dissertation director, has remained a dependable source of advice and counsel throughout the years, and to her I dedicate this paper. I also dedicate this paper to the memory of three women who were profoundly instrumental in securing women's studies at the University of Washington, and my role in it: Carol Eastman (1937–97), Melinda Denton (1944–94), and Naomi Gottlieb (1925–95). I also want to acknowledge the others who were supporters from the beginning of my years at the University of Washington, especially Carolyn Allen, Marilyn Bentz, Clare Bright, Ingrith Deyrup-Olsen, Donna Gerstenberger, Sydney Kaplan, Thelma Kennedy, Mark McDermott, Karen Rudolph, Davida Teller, James Vasquez, Carolyn Woodward, Artee Young, and those who preferred to remain in the background as we tried collective governance in the midst of the pressure to conform to patriarchy. Special thanks to Mary Saucier for helping with the final revision and editing of this paper.

1 Sue-Ellen Jacobs, *Women in Perspective: A Guide for Cross-Cultural Studies* (Urbana: University of Illinois Press, 1974).

2 Sue-Ellen Jacobs, "Doing It Our Way and Mostly for Our Own," *Human Organization* 33, no. 4 (Winter 1974): 380–82; Sue-Ellen Jacobs, "Our Babies Shall Not Die: A Community's Response to Medical Neglect," *Human Organization* 38, no. 2 (Summer 1979): 120–33.

3 It would be late in the 1980s before the Association for Feminist Anthropology (AFA) would be developed within the American Anthropological Association (the principal professional association of anthropologists). In the 1970s there were many publications by feminist anthropologists, which, in turn, informed the general development of women studies. But some of us felt that it was better to work through the various collectives within the AAA than to form a separate organization— until at last we realized that the "alpha males" of our discipline were simply determined to prevent both feminist and minority research from becoming part of the canon—i.e., the principal introductory texts in our field. It took the formation of the AFA and head-to-head sessions at the annual meetings among those alpha males, respected senior women anthropologists, and publishing houses before change began to be noticed. Even today, there are courses still taught in anthropology departments where feminist theory and other writings are treated as faddish if mentioned at all. Most anthropology department faculty are still well over 50 percent male.

4 These students left the University of Washington for graduate studies elsewhere when it became clear to them that the male faculty

intended retribution for their participation in campus activism. Remnants of that time still exist, with the most recent being attempts to defame the character of one of those students, now a widely published senior anthropologist with numerous awards.

5 I often tell people that I found that I could not serve both a demanding master and a demanding mistress; so, of course, I chose the mistress.

6 These days, the teaching load in women studies and most of the other social sciences departments takes into account the considerable amount of work required to manage and teach our large lecture courses. Junior faculty are protected from overwork on service, as much as possible, and they are given competitive free time for research. These new measures were put into place collegewide long after our first historian, and many other dedicated junior faculty throughout the college, had left. Our university also instituted a mentoring system, so senior faculty (or at least a departmental chair) could remain vigilant about junior faculty work loads, and provide advice about publishing and teaching; in short, help junior faculty have the best chance for success at tenure and promotion time.

7 At the University of Washington, an adjunct faculty member is someone whose full appointment is in one unit or department, but is willing to give support to another unit or department in a variety of ways, e.g., by joint-listing courses; supervising students' thesis or independent study research; or serving on search, tenure review, and other committees. "Adjunct appointments do not confer governance or voting privileges or eligibility for tenure in the secondary department. These appointments are annual. The question of their renewal shall be considered each year by the faculty of the secondary department." *University Handbook,* vol. 2 (1997), 33. Adjunct faculty have always lent status to our department by agreeing to be listed in published literature; and now we lend status to faculty in other departments whose work in feminist or women studies we recognize by appointing them as adjunct members of our department.

8 Research assistant professors are reviewed for reappointment and for promotion, but do not teach. They are generally on soft money or are seeking funding from grants.

9 For examples of affirmations of this position, see Joan Wallach Scott, guest editor, "Women Studies on the Edge," *Differences: A Journal of Feminist Cultural Studies* 9, no. 3 (Fall 1997). For examples of naysaying, see Elizabeth Fox-Genovese, *Feminism Without Illusions: A Critique of Individualism* (Chapel Hill: University of North Carolina

Press, 1991) and Elizabeth Fox-Genovese, *Feminism Is Not the Story of My Life: How Today's Feminist Elite Has Lost Touch With the Real Concerns of Women* (New York: Doubleday, 1996).

10 Joy Harjo and Carol Bird, eds., *Reinventing the Enemy's Language: Contemporary Native Women's Writing of North America* (New York: Norton, 1997).

11 These early works include Paula G. Allen, *The Woman Who Owned Shadows* (San Francisco: Spinsters, Ink., 1983); Paula G. Allen, *The Sacred Hoop: Recovering the Feminine in American Indian Traditions* (Boston: Beacon Press, 1986); Maya Angelou, *I Know Why the Caged Bird Sings* (New York: Bantam Books, 1971); Ellen Cantarow, *Moving the Mountain: Women Working for Social Change* (New York: The Feminist Press, 1980); Angela Y. Davis, *Women, Race, and Class* (New York: Random House, 1981); Angela Y. Davis, *Violence against Women and the Ongoing Challenge to Racism,* (Latham, N.Y.: Kitchen Table, Women of Color Press, 1985); bell hooks, *Ain't I a Woman: Black Women and Feminism* (Boston: South End Press, 1981); bell hooks, *Feminist Theory from Margin to Center* (Boston: South End Press, 1984); Cherrie Moraga and Gloria Anzaldúa, eds., *This Bridge Called My Back: Writings by Radical Women of Color* (Watertown, Mass.: Persephone Press, 1981); Tillie Olsen, *Silences* (New York : Delacorte Press/Seymour Lawrence, 1978); Dorothy Ster-ling, *Black Foremothers: Three Lives* (New York: The Feminist Press, 1979); and Alice Walker, *In Search of Our Mothers' Gardens: Womanist Prose* (San Diego: Harcourt Brace Jovanovich, 1983).

12 Some even call themselves girls, using this word today in the same self-determined way that we used *women* in the 1970s. For excellent articles dealing with "girl culture," see the spring 1998 special issue of *Signs,* "Feminisms and Youth Cultures," edited by Kum-Kum Bhavani, Kathryn R. Kent, and Frances Winddance Twine.

13 Sue-Ellen Jacobs, "Continuity and Change in Gender Roles at San Juan Pueblo," in *Native American Women and Power,* ed. Laura Klein and Lillian Ackerman (Norman, Okla.: University of Oklahoma Press, 1995), 177–213; and Sue-Ellen Jacobs, "Being a Grandmother in the Tewa World," *American Indian Culture and Research Journal* 19, no. 2 (1995): 67–83.

Yolanda T. Moses

1 My mother came to my rescue for the first time when she managed to get a Parents and Teachers Association scholarship for me at the end of my high school years, rather than the secretarial scholarship that the school had offered. This time, my mother clipped a small article in the *Riverside Press-Enterprise,* a regional newspaper, advertising a program that the Ford Foundation was establishing

to help create a minority professoriat. My mother urged me to look
into this because she knew that I
was unhappy with my position.

2 In response to my application, I
received an invitation a few
months later to fly to New York
City for interviews. There, I was
asked why I wanted to be a professor and how that would make a
difference to my life and the lives
of others. I had two advantages
that many of the 780 other applicants did not. First, I had been
working in the real world for two
years; and second, I was involved
in community volunteer work.
Several weeks later, I was one of
the 75 people nationally awarded a
fellowship. Today that program is
the prestigious National Research
Council Minority Fellowship Program. Although the fellowship
paid tuition and a stipend for
four years, I had to figure out
where I wanted to study, and what
field I wanted to enter. This all
occurred in the spring of 1970,
when I was active in the National
Organization for Women, Los
Angeles, as well as in Watts at a
community parole center called
Ujima, which, in Swahili, means
"collective work and responsibility." It was at Ujima that I met my
husband-to-be, a German-
Hungarian from small-town rural
Iowa.

3 Louise Lamphere and Michelle
Zimbalist Rosaldo, eds., *Woman,
Culture, and Society* (Stanford, Calif.:
Standford University Press,
1974).

Nona Glazer

1 One of my mentors at UO
wanted me to do a graduate
research degree in social work at
Columbia University or at the
University of California, Berkeley, but refused to support my
studying for a Ph.D. in sociology
anywhere. At Cornell, where I
was in a joint sociology and
anthropology department, I was
given enormous support for
doing research through grants
and jobs, and only modest support for teaching, mostly at
women's colleges or small, badly
paying elite liberal arts colleges
far from any large city. Only one
woman in my cohort at Cornell
went to a teaching position at a
first-rate institution.

2 I had mixed training: I had both a
psychology undergraduate degree
and a sociology graduate degree—
and I deliberately did my doctorate in a sociology and anthropology department, because I wanted
to study in both fields. At the
London School of Economics and
Political Science (1959–60), I
studied mostly anthropology, and
at Cornell, I had intended to
minor in American history (as
well as in anthropology, in addition to majoring in sociology),
but their program at that time was
antagonistic to emerging revi-
sionist understandings of American history.

3 I moved back toward historically
based analyses in the tradition of
Marx and C. Wright Mills.
Eventually, I even taught qualitative

methods to graduate students after having been hired at PSU to teach statistics and quantitative research methods to undergraduates.

4 Nona Glazer and Helen Waehrer, eds., *Woman in a Man-made World* (Chicago: Rand McNally, 1972).

Nancy Porter

This essay is dedicated to my two youngest colleagues, Francesca Sawaya and Sherrie Gradin, because they asked. And to Meg O'Hara, loved friend and administrator extraordinaire, who died in August 1998.

Mariam K. Chamberlain

1 A full account of the process by which the Ford Foundation placed women's programming on its main agenda is provided in Susan Hartmann's book *The Other Feminists* (New Haven, Conn.: Yale University Press, 1998).

2 As I have since learned, this was a march organized by the National Organization for Women and other feminist groups. Similar marches were held in other cities across the country.

Index